SHINOBU OHTAKA

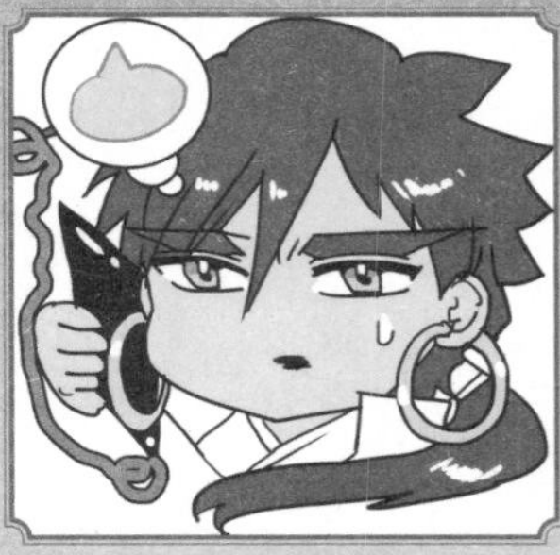

Magi *volume 31 even surprises the conqueror! Read with caution!*

MAGI
Volume 31
Shonen Sunday Edition

Story and Art by
SHINOBU OHTAKA

Original Japanese edition published by SHOGAKUKAN.
English translation rights in the United States of America, Canada, the United Kingdom, Ireland, Australia and New Zealand arranged with SHOGAKUKAN.

ORIGINAL COVER DESIGN / Yasuo SHIMURA+Bay Bridge Studio

Translation & English Adaptation ◆ John Werry
Touch-up Art & Lettering ◆ Stephen Dutro
Editor ◆ Mike Montesa

Printed in Canada

Published by VIZ Media, LLC
P.O. Box 77010
San Francisco, CA 94107

10 9 8 7 6 5 4 3 2 1
First printing, August 2018

WWW.SHONENSUNDAY.COM

ratings.viz.com
RATED T TEEN

PARENTAL ADVISORY
MAGI is rated T for Teen. This volume contains suggestive themes.

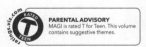

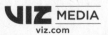

viz.com

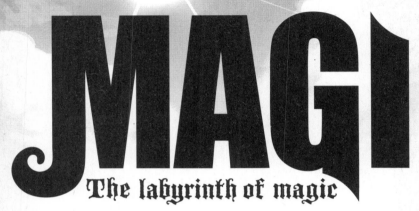

MAGI
The labyrinth of magic

31

Story & Art by
SHINOBU OHTAKA

MAGI
The labyrinth of magic
31

CONTENTS

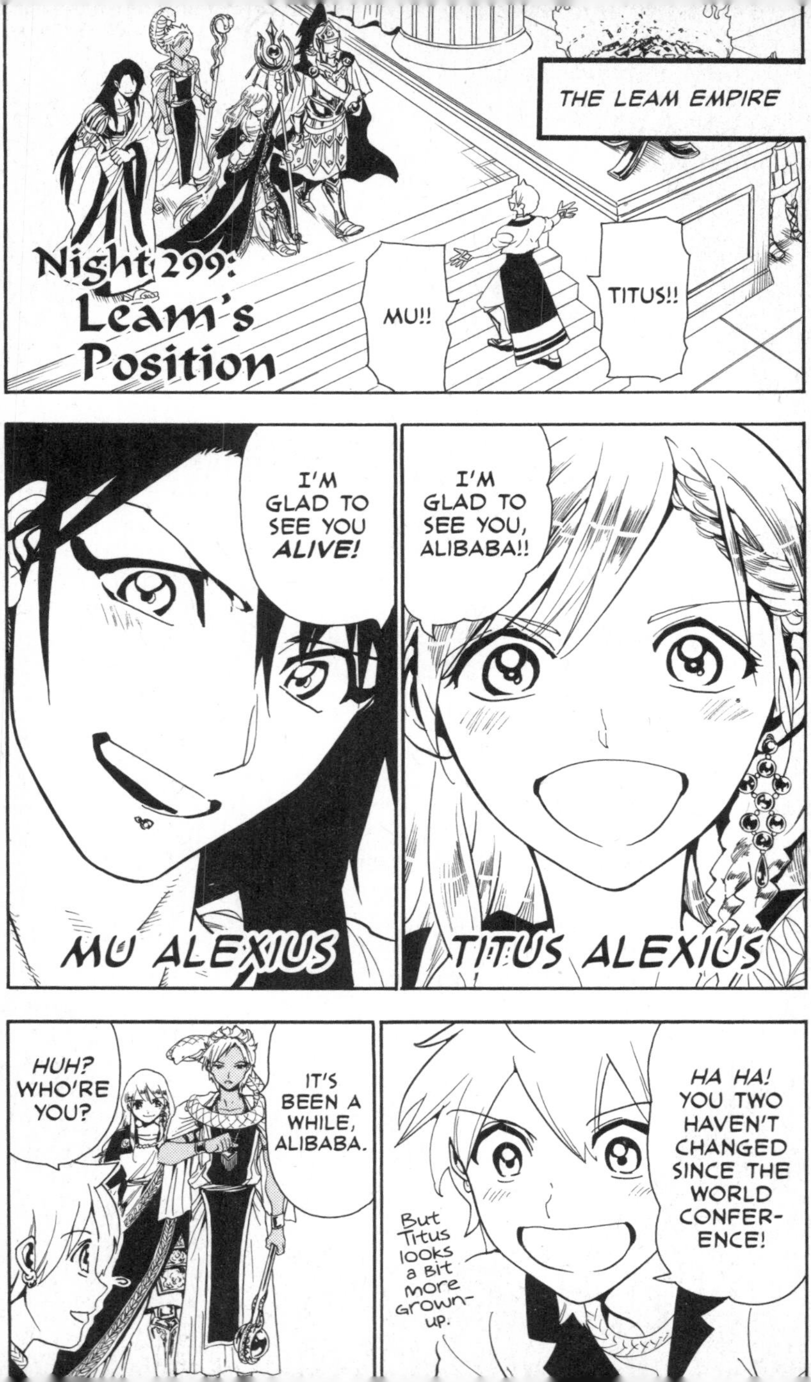
THE LEAM EMPIRE
TITUS!!
MU!!
Night 299: Leam's Position
I'M GLAD TO SEE YOU, ALIBABA!!
TITUS ALEXIUS
I'M GLAD TO SEE YOU ALIVE!
MU ALEXIUS
HA HA! YOU TWO HAVEN'T CHANGED SINCE THE WORLD CONFER-ENCE!
But Titus looks a bit more Grown-up.
IT'S BEEN A WHILE, ALIBABA.
HUH? WHO'RE YOU?

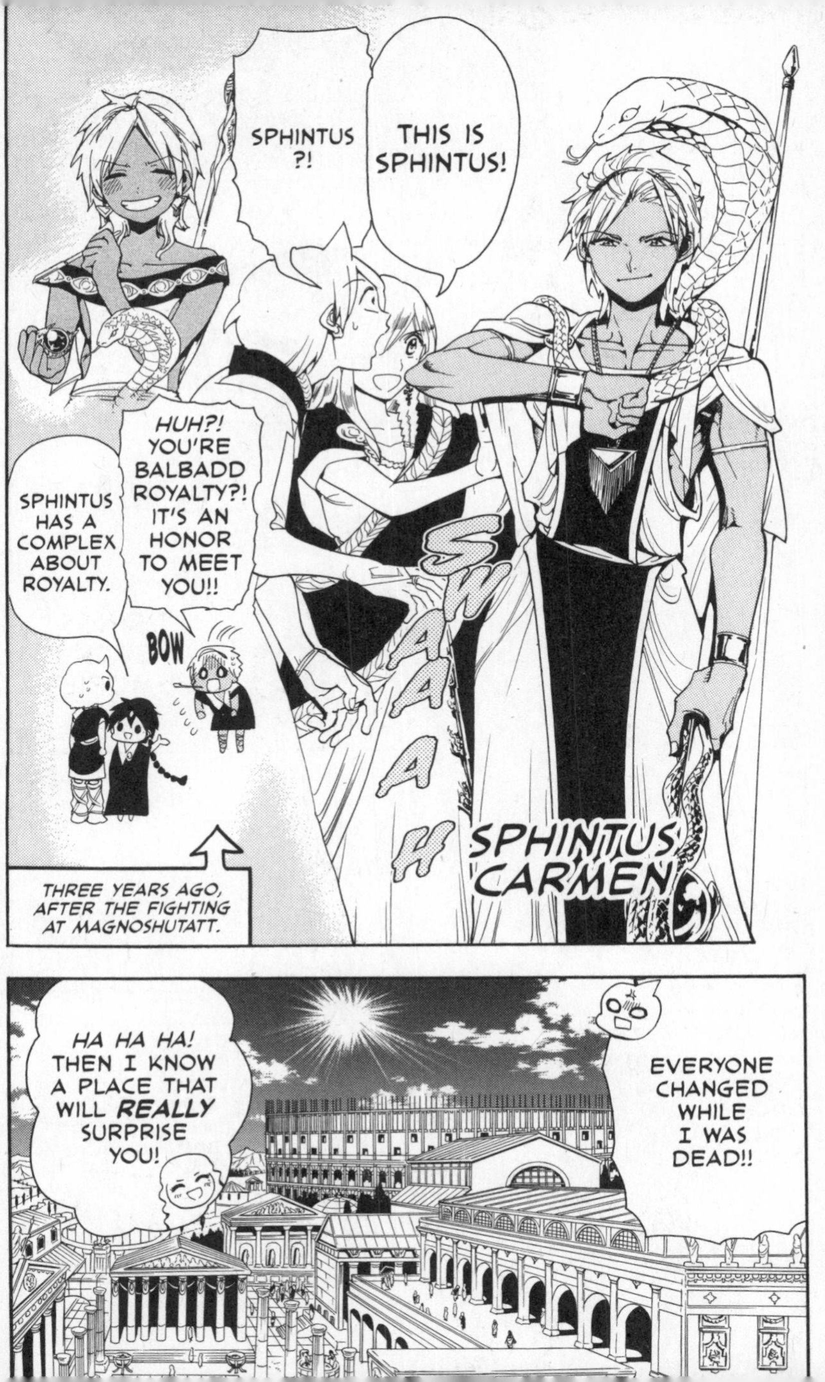
THIS IS SPHINTUS!
SPHINTUS?!
SWAAAH
SPHINTUS CARMEN
HUH?! YOU'RE BALBADD ROYALTY?! IT'S AN HONOR TO MEET YOU!!
BOW
SPHINTUS HAS A COMPLEX ABOUT ROYALTY.
THREE YEARS AGO, AFTER THE FIGHTING AT MAGNOSHUTATT.
EVERYONE CHANGED WHILE I WAS DEAD!!
HA HA HA! THEN I KNOW A PLACE THAT WILL REALLY SURPRISE YOU!

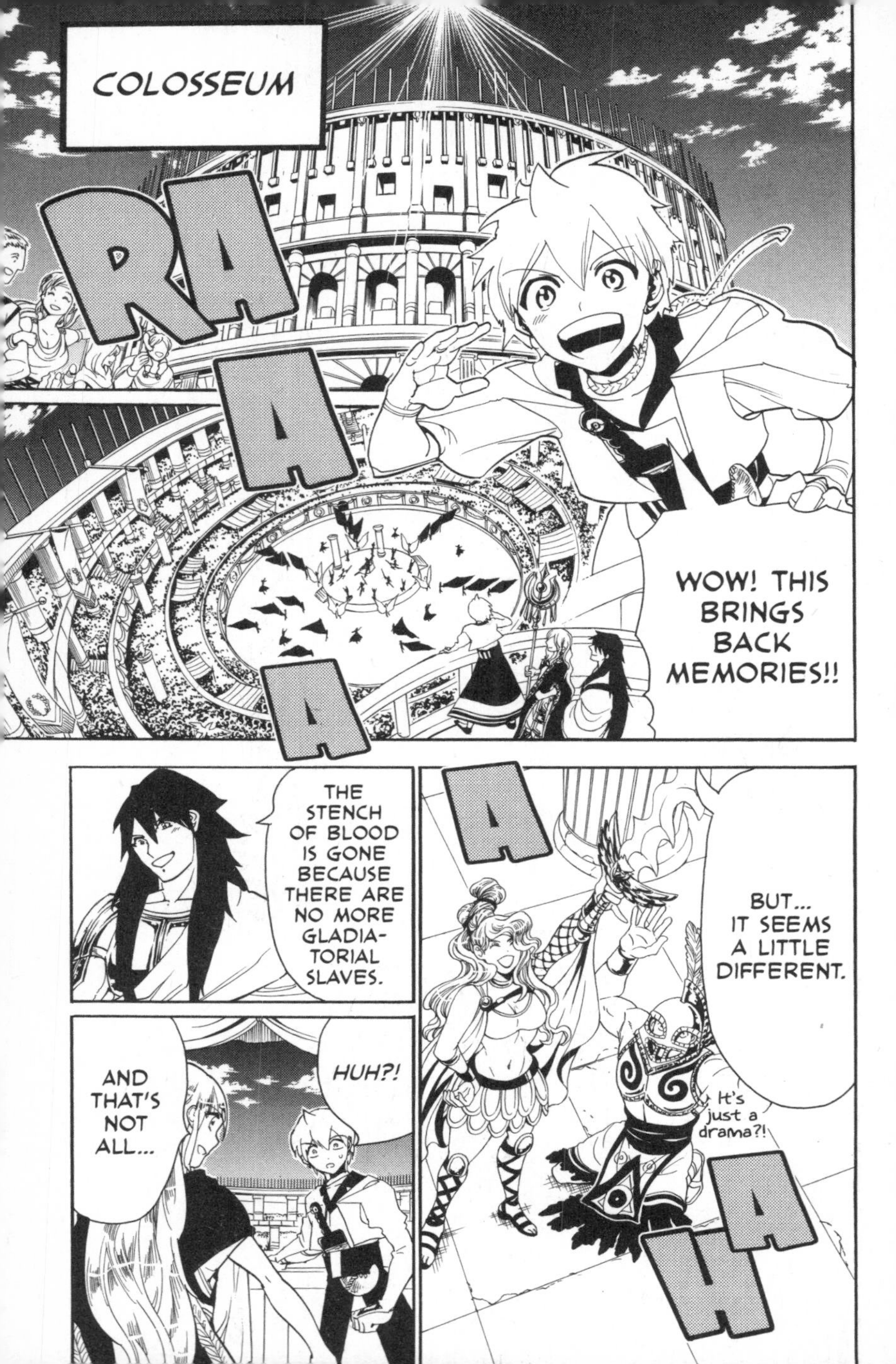
COLOSSEUM
RA
A
A
WOW! THIS BRINGS BACK MEMORIES!!
A
BUT... IT SEEMS A LITTLE DIFFERENT.
It's just a drama?!
AH
THE STENCH OF BLOOD IS GONE BECAUSE THERE ARE NO MORE GLADIA-TORIAL SLAVES.
HUH?!
AND THAT'S NOT ALL...

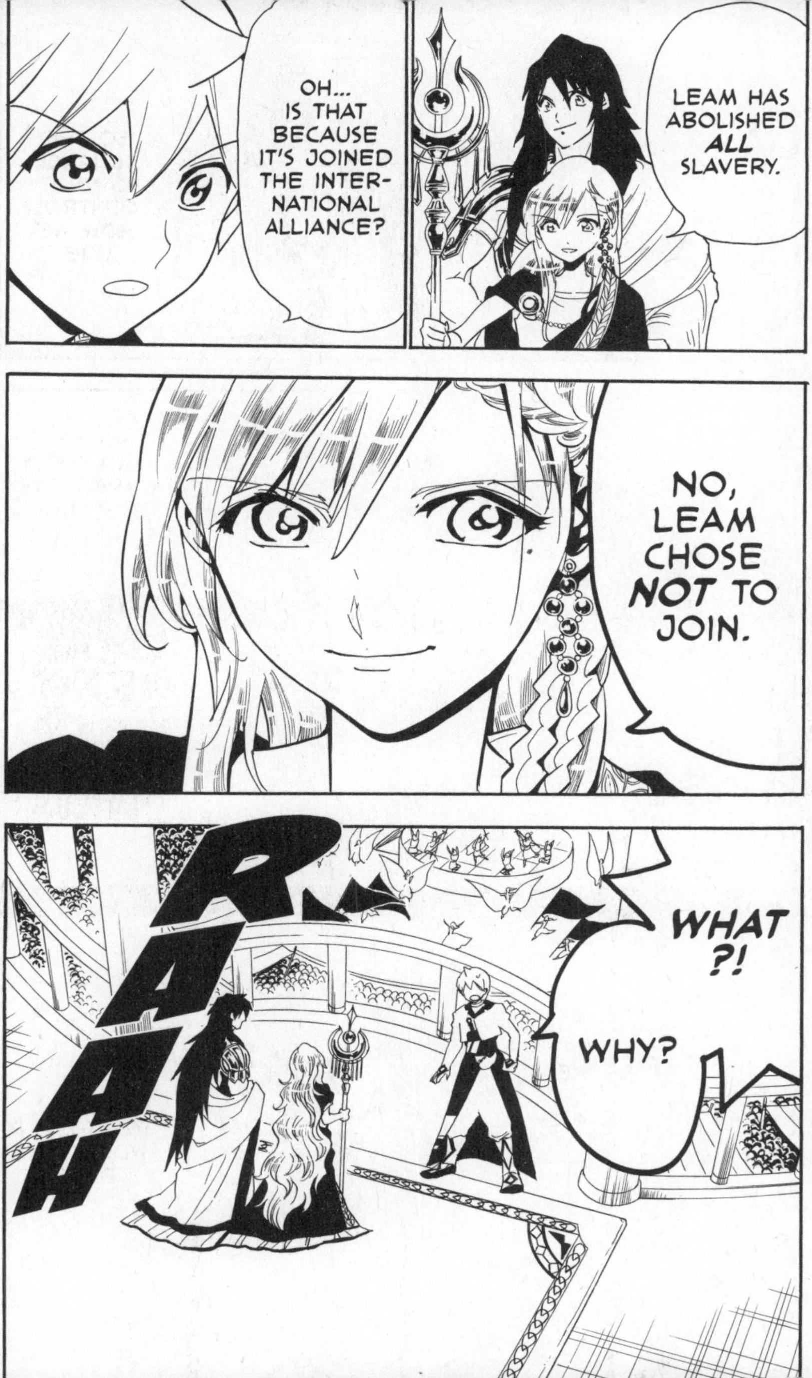
LEAM HAS ABOLISHED *ALL* SLAVERY.
OH... IS THAT BECAUSE IT'S JOINED THE INTER-NATIONAL ALLIANCE?
NO, LEAM CHOSE *NOT* TO JOIN.
WHAT?!
WHY?
RAAH

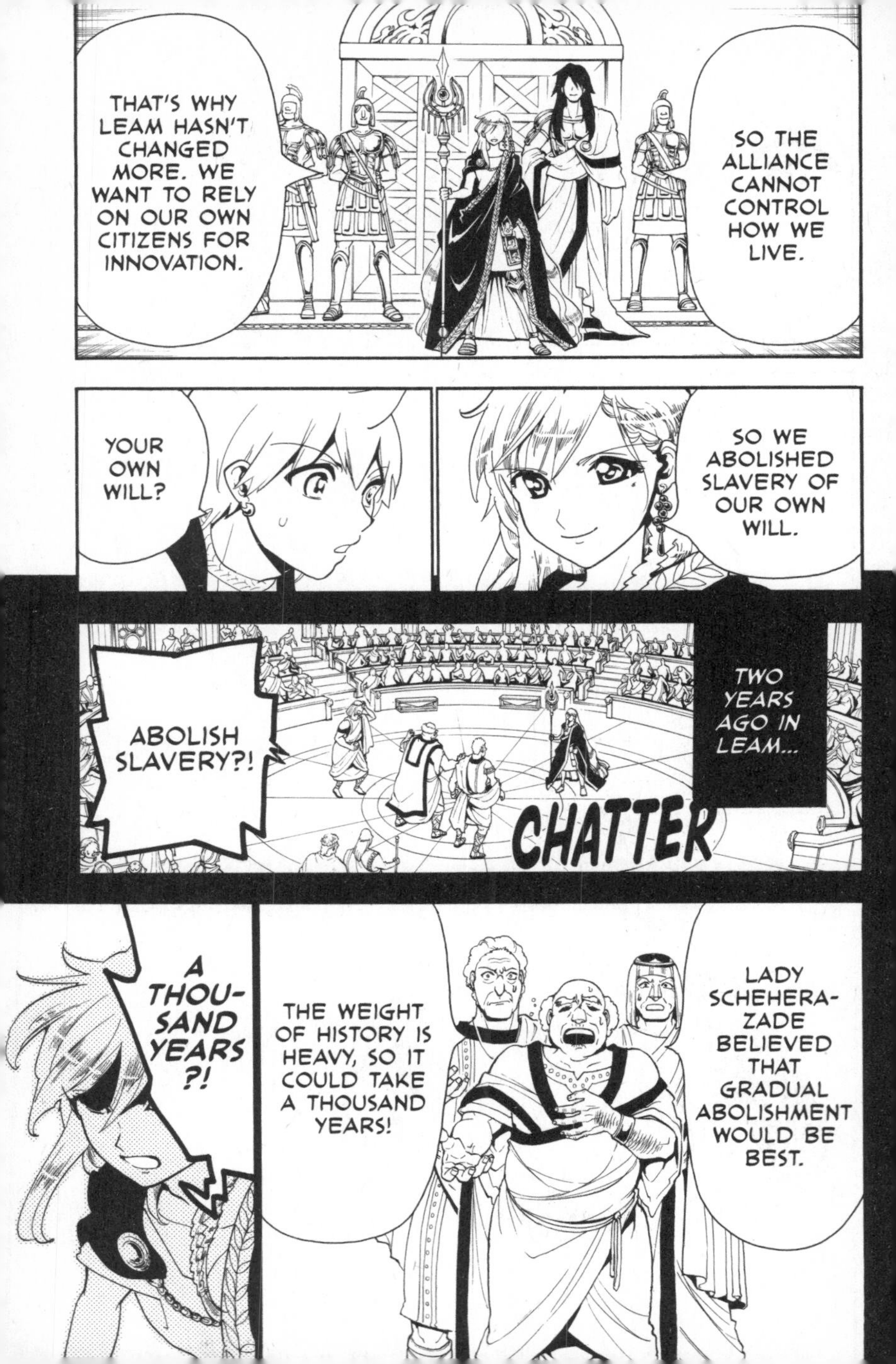
SO THE ALLIANCE CANNOT CONTROL HOW WE LIVE.
THAT'S WHY LEAM HASN'T CHANGED MORE. WE WANT TO RELY ON OUR OWN CITIZENS FOR INNOVATION.
SO WE ABOLISHED SLAVERY OF OUR OWN WILL.
YOUR OWN WILL?
TWO YEARS AGO IN LEAM...
CHATTER
ABOLISH SLAVERY?!
LADY SCHEHERAZADE BELIEVED THAT GRADUAL ABOLISHMENT WOULD BE BEST.
THE WEIGHT OF HISTORY IS HEAVY, SO IT COULD TAKE A THOUSAND YEARS!
A THOUSAND YEARS?!

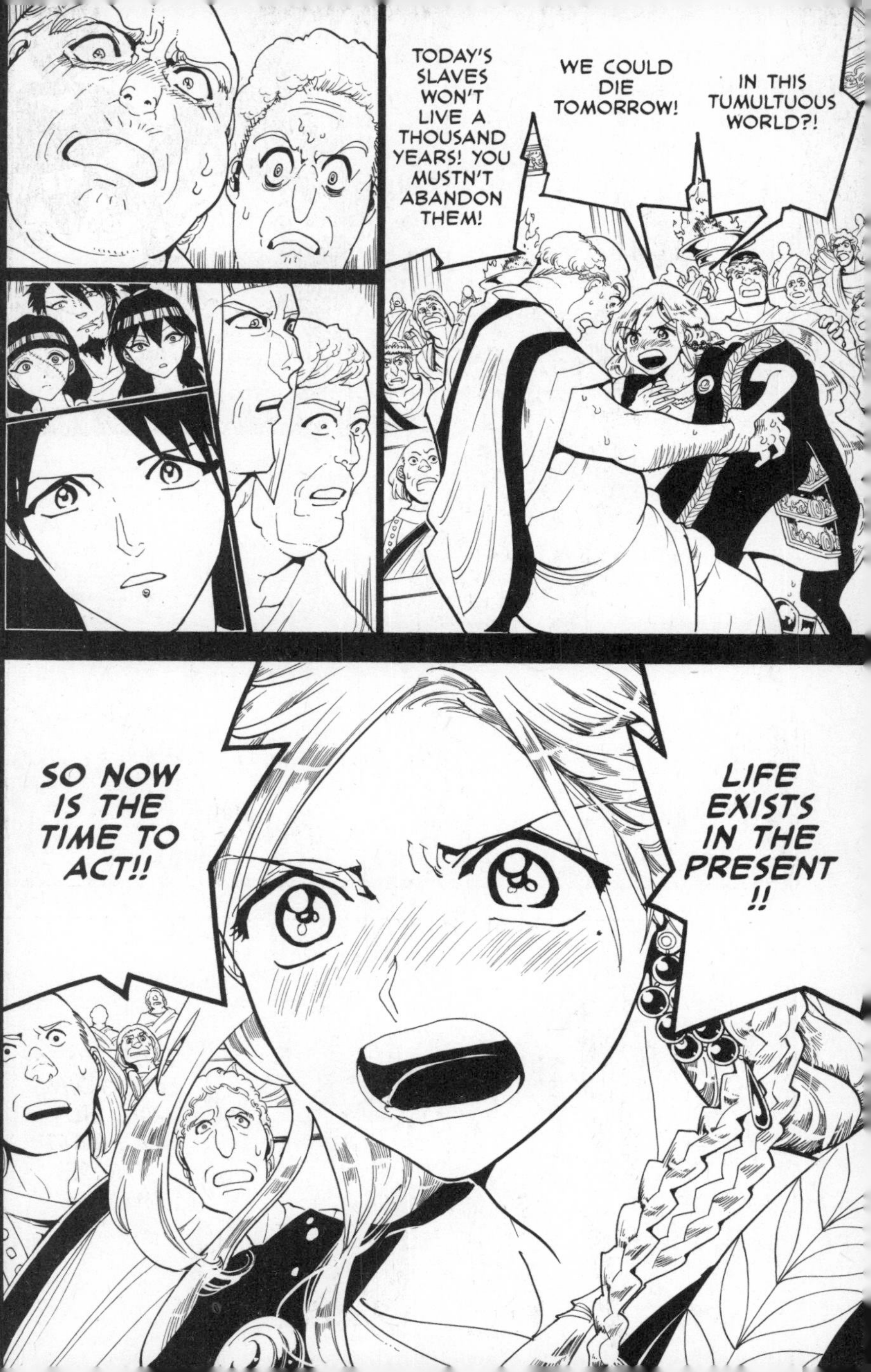
IN THIS TUMULTUOUS WORLD?!
WE COULD DIE TOMORROW!
TODAY'S SLAVES WON'T LIVE A THOUSAND YEARS! YOU MUSTN'T ABANDON THEM!
LIFE EXISTS IN THE PRESENT!!
SO NOW IS THE TIME TO ACT!!

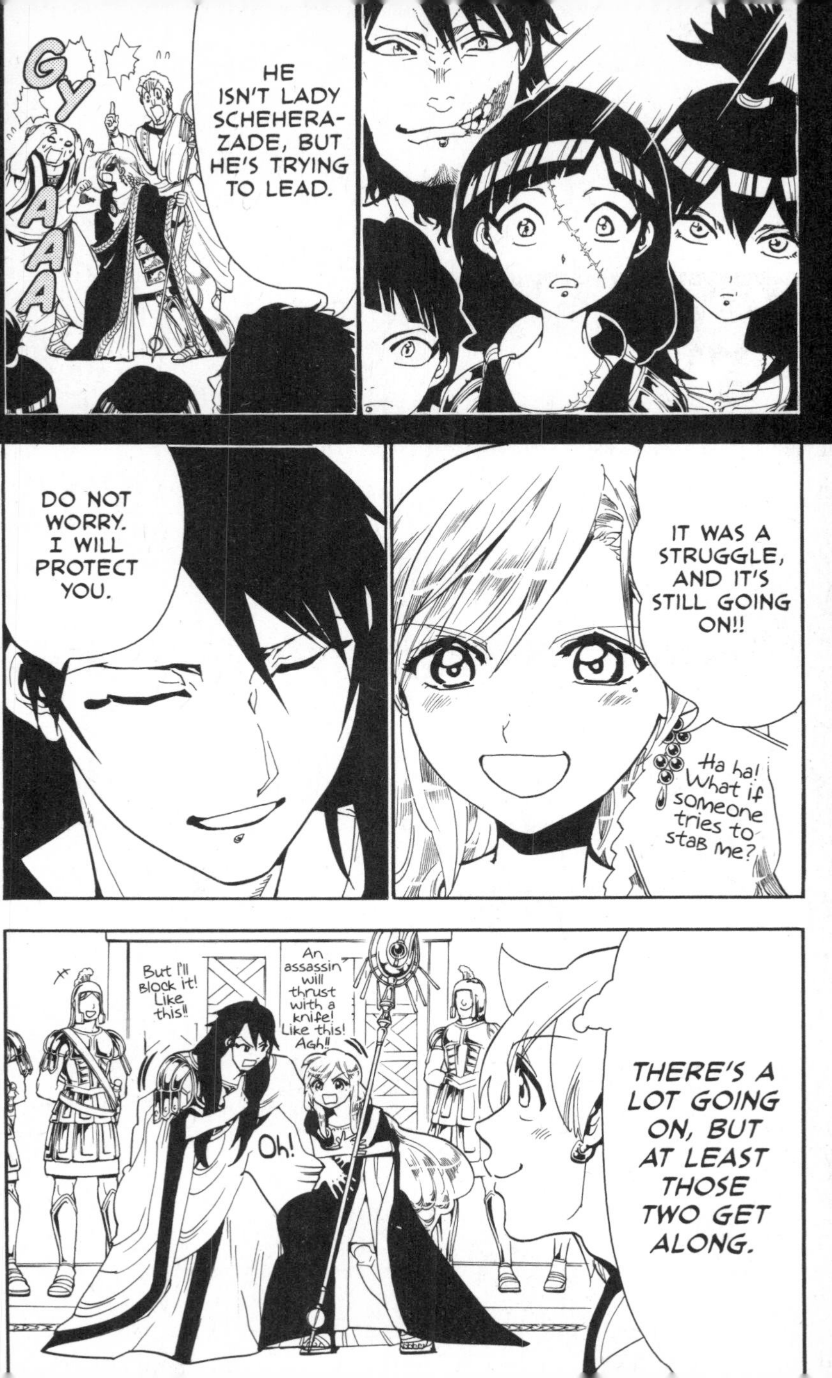
HE ISN'T LADY SCHEHERAZADE, BUT HE'S TRYING TO LEAD.
GYAAAA
IT WAS A STRUGGLE, AND IT'S STILL GOING ON!!
Ha ha! What if someone tries to stab me?
DO NOT WORRY. I WILL PROTECT YOU.
THERE'S A LOT GOING ON, BUT AT LEAST THOSE TWO GET ALONG.
An assassin will thrust with a knife! Like this! Agh!!
But I'll block it! Like this!!
Oh!

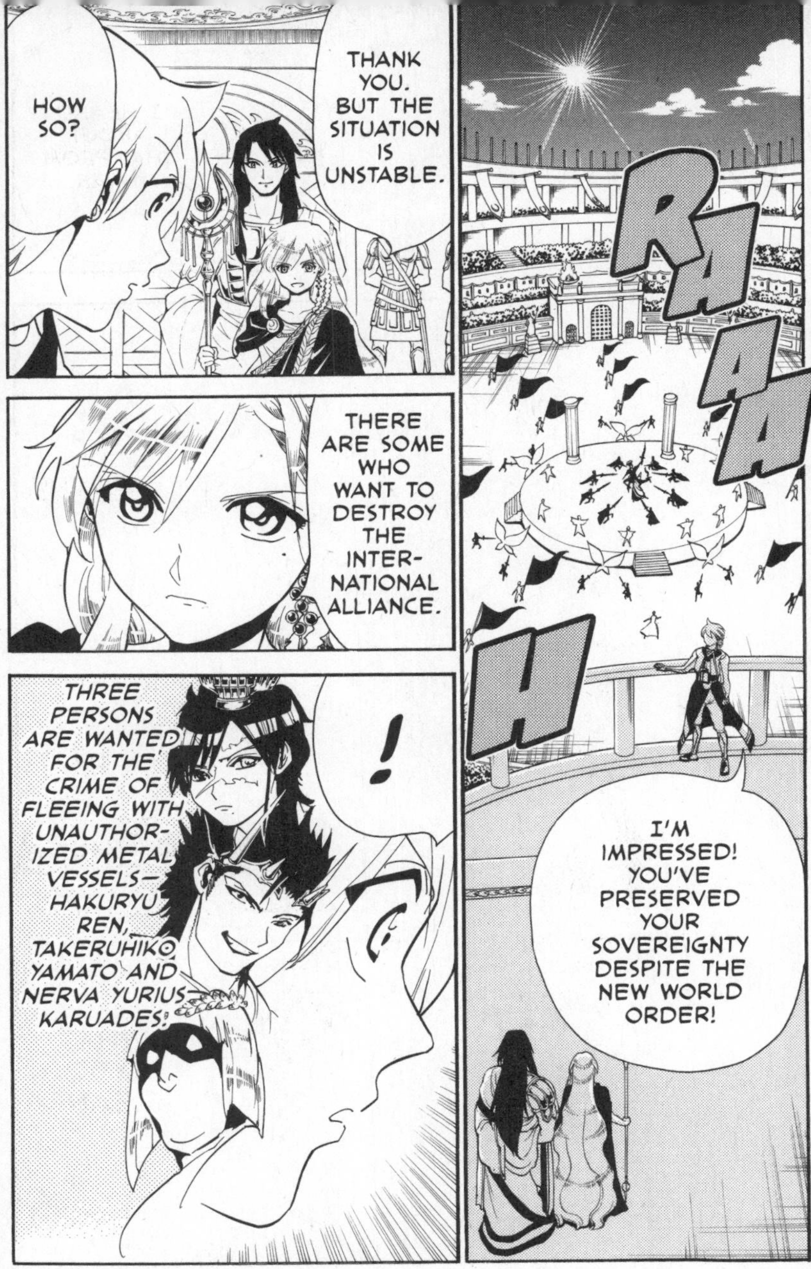
RAAAH
I'M IMPRESSED! YOU'VE PRESERVED YOUR SOVEREIGNTY DESPITE THE NEW WORLD ORDER!
THANK YOU. BUT THE SITUATION IS UNSTABLE.
HOW SO?
THERE ARE SOME WHO WANT TO DESTROY THE INTER-NATIONAL ALLIANCE.
!
THREE PERSONS ARE WANTED FOR THE CRIME OF FLEEING WITH UNAUTHOR-IZED METAL VESSELS— HAKURYU REN, TAKERUHIKO YAMATO AND NERVA YURIUS KARUADES!

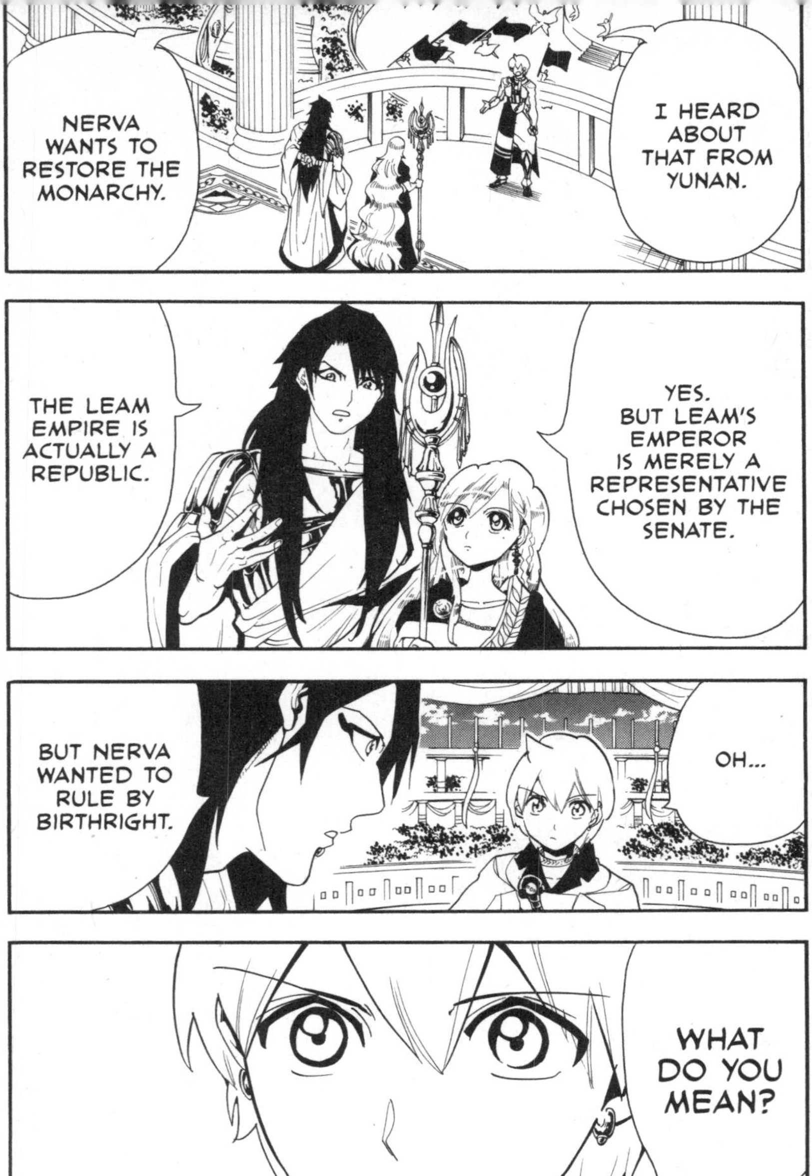
I HEARD ABOUT THAT FROM YUNAN.
NERVA WANTS TO RESTORE THE MONARCHY.
YES. BUT LEAM'S EMPEROR IS MERELY A REPRESENTATIVE CHOSEN BY THE SENATE.
THE LEAM EMPIRE IS ACTUALLY A REPUBLIC.
OH...
BUT NERVA WANTED TO RULE BY BIRTHRIGHT.
WHAT DO YOU MEAN?

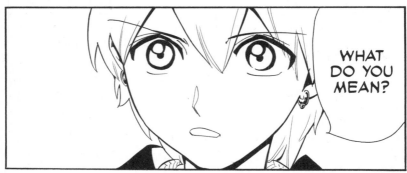

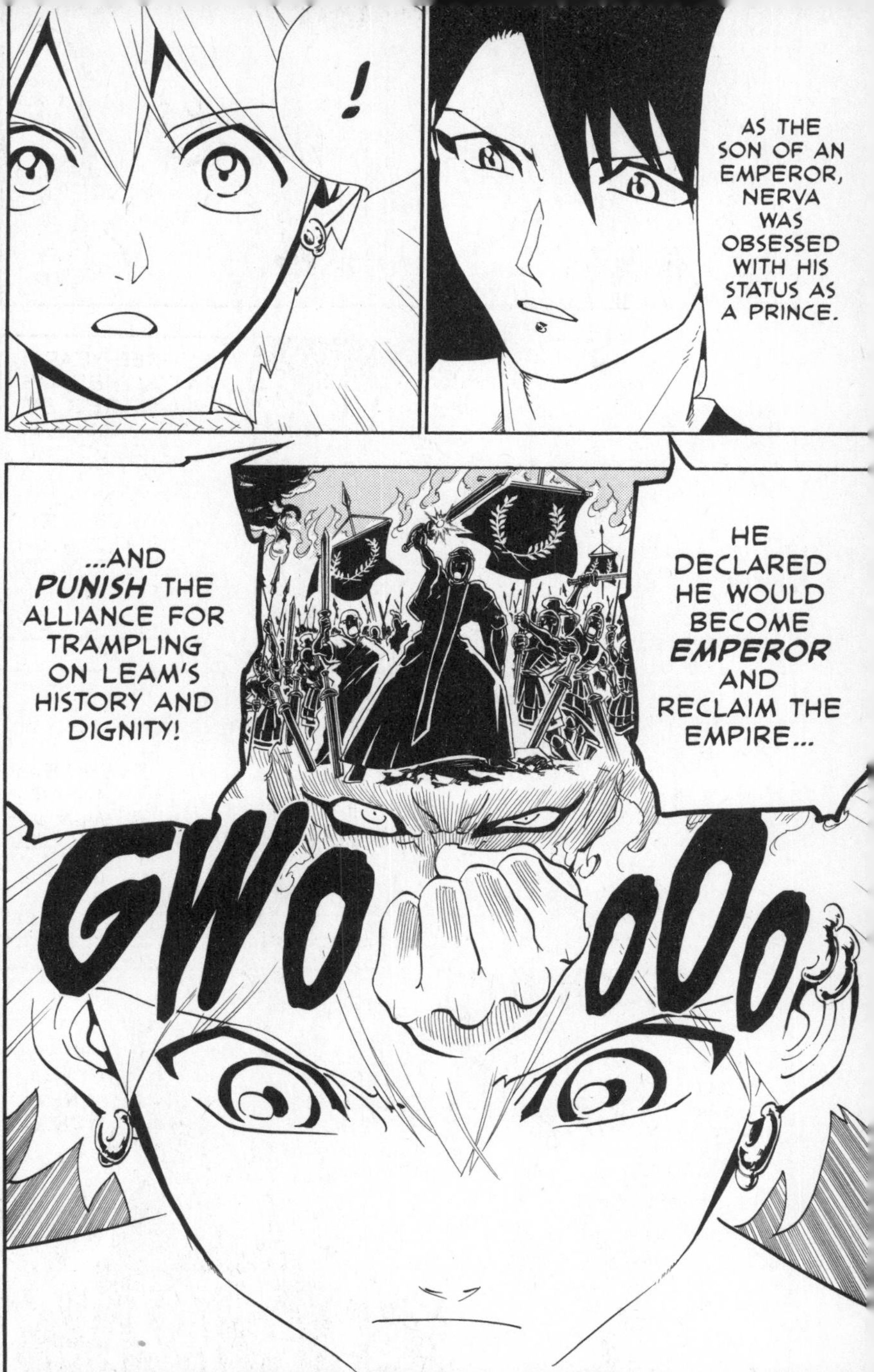
AS THE SON OF AN EMPEROR, NERVA WAS OBSESSED WITH HIS STATUS AS A PRINCE.
!
HE DECLARED HE WOULD BECOME EMPEROR AND RECLAIM THE EMPIRE...
...AND PUNISH THE ALLIANCE FOR TRAMPLING ON LEAM'S HISTORY AND DIGNITY!
GWOOOO

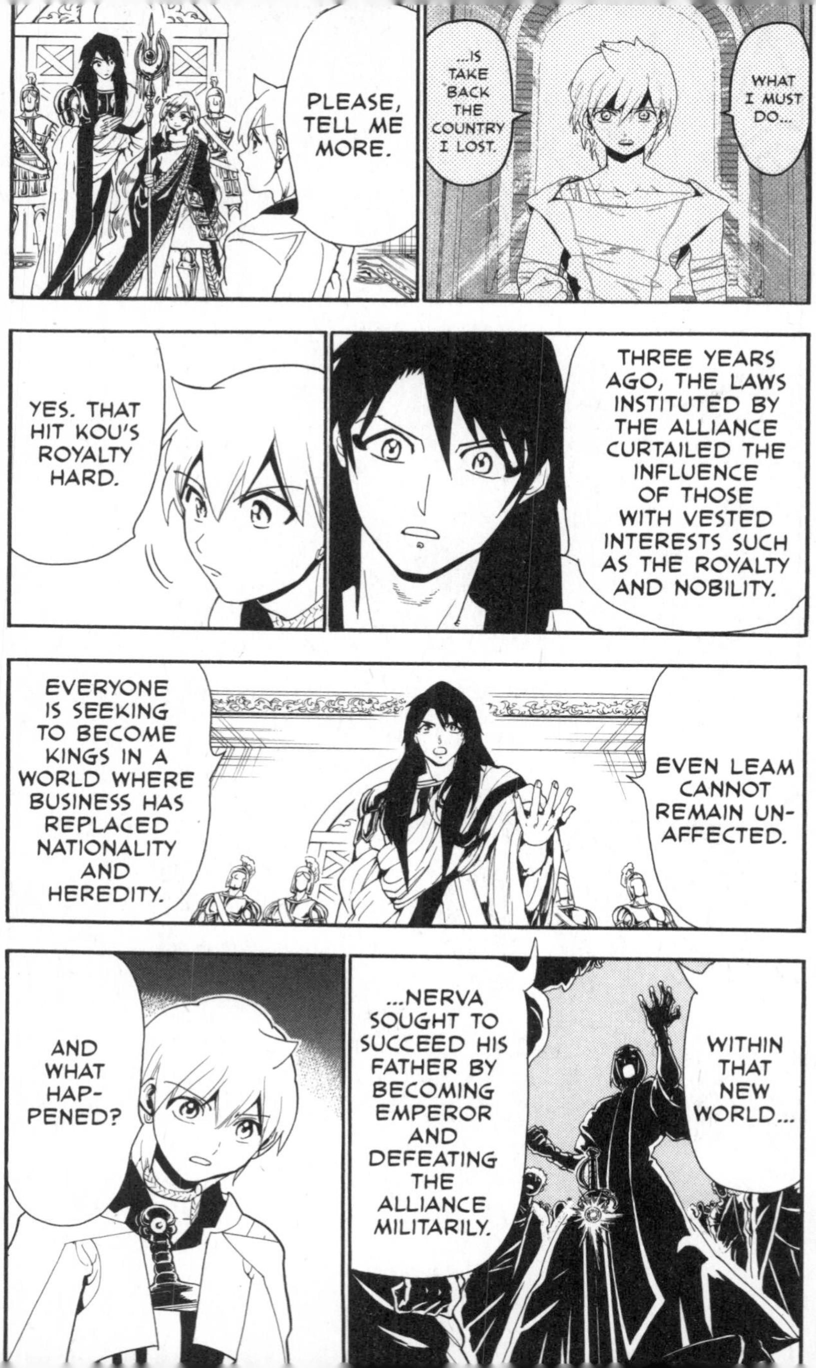
WHAT I MUST DO...
...IS TAKE BACK THE COUNTRY I LOST.
PLEASE, TELL ME MORE.
THREE YEARS AGO, THE LAWS INSTITUTED BY THE ALLIANCE CURTAILED THE INFLUENCE OF THOSE WITH VESTED INTERESTS SUCH AS THE ROYALTY AND NOBILITY.
YES. THAT HIT KOU'S ROYALTY HARD.
EVEN LEAM CANNOT REMAIN UN-AFFECTED.
EVERYONE IS SEEKING TO BECOME KINGS IN A WORLD WHERE BUSINESS HAS REPLACED NATIONALITY AND HEREDITY.
WITHIN THAT NEW WORLD...
...NERVA SOUGHT TO SUCCEED HIS FATHER BY BECOMING EMPEROR AND DEFEATING THE ALLIANCE MILITARILY.
AND WHAT HAP-PENED?

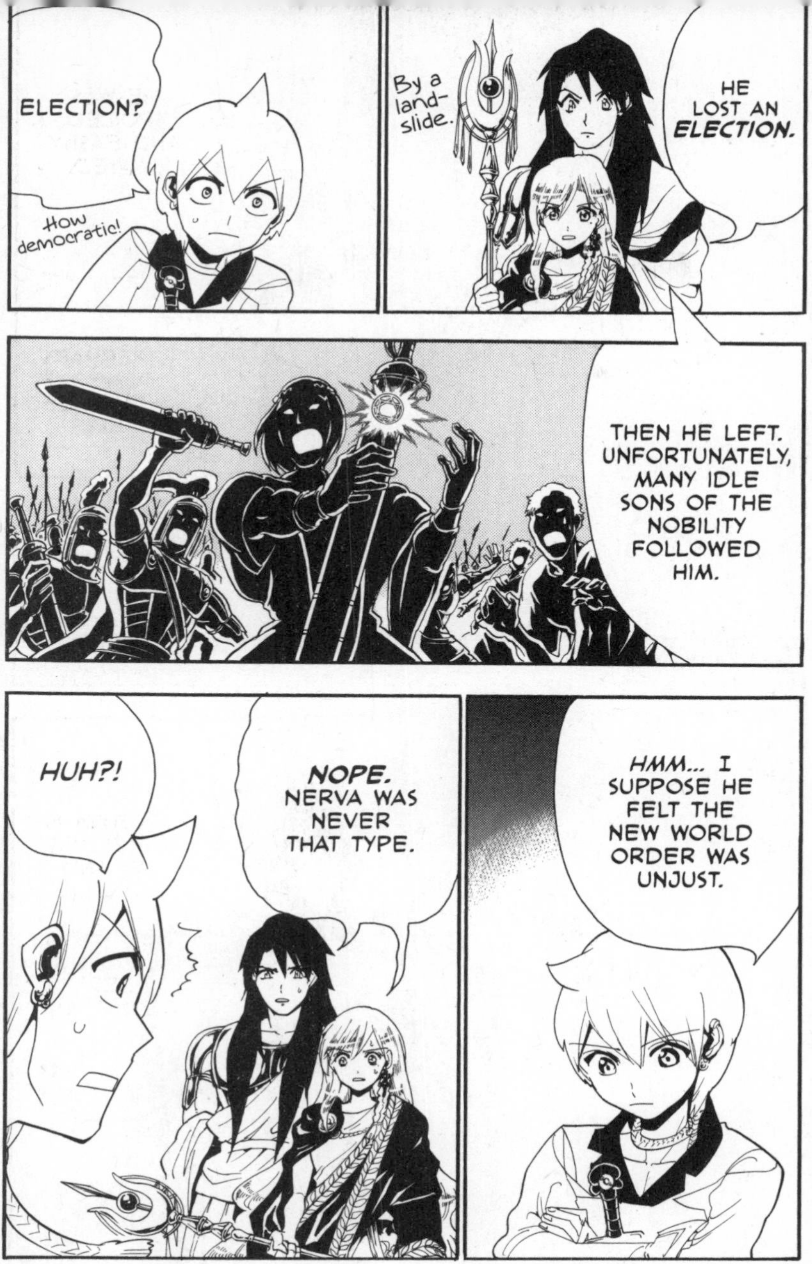
HE LOST AN ELECTION.
By a land-slide.
ELECTION?
How democratic!
THEN HE LEFT. UNFORTUNATELY, MANY IDLE SONS OF THE NOBILITY FOLLOWED HIM.
HMM... I SUPPOSE HE FELT THE NEW WORLD ORDER WAS UNJUST.
NOPE. NERVA WAS NEVER THAT TYPE.
HUH?!

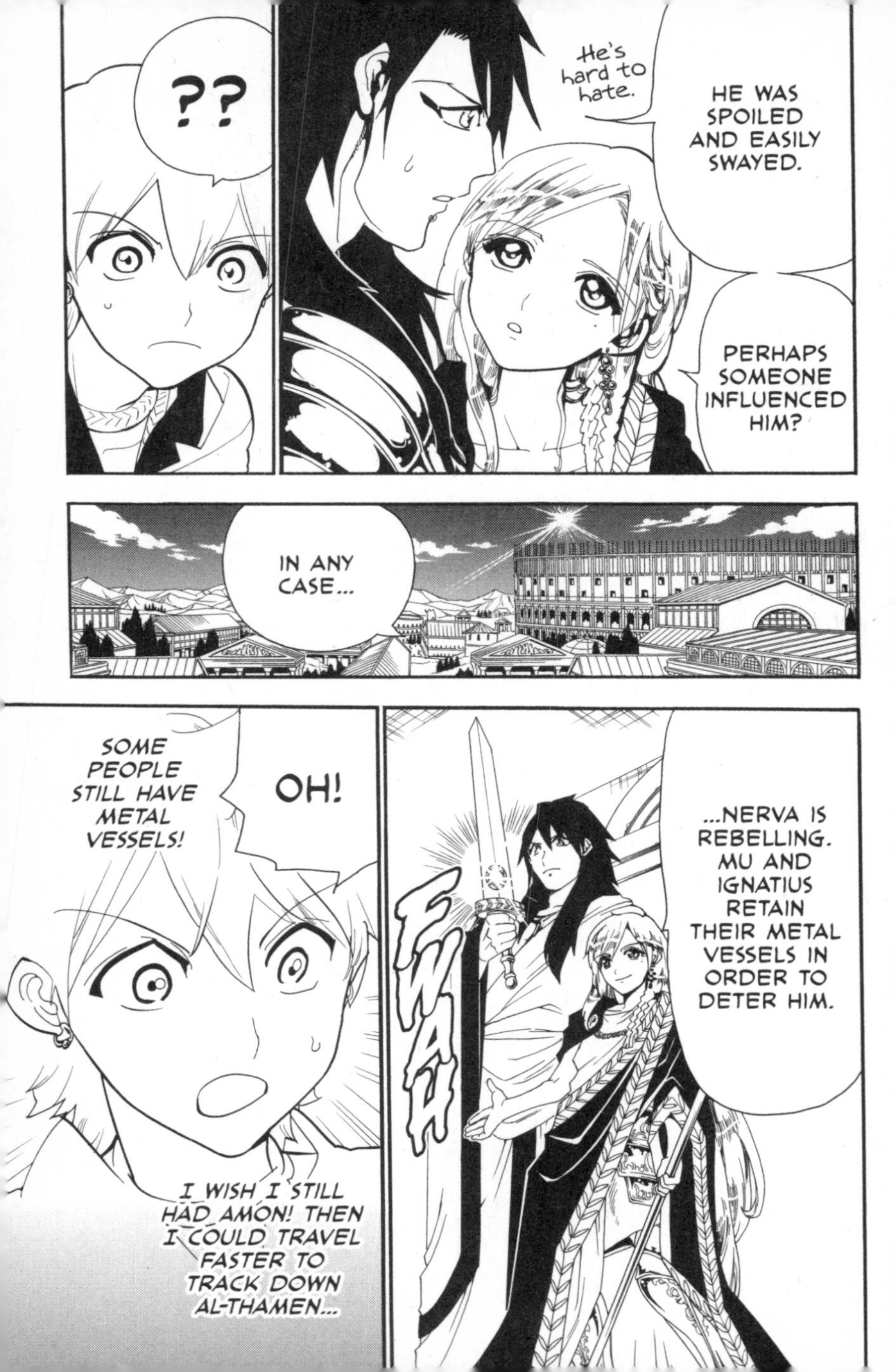
HE WAS SPOILED AND EASILY SWAYED.
He's hard to hate.
PERHAPS SOMEONE INFLUENCED HIM?
??
IN ANY CASE...
...NERVA IS REBELLING. MU AND IGNATIUS RETAIN THEIR METAL VESSELS IN ORDER TO DETER HIM.
OH!
SOME PEOPLE STILL HAVE METAL VESSELS!
I WISH I STILL HAD AMON! THEN I COULD TRAVEL FASTER TO TRACK DOWN AL-THAMEN...

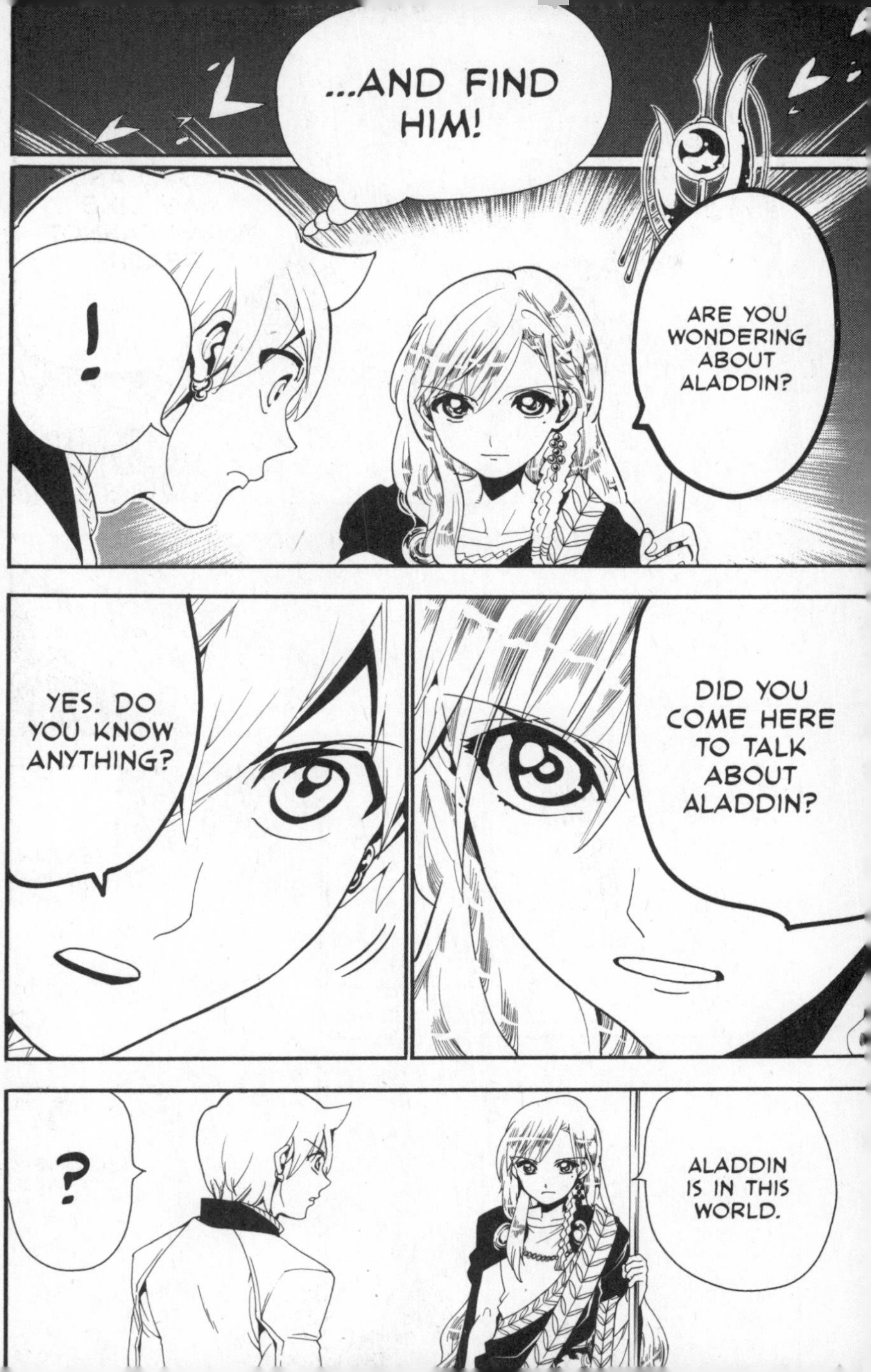
...AND FIND HIM!
ARE YOU WONDERING ABOUT ALADDIN?
!
DID YOU COME HERE TO TALK ABOUT ALADDIN?
YES. DO YOU KNOW ANYTHING?
ALADDIN IS IN THIS WORLD.
?

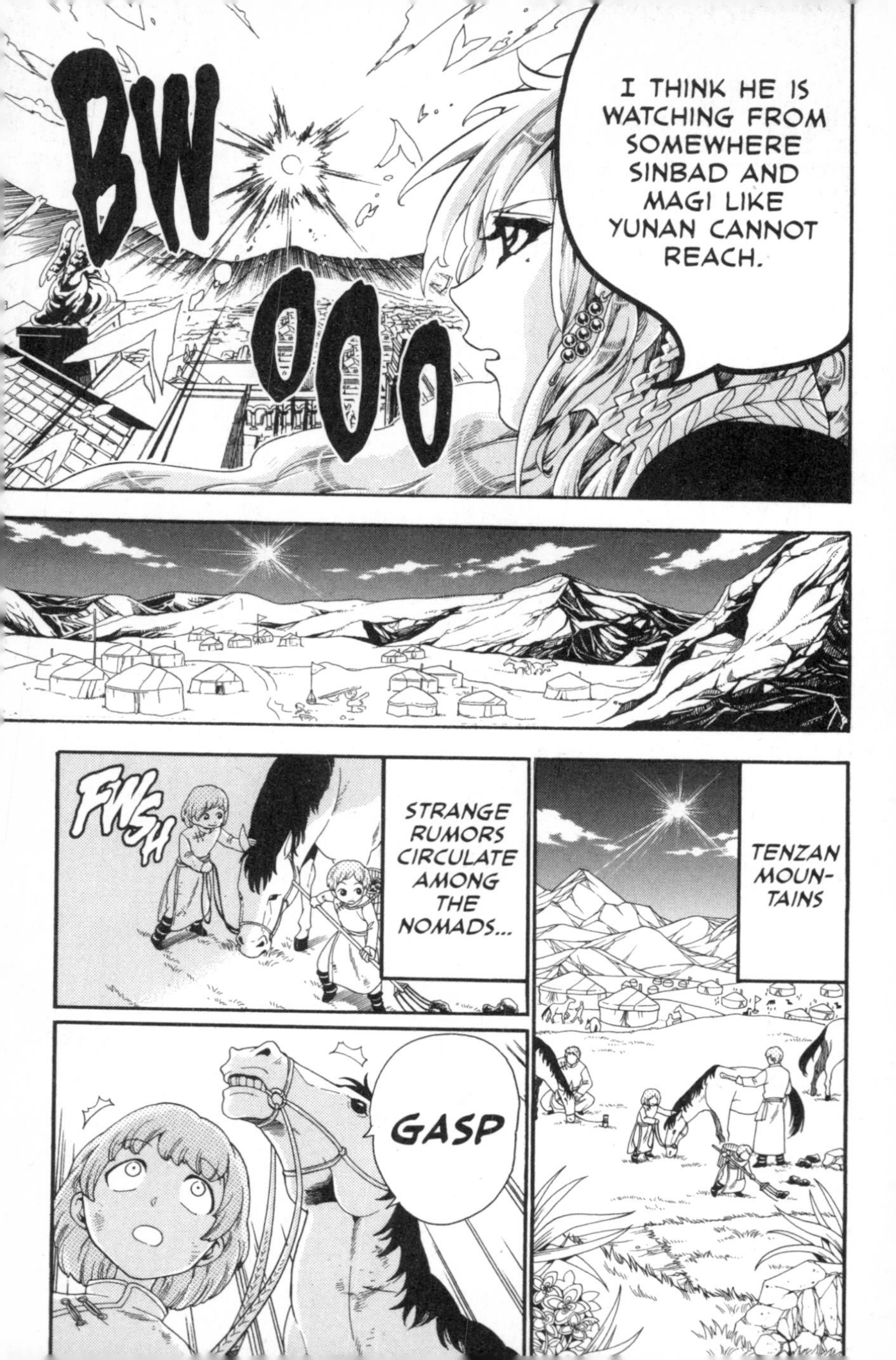
I THINK HE IS WATCHING FROM SOMEWHERE SINBAD AND MAGI LIKE YUNAN CANNOT REACH.
BWOOO
TENZAN MOUNTAINS
STRANGE RUMORS CIRCULATE AMONG THE NOMADS...
FWSH
GASP

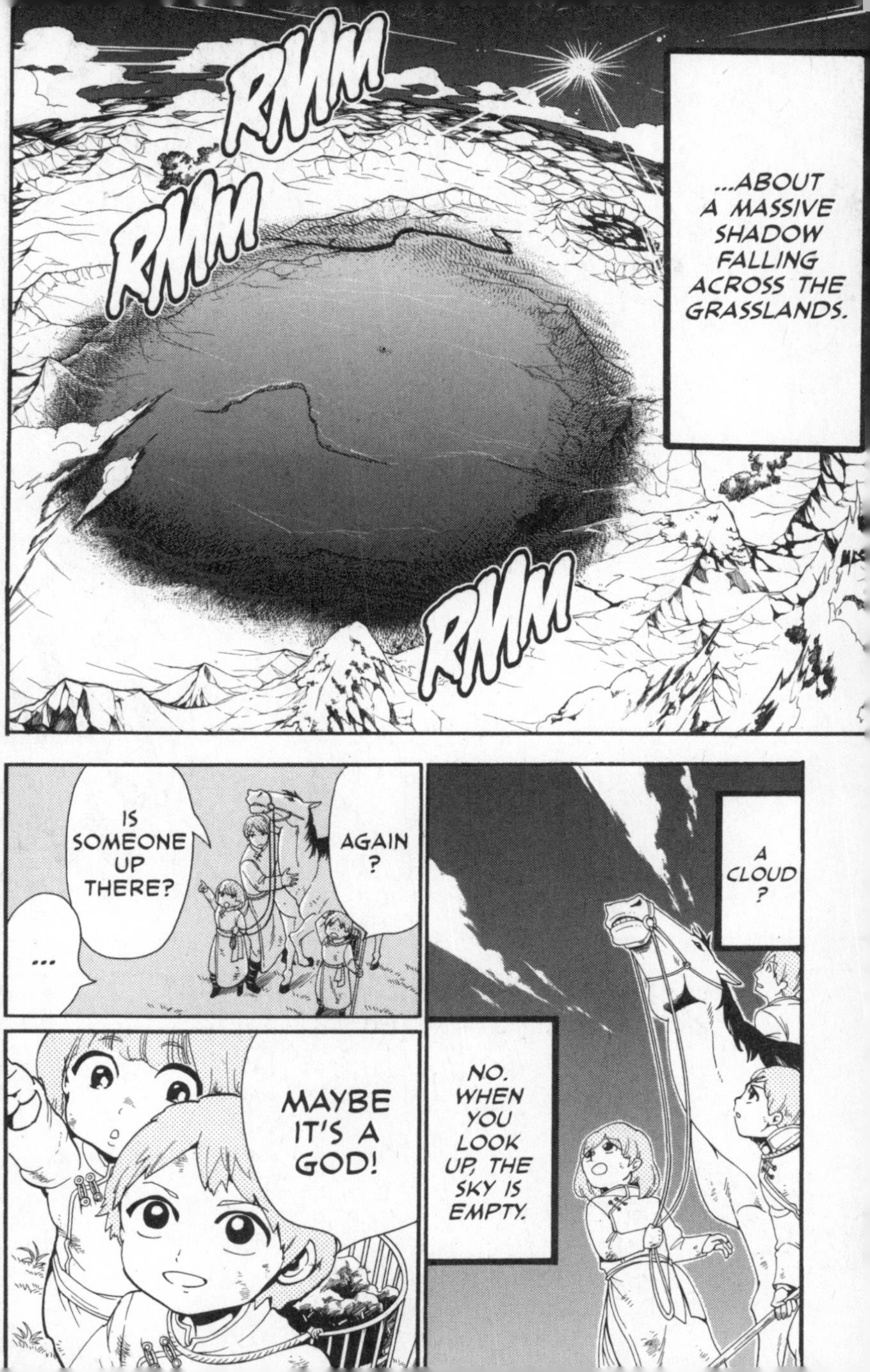
...ABOUT A MASSIVE SHADOW FALLING ACROSS THE GRASSLANDS.
RMM
RMM
RMM
A CLOUD?
NO. WHEN YOU LOOK UP, THE SKY IS EMPTY.
AGAIN?
IS SOMEONE UP THERE?
...
MAYBE IT'S A GOD!

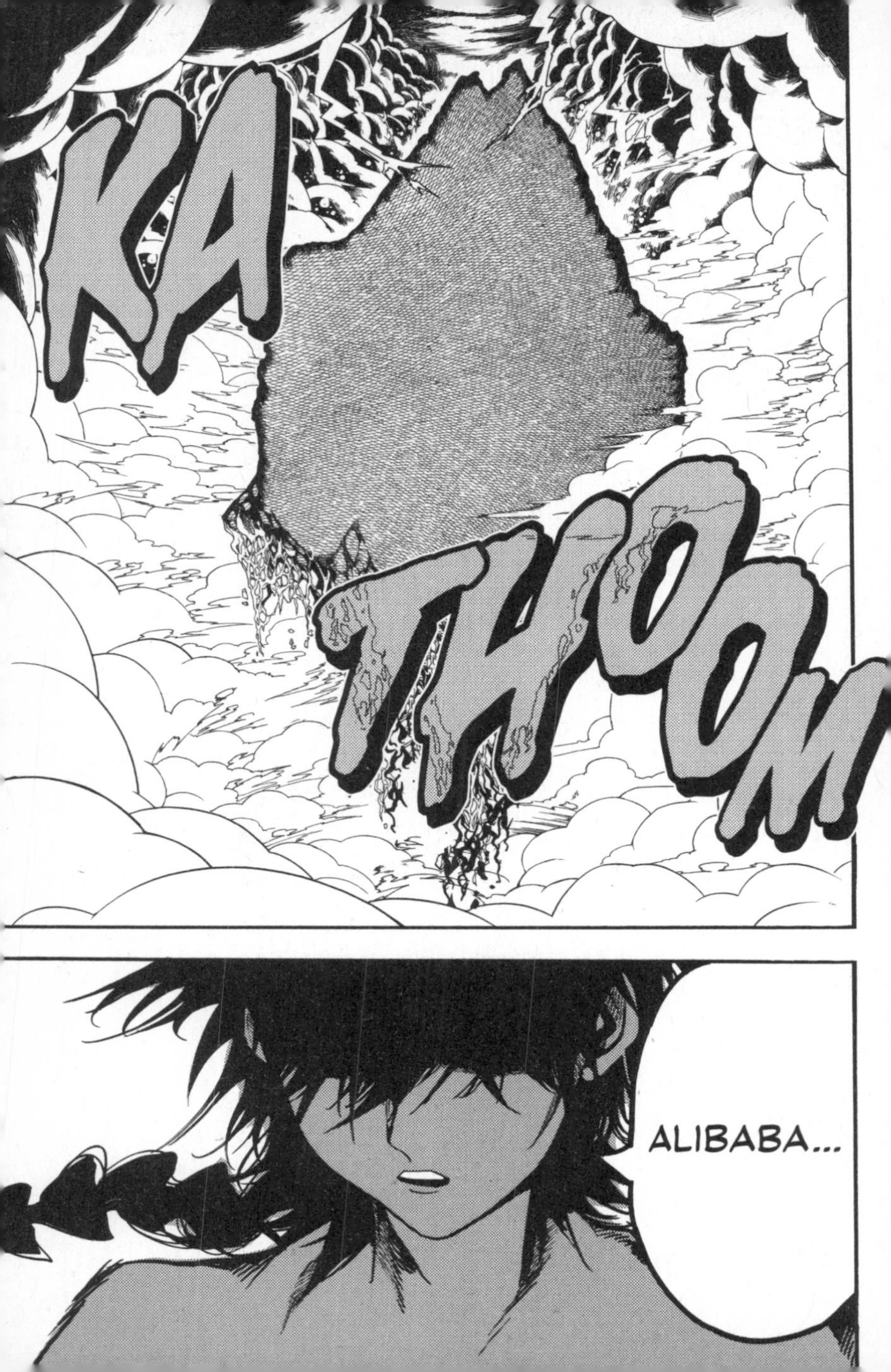
KA
THOOM
ALIBABA...

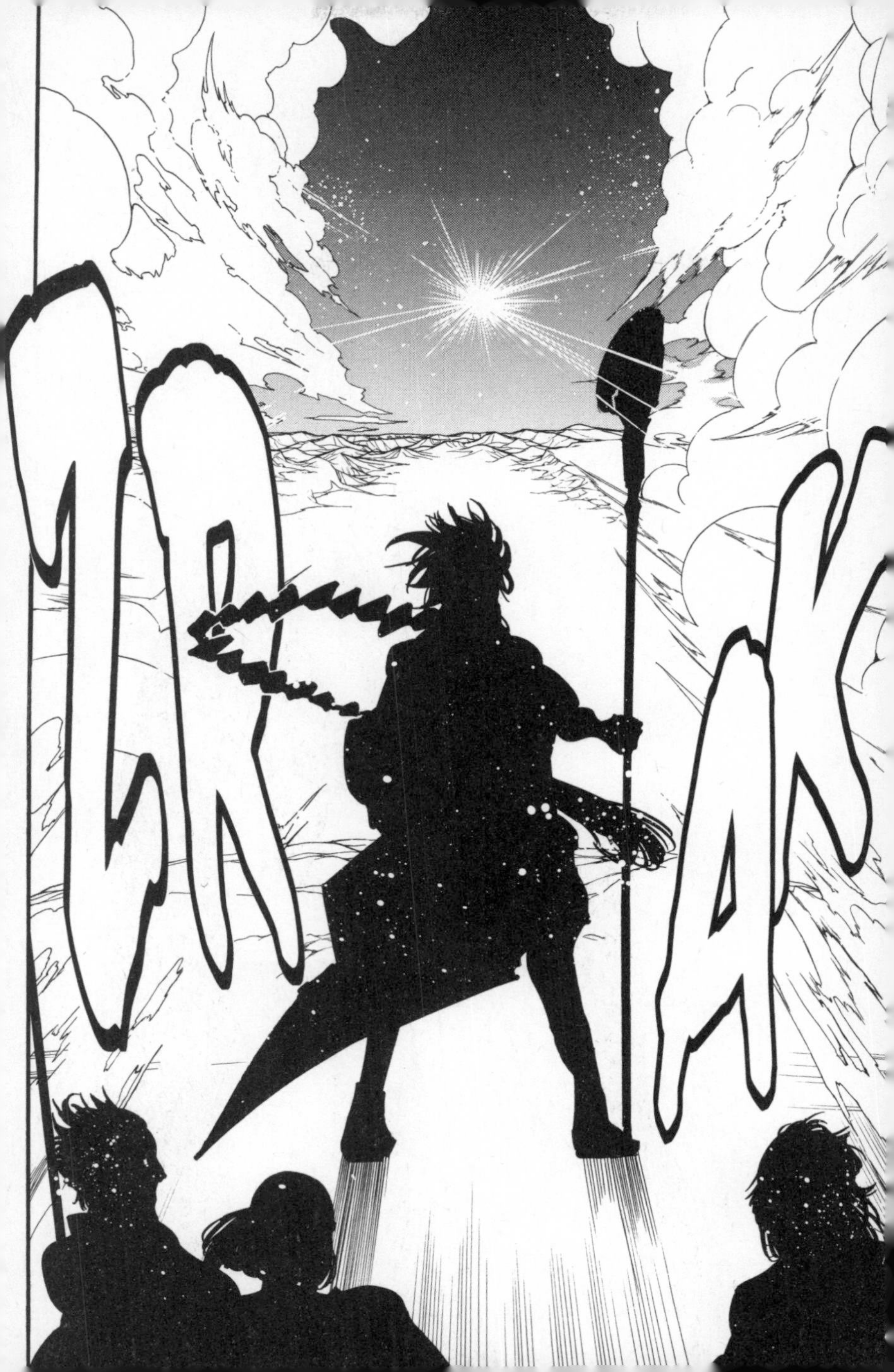
CRAK

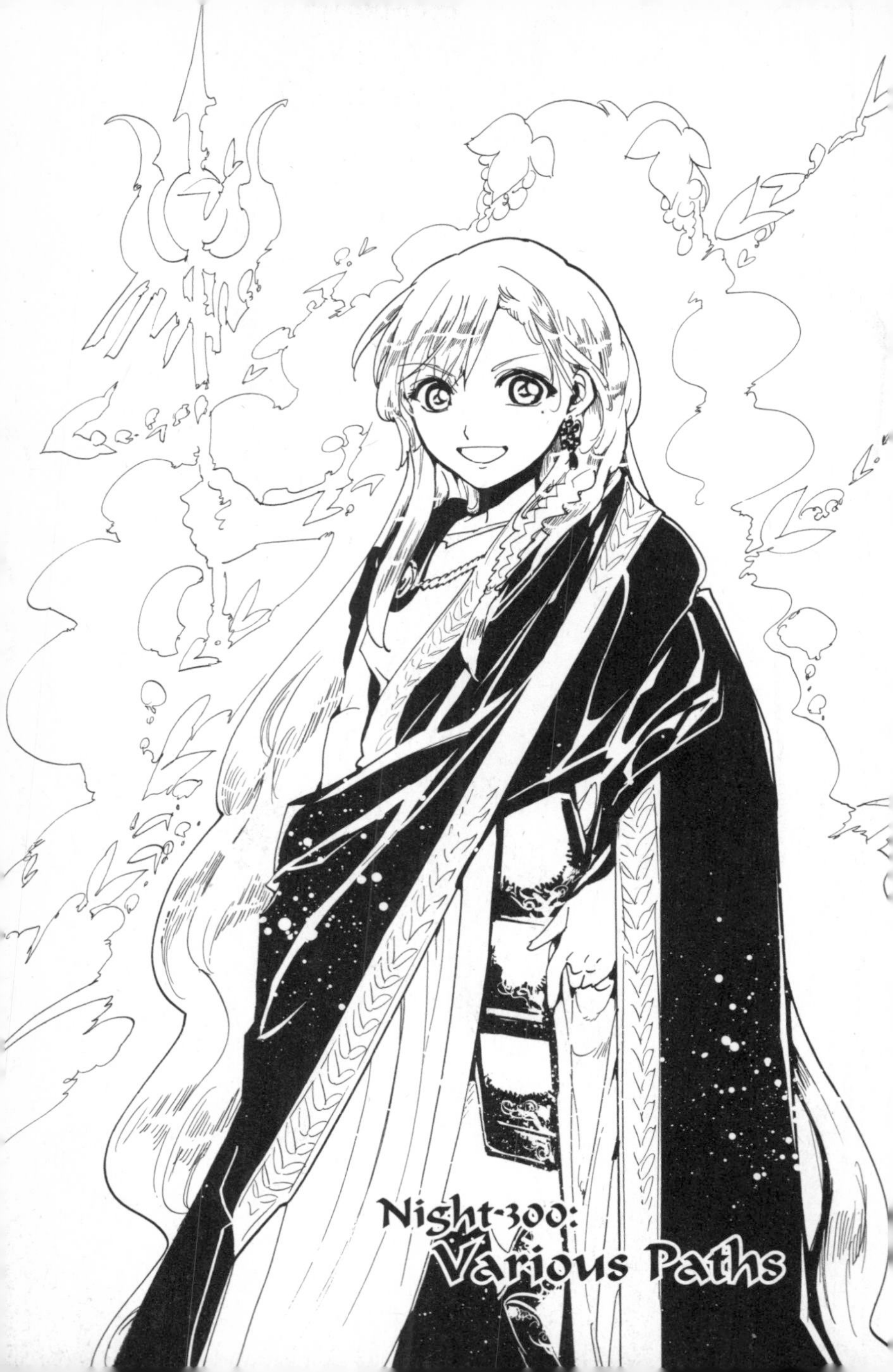
Night 300:
Various Paths

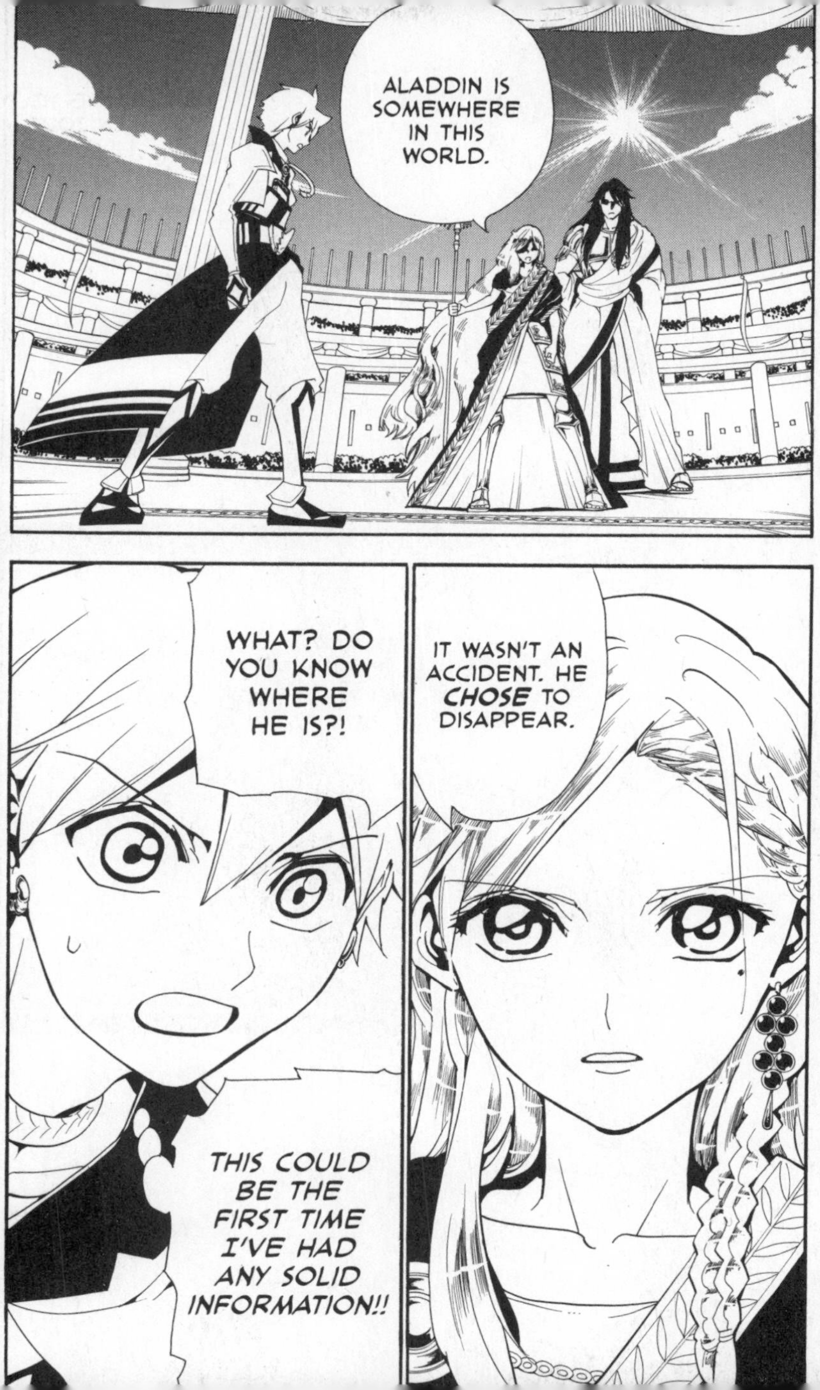
ALADDIN IS SOMEWHERE IN THIS WORLD.
IT WASN'T AN ACCIDENT. HE *CHOSE* TO DISAPPEAR.
WHAT? DO YOU KNOW WHERE HE IS?!
THIS COULD BE THE FIRST TIME I'VE HAD ANY SOLID INFORMATION!!

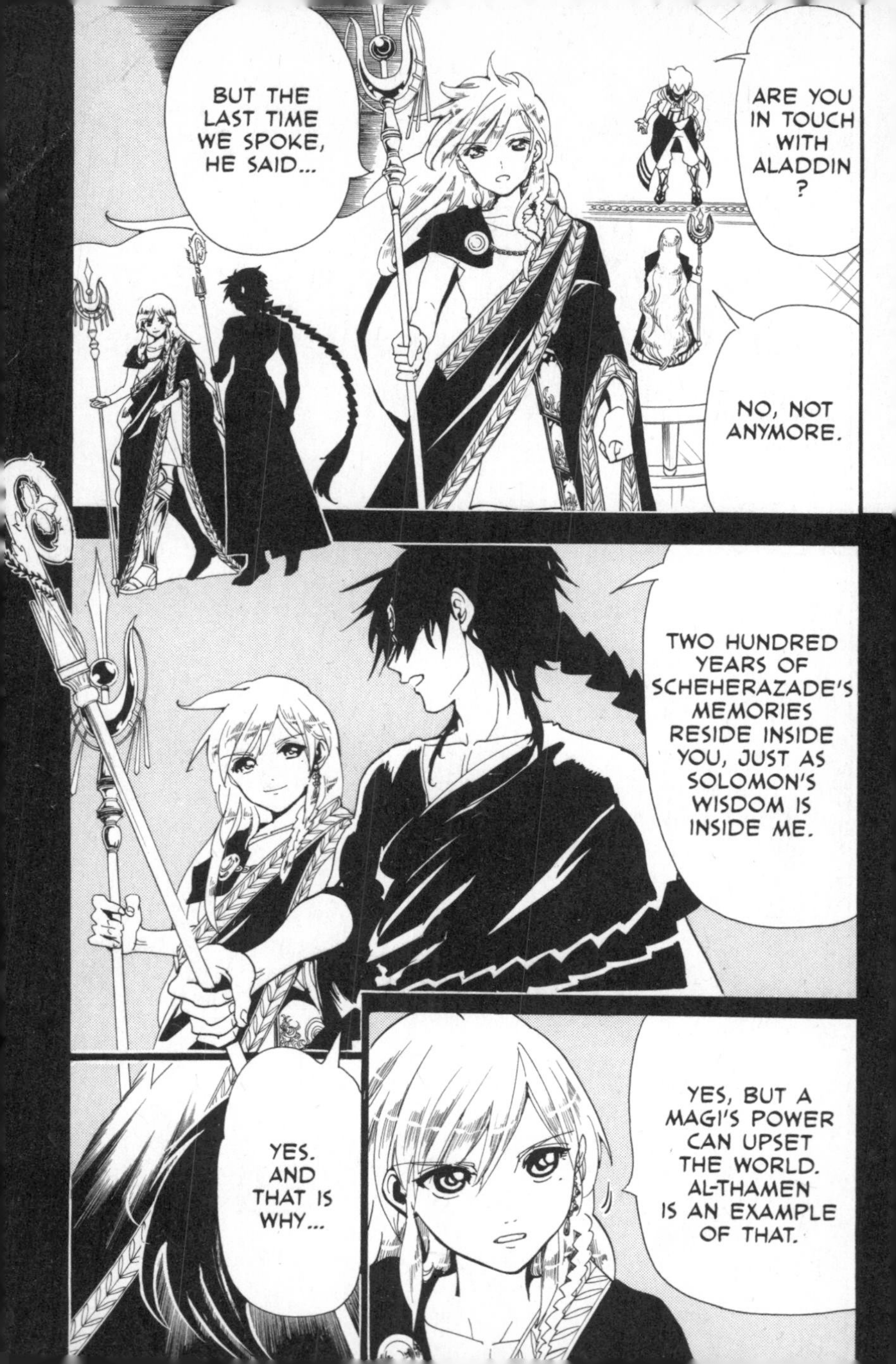
ARE YOU IN TOUCH WITH ALADDIN?
NO, NOT ANYMORE.
BUT THE LAST TIME WE SPOKE, HE SAID...
TWO HUNDRED YEARS OF SCHEHERAZADE'S MEMORIES RESIDE INSIDE YOU, JUST AS SOLOMON'S WISDOM IS INSIDE ME.
YES, BUT A MAGI'S POWER CAN UPSET THE WORLD. AL-THAMEN IS AN EXAMPLE OF THAT.
YES. AND THAT IS WHY...

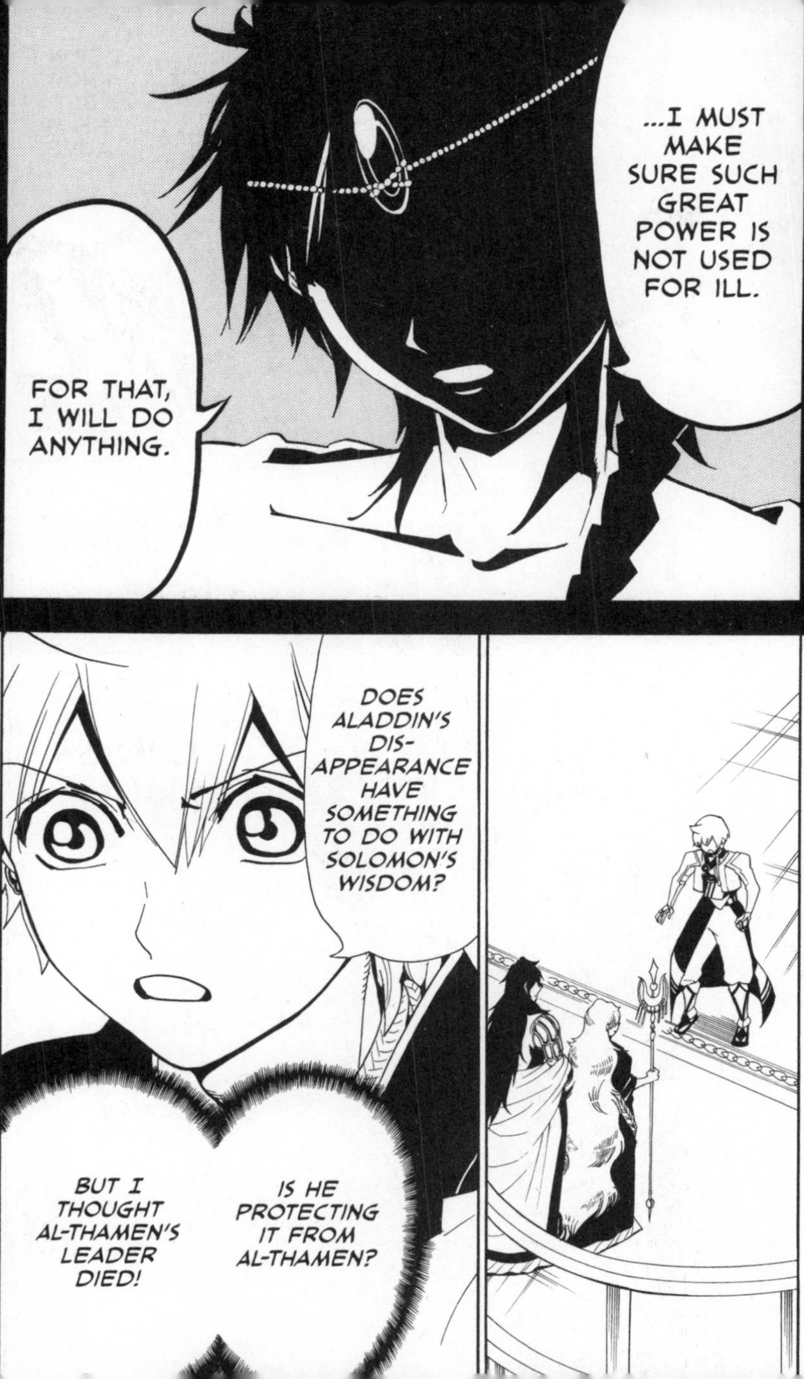
...I MUST MAKE SURE SUCH GREAT POWER IS NOT USED FOR ILL.
FOR THAT, I WILL DO ANYTHING.
DOES ALADDIN'S DIS-APPEARANCE HAVE SOMETHING TO DO WITH SOLOMON'S WISDOM?
IS HE PROTECTING IT FROM AL-THAMEN?
BUT I THOUGHT AL-THAMEN'S LEADER DIED!

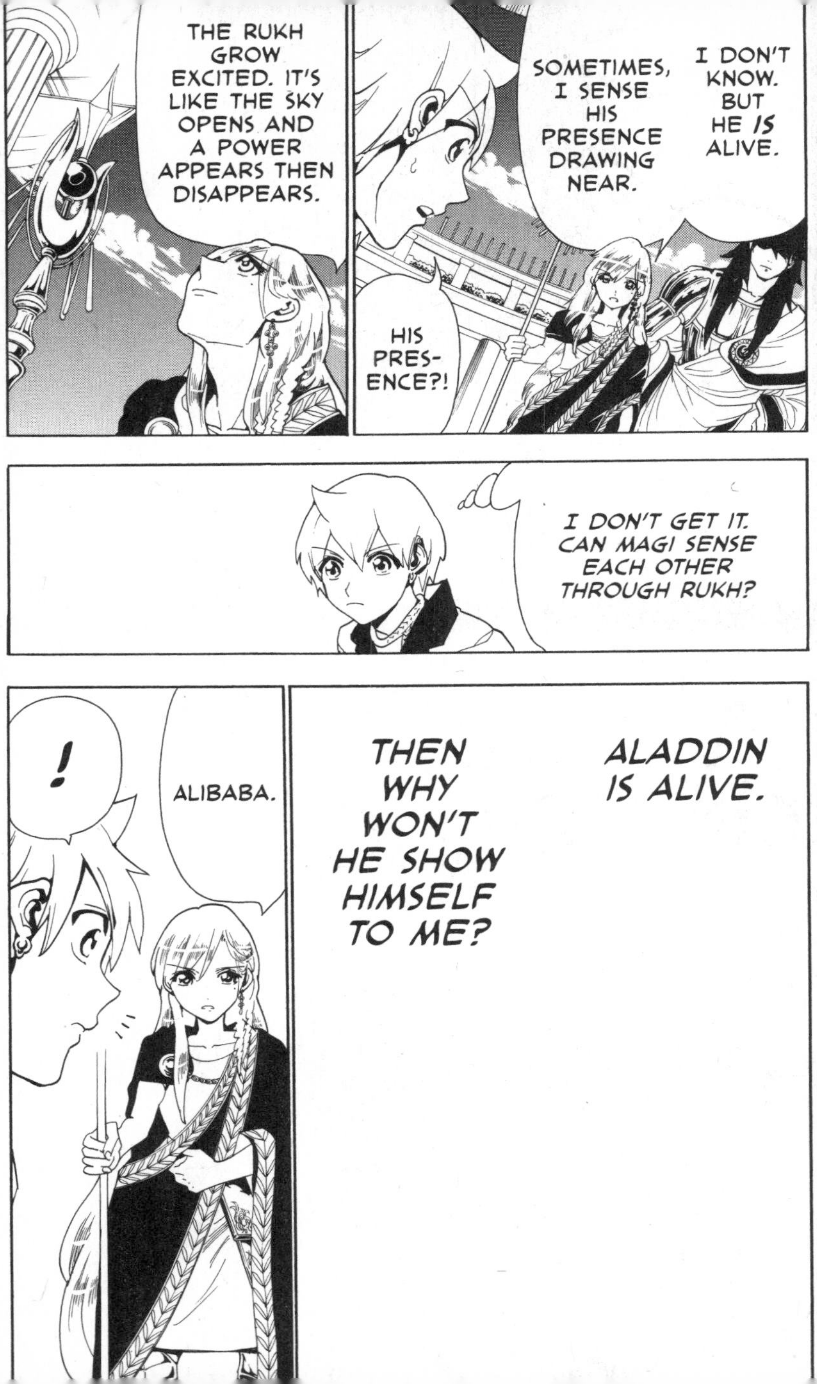
I DON'T KNOW. BUT HE IS ALIVE.
SOMETIMES, I SENSE HIS PRESENCE DRAWING NEAR.
HIS PRES-ENCE?!
THE RUKH GROW EXCITED. IT'S LIKE THE SKY OPENS AND A POWER APPEARS THEN DISAPPEARS.
I DON'T GET IT. CAN MAGI SENSE EACH OTHER THROUGH RUKH?
ALADDIN IS ALIVE.
THEN WHY WON'T HE SHOW HIMSELF TO ME?
ALIBABA.
!

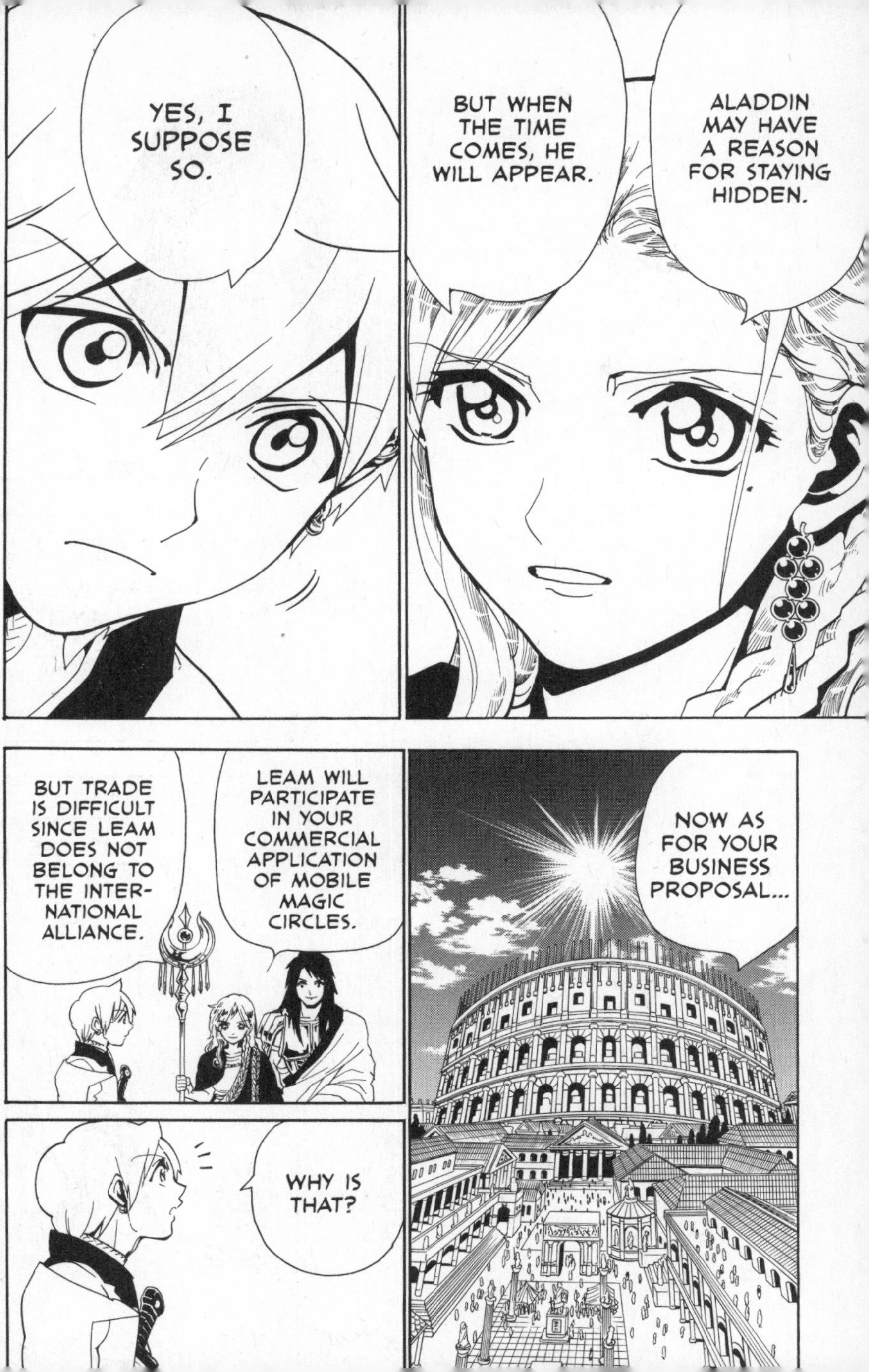
ALADDIN MAY HAVE A REASON FOR STAYING HIDDEN.
BUT WHEN THE TIME COMES, HE WILL APPEAR.
YES, I SUPPOSE SO.
NOW AS FOR YOUR BUSINESS PROPOSAL...
LEAM WILL PARTICIPATE IN YOUR COMMERCIAL APPLICATION OF MOBILE MAGIC CIRCLES.
BUT TRADE IS DIFFICULT SINCE LEAM DOES NOT BELONG TO THE INTER-NATIONAL ALLIANCE.
WHY IS THAT?

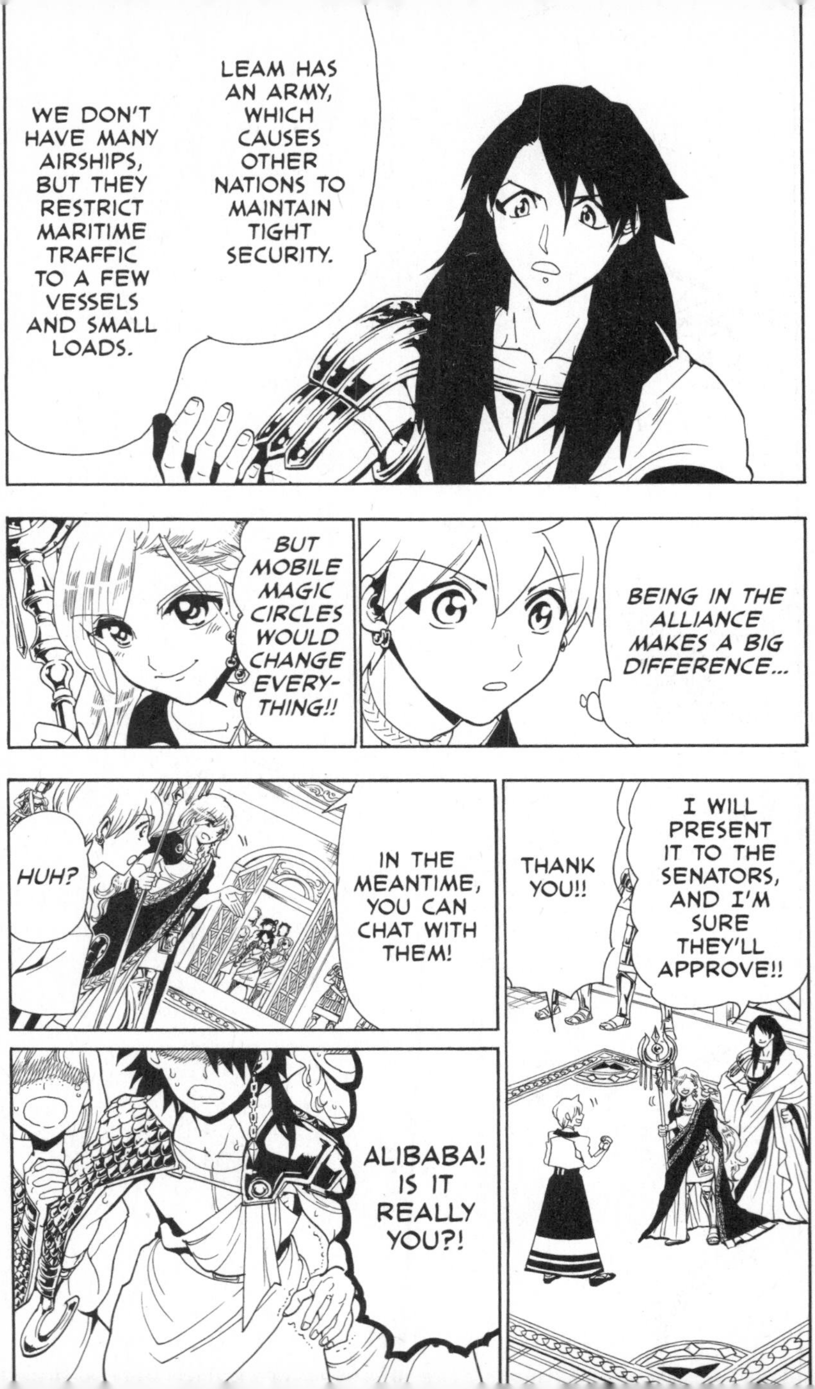
LEAM HAS AN ARMY, WHICH CAUSES OTHER NATIONS TO MAINTAIN TIGHT SECURITY.
WE DON'T HAVE MANY AIRSHIPS, BUT THEY RESTRICT MARITIME TRAFFIC TO A FEW VESSELS AND SMALL LOADS.
BEING IN THE ALLIANCE MAKES A BIG DIFFERENCE...
BUT MOBILE MAGIC CIRCLES WOULD CHANGE EVERY-THING!!
I WILL PRESENT IT TO THE SENATORS, AND I'M SURE THEY'LL APPROVE!!
THANK YOU!!
IN THE MEANTIME, YOU CAN CHAT WITH THEM!
HUH?
ALIBABA! IS IT REALLY YOU?!

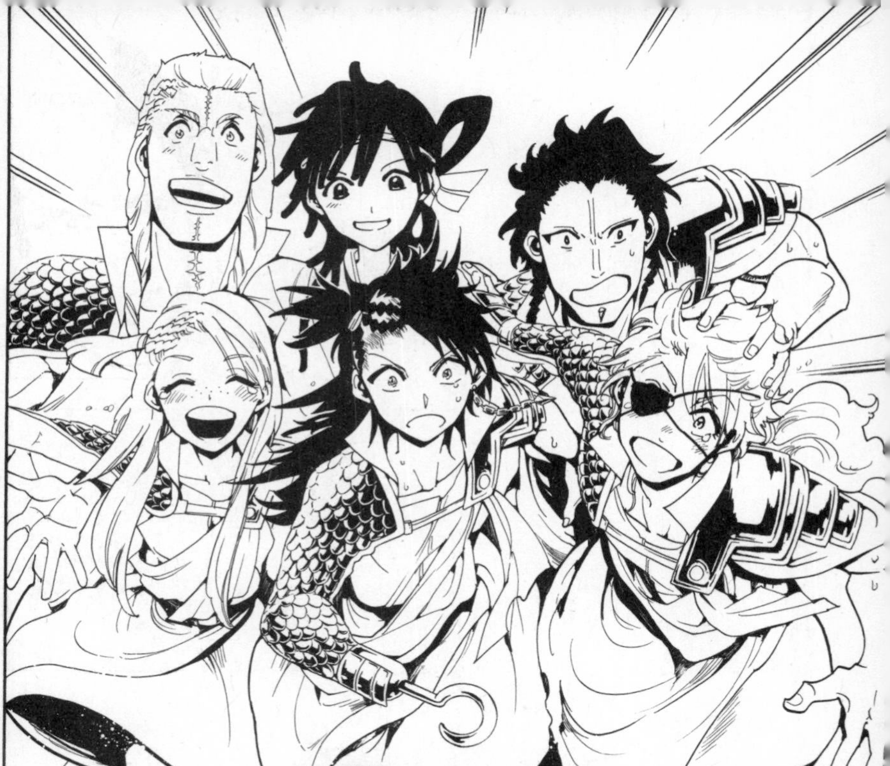

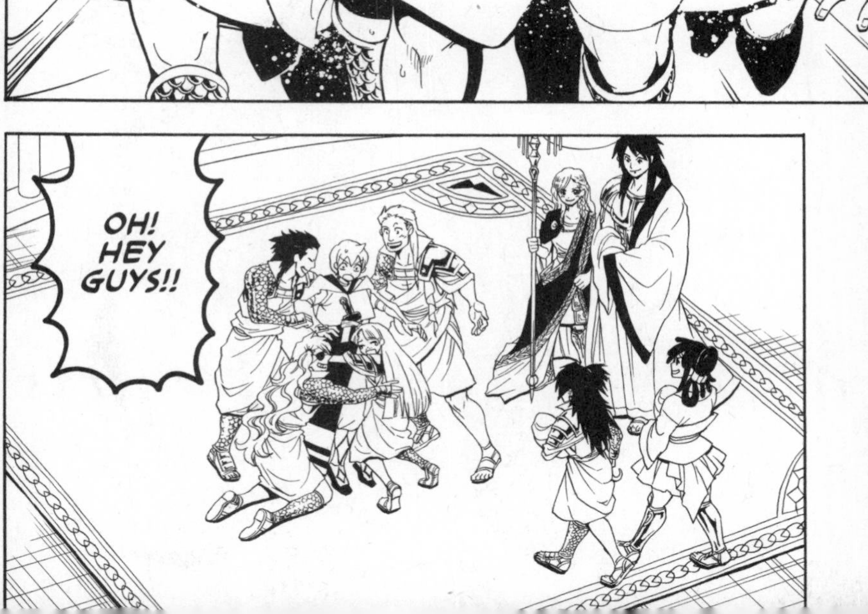
OH! HEY GUYS!!

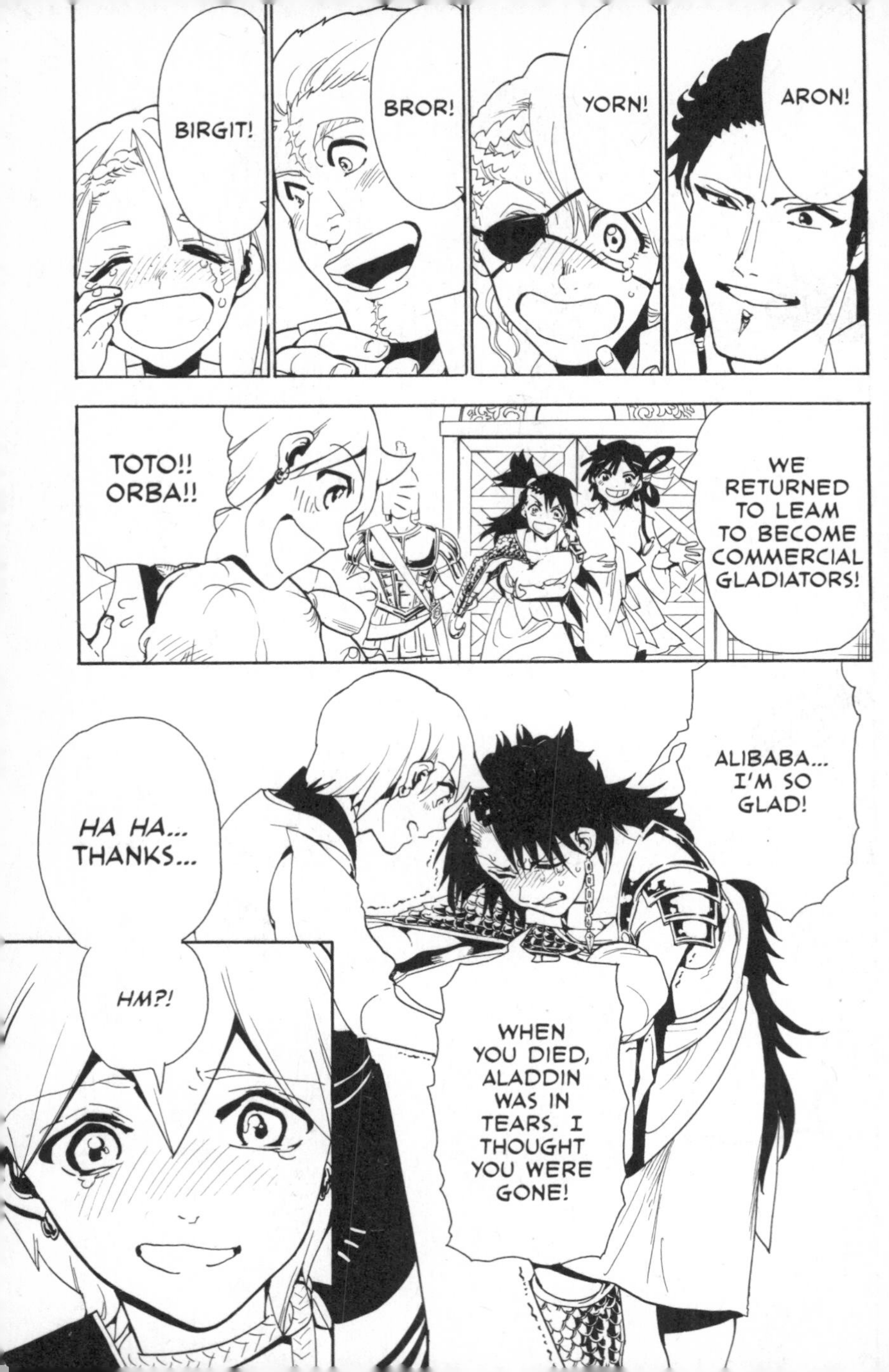
ARON!
YORN!
BROR!
BIRGIT!
WE RETURNED TO LEAM TO BECOME COMMERCIAL GLADIATORS!
TOTO!! ORBA!!
ALIBABA... I'M SO GLAD!
WHEN YOU DIED, ALADDIN WAS IN TEARS. I THOUGHT YOU WERE GONE!
HA HA... THANKS...
HM?!

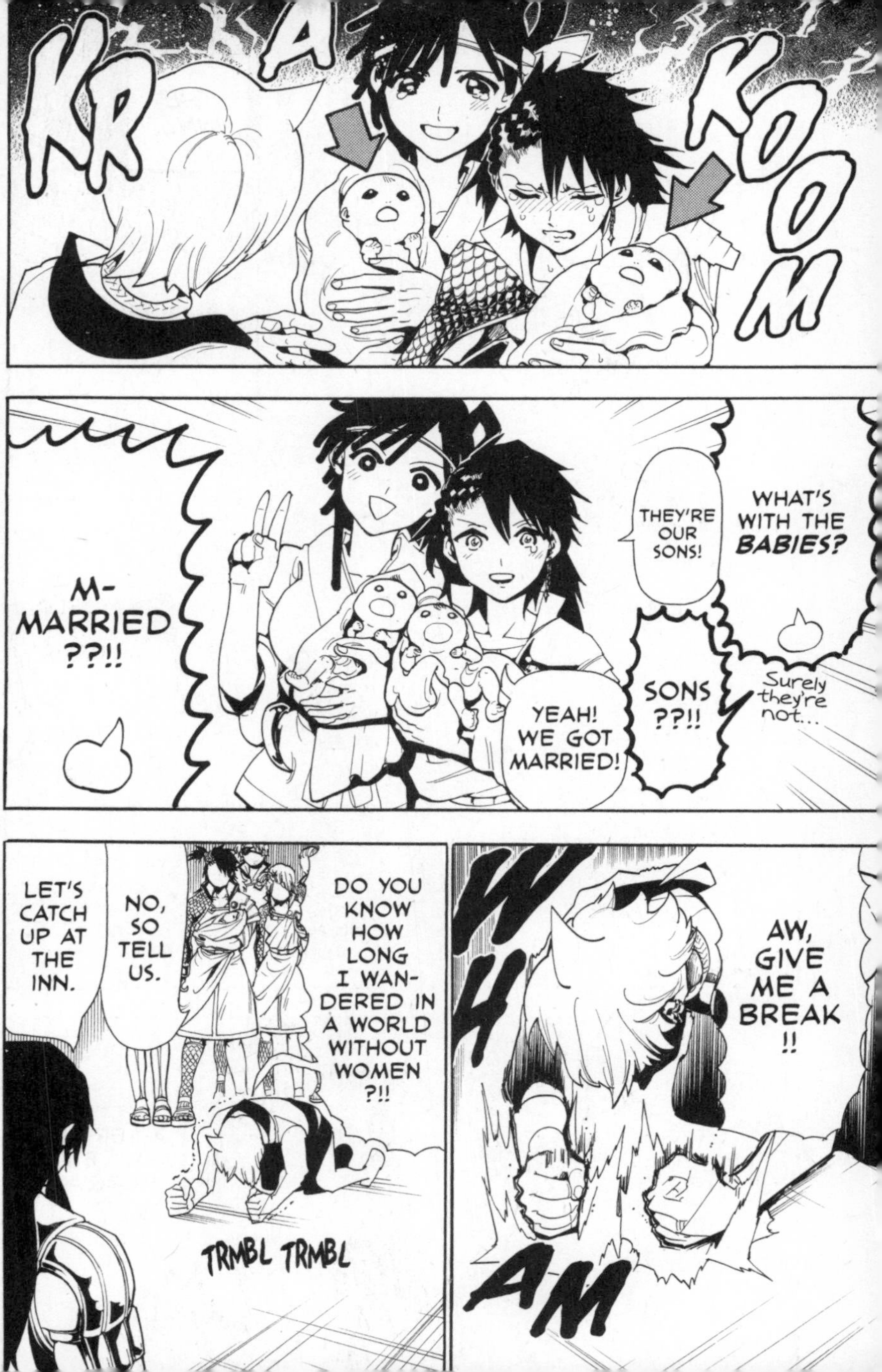
KRAKOOM
WHAT'S WITH THE BABIES?
THEY'RE OUR SONS!
Surely they're not...
SONS??!!
YEAH! WE GOT MARRIED!
M-MARRIED??!!
WHAM
AW, GIVE ME A BREAK!!
DO YOU KNOW HOW LONG I WANDERED IN A WORLD WITHOUT WOMEN?!!
NO, SO TELL US.
LET'S CATCH UP AT THE INN.
TRMBL TRMBL

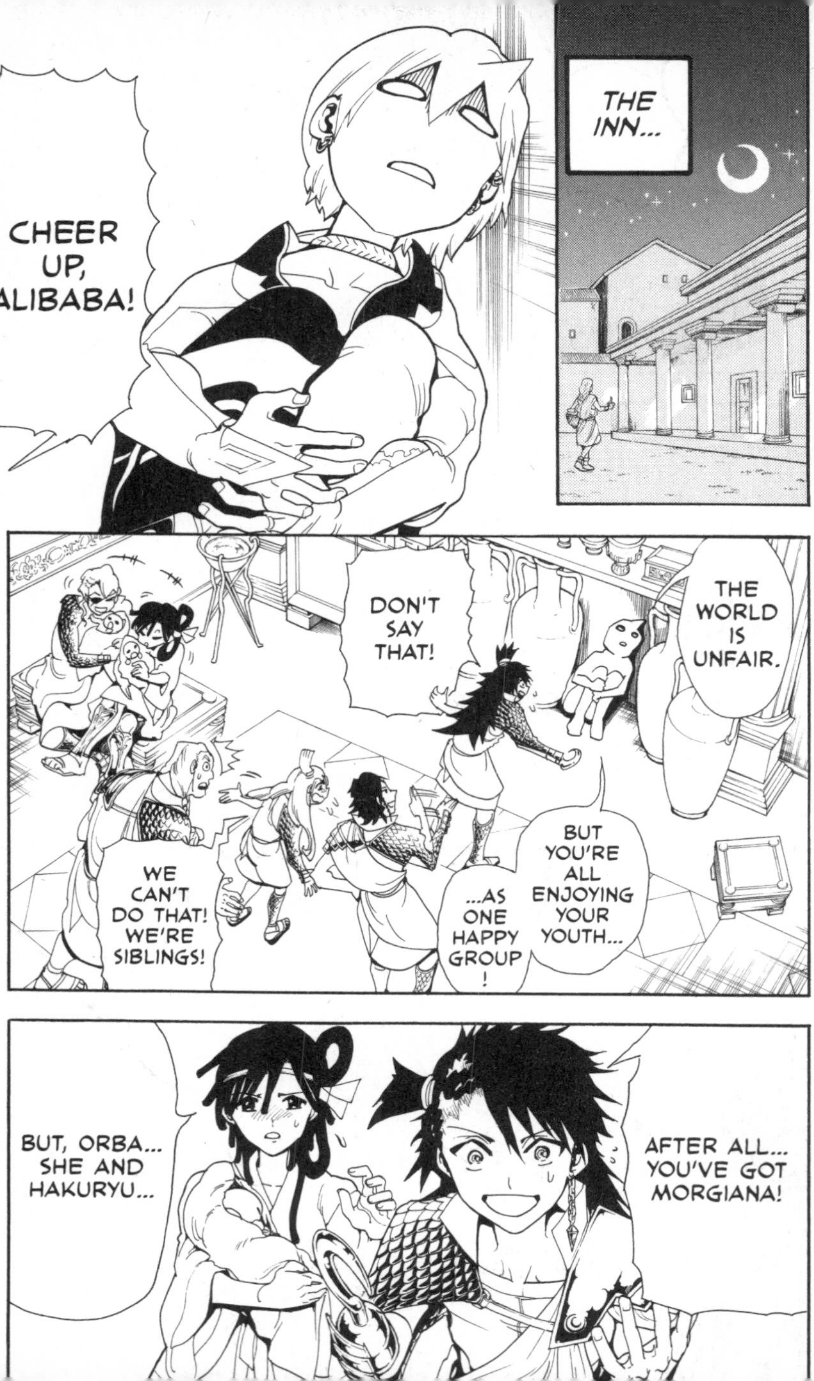
THE INN...
CHEER UP, ALIBABA!
THE WORLD IS UNFAIR.
DON'T SAY THAT!
BUT YOU'RE ALL ENJOYING YOUR YOUTH...
...AS ONE HAPPY GROUP!
WE CAN'T DO THAT! WE'RE SIBLINGS!
AFTER ALL... YOU'VE GOT MORGIANA!
BUT, ORBA... SHE AND HAKURYU...

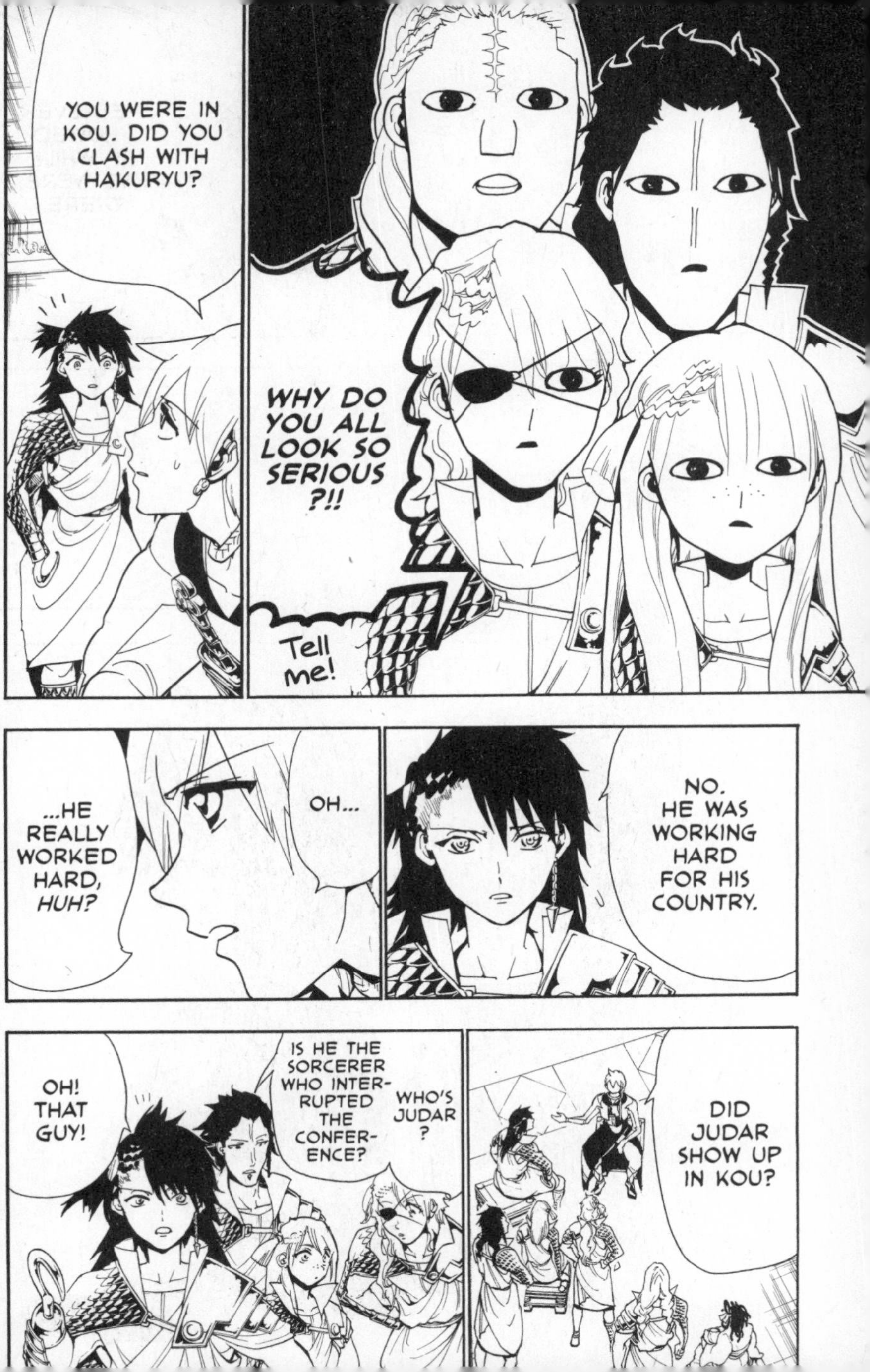
WHY DO YOU ALL LOOK SO SERIOUS ?!!
Tell me!
YOU WERE IN KOU. DID YOU CLASH WITH HAKURYU?
NO. HE WAS WORKING HARD FOR HIS COUNTRY.
OH...
...HE REALLY WORKED HARD, *HUH?*
DID JUDAR SHOW UP IN KOU?
WHO'S JUDAR ?
IS HE THE SORCERER WHO INTERRUPTED THE CONFERENCE?
OH! THAT GUY!

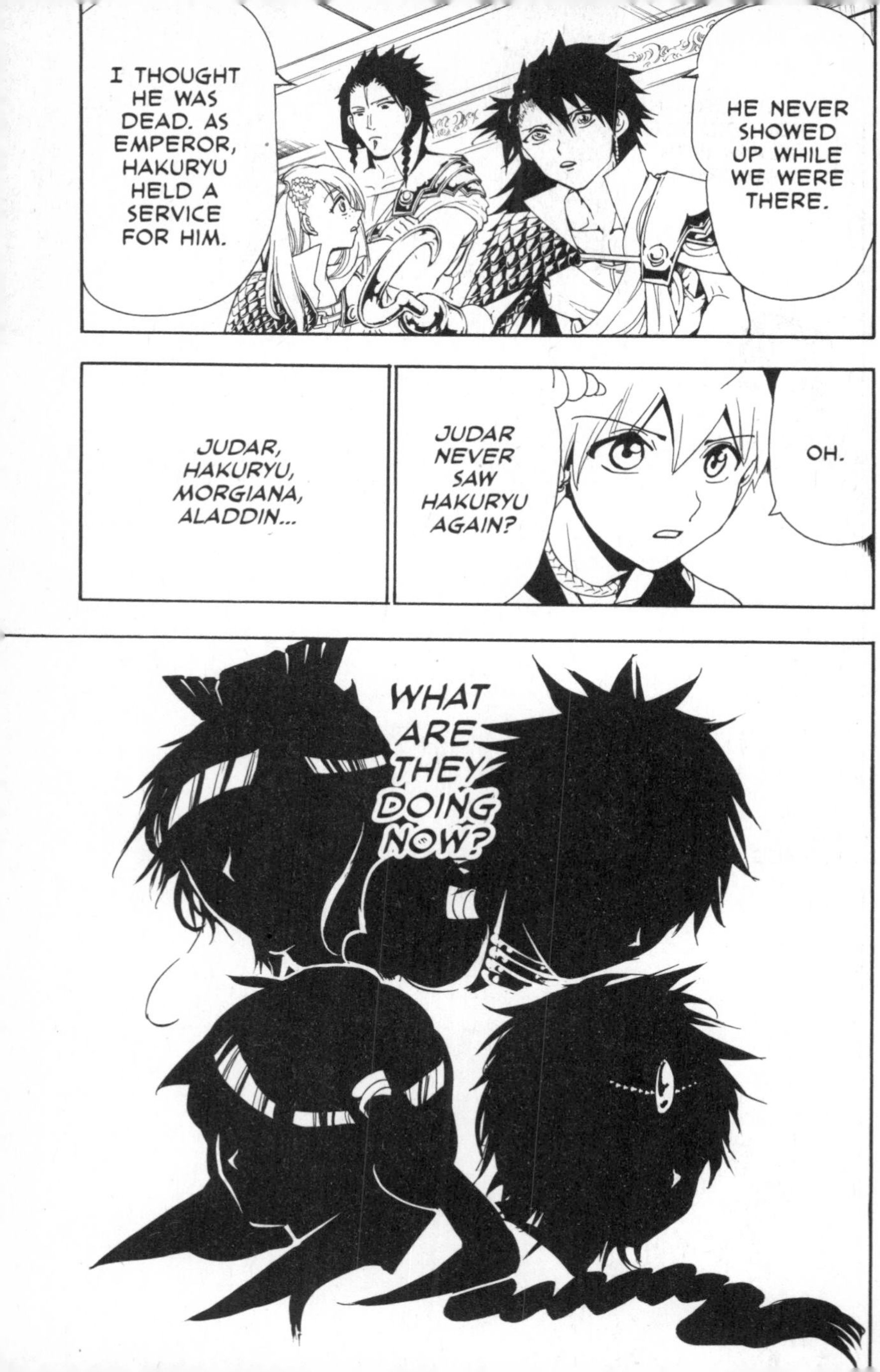
HE NEVER SHOWED UP WHILE WE WERE THERE.
I THOUGHT HE WAS DEAD. AS EMPEROR, HAKURYU HELD A SERVICE FOR HIM.
OH.
JUDAR NEVER SAW HAKURYU AGAIN?
JUDAR, HAKURYU, MORGIANA, ALADDIN...
WHAT ARE THEY DOING NOW?

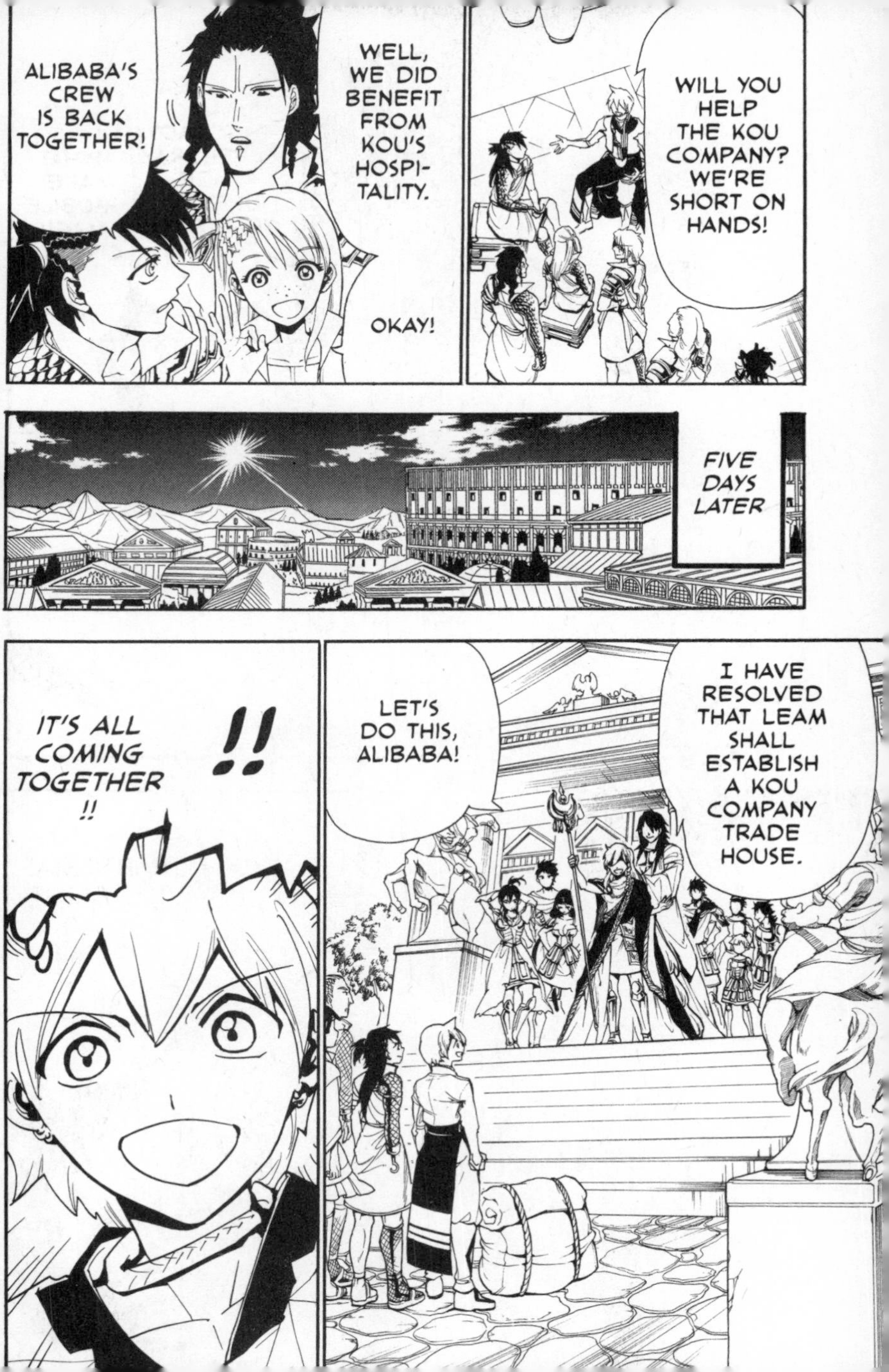
WILL YOU HELP THE KOU COMPANY? WE'RE SHORT ON HANDS!
WELL, WE DID BENEFIT FROM KOU'S HOSPI-TALITY.
OKAY!
ALIBABA'S CREW IS BACK TOGETHER!
FIVE DAYS LATER
I HAVE RESOLVED THAT LEAM SHALL ESTABLISH A KOU COMPANY TRADE HOUSE.
LET'S DO THIS, ALIBABA!
!!
IT'S ALL COMING TOGETHER !!

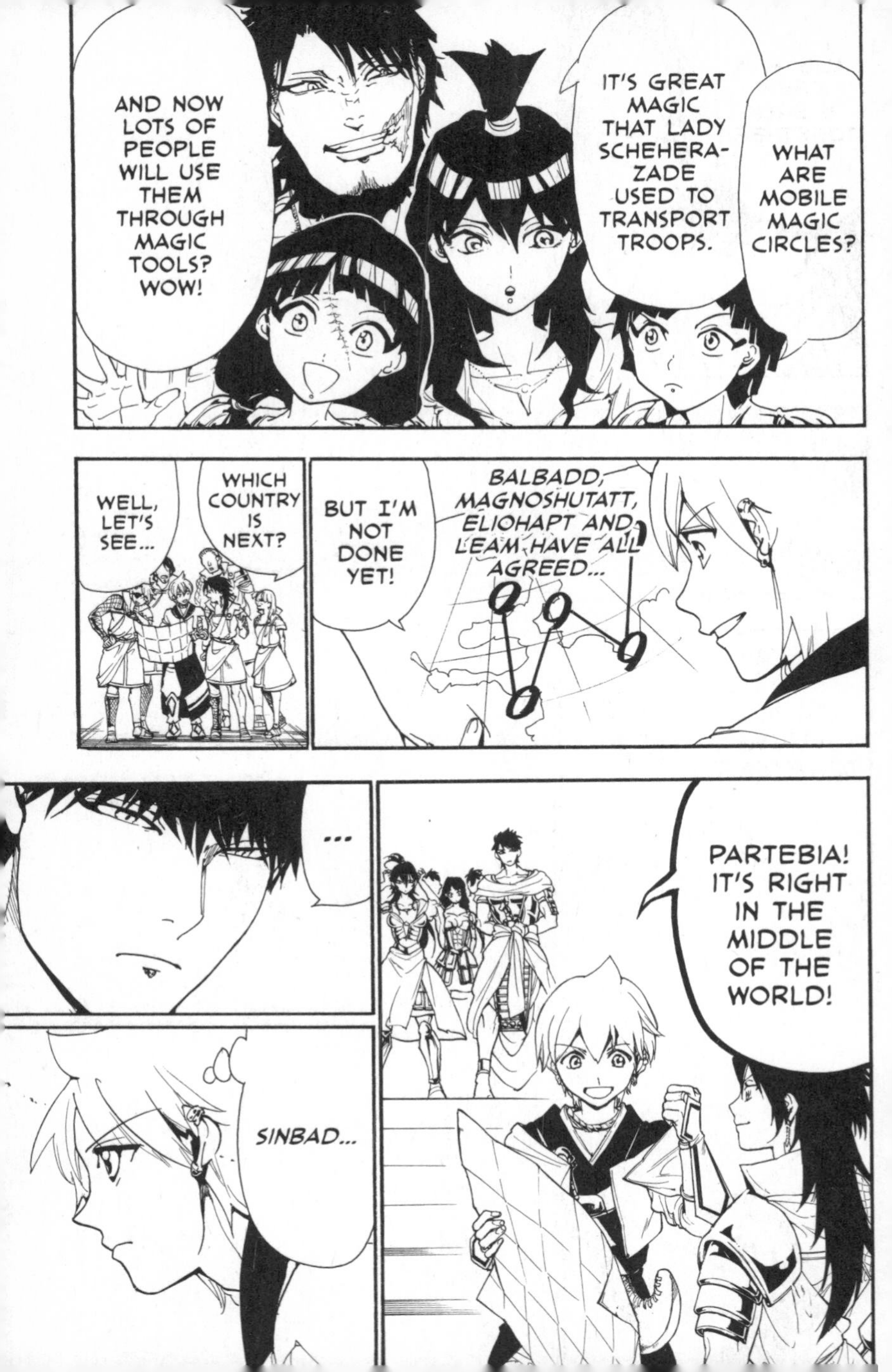
WHAT ARE MOBILE MAGIC CIRCLES?
IT'S GREAT MAGIC THAT LADY SCHEHERAZADE USED TO TRANSPORT TROOPS.
AND NOW LOTS OF PEOPLE WILL USE THEM THROUGH MAGIC TOOLS? WOW!
BALBADD, MAGNOSHUTATT, ELIOHAPT AND LEAM HAVE ALL AGREED...
BUT I'M NOT DONE YET!
WHICH COUNTRY IS NEXT?
WELL, LET'S SEE...
PARTEBIA! IT'S RIGHT IN THE MIDDLE OF THE WORLD!
...
SINBAD...

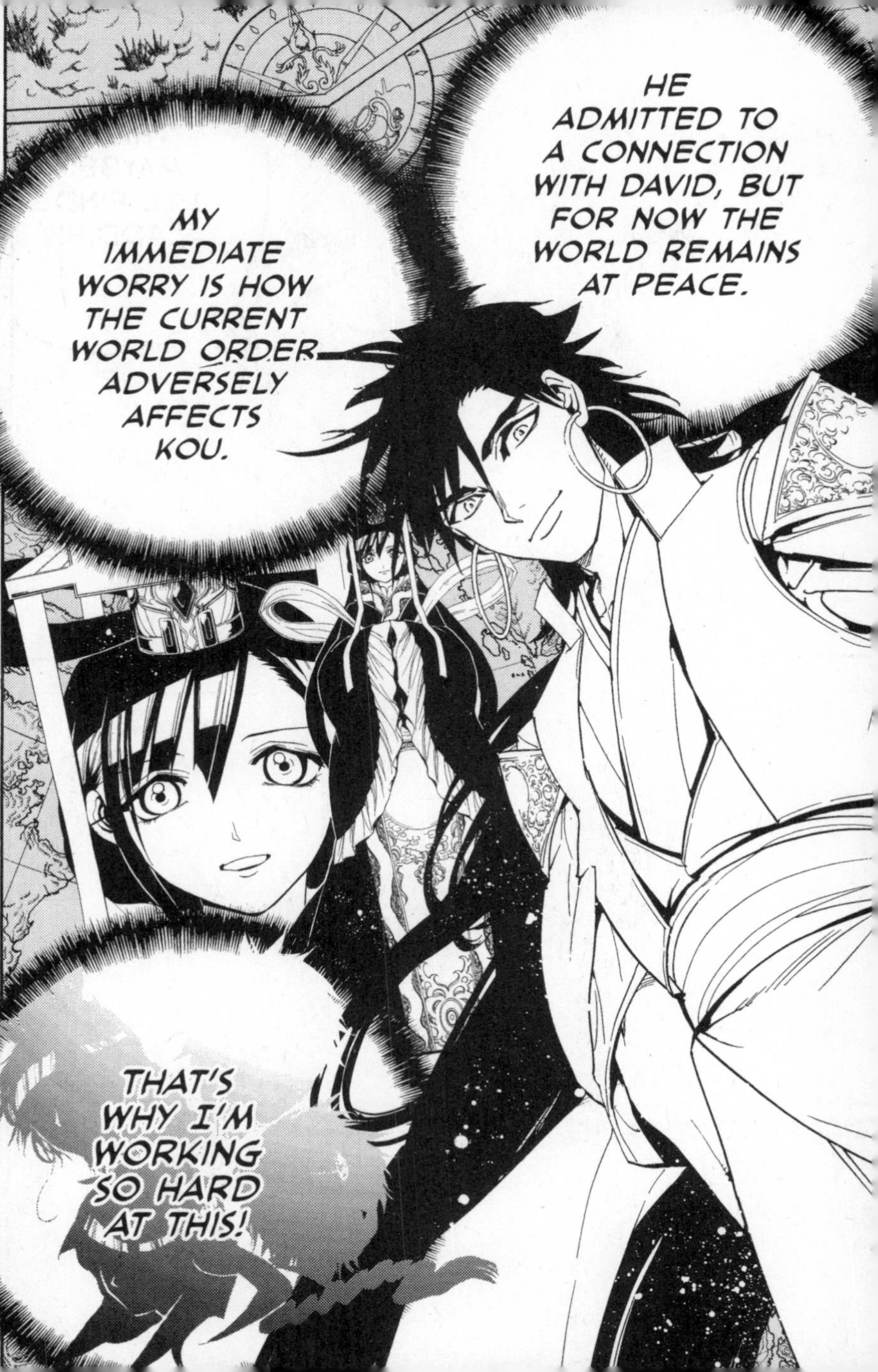
HE ADMITTED TO A CONNECTION WITH DAVID, BUT FOR NOW THE WORLD REMAINS AT PEACE.
MY IMMEDIATE WORRY IS HOW THE CURRENT WORLD ORDER ADVERSELY AFFECTS KOU.
THAT'S WHY I'M WORKING SO HARD AT THIS!

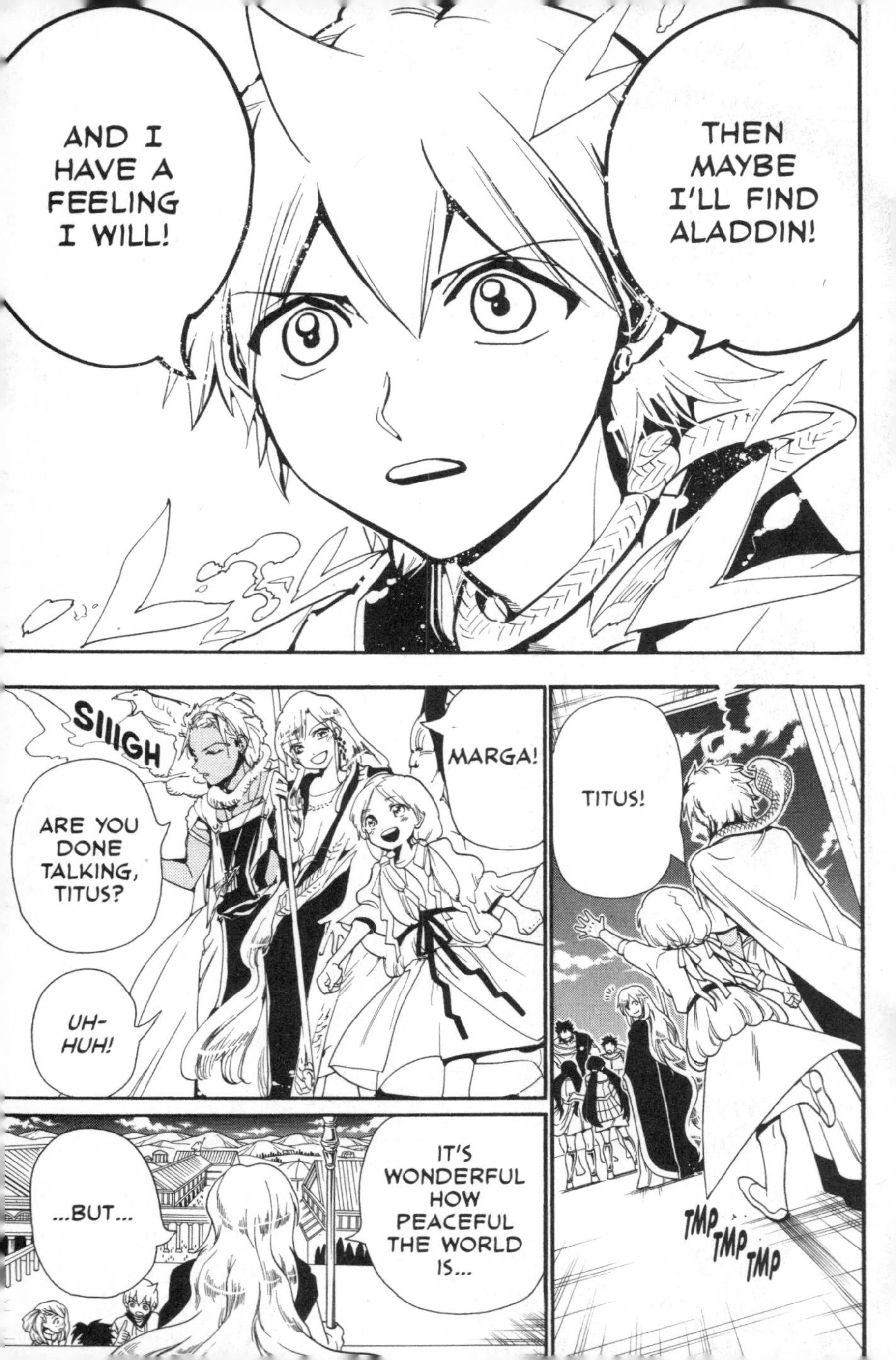
THEN MAYBE I'LL FIND ALADDIN!
AND I HAVE A FEELING I WILL!
TITUS!
TMP TMP TMP
MARGA!
SIIIGH
ARE YOU DONE TALKING, TITUS?
UH-HUH!
IT'S WONDERFUL HOW PEACEFUL THE WORLD IS...
...BUT...

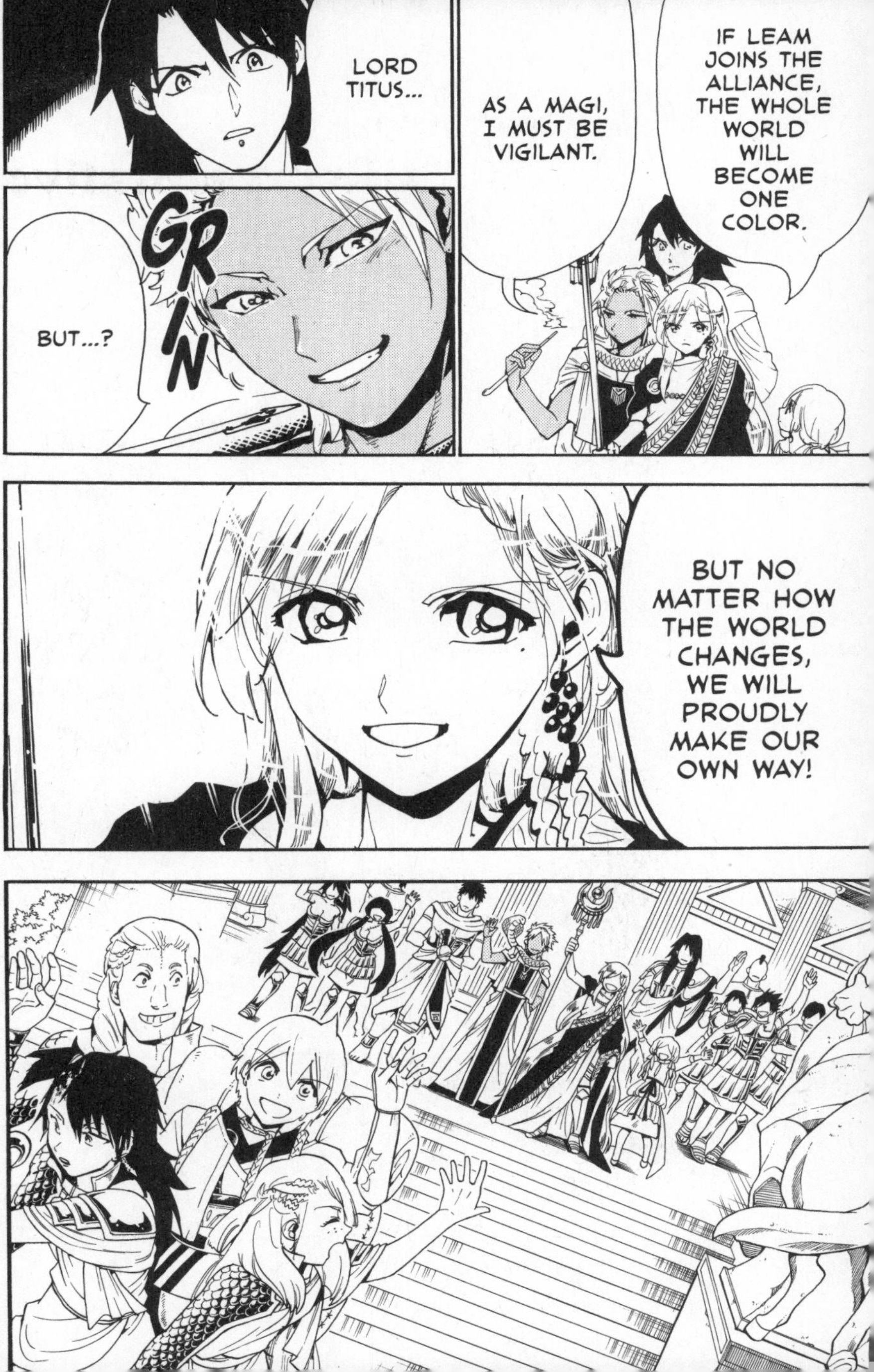
IF LEAM JOINS THE ALLIANCE, THE WHOLE WORLD WILL BECOME ONE COLOR.
AS A MAGI, I MUST BE VIGILANT.
LORD TITUS...
GRIN
BUT...?
BUT NO MATTER HOW THE WORLD CHANGES, WE WILL PROUDLY MAKE OUR OWN WAY!

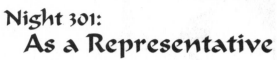

Night 301:
As a Representative

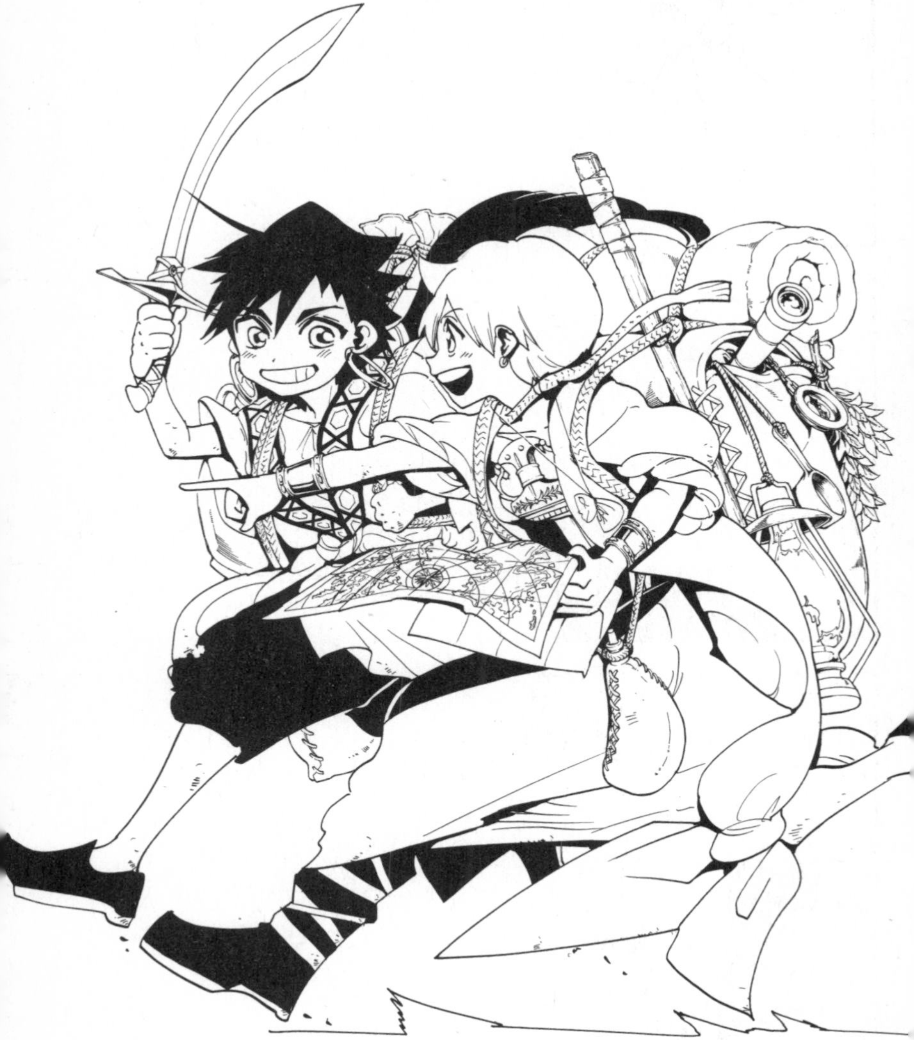

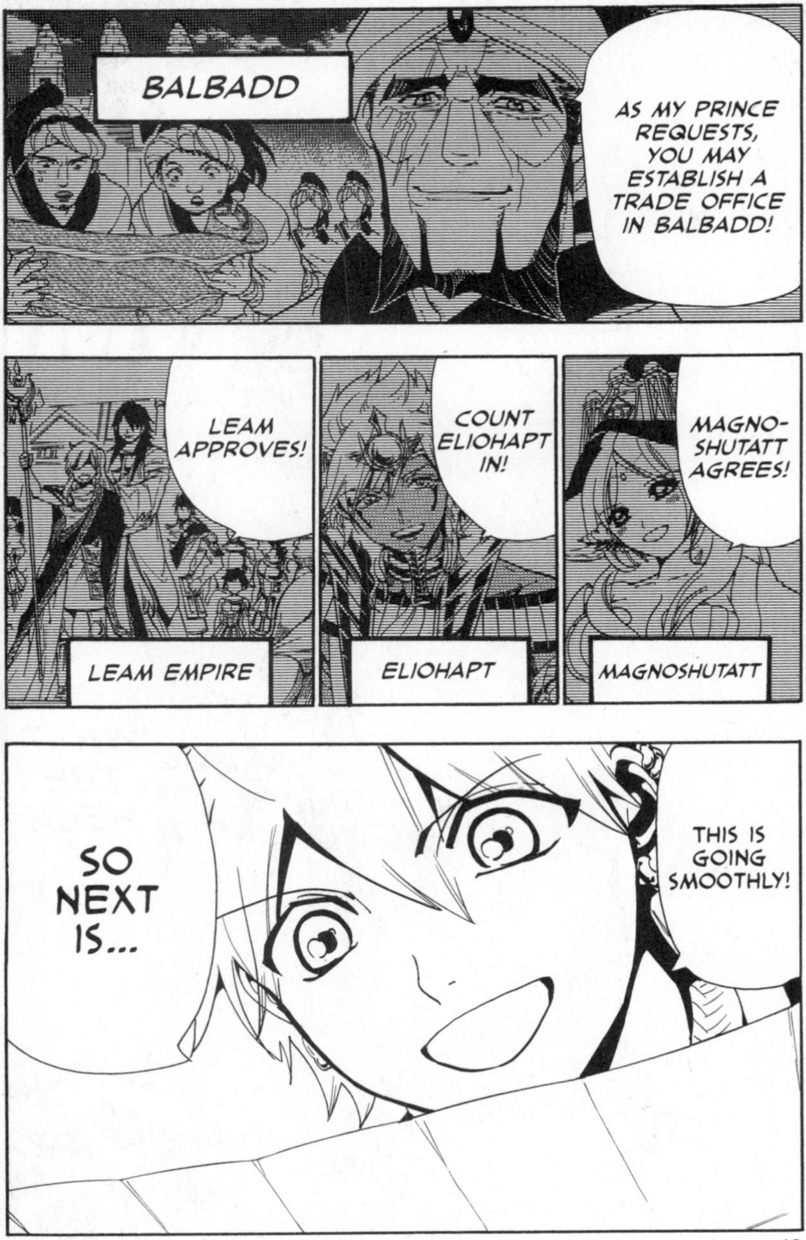
AS MY PRINCE REQUESTS, YOU MAY ESTABLISH A TRADE OFFICE IN BALBADD!
BALBADD
MAGNO-SHUTATT AGREES!
MAGNOSHUTATT
COUNT ELIOHAPT IN!
ELIOHAPT
LEAM APPROVES!
LEAM EMPIRE
THIS IS GOING SMOOTHLY!
SO NEXT IS...

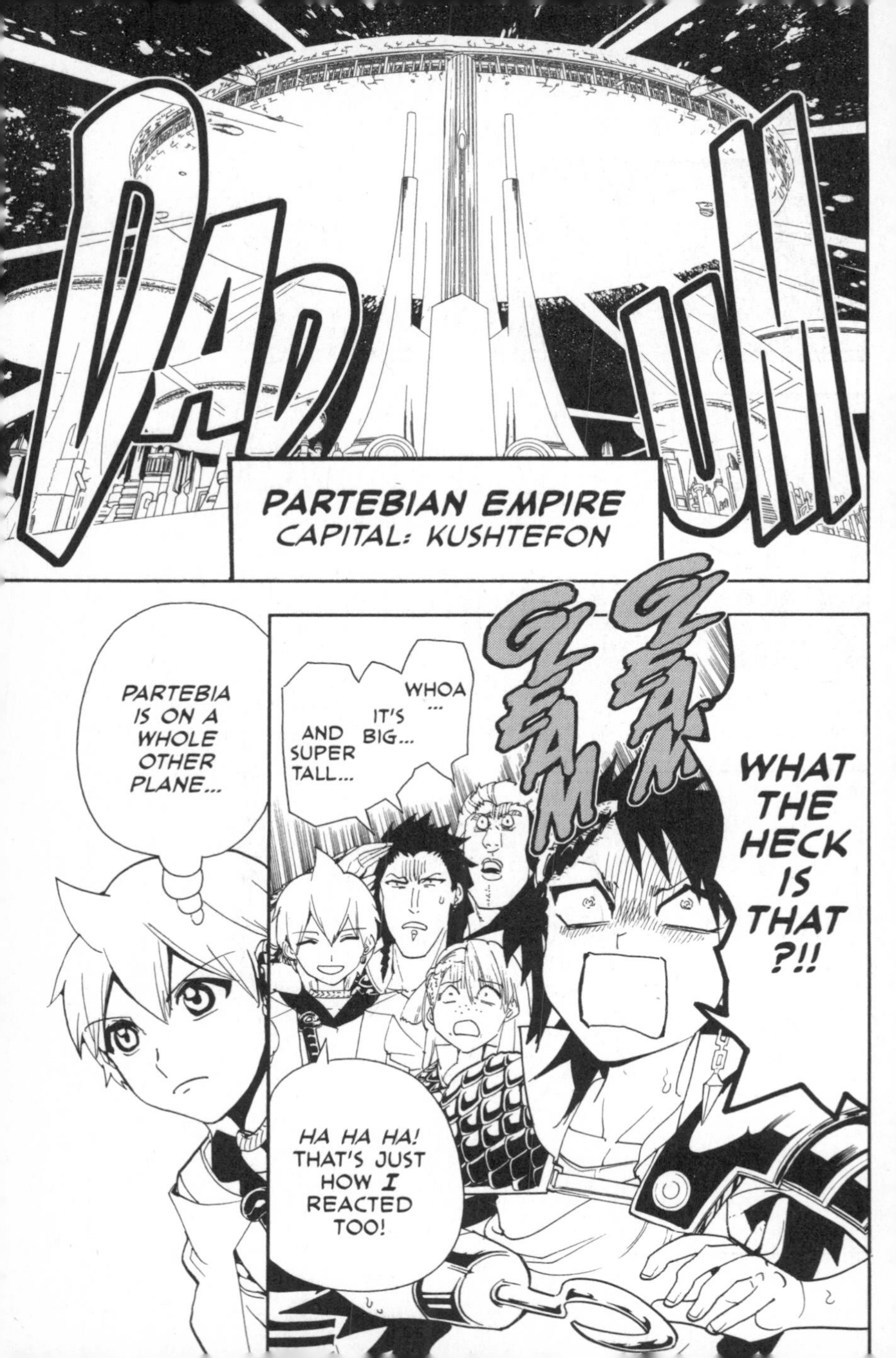
PARTEBIAN EMPIRE
CAPITAL: KUSHTEFON
GLEAM GLEAM
WHAT THE HECK IS THAT?!!
WHOA... IT'S BIG... AND SUPER TALL...
PARTEBIA IS ON A WHOLE OTHER PLANE...
HA HA HA! THAT'S JUST HOW I REACTED TOO!

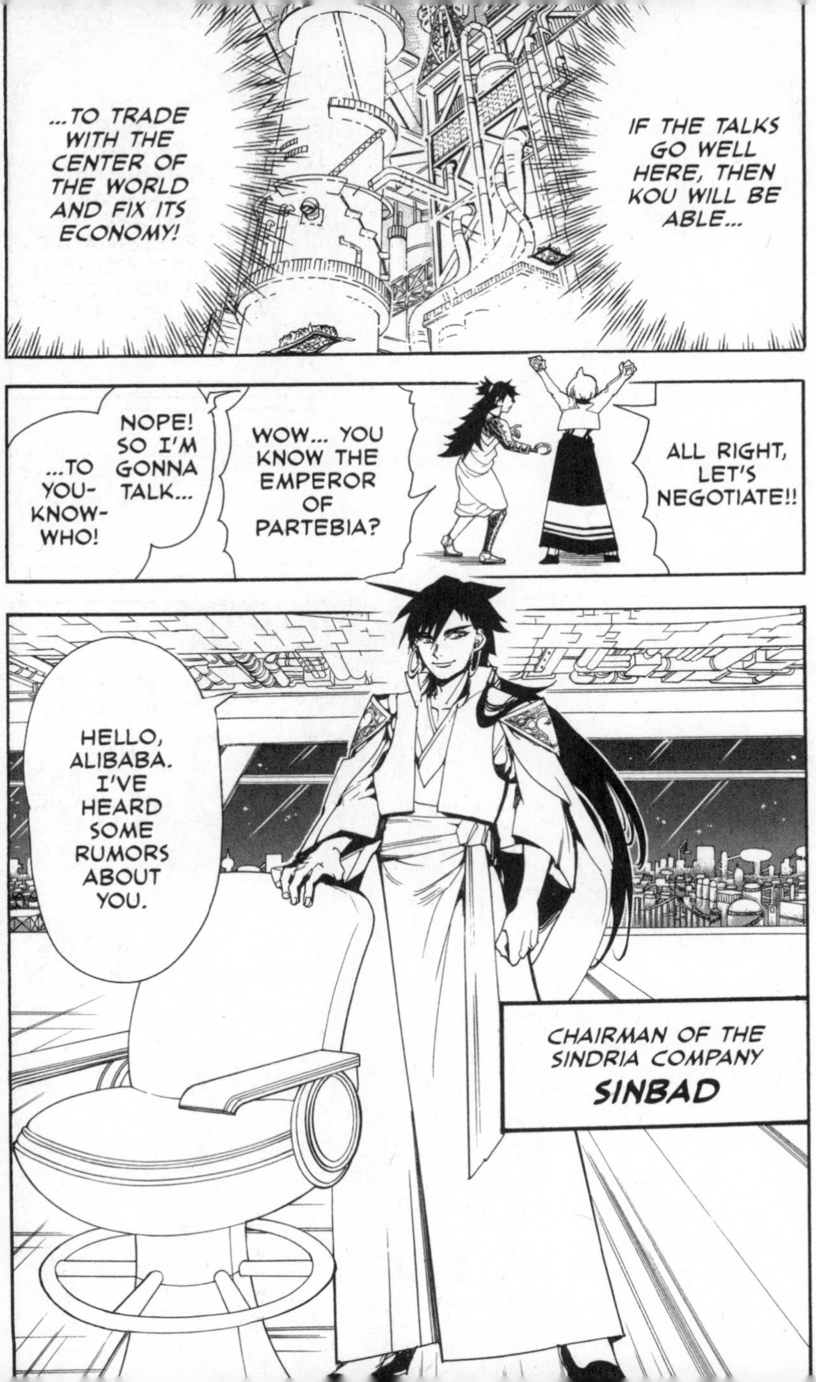
IF THE TALKS GO WELL HERE, THEN KOU WILL BE ABLE...
...TO TRADE WITH THE CENTER OF THE WORLD AND FIX ITS ECONOMY!
ALL RIGHT, LET'S NEGOTIATE!!
WOW... YOU KNOW THE EMPEROR OF PARTEBIA?
NOPE! SO I'M GONNA TALK...
...TO YOU-KNOW-WHO!
HELLO, ALIBABA. I'VE HEARD SOME RUMORS ABOUT YOU.
CHAIRMAN OF THE SINDRIA COMPANY
SINBAD

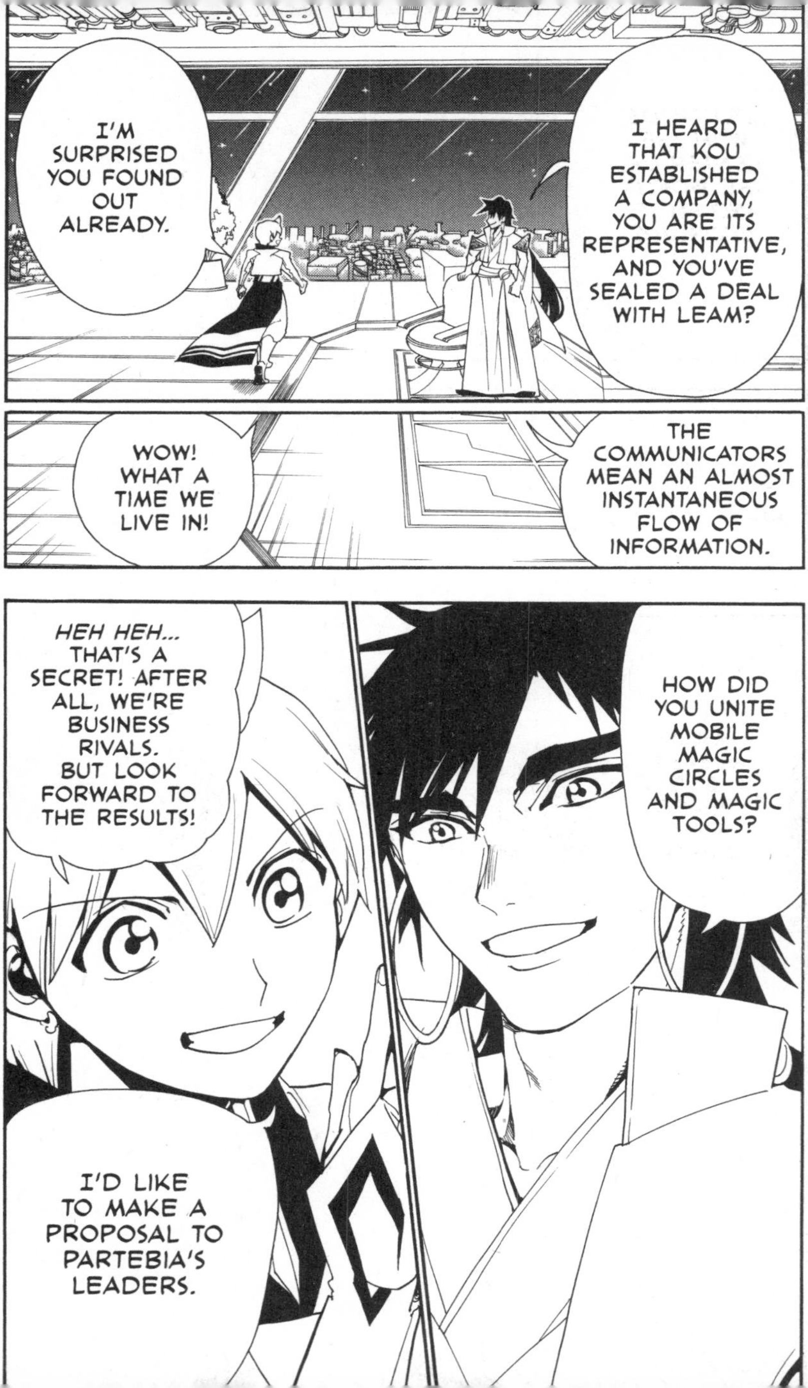
I HEARD THAT KOU ESTABLISHED A COMPANY, YOU ARE ITS REPRESENTATIVE, AND YOU'VE SEALED A DEAL WITH LEAM?
I'M SURPRISED YOU FOUND OUT ALREADY.
THE COMMUNICATORS MEAN AN ALMOST INSTANTANEOUS FLOW OF INFORMATION.
WOW! WHAT A TIME WE LIVE IN!
HOW DID YOU UNITE MOBILE MAGIC CIRCLES AND MAGIC TOOLS?
HEH HEH... THAT'S A SECRET! AFTER ALL, WE'RE BUSINESS RIVALS. BUT LOOK FORWARD TO THE RESULTS!
I'D LIKE TO MAKE A PROPOSAL TO PARTEBIA'S LEADERS.

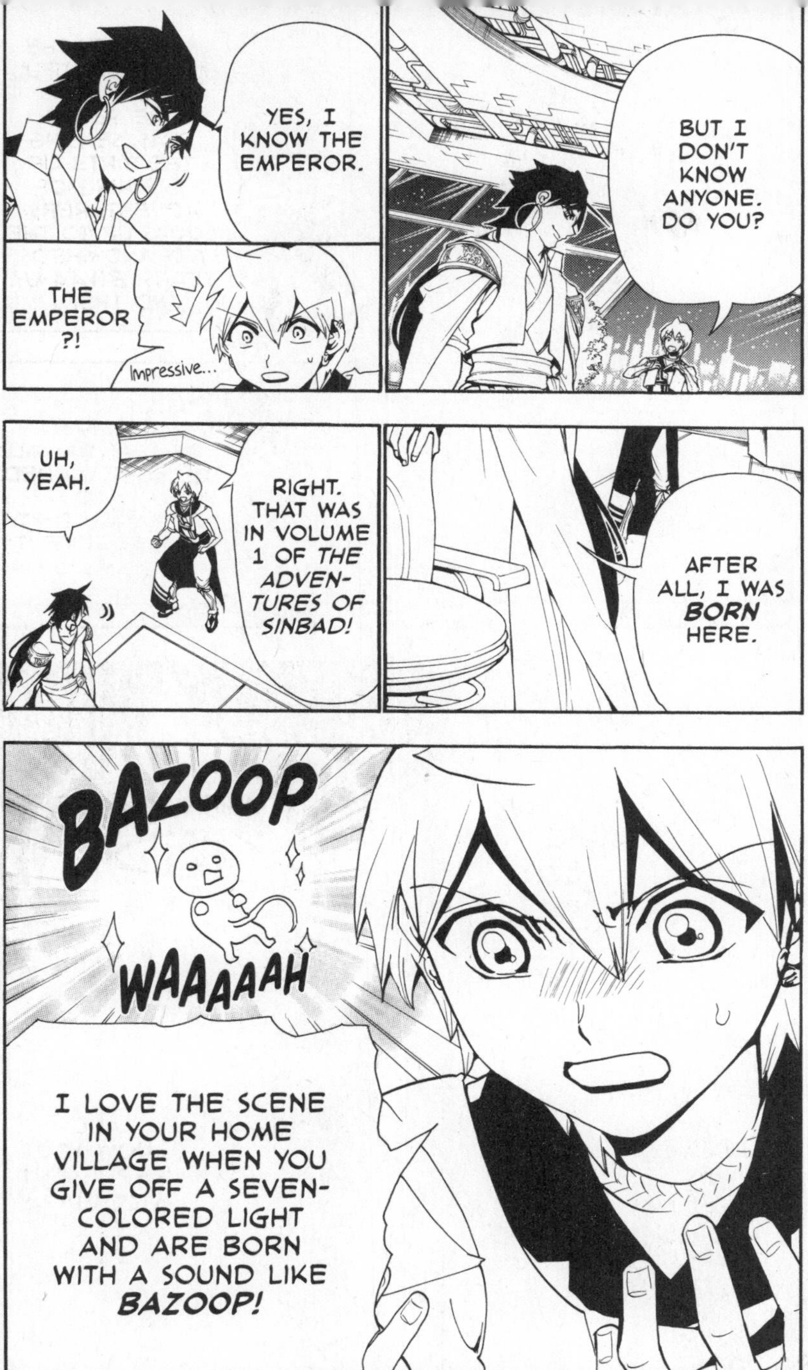
BUT I DON'T KNOW ANYONE. DO YOU?
YES, I KNOW THE EMPEROR.
THE EMPEROR ?!
Impressive...
AFTER ALL, I WAS *BORN* HERE.
RIGHT. THAT WAS IN VOLUME 1 OF *THE ADVENTURES OF SINBAD!*
UH, YEAH.
BAZOOP
WAAAAAH
I LOVE THE SCENE IN YOUR HOME VILLAGE WHEN YOU GIVE OFF A SEVEN-COLORED LIGHT AND ARE BORN WITH A SOUND LIKE *BAZOOP!*

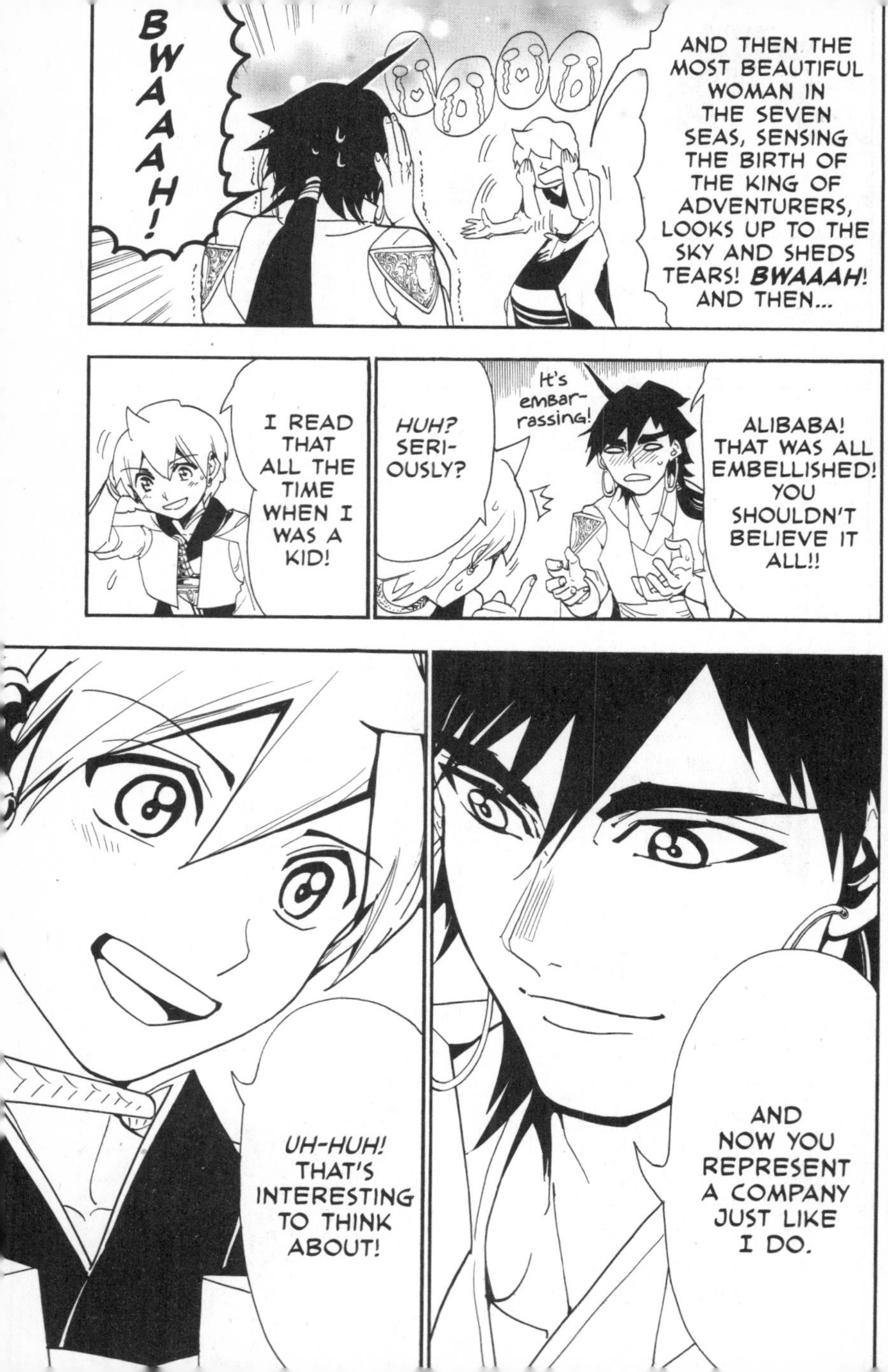
AND THEN THE MOST BEAUTIFUL WOMAN IN THE SEVEN SEAS, SENSING THE BIRTH OF THE KING OF ADVENTURERS, LOOKS UP TO THE SKY AND SHEDS TEARS! BWAAAH! AND THEN...
BWAAAAH!
ALIBABA! THAT WAS ALL EMBELLISHED! YOU SHOULDN'T BELIEVE IT ALL!!
It's embarrassing!
HUH? SERIOUSLY?
I READ THAT ALL THE TIME WHEN I WAS A KID!
AND NOW YOU REPRESENT A COMPANY JUST LIKE I DO.
UH-HUH! THAT'S INTERESTING TO THINK ABOUT!

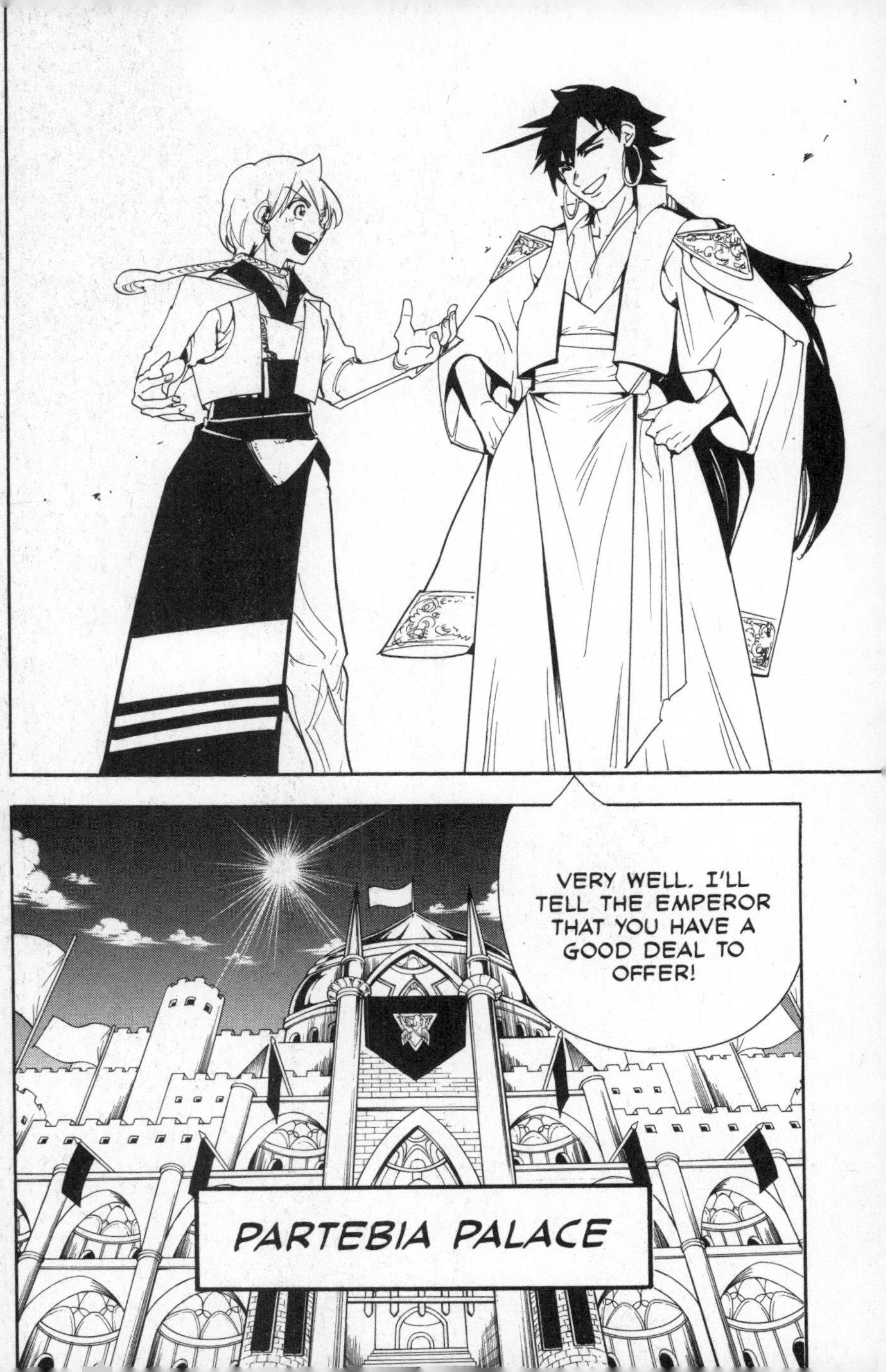
VERY WELL. I'LL TELL THE EMPEROR THAT YOU HAVE A GOOD DEAL TO OFFER!
PARTEBIA PALACE

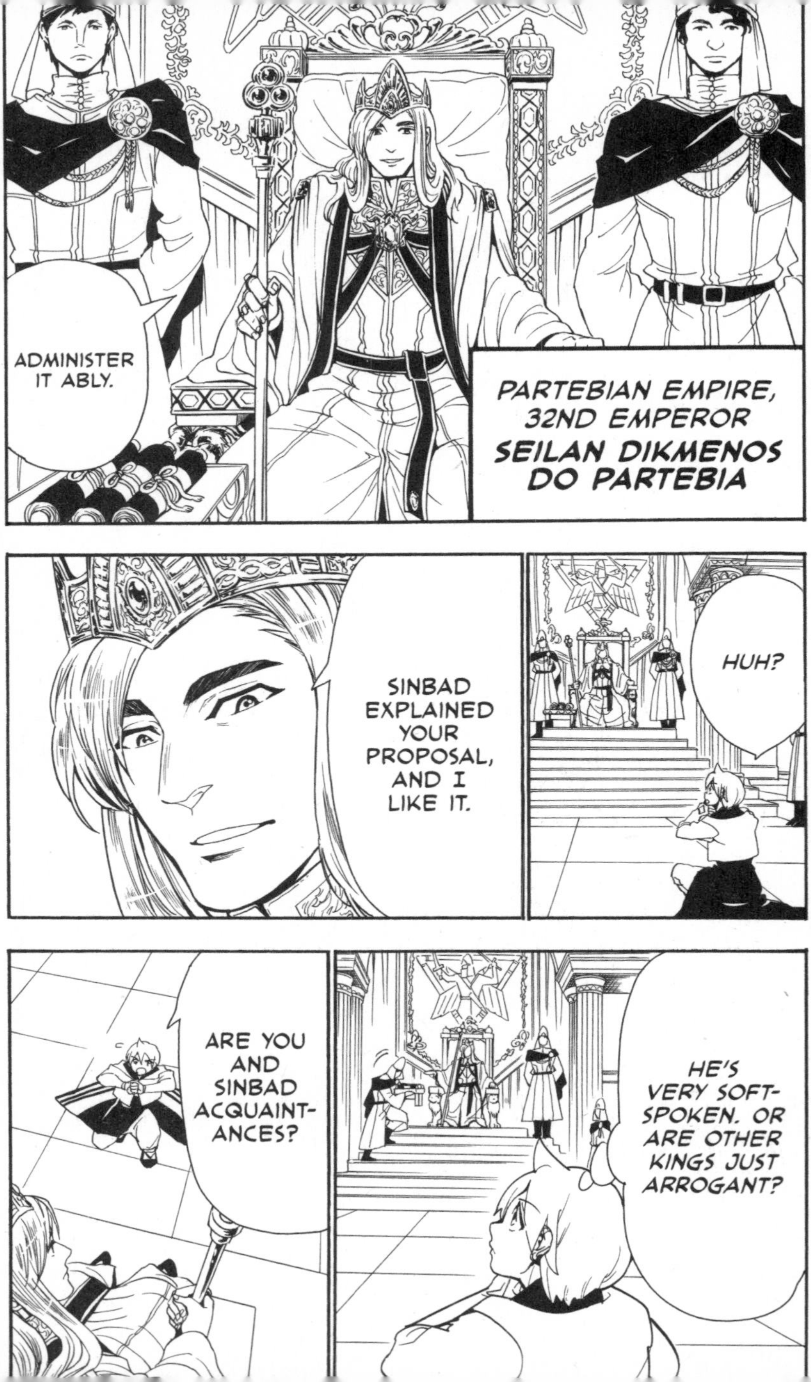
PARTEBIAN EMPIRE, 32ND EMPEROR SEILAN DIKMENOS DO PARTEBIA
ADMINISTER IT ABLY.
HUH?
SINBAD EXPLAINED YOUR PROPOSAL, AND I LIKE IT.
HE'S VERY SOFT-SPOKEN. OR ARE OTHER KINGS JUST ARROGANT?
ARE YOU AND SINBAD ACQUAINT-ANCES?

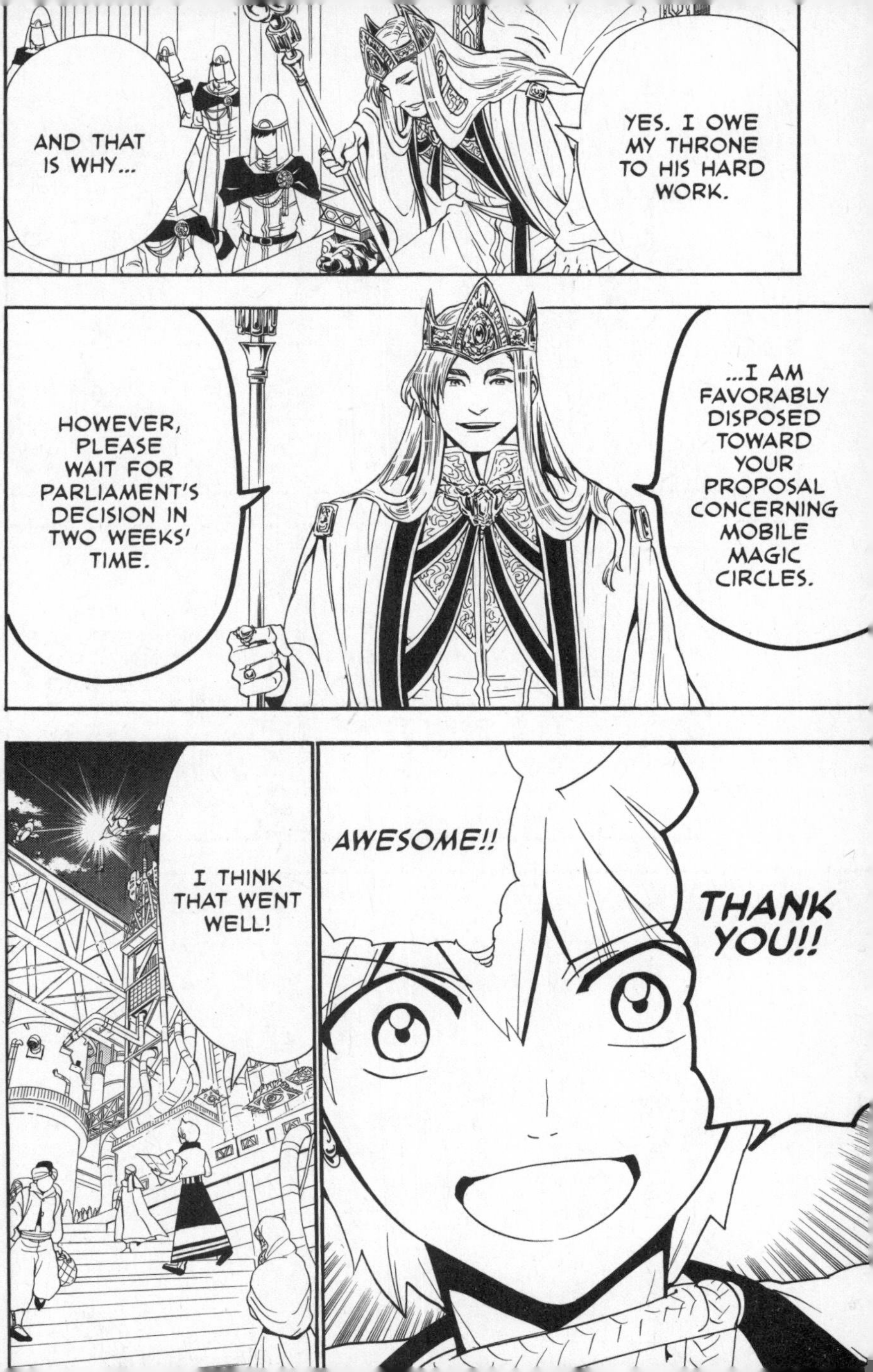
YES. I OWE MY THRONE TO HIS HARD WORK.
AND THAT IS WHY...
...I AM FAVORABLY DISPOSED TOWARD YOUR PROPOSAL CONCERNING MOBILE MAGIC CIRCLES.
HOWEVER, PLEASE WAIT FOR PARLIAMENT'S DECISION IN TWO WEEKS' TIME.
THANK YOU!!
AWESOME!!
I THINK THAT WENT WELL!

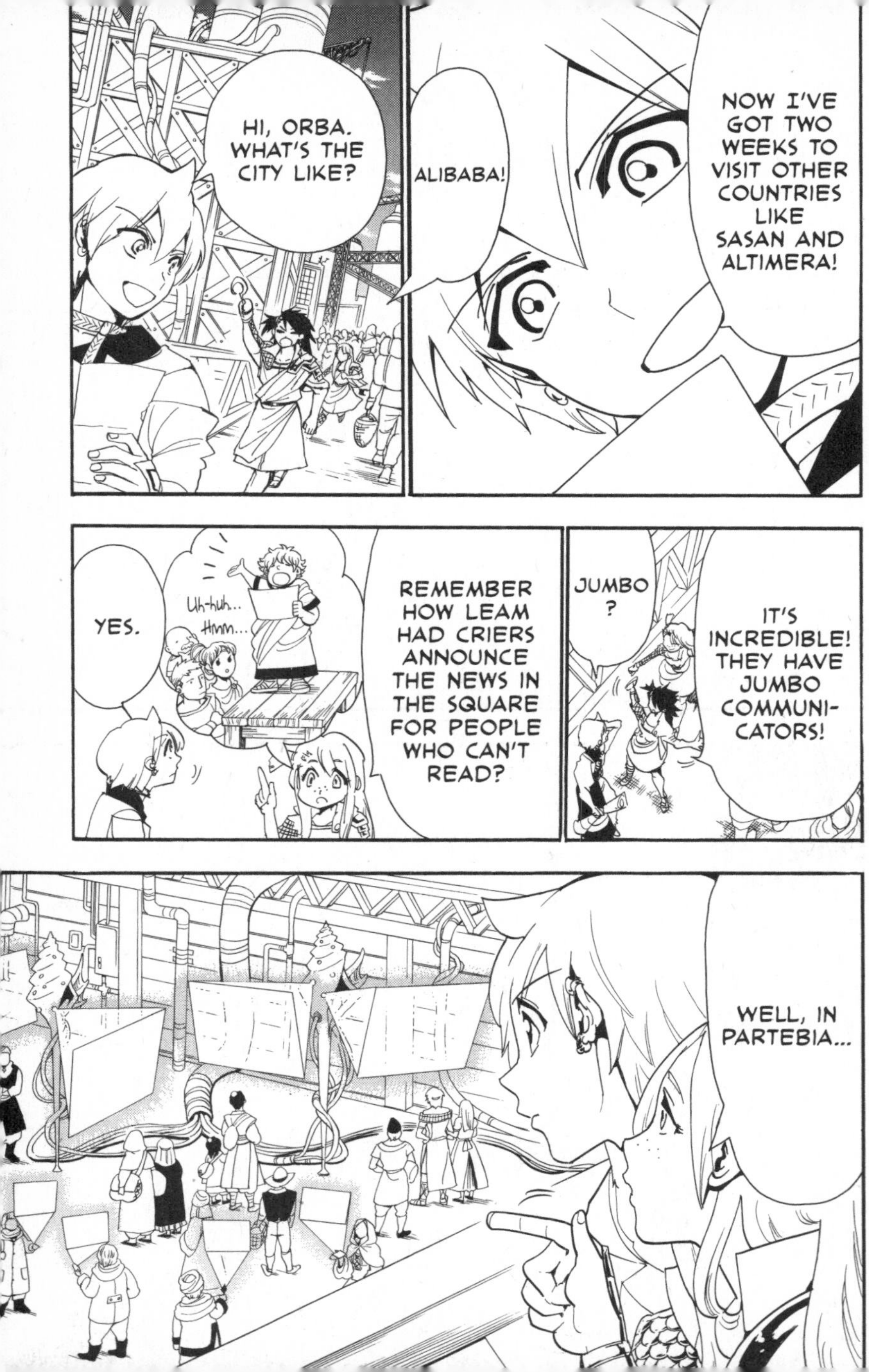
NOW I'VE GOT TWO WEEKS TO VISIT OTHER COUNTRIES LIKE SASAN AND ALTIMERA!
ALIBABA!
HI, ORBA. WHAT'S THE CITY LIKE?
IT'S INCREDIBLE! THEY HAVE JUMBO COMMUNICATORS!
JUMBO?
REMEMBER HOW LEAM HAD CRIERS ANNOUNCE THE NEWS IN THE SQUARE FOR PEOPLE WHO CAN'T READ?
Uh-huh... Hmm...
YES.
WELL, IN PARTEBIA...

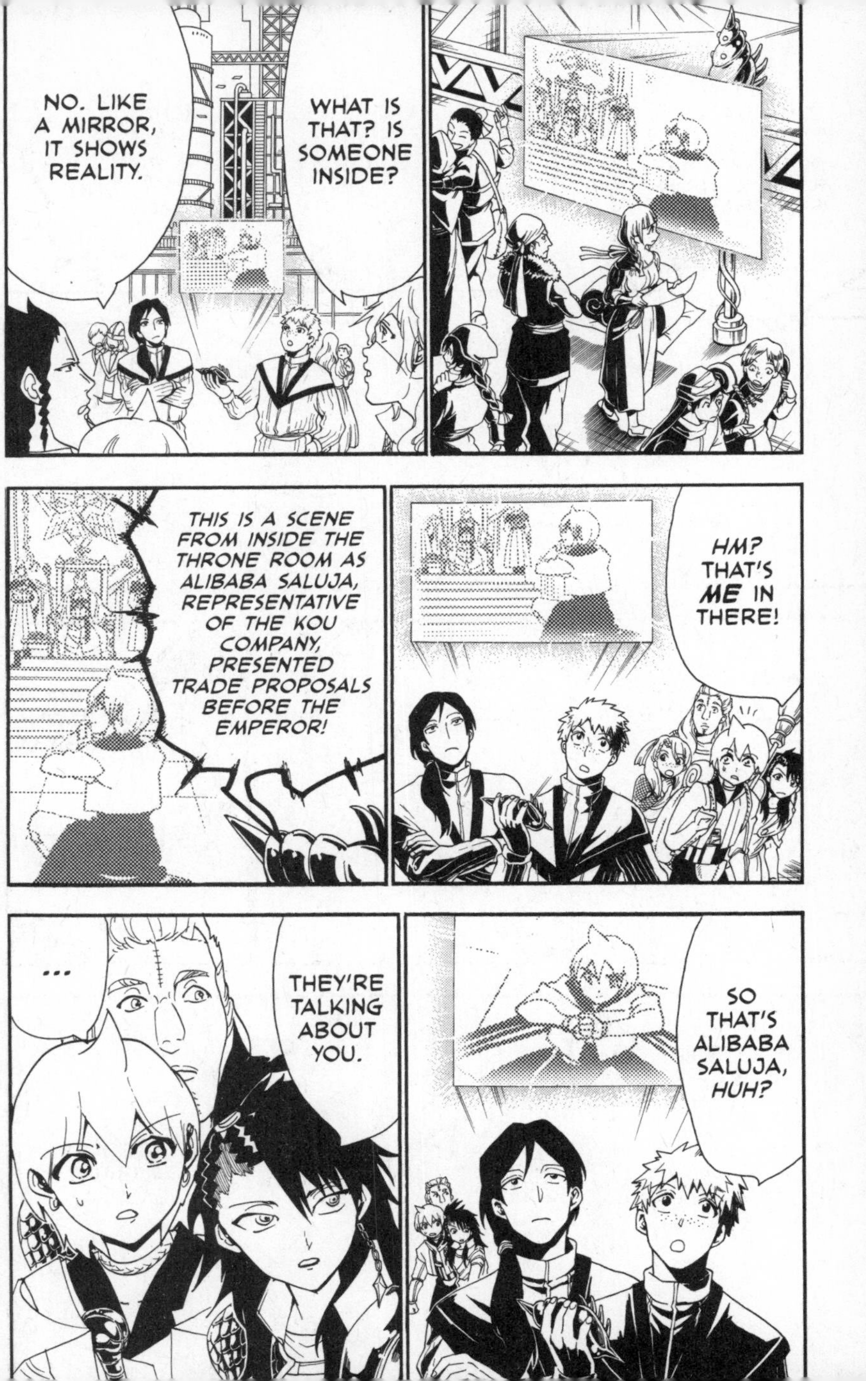
WHAT IS THAT? IS SOMEONE INSIDE?
NO. LIKE A MIRROR, IT SHOWS REALITY.
HM? THAT'S *ME* IN THERE!
THIS IS A SCENE FROM INSIDE THE THRONE ROOM AS ALIBABA SALUJA, REPRESENTATIVE OF THE KOU COMPANY, PRESENTED TRADE PROPOSALS BEFORE THE EMPEROR!
SO THAT'S ALIBABA SALUJA, HUH?
THEY'RE TALKING ABOUT YOU.
...

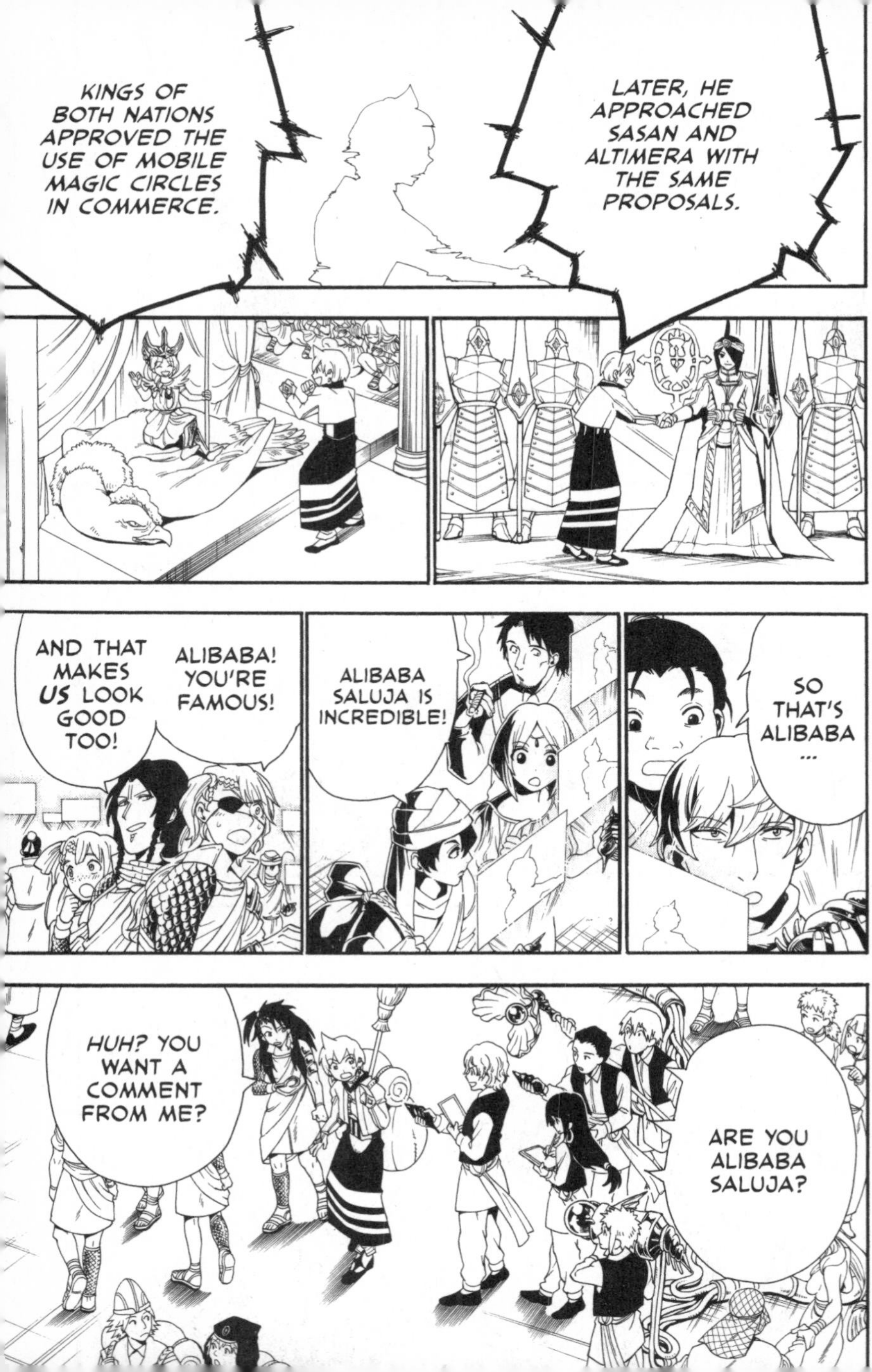
LATER, HE APPROACHED SASAN AND ALTIMERA WITH THE SAME PROPOSALS.
KINGS OF BOTH NATIONS APPROVED THE USE OF MOBILE MAGIC CIRCLES IN COMMERCE.
SO THAT'S ALIBABA...
ALIBABA SALUJA IS INCREDIBLE!
ALIBABA! YOU'RE FAMOUS!
AND THAT MAKES *US* LOOK GOOD TOO!
ARE YOU ALIBABA SALUJA?
HUH? YOU WANT A COMMENT FROM ME?

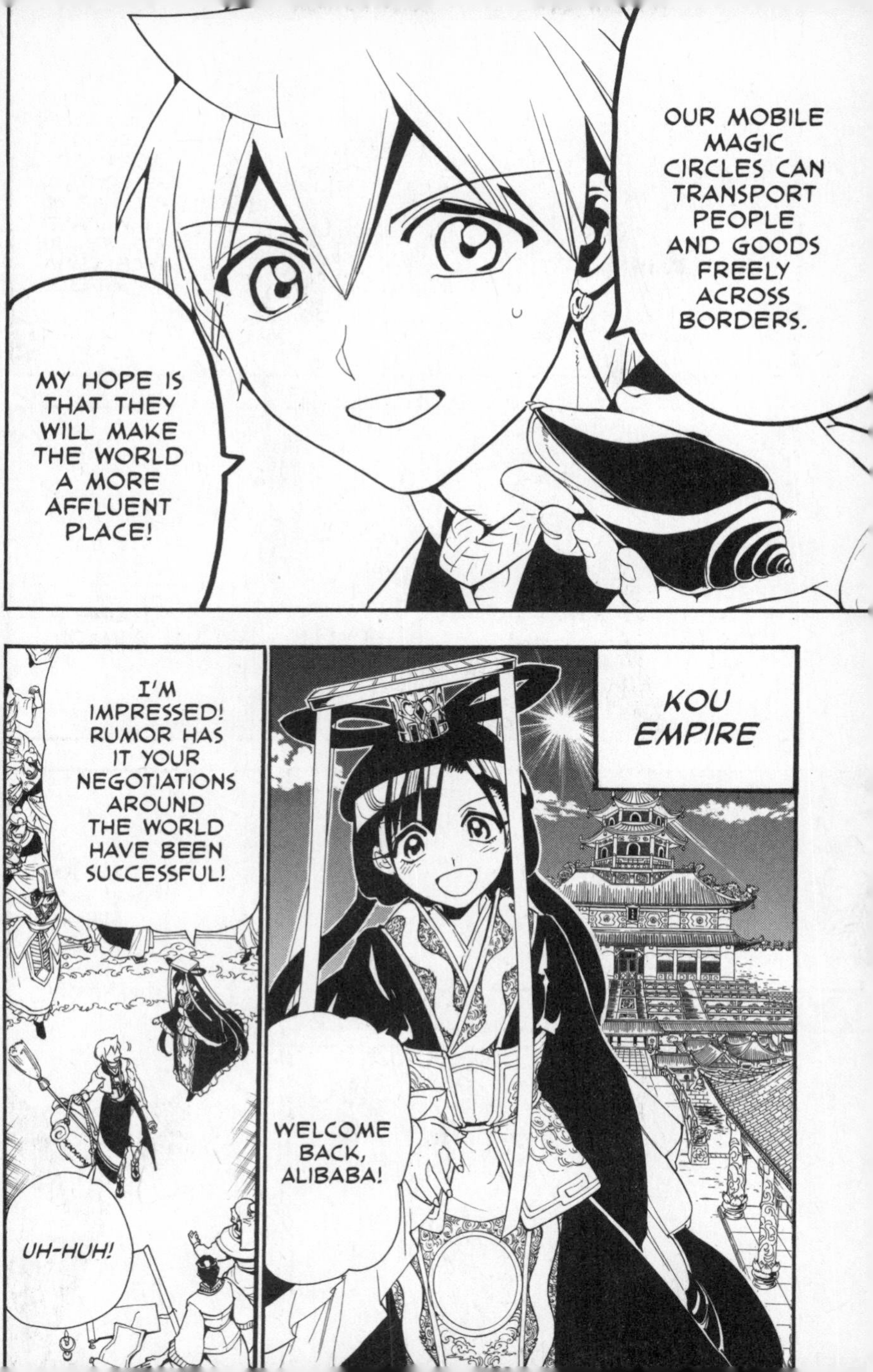
OUR MOBILE MAGIC CIRCLES CAN TRANSPORT PEOPLE AND GOODS FREELY ACROSS BORDERS.
MY HOPE IS THAT THEY WILL MAKE THE WORLD A MORE AFFLUENT PLACE!
KOU EMPIRE
WELCOME BACK, ALIBABA!
I'M IMPRESSED! RUMOR HAS IT YOUR NEGOTIATIONS AROUND THE WORLD HAVE BEEN SUCCESSFUL!
UH-HUH!

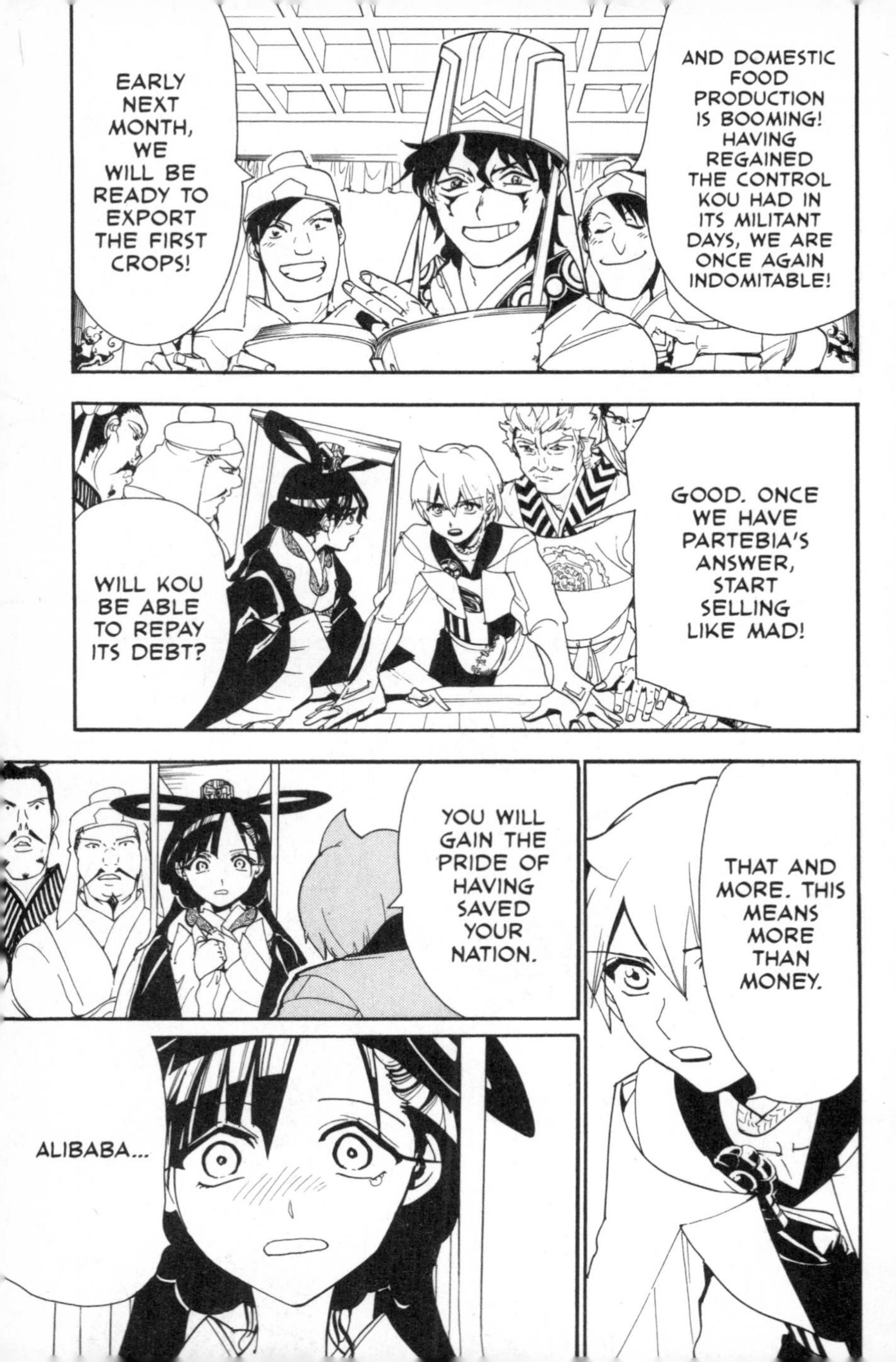
AND DOMESTIC FOOD PRODUCTION IS BOOMING! HAVING REGAINED THE CONTROL KOU HAD IN ITS MILITANT DAYS, WE ARE ONCE AGAIN INDOMITABLE!
EARLY NEXT MONTH, WE WILL BE READY TO EXPORT THE FIRST CROPS!
GOOD. ONCE WE HAVE PARTEBIA'S ANSWER, START SELLING LIKE MAD!
WILL KOU BE ABLE TO REPAY ITS DEBT?
THAT AND MORE. THIS MEANS MORE THAN MONEY.
YOU WILL GAIN THE PRIDE OF HAVING SAVED YOUR NATION.
ALIBABA...

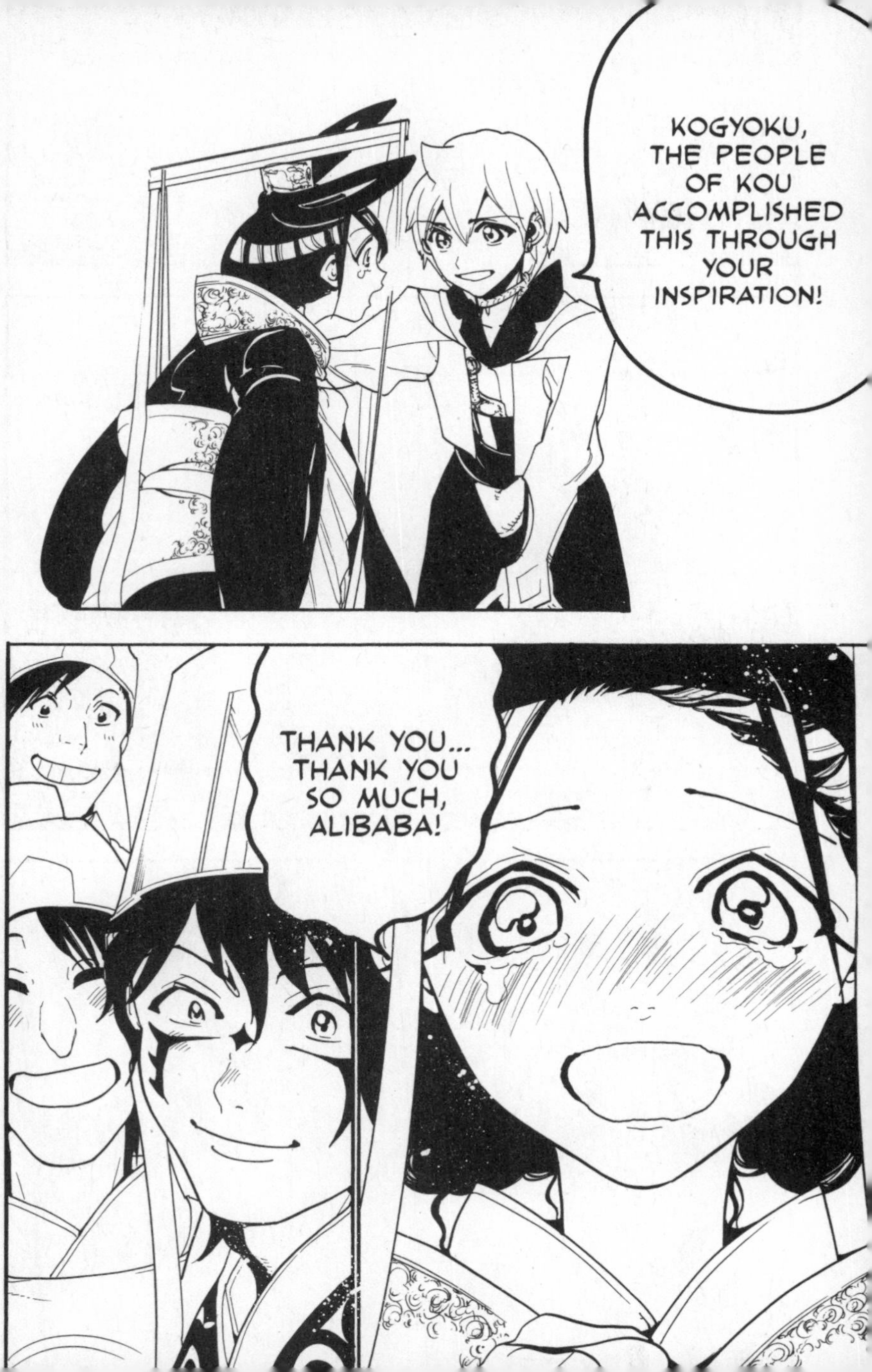
KOGYOKU, THE PEOPLE OF KOU ACCOMPLISHED THIS THROUGH YOUR INSPIRATION!
THANK YOU... THANK YOU SO MUCH, ALIBABA!

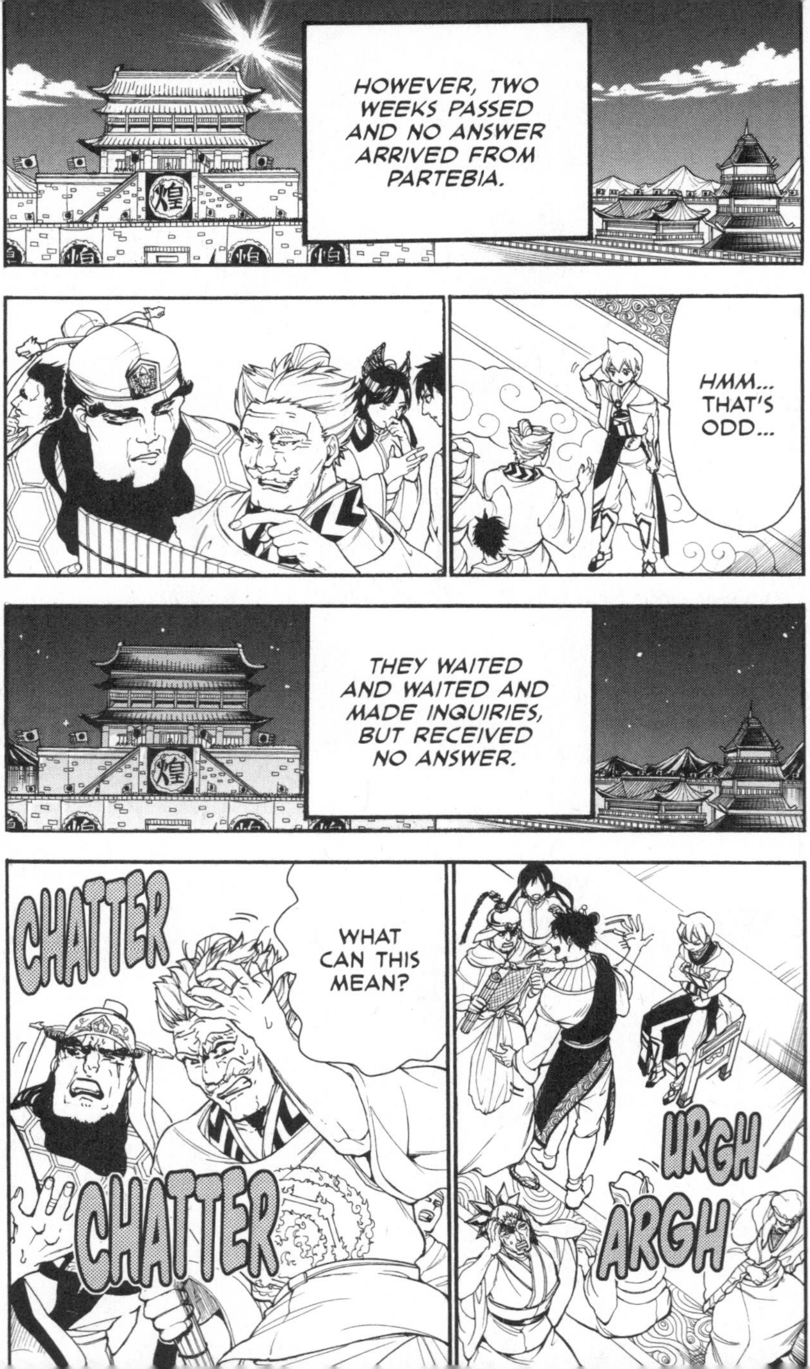
HOWEVER, TWO WEEKS PASSED AND NO ANSWER ARRIVED FROM PARTEBIA.
HMM... THAT'S ODD...
THEY WAITED AND WAITED AND MADE INQUIRIES, BUT RECEIVED NO ANSWER.
URGH
ARGH
CHATTER
WHAT CAN THIS MEAN?
CHATTER

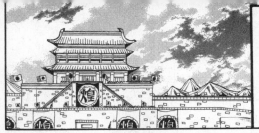

FOUR WEEKS LATER, A MISSIVE ARRIVED.

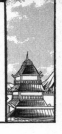

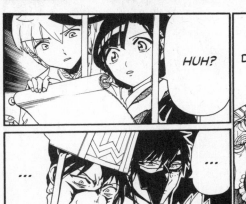

HUH?

WHAT DOES IT SAY?!

...

...

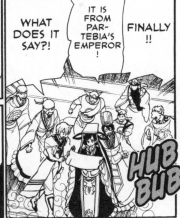

WHAT DOES IT SAY?!

IT IS FROM PARTEBIA'S EMPEROR!

FINALLY!!

HUB BUB

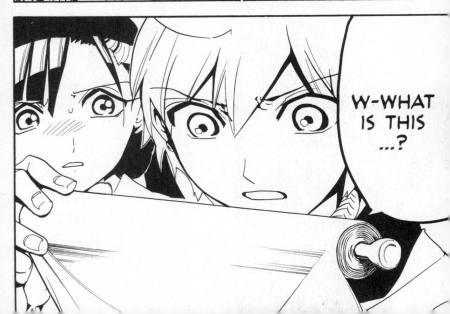

W-WHAT IS THIS ...?

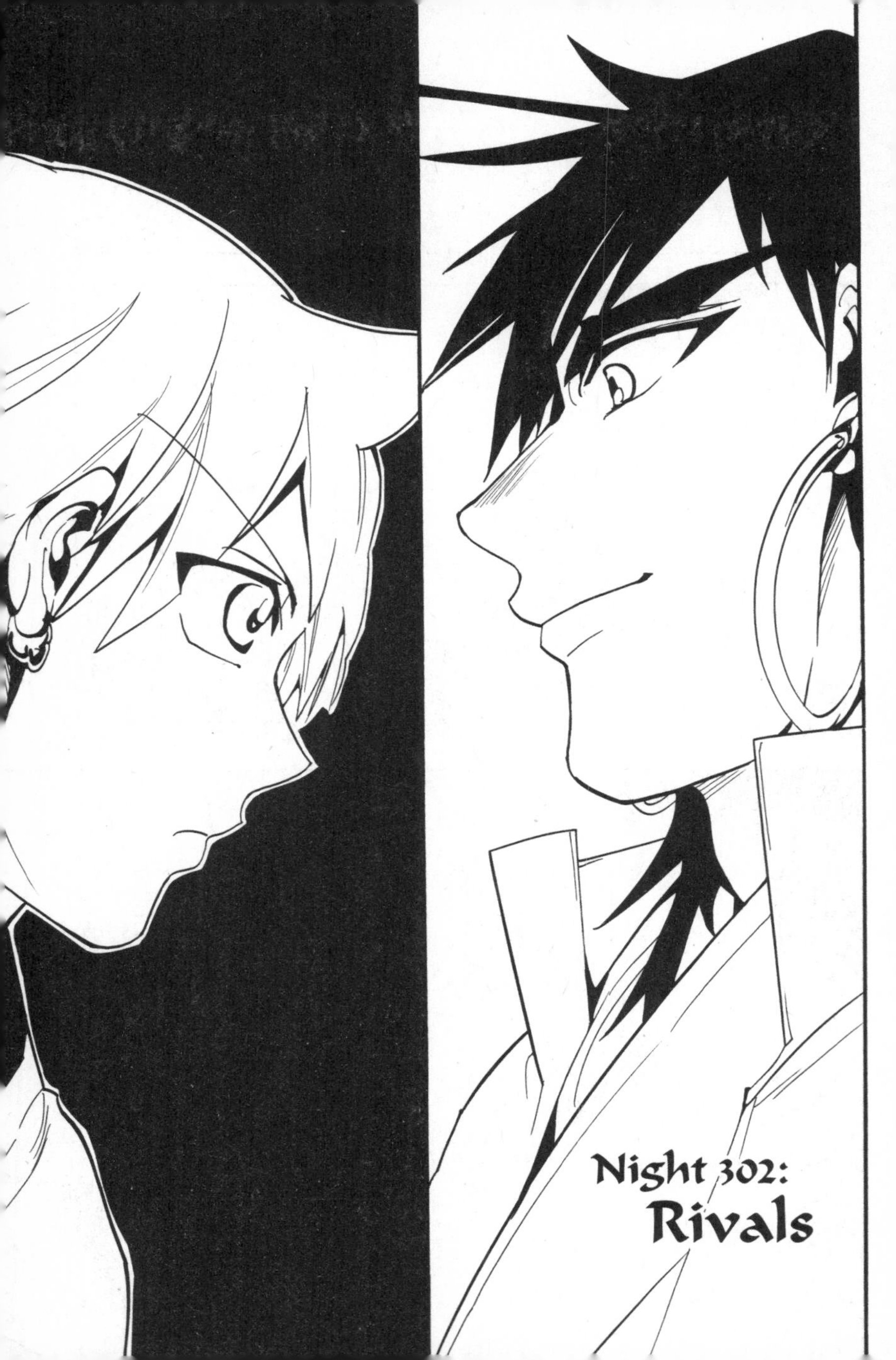
Night 302:
Rivals

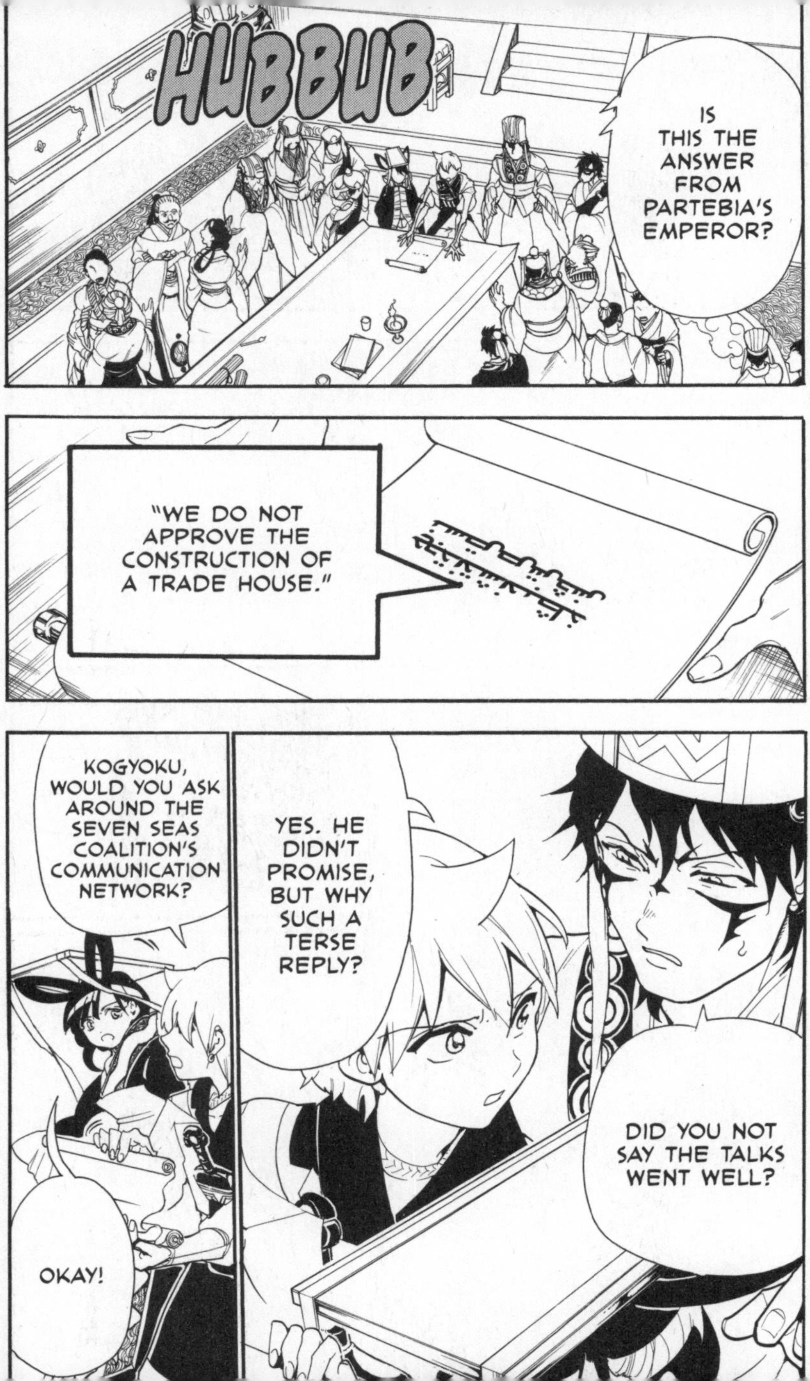
IS THIS THE ANSWER FROM PARTEBIA'S EMPEROR?
HUBBUB
"WE DO NOT APPROVE THE CONSTRUCTION OF A TRADE HOUSE."
YES. HE DIDN'T PROMISE, BUT WHY SUCH A TERSE REPLY?
DID YOU NOT SAY THE TALKS WENT WELL?
KOGYOKU, WOULD YOU ASK AROUND THE SEVEN SEAS COALITION'S COMMUNICATION NETWORK?
OKAY!

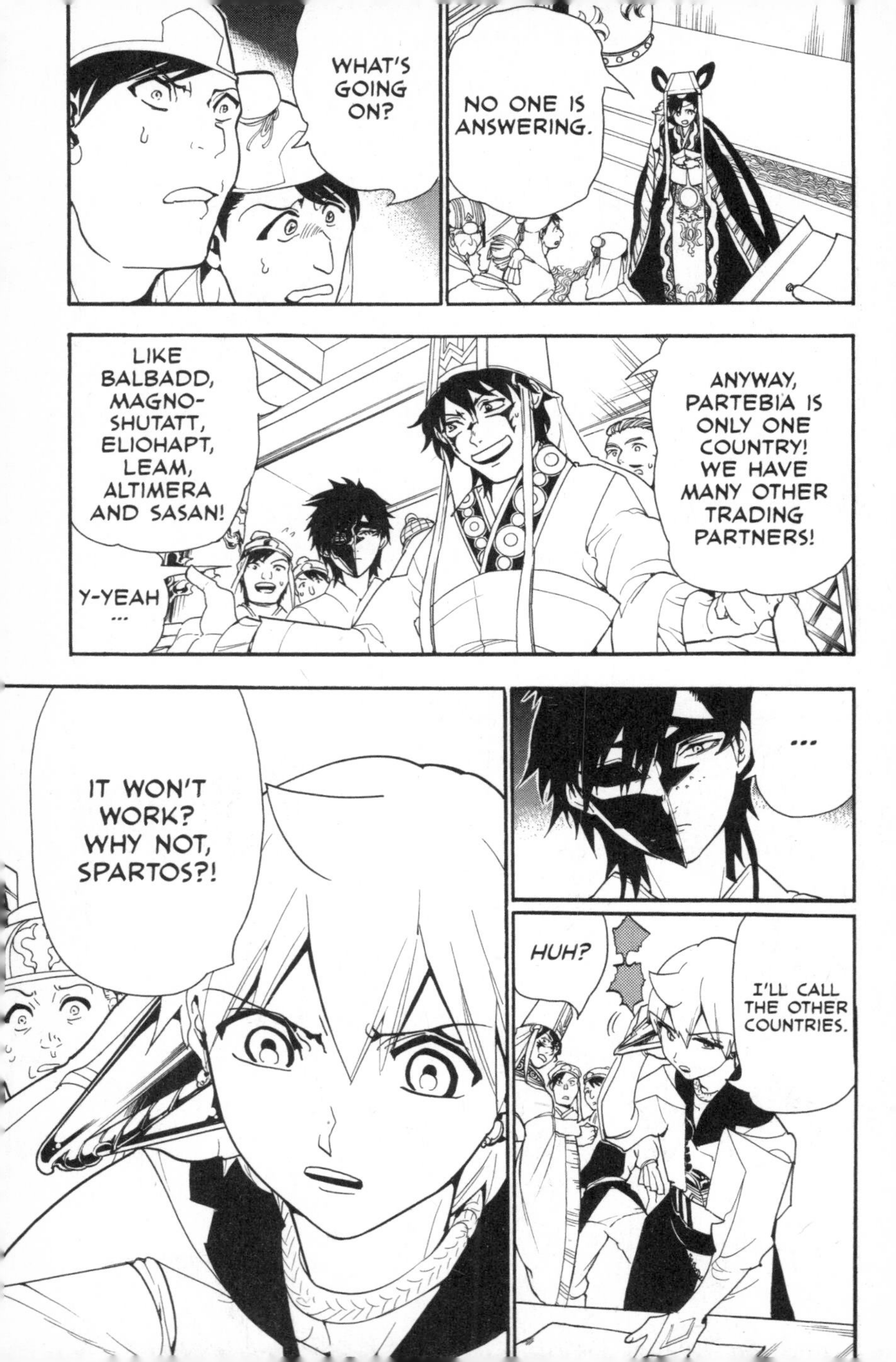
NO ONE IS ANSWERING.
WHAT'S GOING ON?
ANYWAY, PARTEBIA IS ONLY ONE COUNTRY! WE HAVE MANY OTHER TRADING PARTNERS!
LIKE BALBADD, MAGNO-SHUTATT, ELIOHAPT, LEAM, ALTIMERA AND SASAN!
Y-YEAH ...
...
I'LL CALL THE OTHER COUNTRIES.
HUH?
IT WON'T WORK? WHY NOT, SPARTOS?!

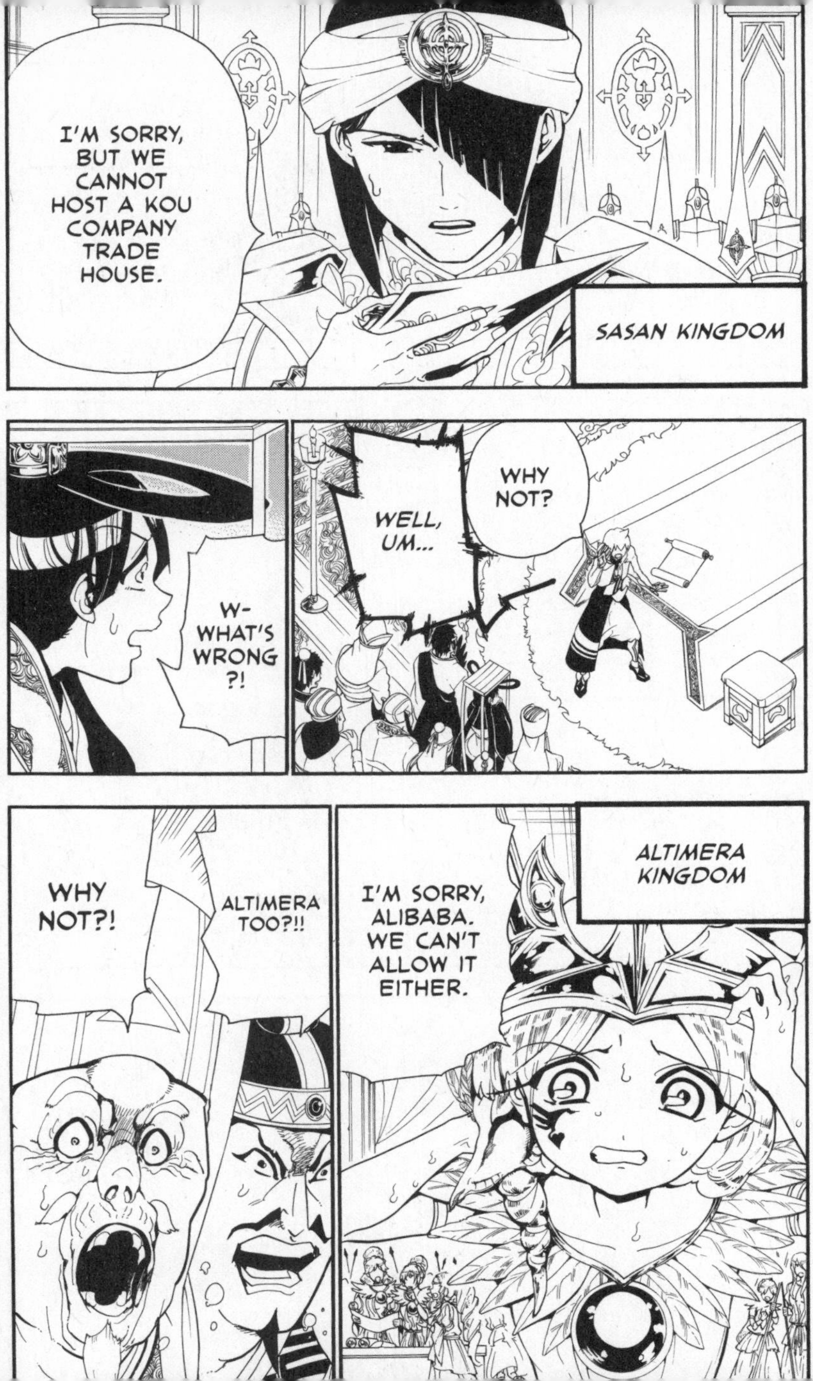
SASAN KINGDOM
I'M SORRY, BUT WE CANNOT HOST A KOU COMPANY TRADE HOUSE.
WHY NOT?
WELL, UM...
W- WHAT'S WRONG ?!
ALTIMERA KINGDOM
I'M SORRY, ALIBABA. WE CAN'T ALLOW IT EITHER.
ALTIMERA TOO?!!
WHY NOT?!

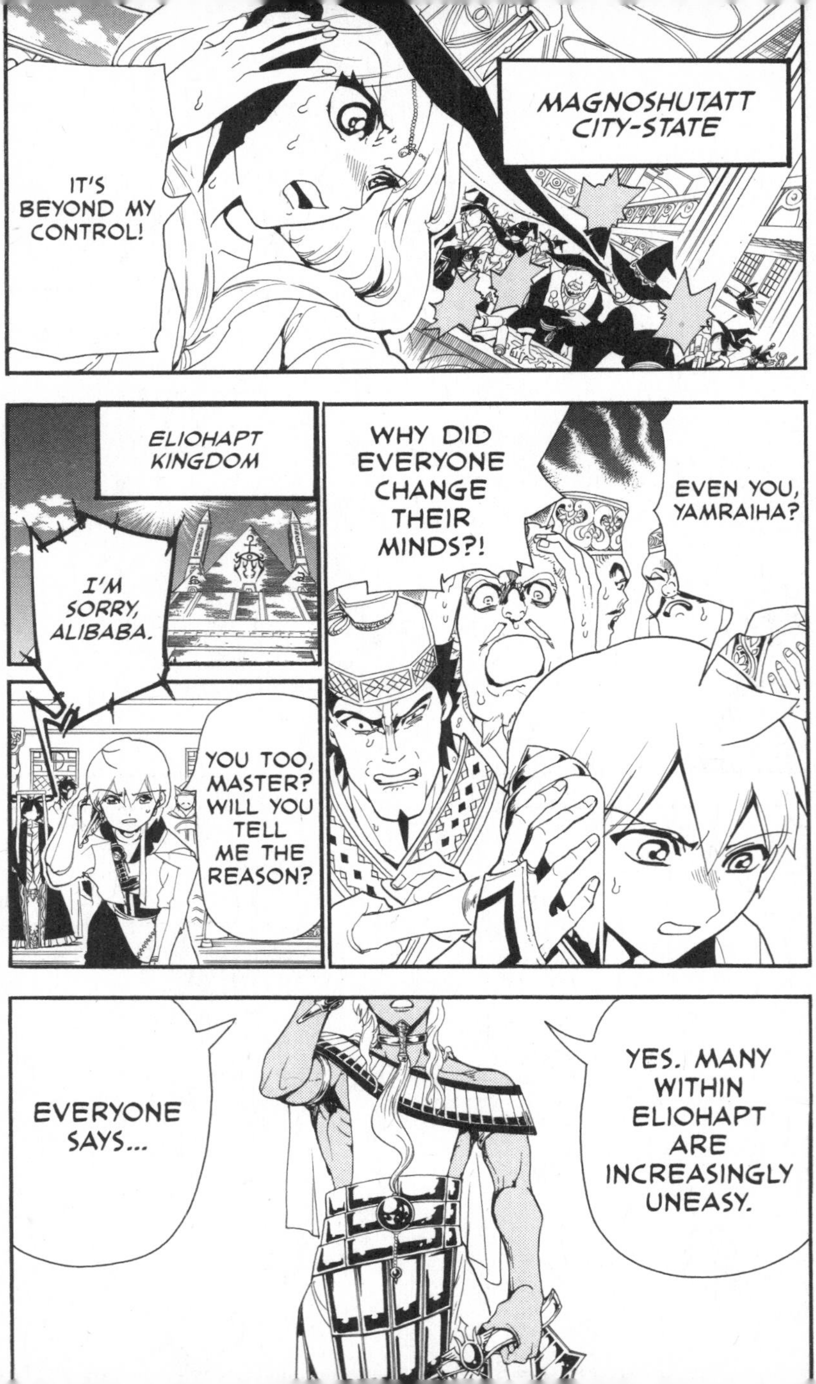
MAGNOSHUTATT CITY-STATE
IT'S BEYOND MY CONTROL!
WHY DID EVERYONE CHANGE THEIR MINDS?!
EVEN YOU, YAMRAIHA?
ELIOHAPT KINGDOM
I'M SORRY, ALIBABA.
YOU TOO, MASTER? WILL YOU TELL ME THE REASON?
YES. MANY WITHIN ELIOHAPT ARE INCREASINGLY UNEASY.
EVERYONE SAYS...

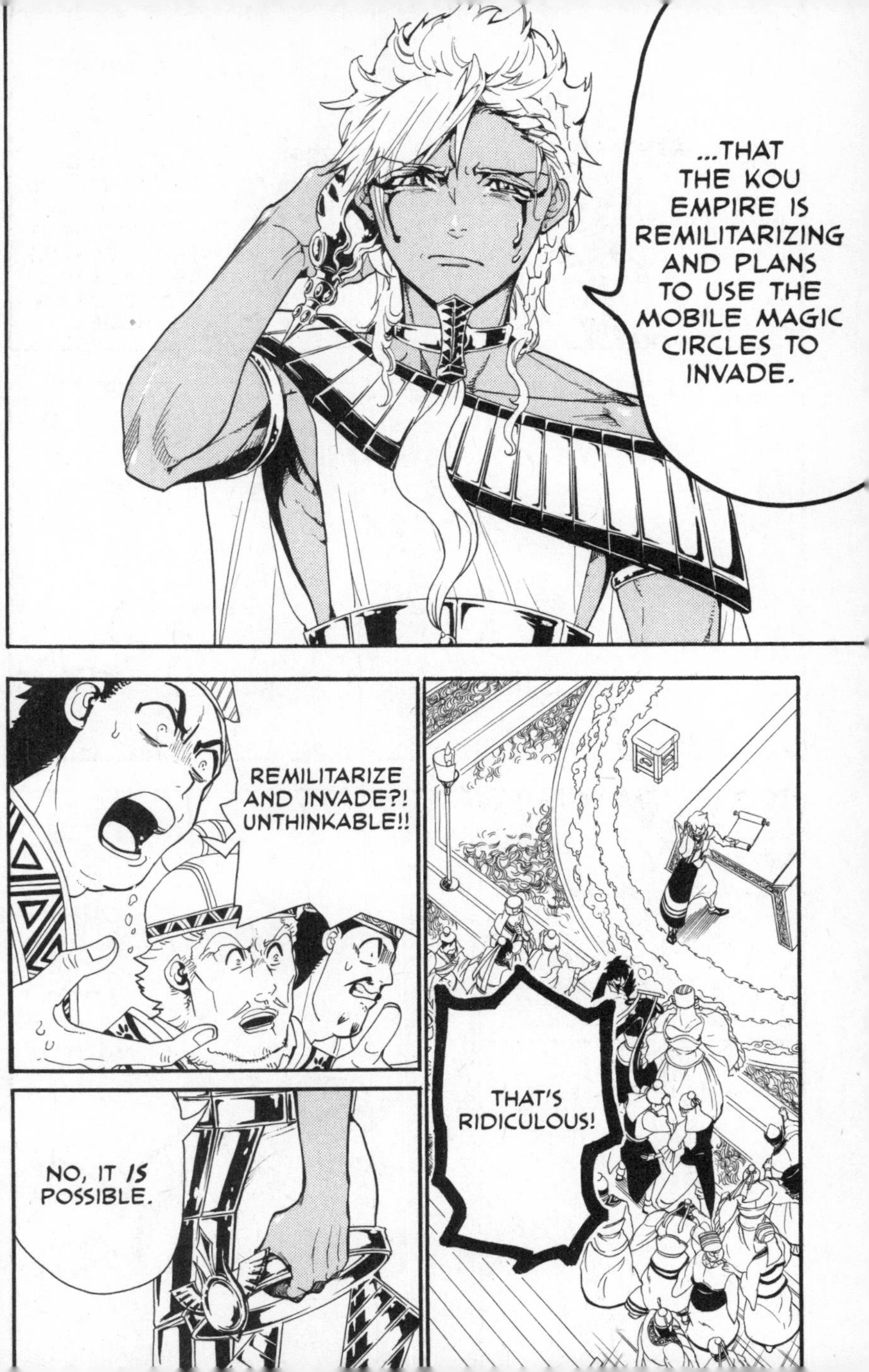
...THAT THE KOU EMPIRE IS REMILITARIZING AND PLANS TO USE THE MOBILE MAGIC CIRCLES TO INVADE.
THAT'S RIDICULOUS!
REMILITARIZE AND INVADE?! UNTHINKABLE!!
NO, IT *IS* POSSIBLE.

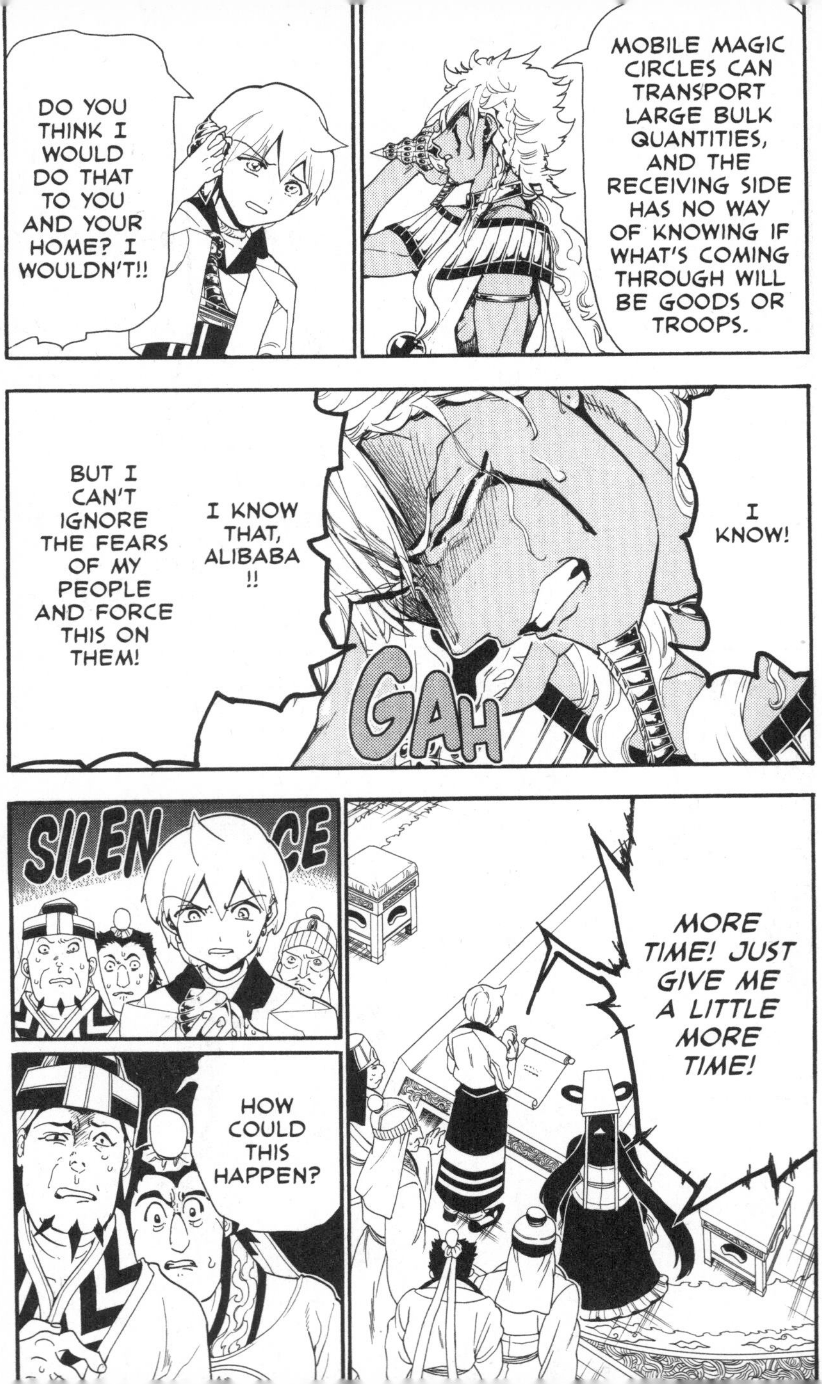
MOBILE MAGIC CIRCLES CAN TRANSPORT LARGE BULK QUANTITIES, AND THE RECEIVING SIDE HAS NO WAY OF KNOWING IF WHAT'S COMING THROUGH WILL BE GOODS OR TROOPS.
DO YOU THINK I WOULD DO THAT TO YOU AND YOUR HOME? I WOULDN'T!!
I KNOW!
I KNOW THAT, ALIBABA!!
BUT I CAN'T IGNORE THE FEARS OF MY PEOPLE AND FORCE THIS ON THEM!
GAH
MORE TIME! JUST GIVE ME A LITTLE MORE TIME!
SILENCE
HOW COULD THIS HAPPEN?

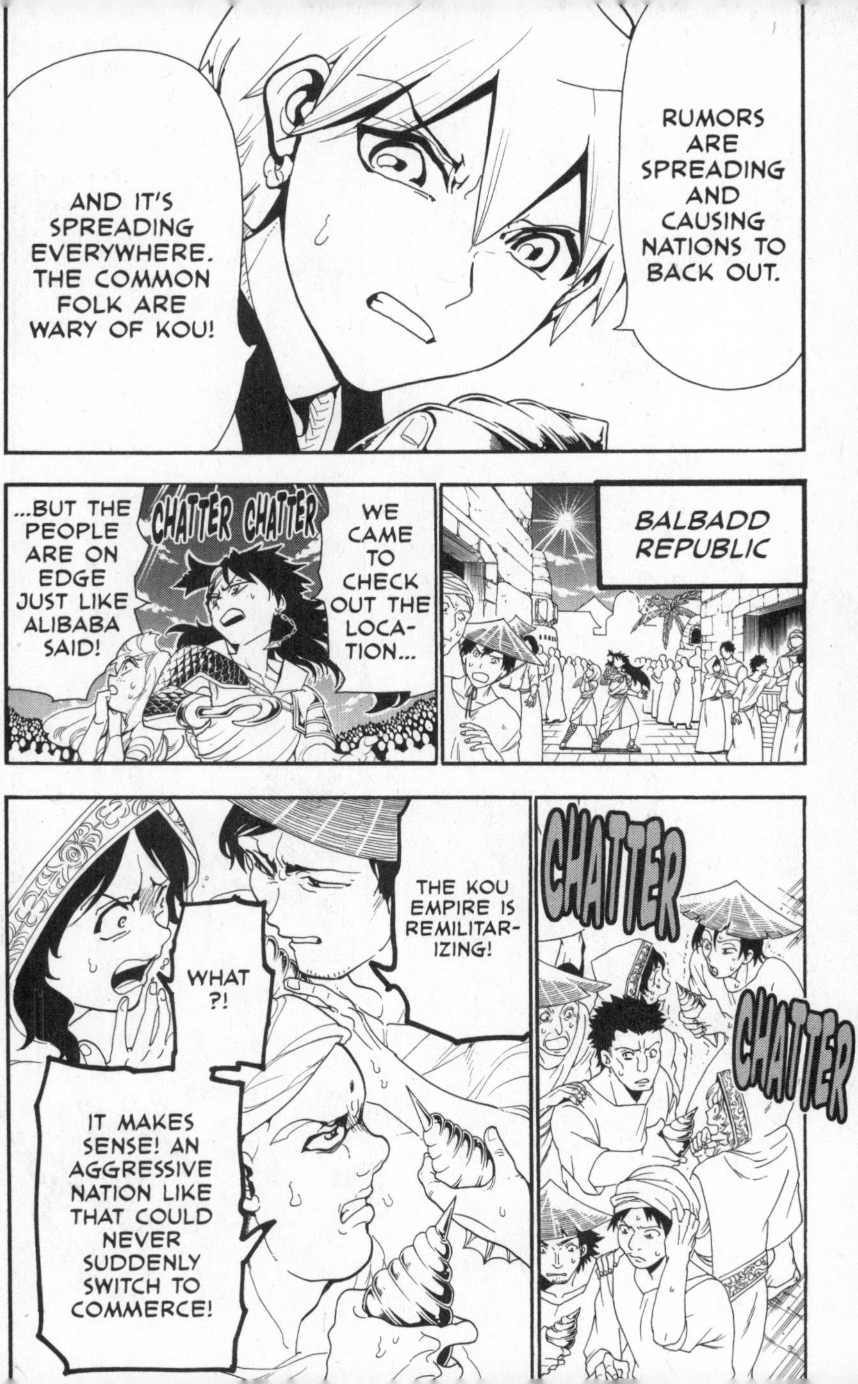
RUMORS ARE SPREADING AND CAUSING NATIONS TO BACK OUT.
AND IT'S SPREADING EVERYWHERE. THE COMMON FOLK ARE WARY OF KOU!
BALBADD REPUBLIC
WE CAME TO CHECK OUT THE LOCA-TION...
CHATTER CHATTER
...BUT THE PEOPLE ARE ON EDGE JUST LIKE ALIBABA SAID!
CHATTER
CHATTER
THE KOU EMPIRE IS REMILITAR-IZING!
WHAT?!
IT MAKES SENSE! AN AGGRESSIVE NATION LIKE THAT COULD NEVER SUDDENLY SWITCH TO COMMERCE!

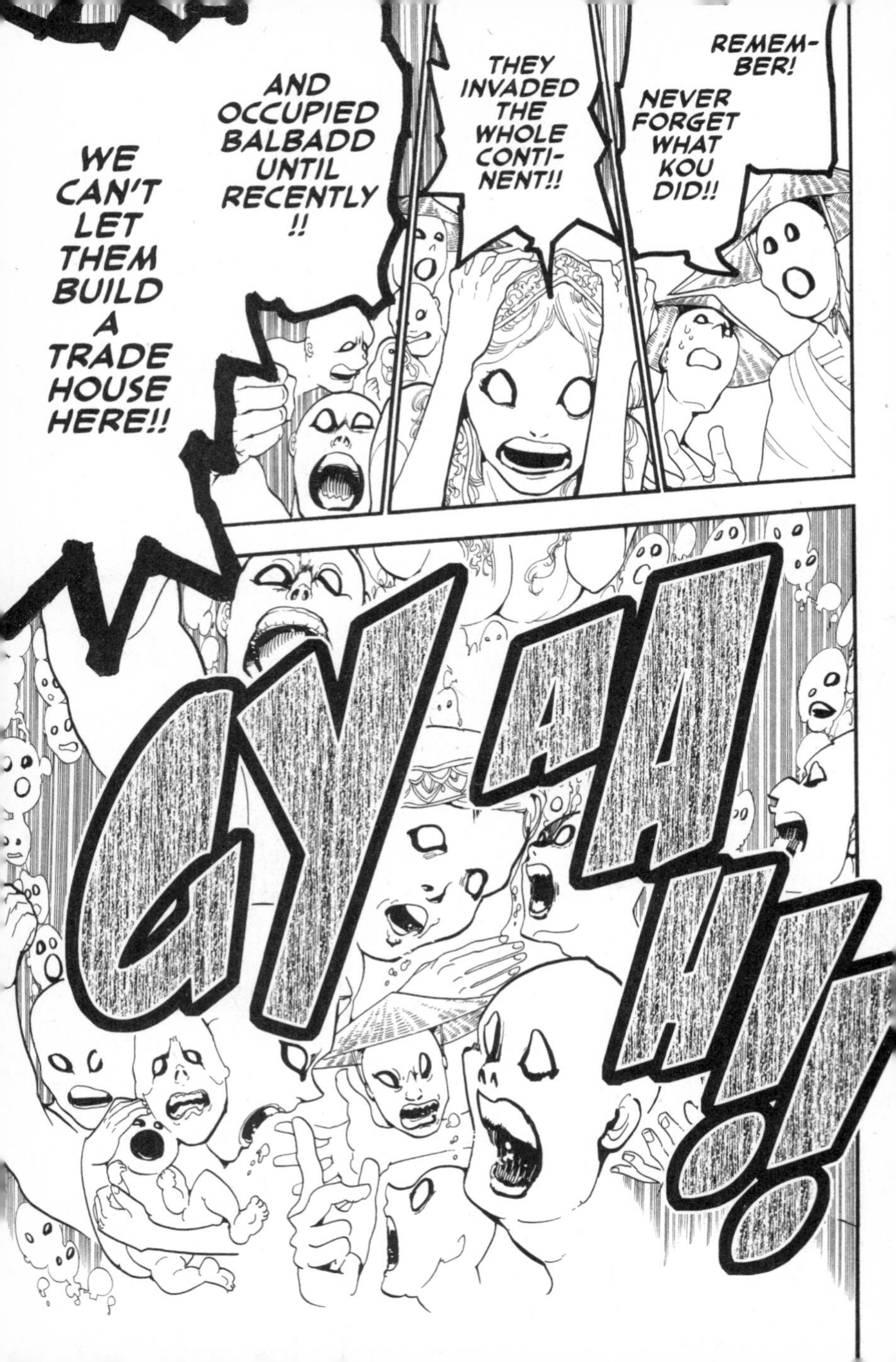
REMEM-
BER!
NEVER FORGET WHAT KOU DID!!
THEY INVADED THE WHOLE CONTI-
NENT!!
AND OCCUPIED BALBADD UNTIL RECENTLY!!
WE CAN'T LET THEM BUILD A TRADE HOUSE HERE!!
GYAAAH!!

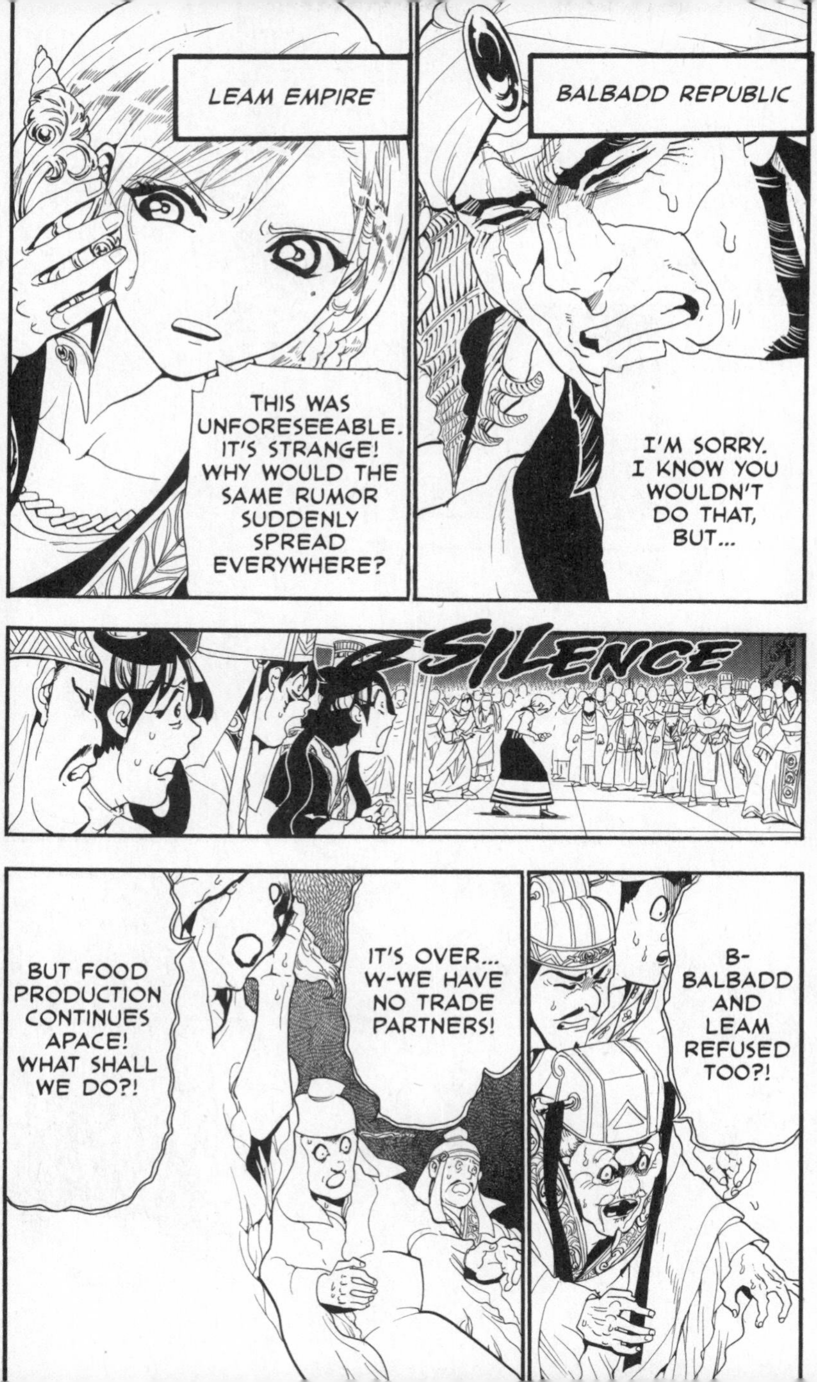
BALBADD REPUBLIC
I'M SORRY. I KNOW YOU WOULDN'T DO THAT, BUT...
LEAM EMPIRE
THIS WAS UNFORESEEABLE. IT'S STRANGE! WHY WOULD THE SAME RUMOR SUDDENLY SPREAD EVERYWHERE?
SILENCE
B-BALBADD AND LEAM REFUSED TOO?!
IT'S OVER... W-WE HAVE NO TRADE PARTNERS!
BUT FOOD PRODUCTION CONTINUES APACE! WHAT SHALL WE DO?!

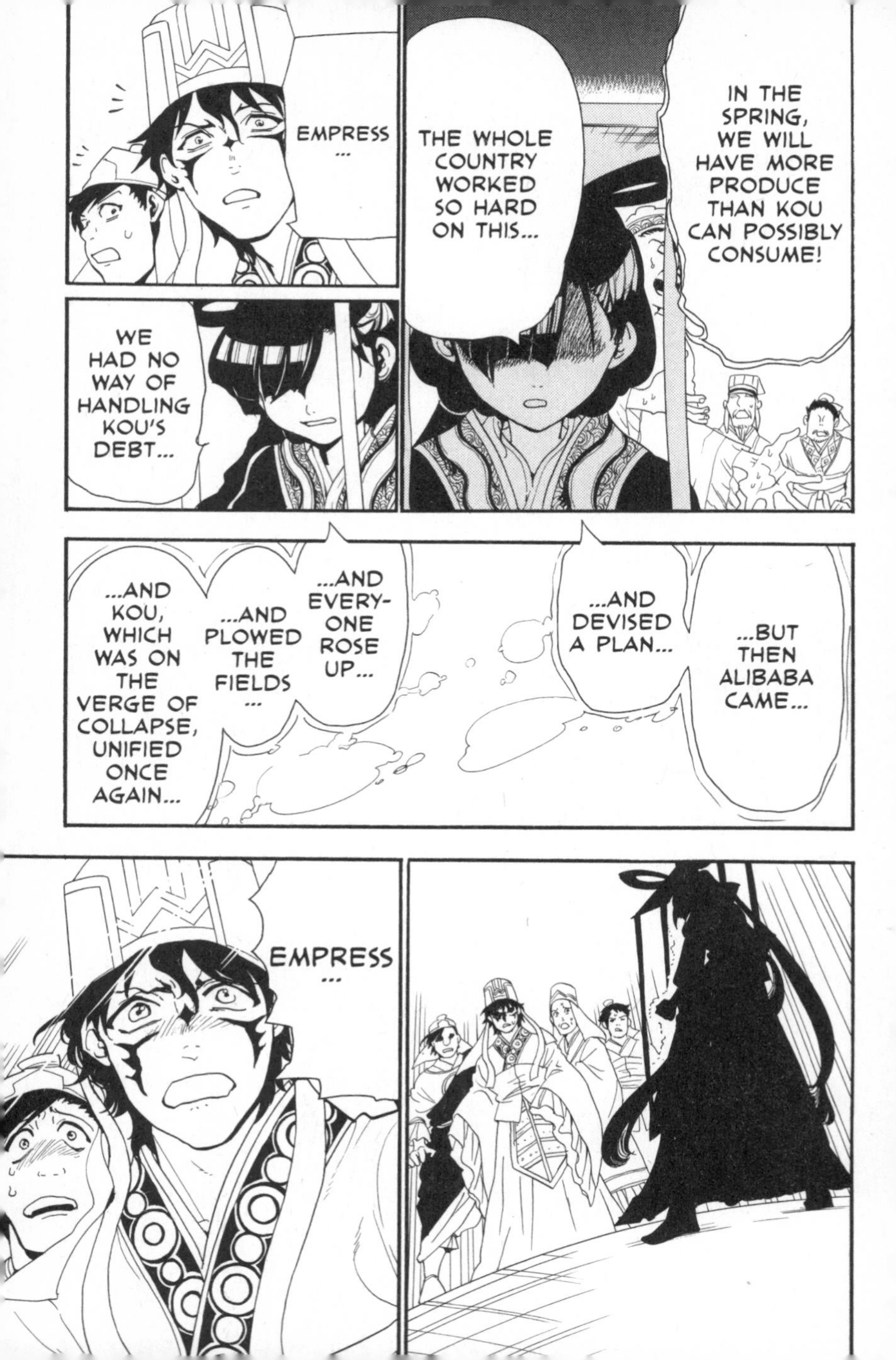
IN THE SPRING, WE WILL HAVE MORE PRODUCE THAN KOU CAN POSSIBLY CONSUME!
THE WHOLE COUNTRY WORKED SO HARD ON THIS...
EMPRESS...
WE HAD NO WAY OF HANDLING KOU'S DEBT...
...BUT THEN ALIBABA CAME...
...AND DEVISED A PLAN...
...AND EVERY-ONE ROSE UP...
...AND PLOWED THE FIELDS...
...AND KOU, WHICH WAS ON THE VERGE OF COLLAPSE, UNIFIED ONCE AGAIN...
EMPRESS...

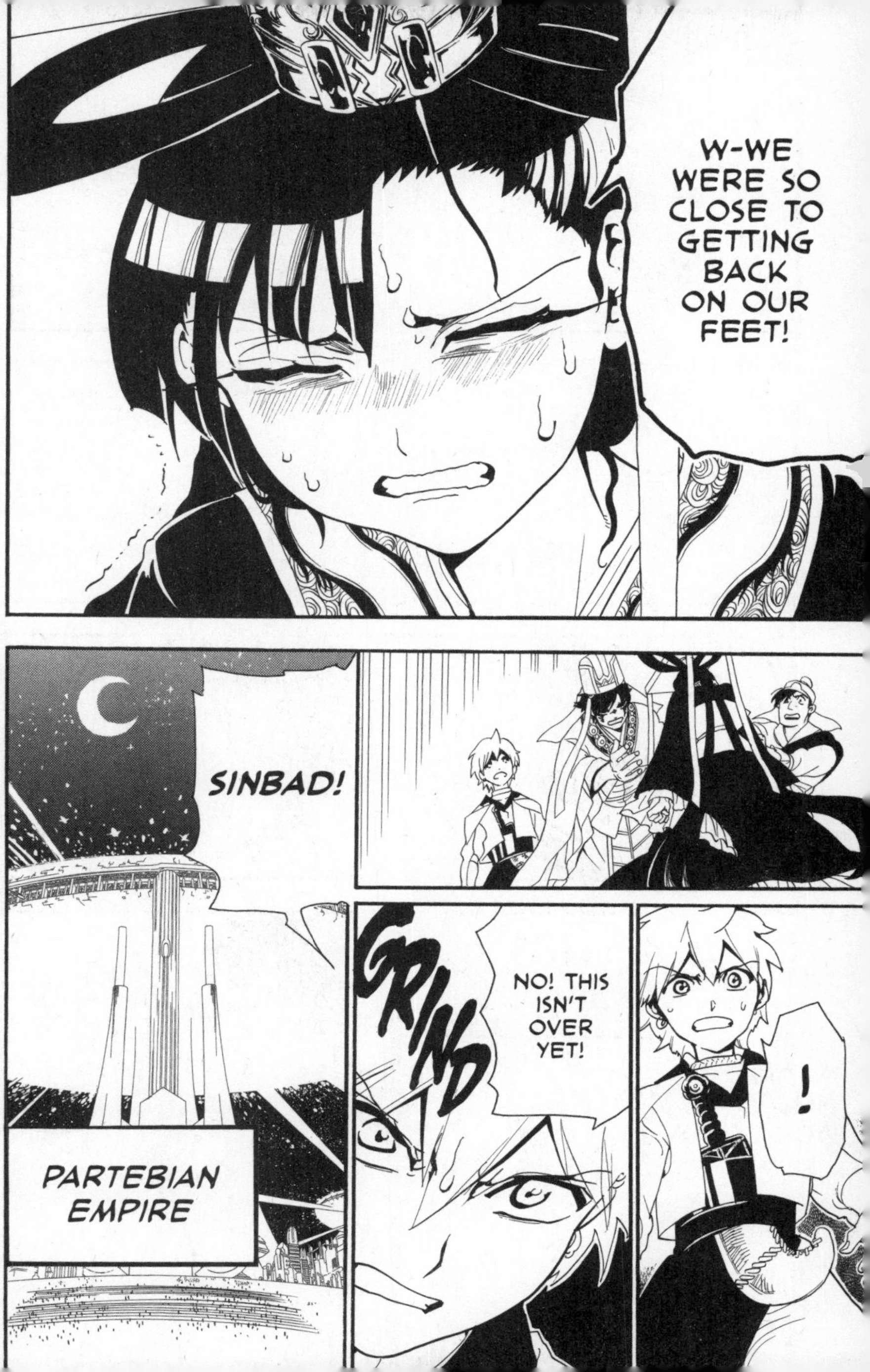
W-WE WERE SO CLOSE TO GETTING BACK ON OUR FEET!
!
GRIND
NO! THIS ISN'T OVER YET!
SINBAD!
PARTEBIAN EMPIRE

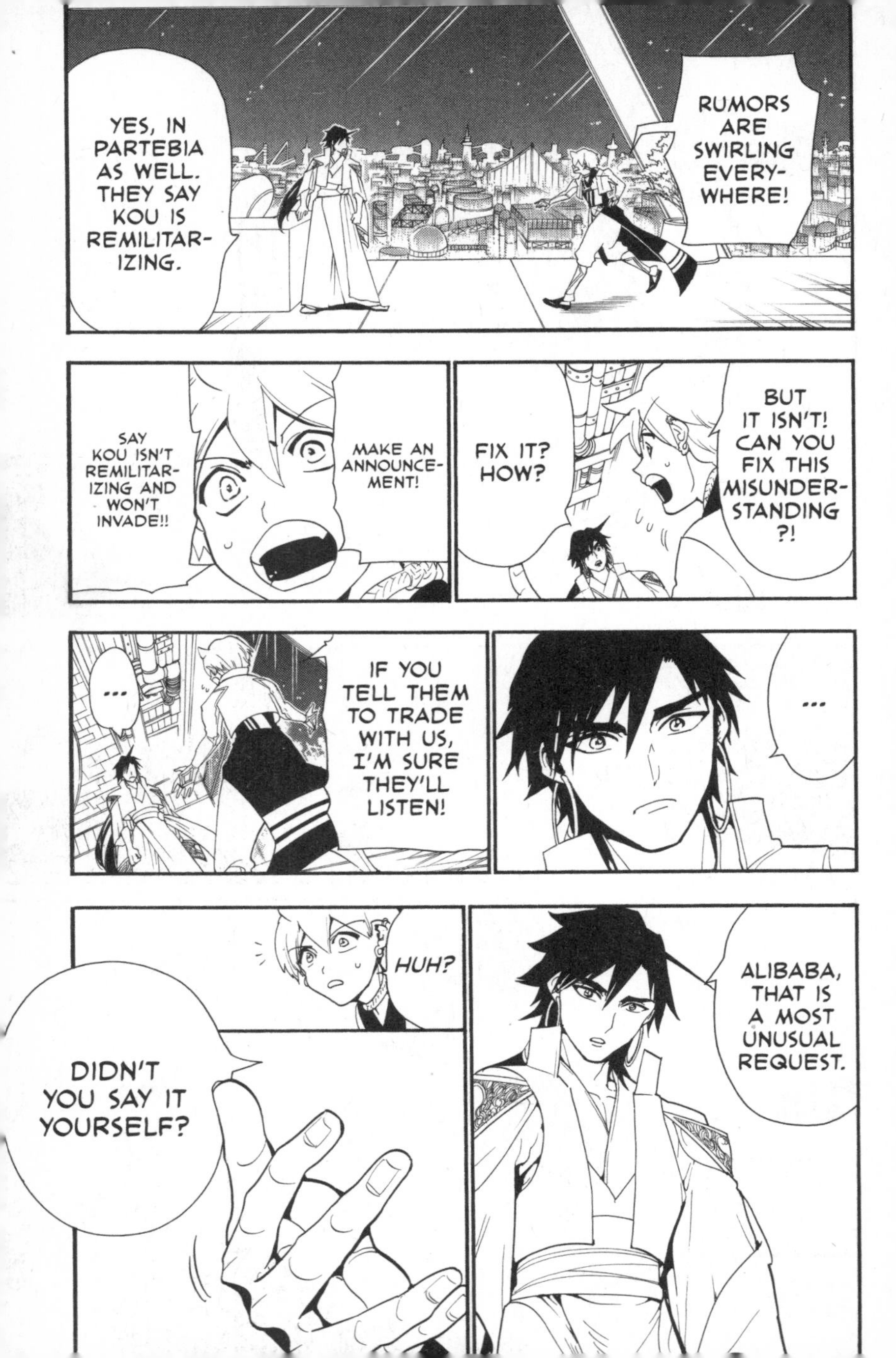
RUMORS ARE SWIRLING EVERYWHERE!
YES, IN PARTEBIA AS WELL. THEY SAY KOU IS REMILITARIZING.
BUT IT ISN'T! CAN YOU FIX THIS MISUNDERSTANDING?!
FIX IT? HOW?
MAKE AN ANNOUNCEMENT!
SAY KOU ISN'T REMILITARIZING AND WON'T INVADE!!
...
IF YOU TELL THEM TO TRADE WITH US, I'M SURE THEY'LL LISTEN!
...
ALIBABA, THAT IS A MOST UNUSUAL REQUEST.
HUH?
DIDN'T YOU SAY IT YOURSELF?

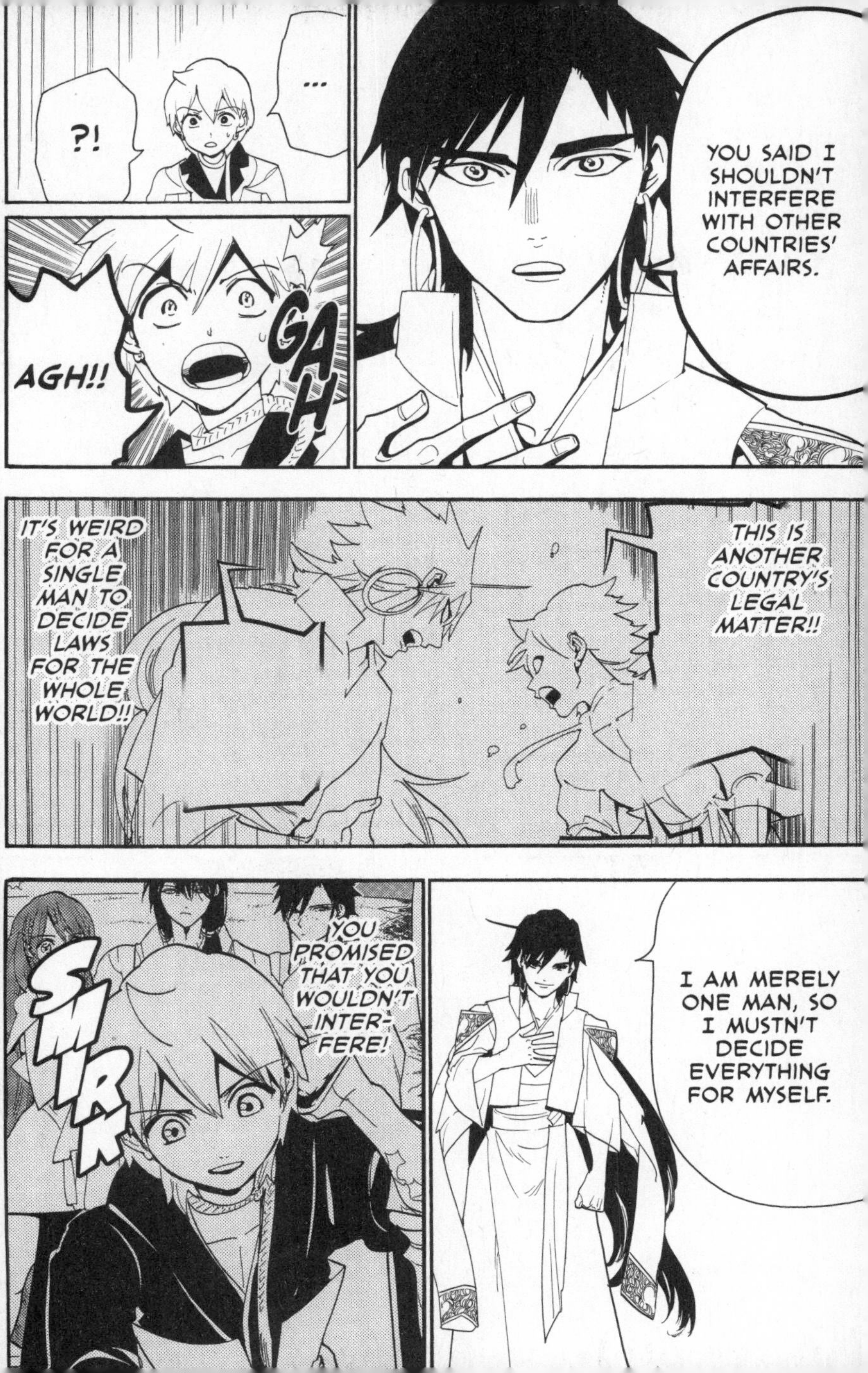
YOU SAID I SHOULDN'T INTERFERE WITH OTHER COUNTRIES' AFFAIRS.
...
?!
GAH
AGH!!
THIS IS ANOTHER COUNTRY'S LEGAL MATTER!!
IT'S WEIRD FOR A SINGLE MAN TO DECIDE LAWS FOR THE WHOLE WORLD!!
I AM MERELY ONE MAN, SO I MUSTN'T DECIDE EVERYTHING FOR MYSELF.
YOU PROMISED THAT YOU WOULDN'T INTER-FERE!
SMIRK

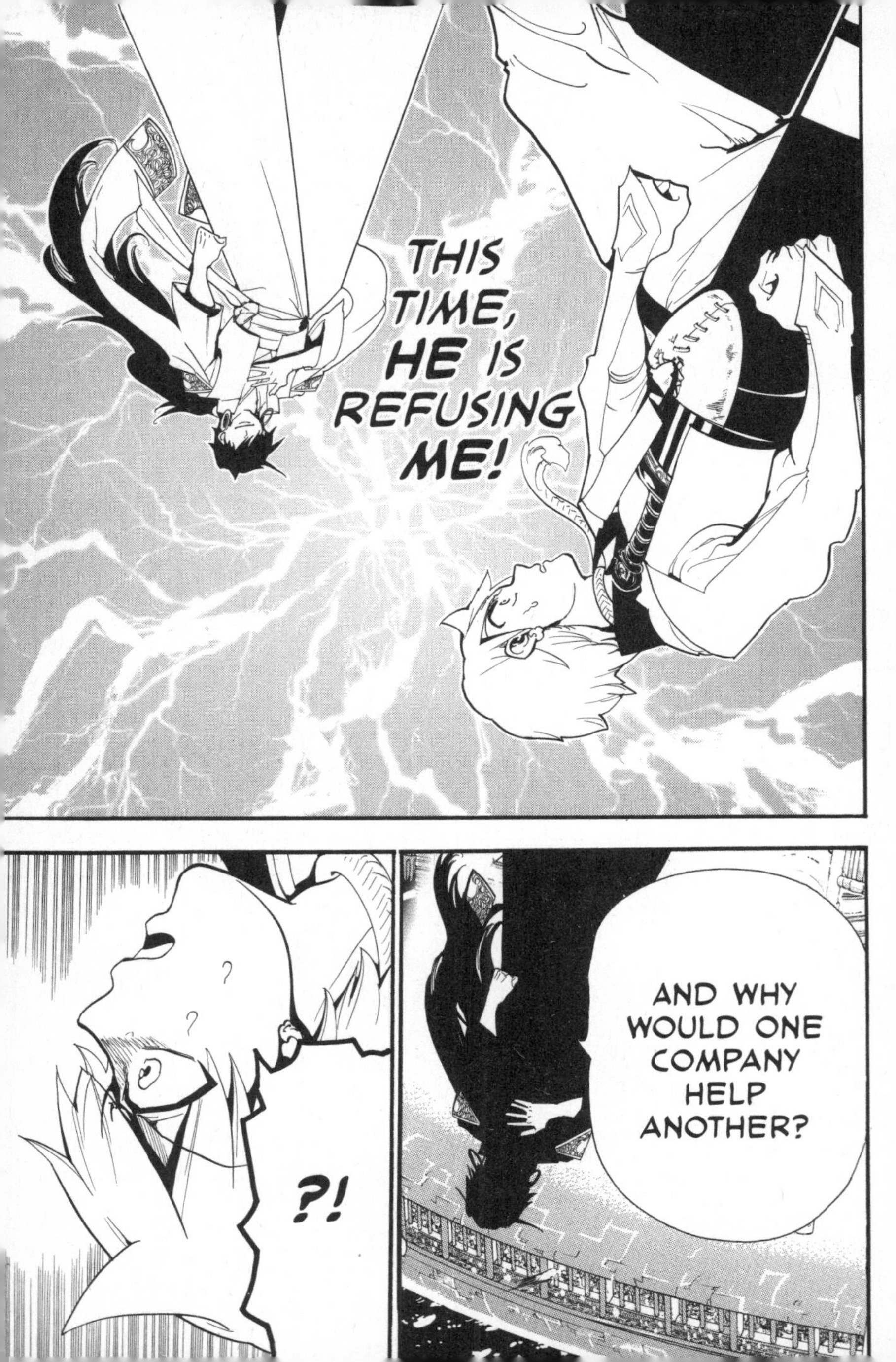
THIS TIME, HE IS REFUSING ME!
AND WHY WOULD ONE COMPANY HELP ANOTHER?
?!

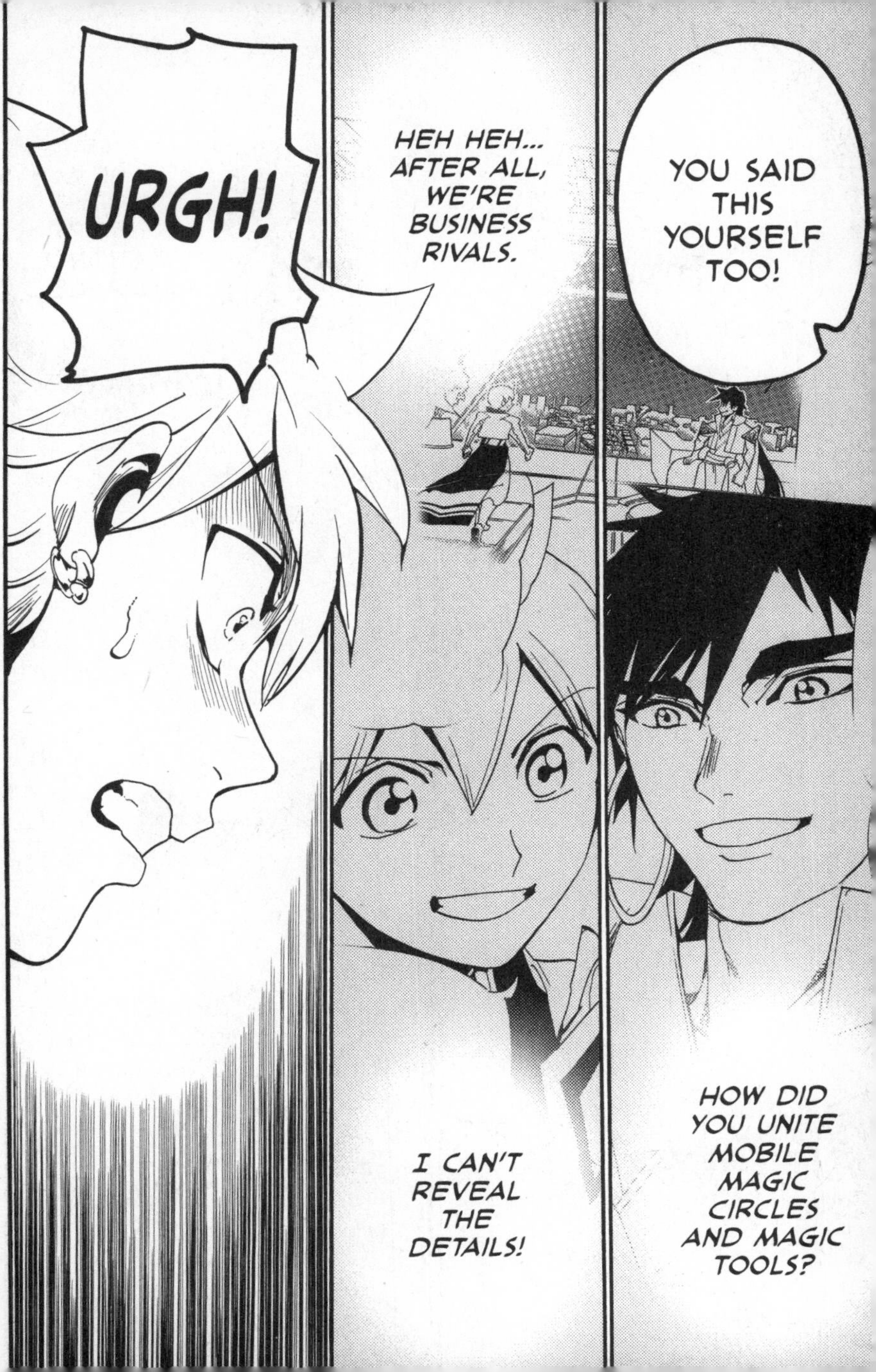
YOU SAID THIS YOURSELF TOO!
HOW DID YOU UNITE MOBILE MAGIC CIRCLES AND MAGIC TOOLS?
HEH HEH... AFTER ALL, WE'RE BUSINESS RIVALS.
I CAN'T REVEAL THE DETAILS!
URGH!

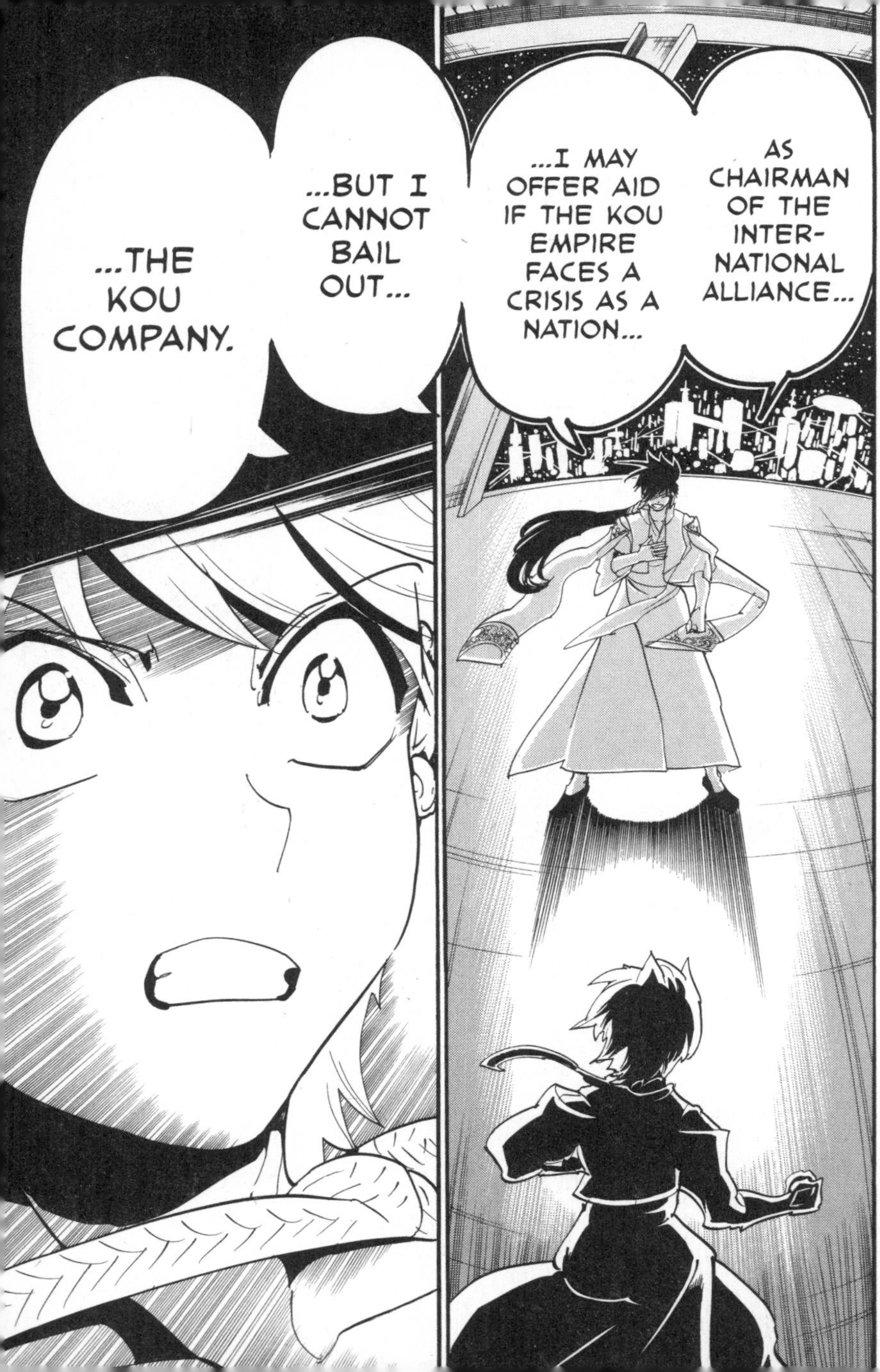
AS CHAIRMAN OF THE INTER- NATIONAL ALLIANCE...
...I MAY OFFER AID IF THE KOU EMPIRE FACES A CRISIS AS A NATION...
...BUT I CANNOT BAIL OUT...
...THE KOU COMPANY.

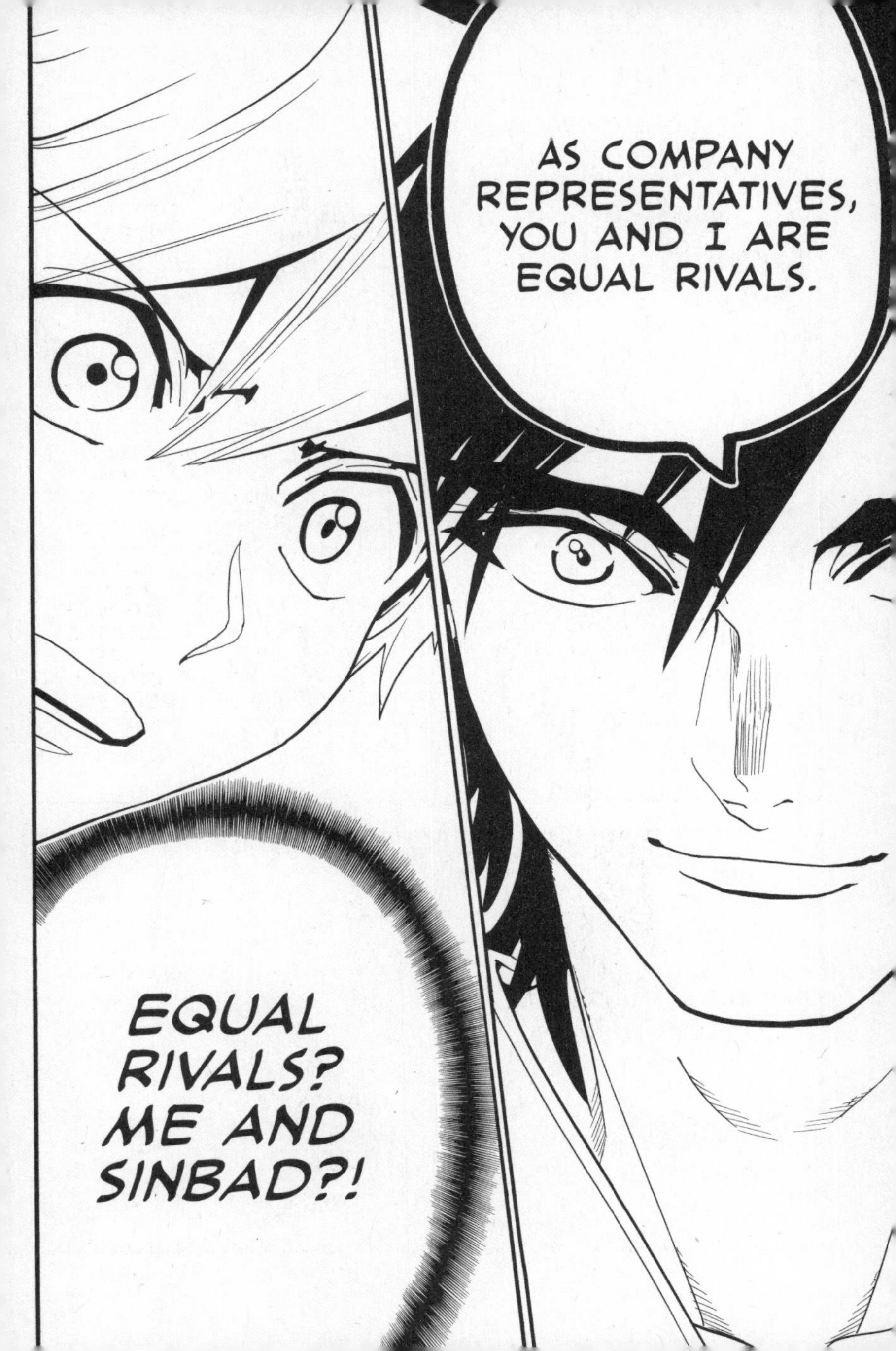
AS COMPANY REPRESENTATIVES, YOU AND I ARE EQUAL RIVALS.
EQUAL RIVALS? ME AND SINBAD?!

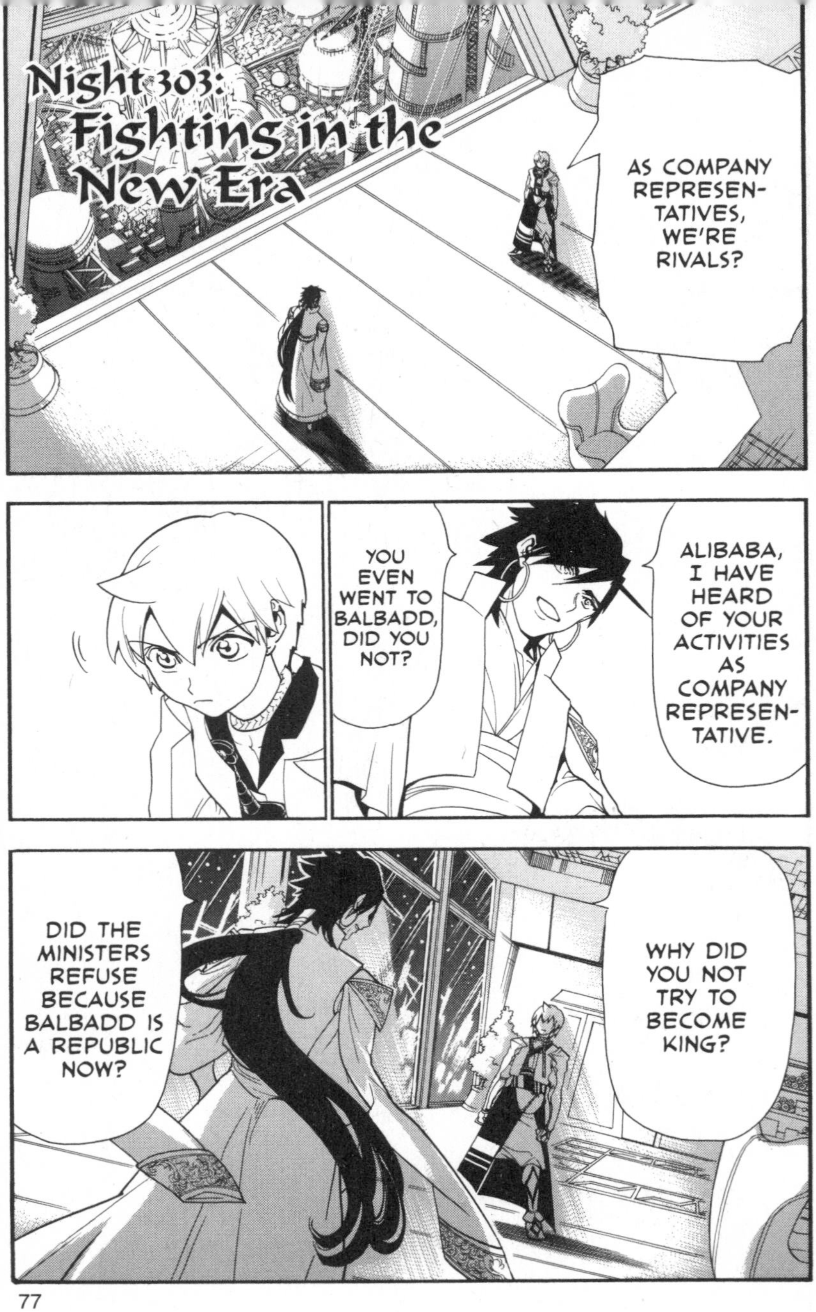
Night 303: Fighting in the New Era
AS COMPANY REPRESENTATIVES, WE'RE RIVALS?
ALIBABA, I HAVE HEARD OF YOUR ACTIVITIES AS COMPANY REPRESENTATIVE.
YOU EVEN WENT TO BALBADD, DID YOU NOT?
WHY DID YOU NOT TRY TO BECOME KING?
DID THE MINISTERS REFUSE BECAUSE BALBADD IS A REPUBLIC NOW?

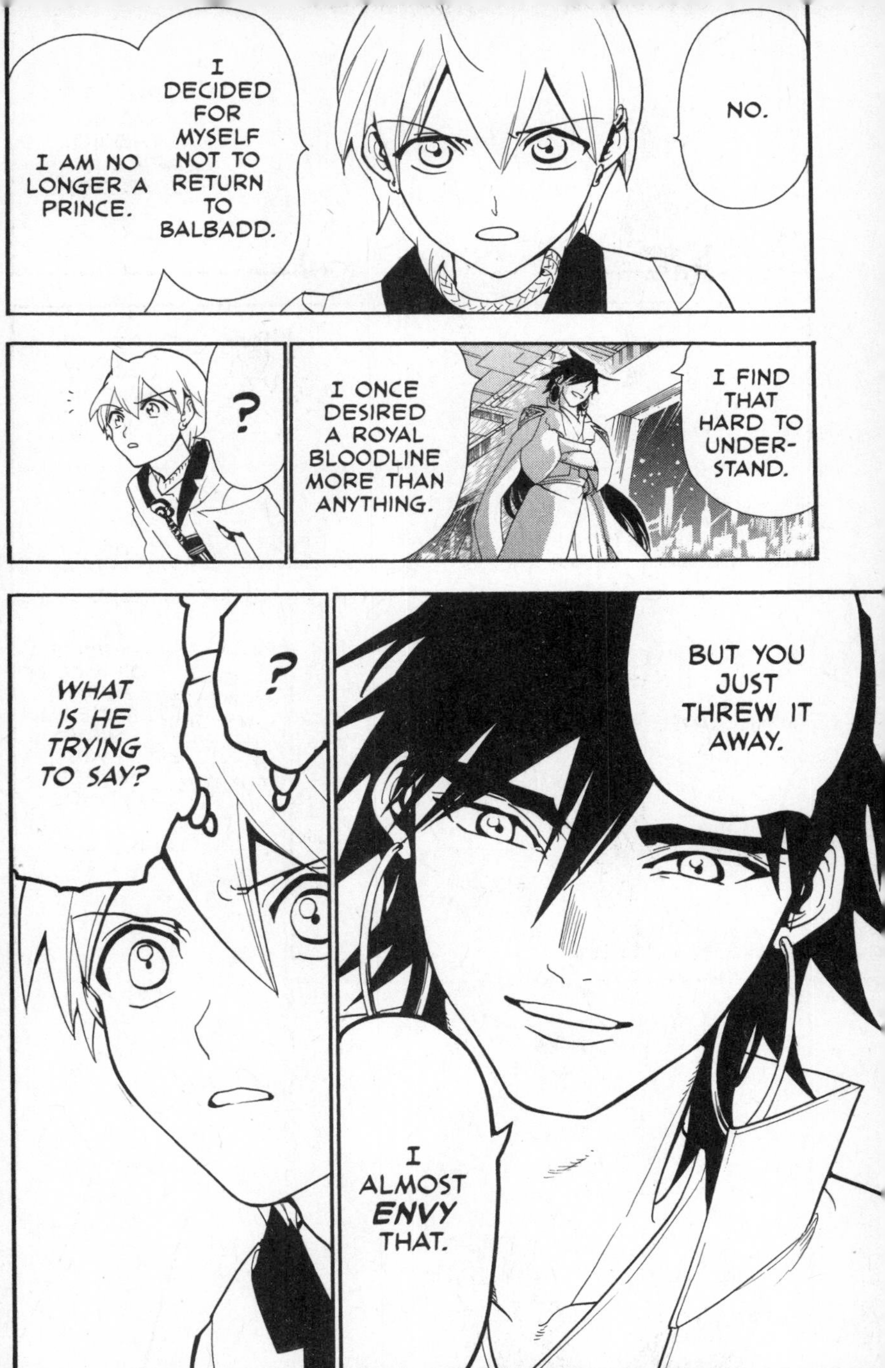
NO.
I DECIDED FOR MYSELF NOT TO RETURN TO BALBADD.
I AM NO LONGER A PRINCE.
I FIND THAT HARD TO UNDERSTAND.
I ONCE DESIRED A ROYAL BLOODLINE MORE THAN ANYTHING.
?
BUT YOU JUST THREW IT AWAY.
I ALMOST *ENVY* THAT.
?
WHAT IS HE TRYING TO SAY?

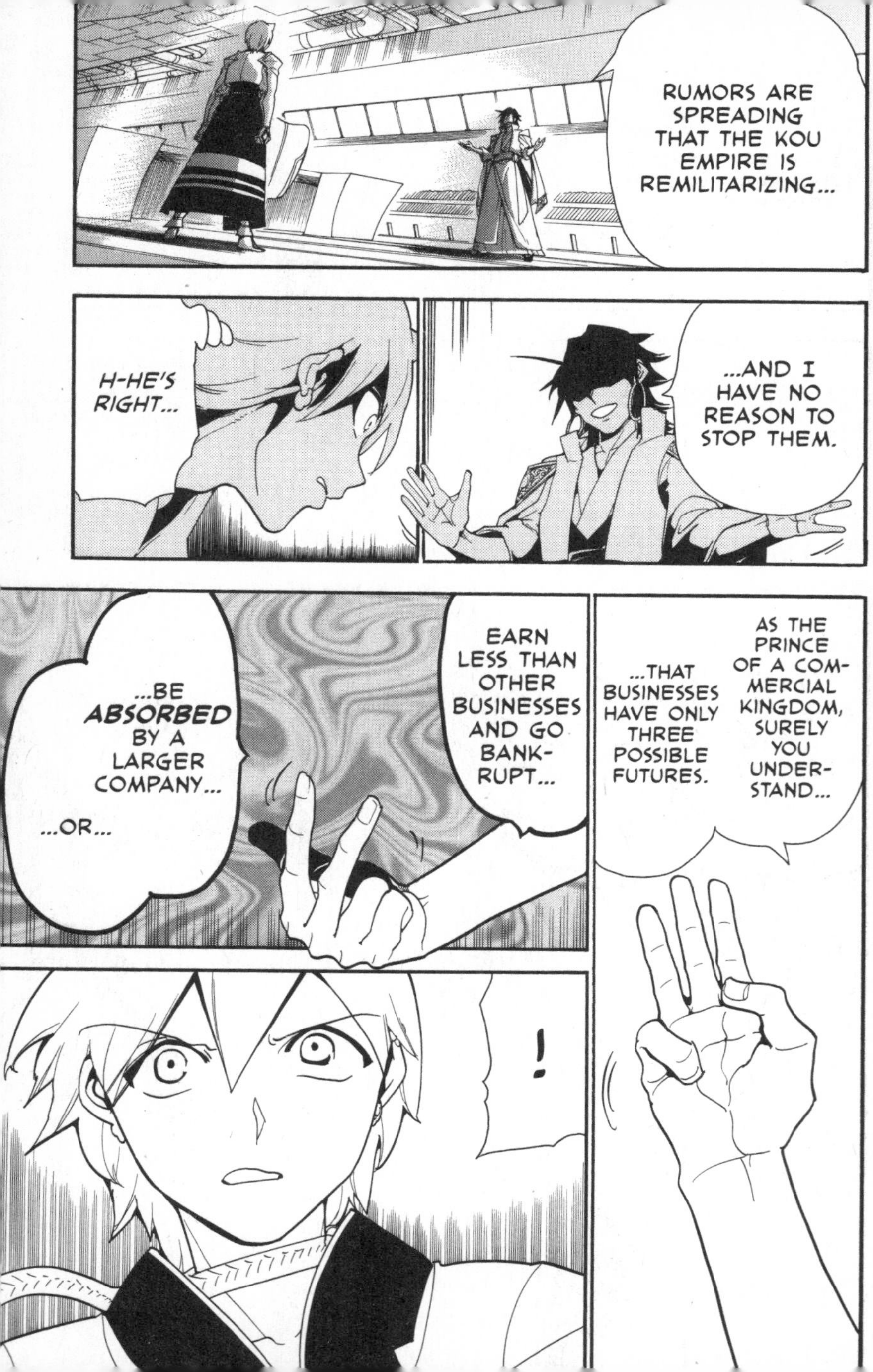
RUMORS ARE SPREADING THAT THE KOU EMPIRE IS REMILITARIZING...
...AND I HAVE NO REASON TO STOP THEM.
H-HE'S RIGHT...
AS THE PRINCE OF A COMMERCIAL KINGDOM, SURELY YOU UNDERSTAND...
...THAT BUSINESSES HAVE ONLY THREE POSSIBLE FUTURES.
EARN LESS THAN OTHER BUSINESSES AND GO BANKRUPT...
...BE *ABSORBED* BY A LARGER COMPANY...
...OR...
!

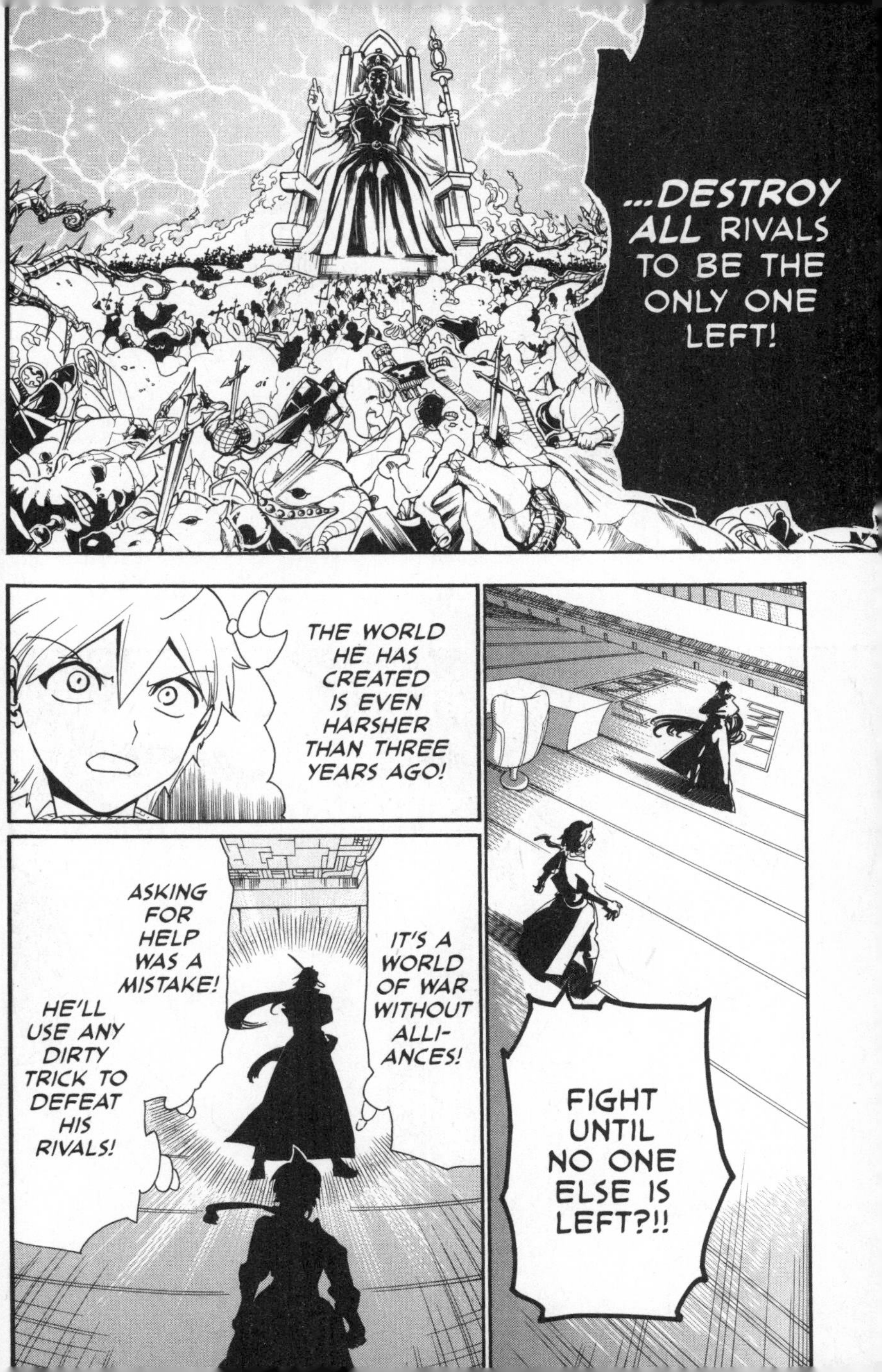
...DESTROY ALL RIVALS TO BE THE ONLY ONE LEFT!
FIGHT UNTIL NO ONE ELSE IS LEFT?!!
THE WORLD HE HAS CREATED IS EVEN HARSHER THAN THREE YEARS AGO!
IT'S A WORLD OF WAR WITHOUT ALLI-ANCES!
ASKING FOR HELP WAS A MISTAKE!
HE'LL USE ANY DIRTY TRICK TO DEFEAT HIS RIVALS!

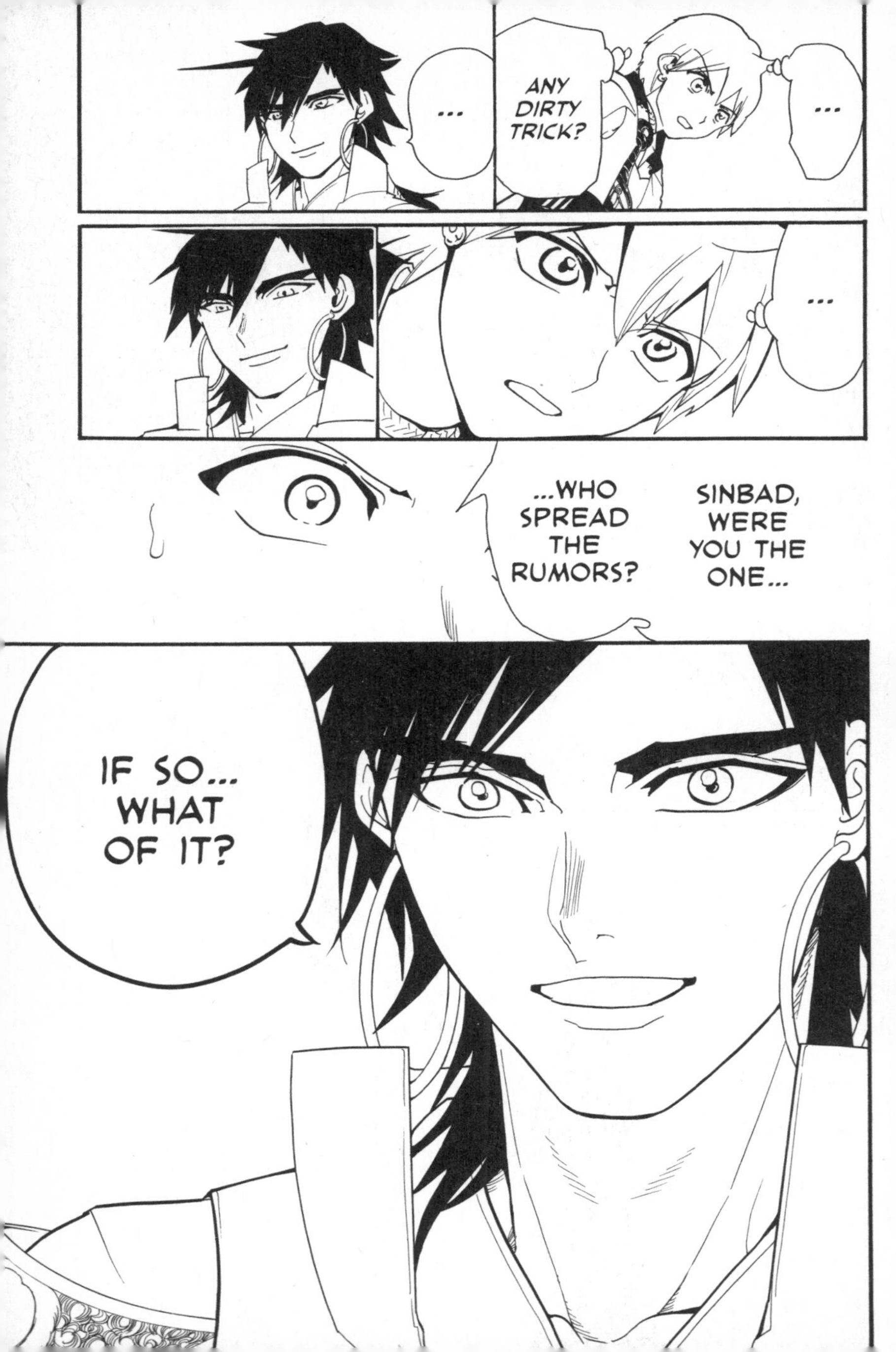
...
ANY DIRTY TRICK?
...
...
SINBAD, WERE YOU THE ONE...
...WHO SPREAD THE RUMORS?
IF SO... WHAT OF IT?

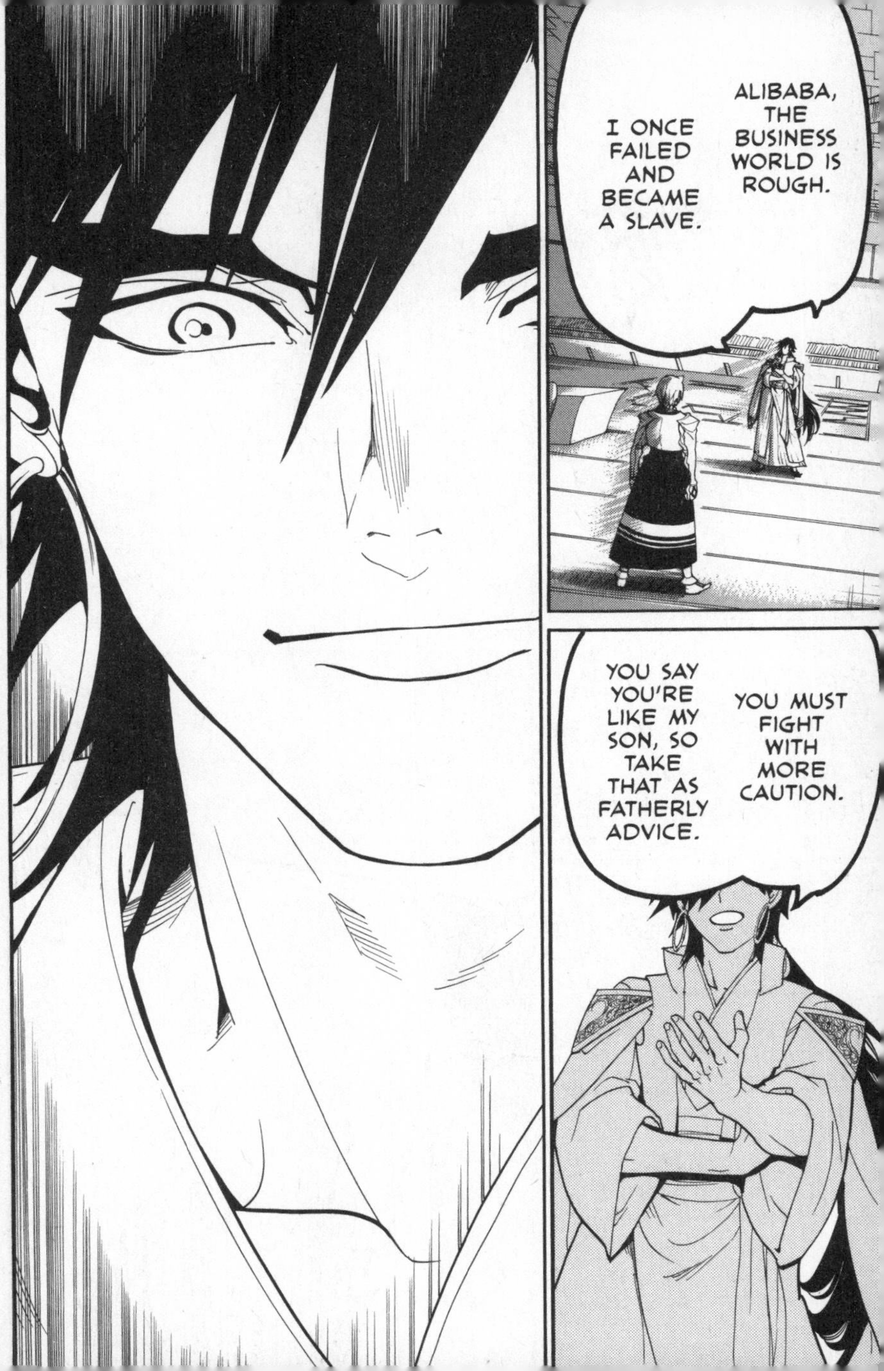
ALIBABA, THE BUSINESS WORLD IS ROUGH.
I ONCE FAILED AND BECAME A SLAVE.
YOU MUST FIGHT WITH MORE CAUTION.
YOU SAY YOU'RE LIKE MY SON, SO TAKE THAT AS FATHERLY ADVICE.

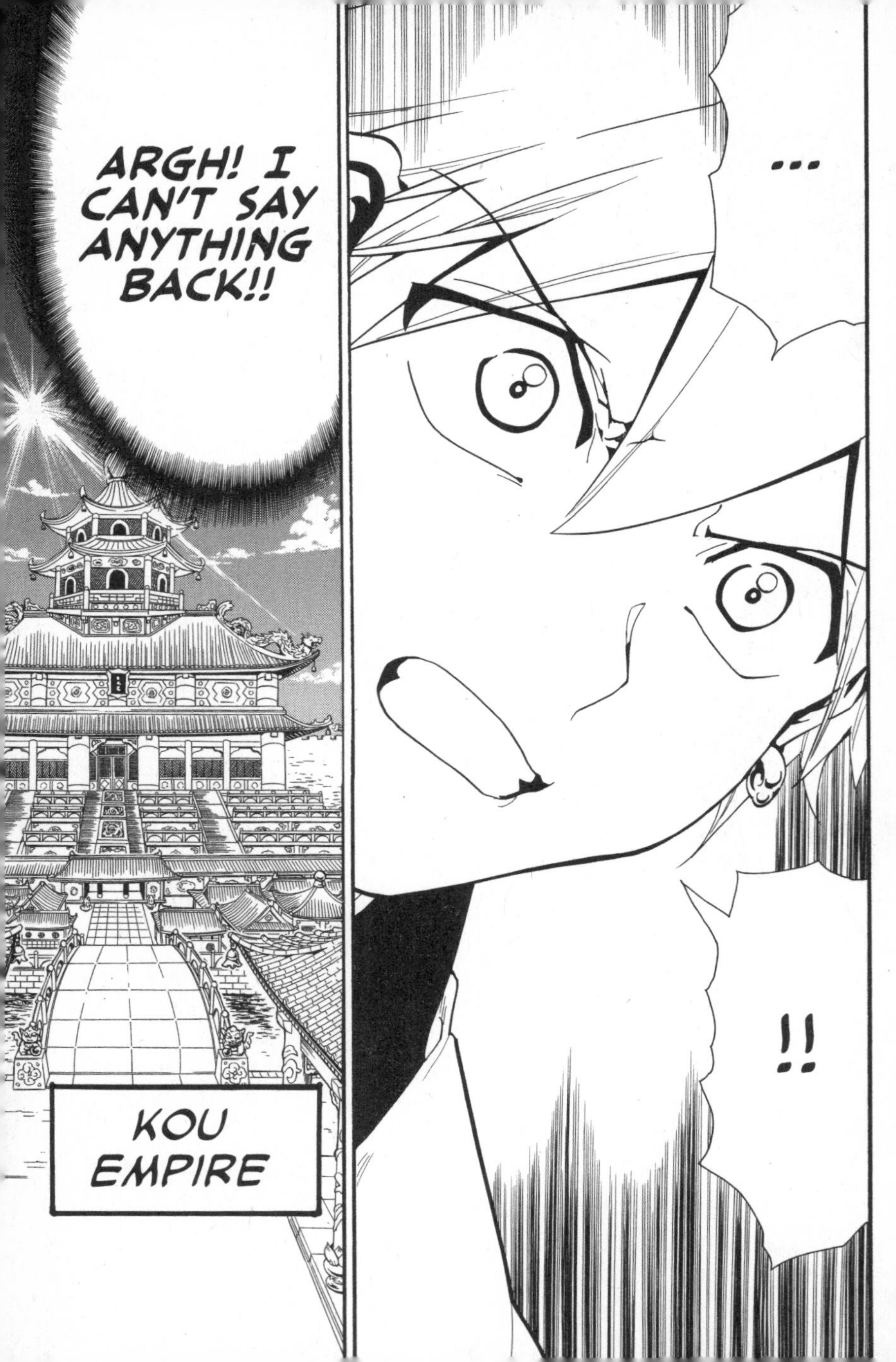
...
!!
ARGH! I CAN'T SAY ANYTHING BACK!!
KOU EMPIRE

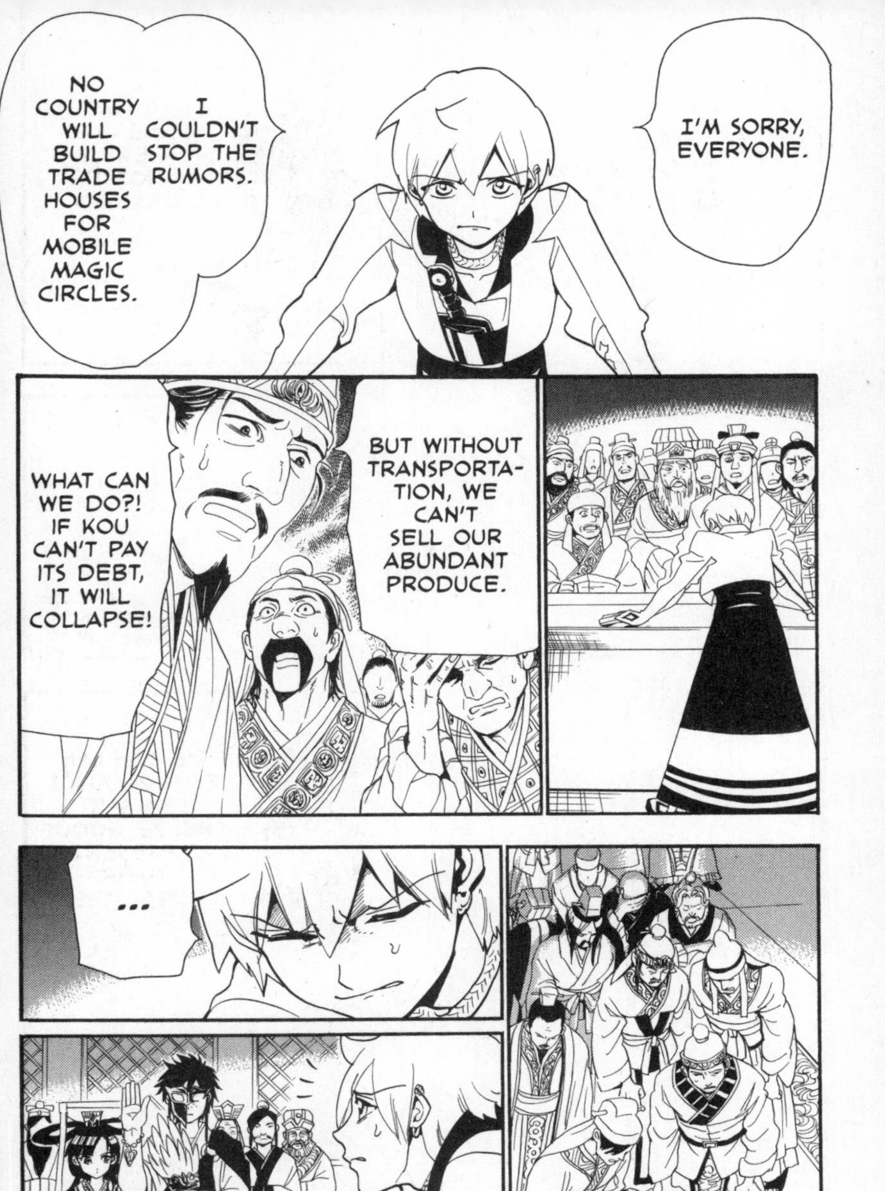
I'M SORRY, EVERYONE.
I COULDN'T STOP THE RUMORS.
NO COUNTRY WILL BUILD TRADE HOUSES FOR MOBILE MAGIC CIRCLES.
BUT WITHOUT TRANSPORTATION, WE CAN'T SELL OUR ABUNDANT PRODUCE.
WHAT CAN WE DO?! IF KOU CAN'T PAY ITS DEBT, IT WILL COLLAPSE!
...

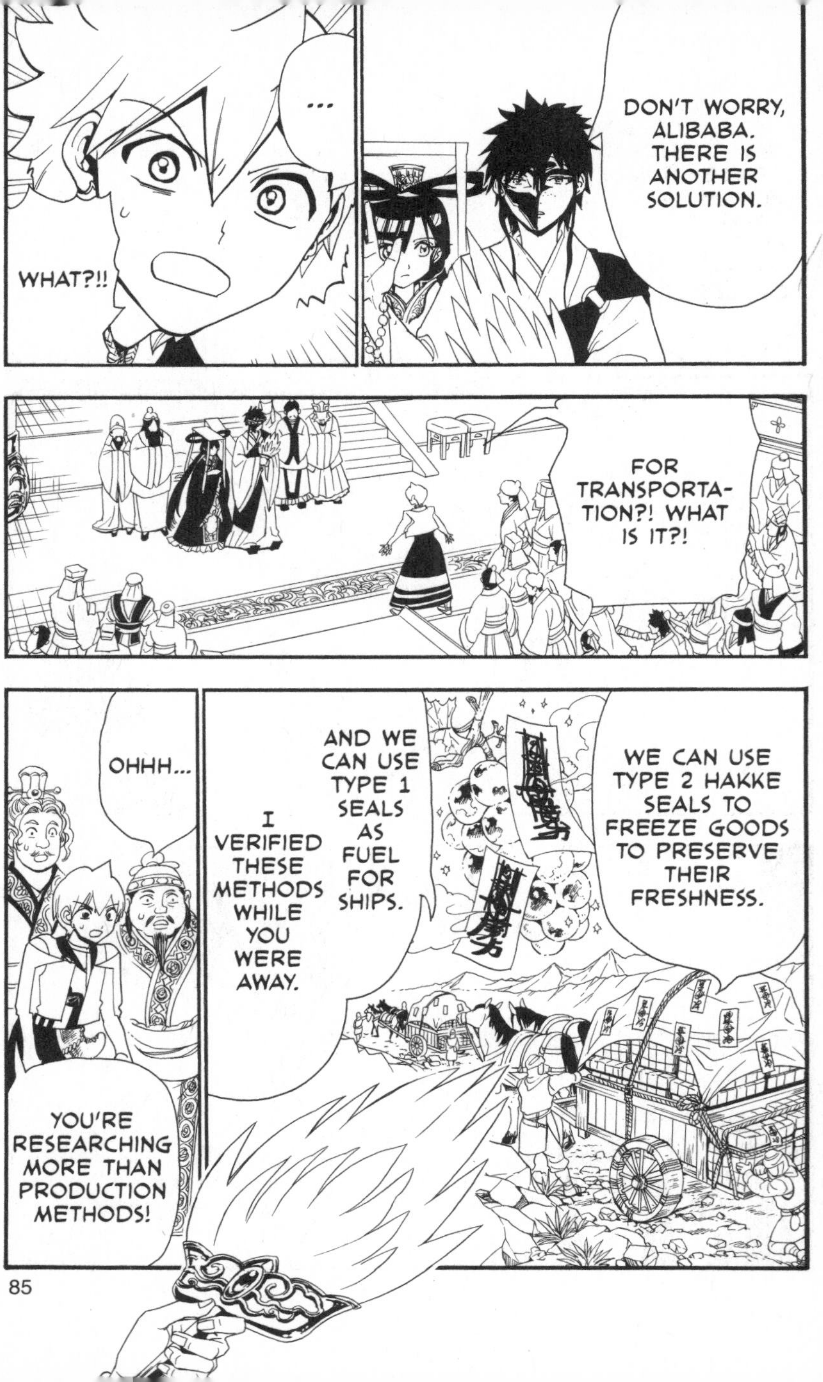
DON'T WORRY, ALIBABA. THERE IS ANOTHER SOLUTION.
...
WHAT?!!
FOR TRANSPORTATION?! WHAT IS IT?!
WE CAN USE TYPE 2 HAKKE SEALS TO FREEZE GOODS TO PRESERVE THEIR FRESHNESS.
AND WE CAN USE TYPE 1 SEALS AS FUEL FOR SHIPS.
I VERIFIED THESE METHODS WHILE YOU WERE AWAY.
OHHH...
YOU'RE RESEARCHING MORE THAN PRODUCTION METHODS!

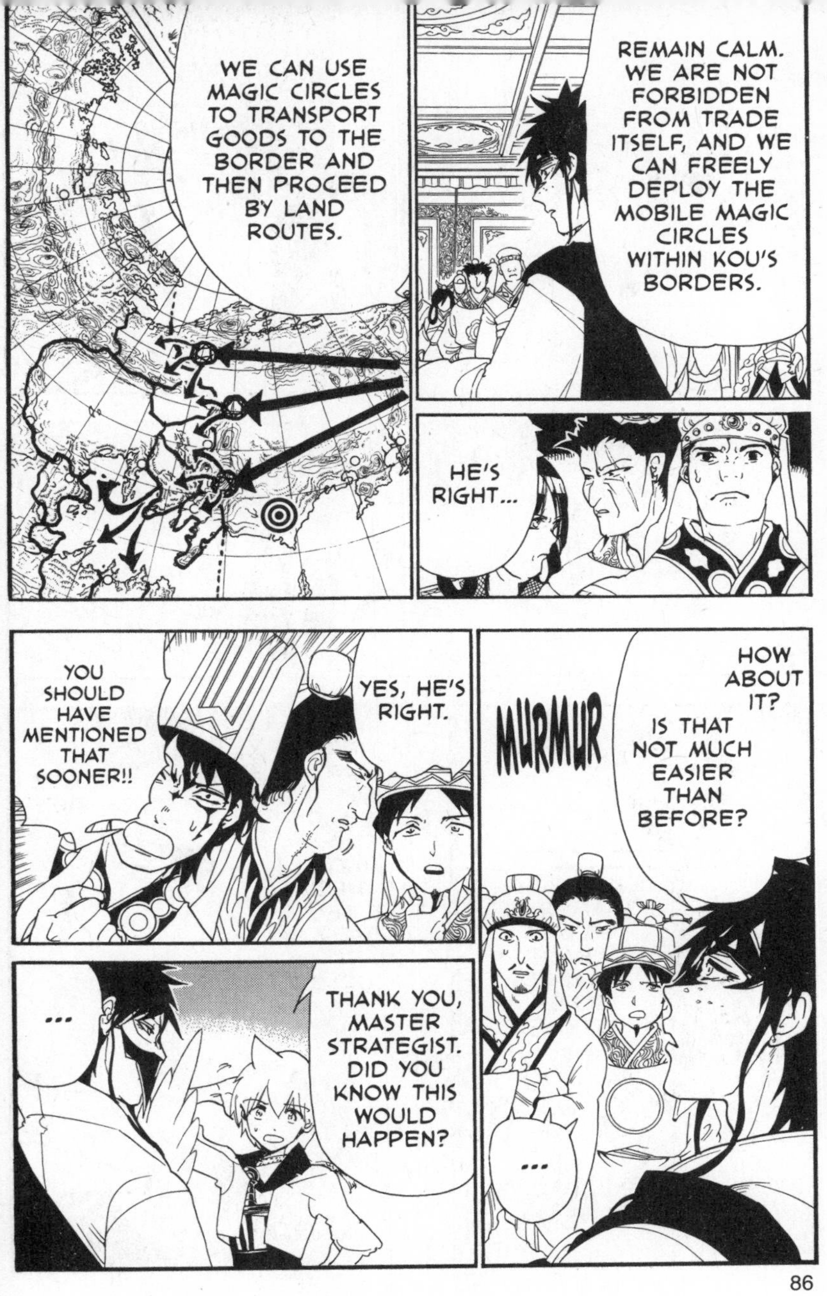
REMAIN CALM. WE ARE NOT FORBIDDEN FROM TRADE ITSELF, AND WE CAN FREELY DEPLOY THE MOBILE MAGIC CIRCLES WITHIN KOU'S BORDERS.
HE'S RIGHT...
WE CAN USE MAGIC CIRCLES TO TRANSPORT GOODS TO THE BORDER AND THEN PROCEED BY LAND ROUTES.
HOW ABOUT IT?
IS THAT NOT MUCH EASIER THAN BEFORE?
MURMUR
YES, HE'S RIGHT.
YOU SHOULD HAVE MENTIONED THAT SOONER!!
...
THANK YOU, MASTER STRATEGIST. DID YOU KNOW THIS WOULD HAPPEN?
...

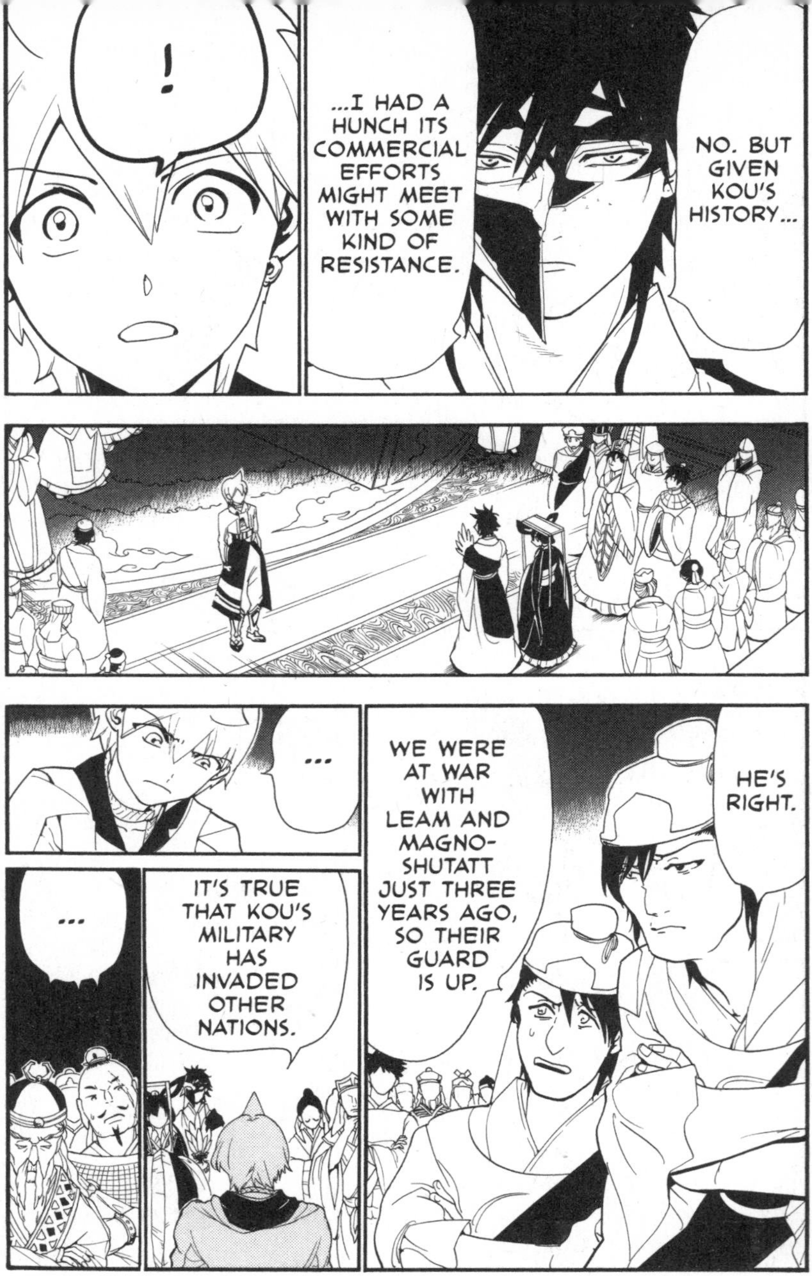
NO. BUT GIVEN KOU'S HISTORY...
...I HAD A HUNCH ITS COMMERCIAL EFFORTS MIGHT MEET WITH SOME KIND OF RESISTANCE.
!
HE'S RIGHT.
WE WERE AT WAR WITH LEAM AND MAGNO-SHUTATT JUST THREE YEARS AGO, SO THEIR GUARD IS UP.
...
IT'S TRUE THAT KOU'S MILITARY HAS INVADED OTHER NATIONS.
...

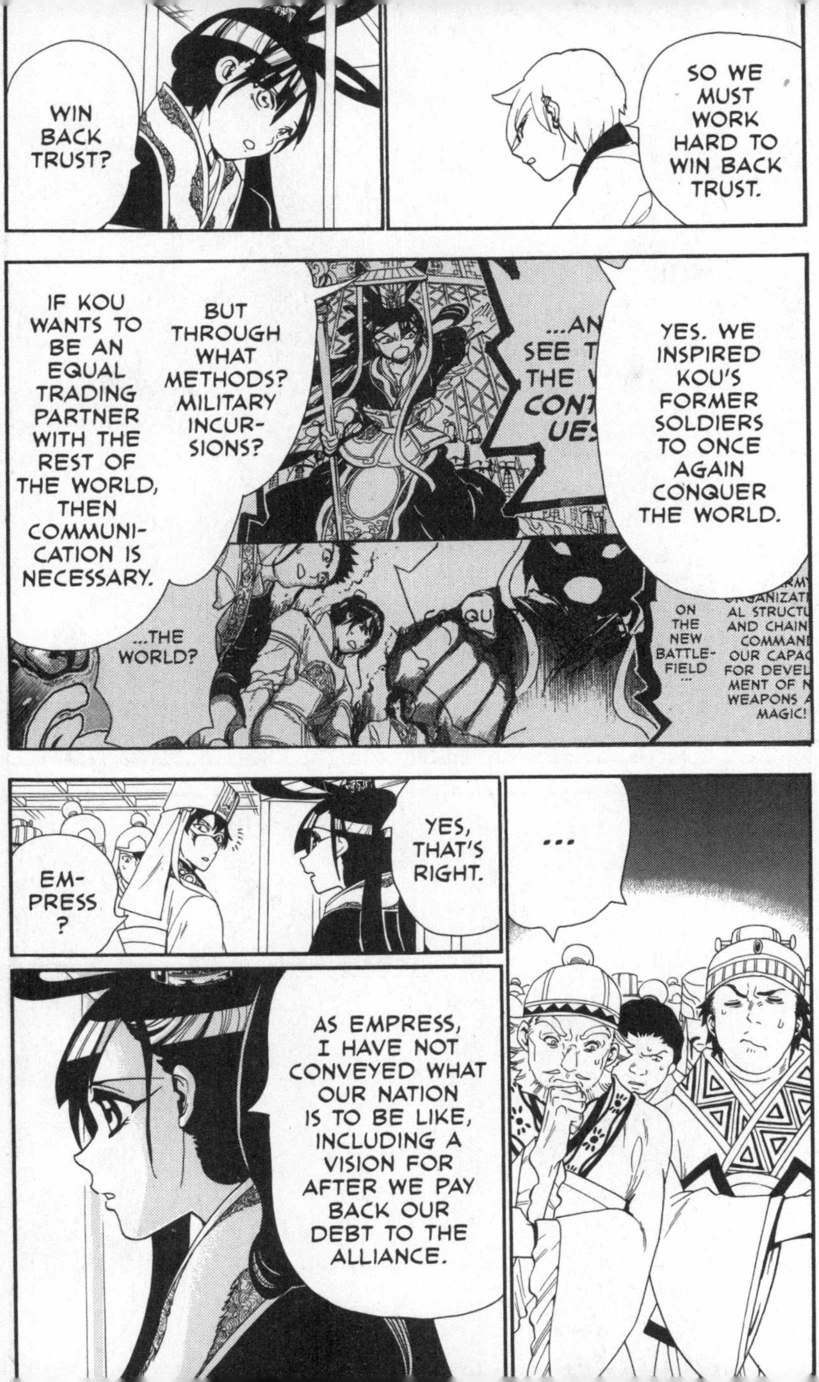
SO WE MUST WORK HARD TO WIN BACK TRUST.
WIN BACK TRUST?
YES. WE INSPIRED KOU'S FORMER SOLDIERS TO ONCE AGAIN CONQUER THE WORLD.
ON THE NEW BATTLE-FIELD ...
BUT THROUGH WHAT METHODS? MILITARY INCURSIONS?
...THE WORLD?
IF KOU WANTS TO BE AN EQUAL TRADING PARTNER WITH THE REST OF THE WORLD, THEN COMMUNICATION IS NECESSARY.
...
YES, THAT'S RIGHT.
EMPRESS?
AS EMPRESS, I HAVE NOT CONVEYED WHAT OUR NATION IS TO BE LIKE, INCLUDING A VISION FOR AFTER WE PAY BACK OUR DEBT TO THE ALLIANCE.

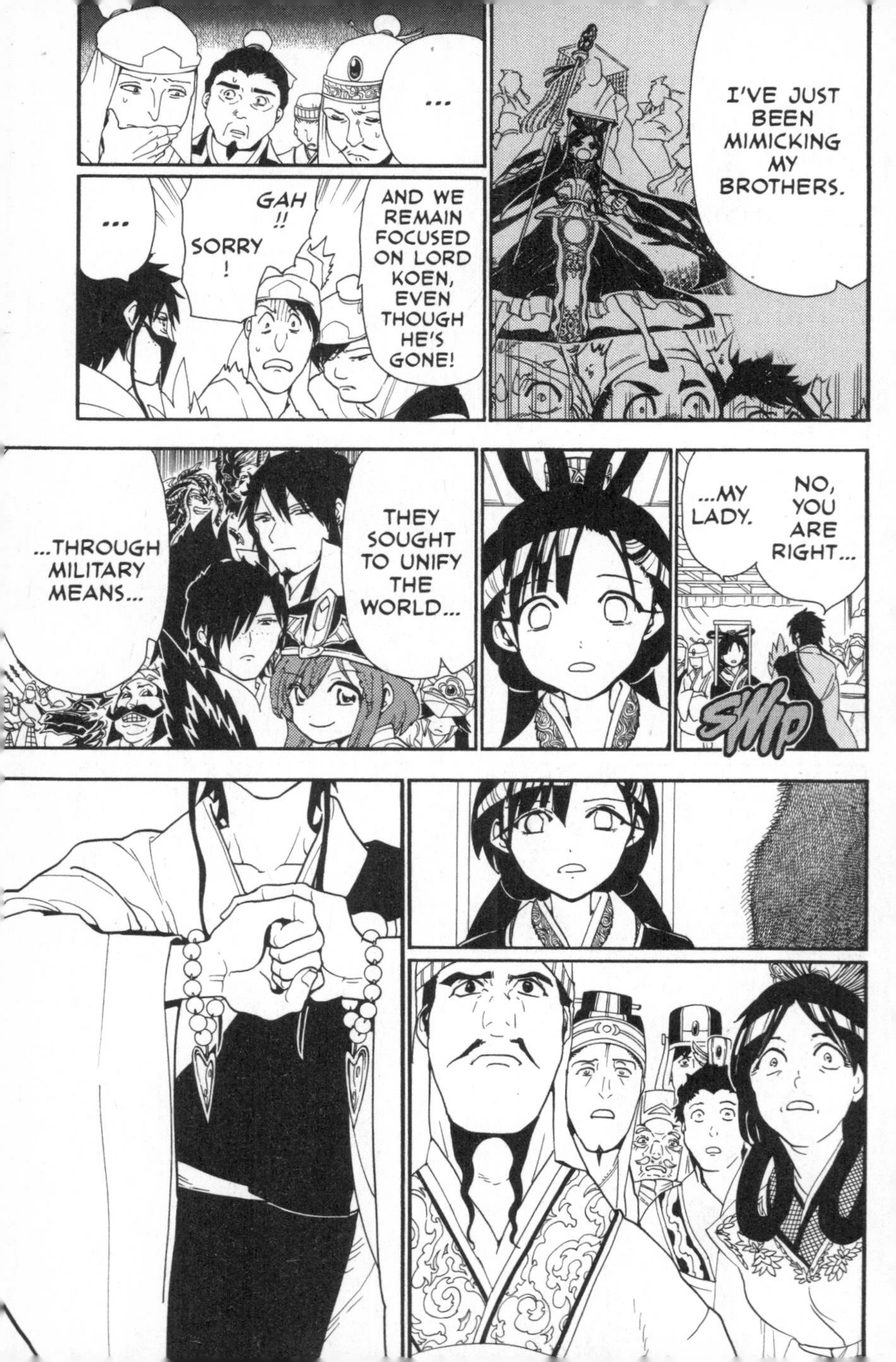
I'VE JUST BEEN MIMICKING MY BROTHERS.
...
AND WE REMAIN FOCUSED ON LORD KOEN, EVEN THOUGH HE'S GONE!
GAH !!
SORRY !
...
NO, YOU ARE RIGHT...
...MY LADY.
SNIP
THEY SOUGHT TO UNIFY THE WORLD...
...THROUGH MILITARY MEANS...

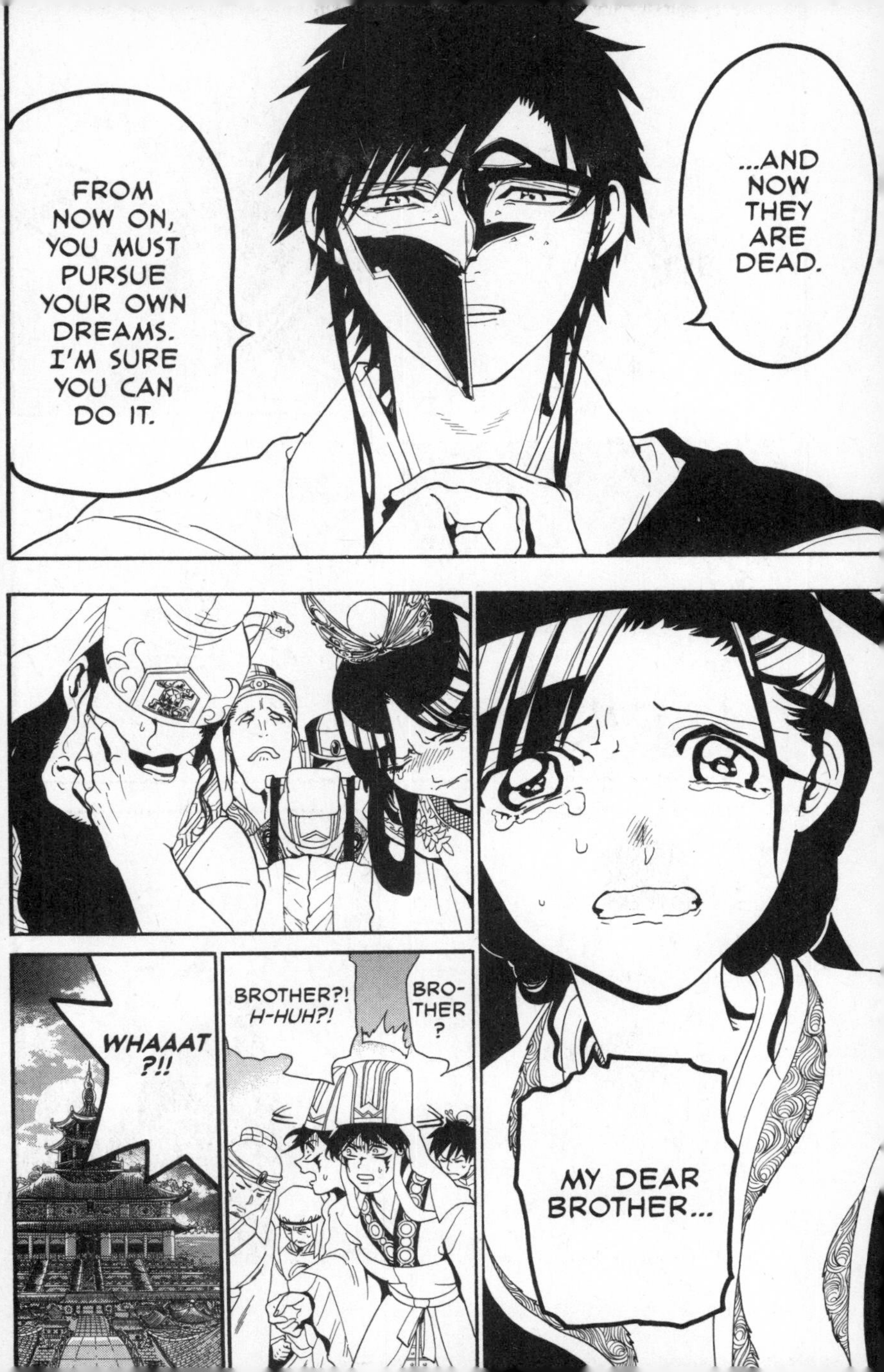
...AND NOW THEY ARE DEAD.
FROM NOW ON, YOU MUST PURSUE YOUR OWN DREAMS. I'M SURE YOU CAN DO IT.
MY DEAR BROTHER...
BRO-THER?
BROTHER?! H-HUH?!
WHAAAT?!!

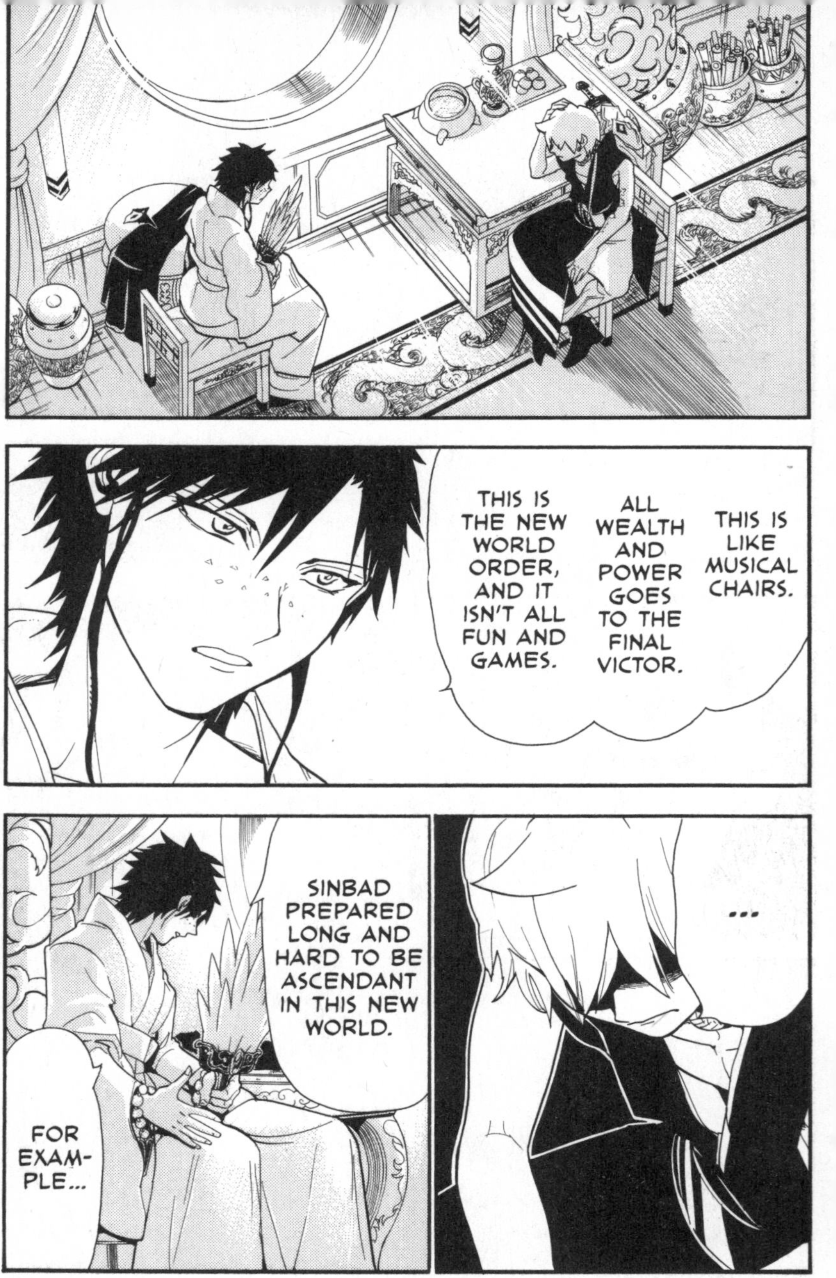
THIS IS LIKE MUSICAL CHAIRS.
ALL WEALTH AND POWER GOES TO THE FINAL VICTOR.
THIS IS THE NEW WORLD ORDER, AND IT ISN'T ALL FUN AND GAMES.
...
SINBAD PREPARED LONG AND HARD TO BE ASCENDANT IN THIS NEW WORLD.
FOR EXAM-PLE...

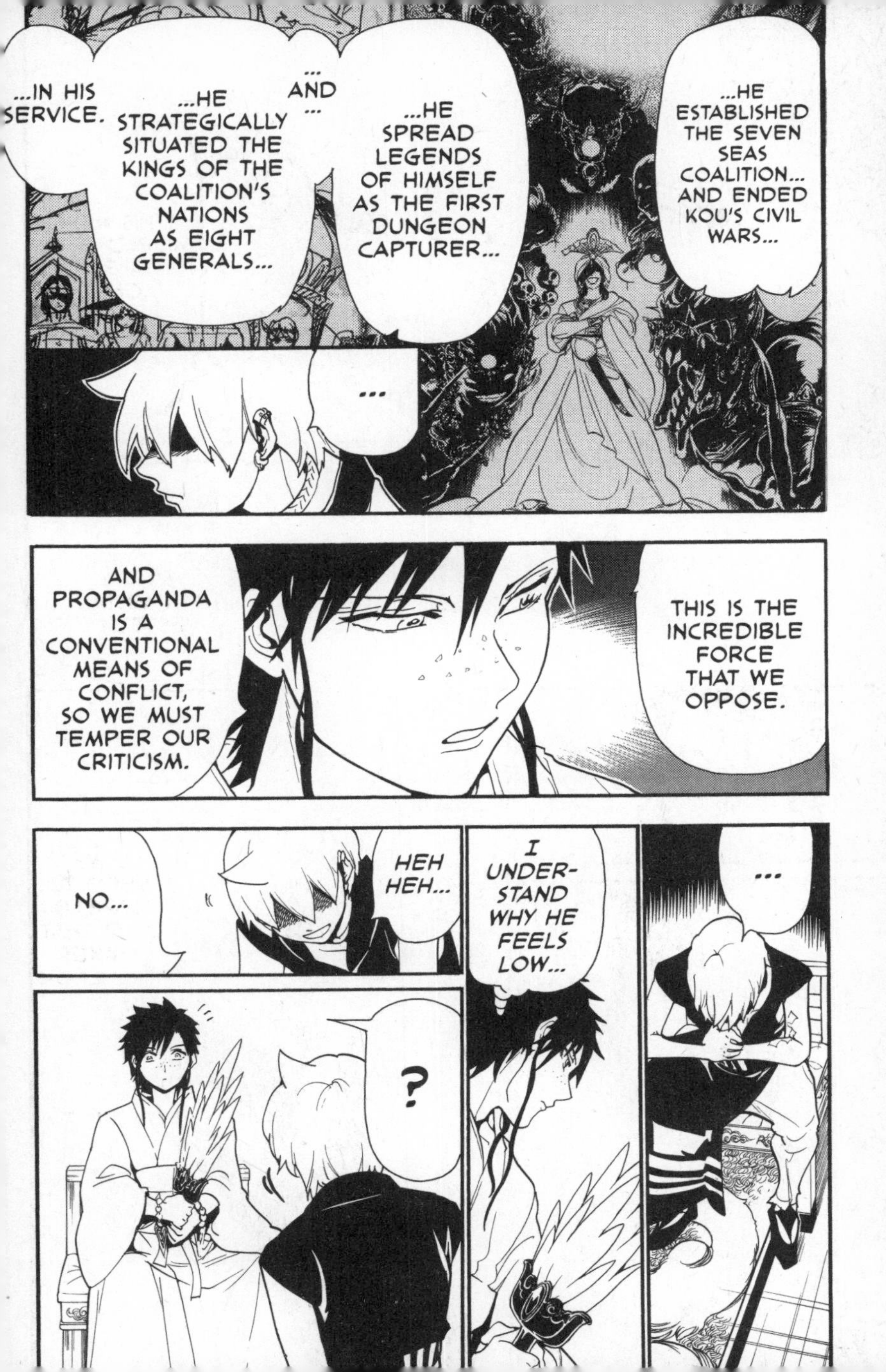
...HE ESTABLISHED THE SEVEN SEAS COALITION... AND ENDED KOU'S CIVIL WARS...
...HE SPREAD LEGENDS OF HIMSELF AS THE FIRST DUNGEON CAPTURER...
...AND...
...HE STRATEGICALLY SITUATED THE KINGS OF THE COALITION'S NATIONS AS EIGHT GENERALS...
...IN HIS SERVICE.
...
THIS IS THE INCREDIBLE FORCE THAT WE OPPOSE.
AND PROPAGANDA IS A CONVENTIONAL MEANS OF CONFLICT, SO WE MUST TEMPER OUR CRITICISM.
...
I UNDER-STAND WHY HE FEELS LOW...
HEH HEH...
NO...
?

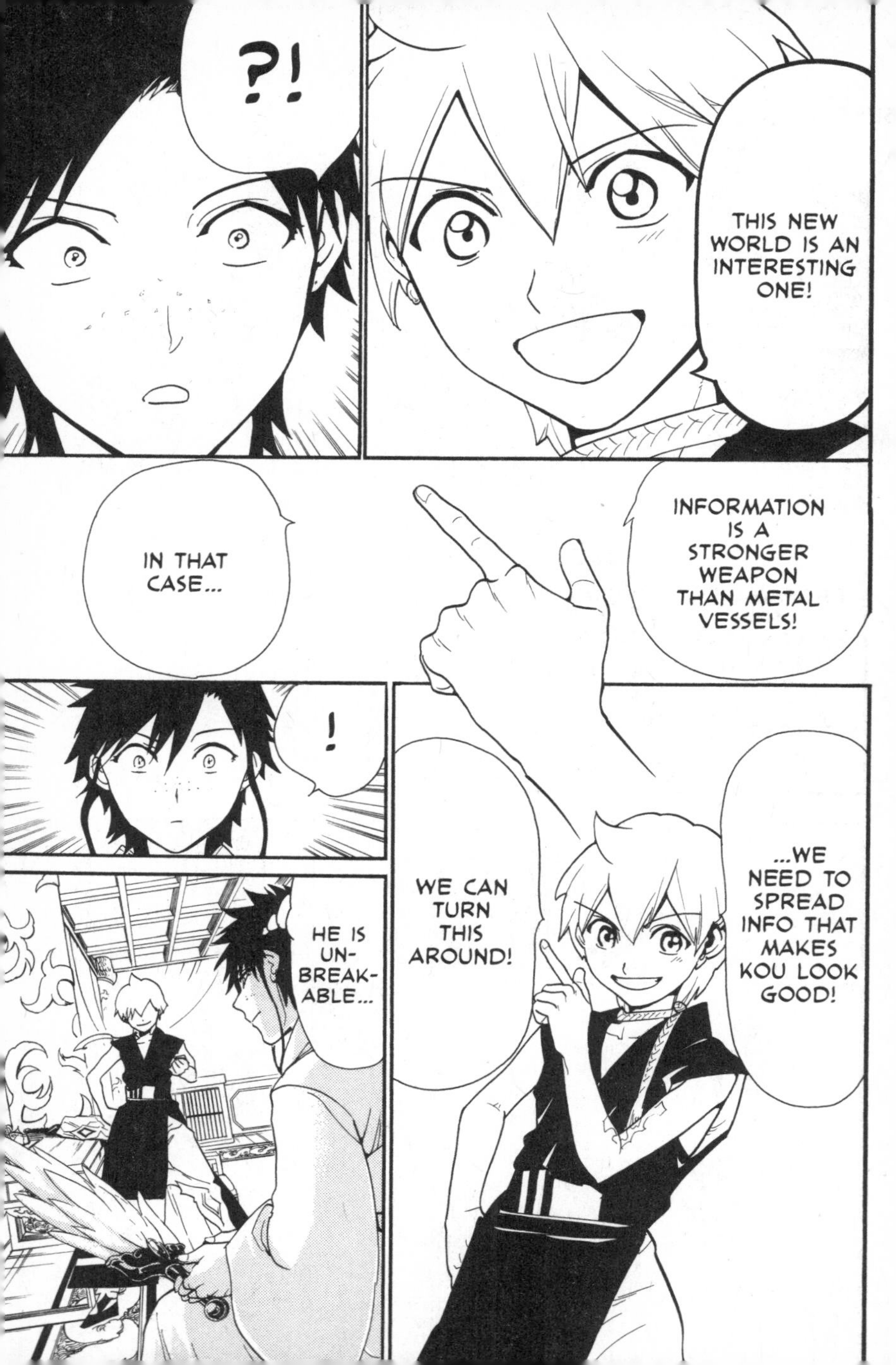
THIS NEW WORLD IS AN INTERESTING ONE!
?!
INFORMATION IS A STRONGER WEAPON THAN METAL VESSELS!
IN THAT CASE...
...WE NEED TO SPREAD INFO THAT MAKES KOU LOOK GOOD!
WE CAN TURN THIS AROUND!
!
HE IS UN-BREAK-ABLE...

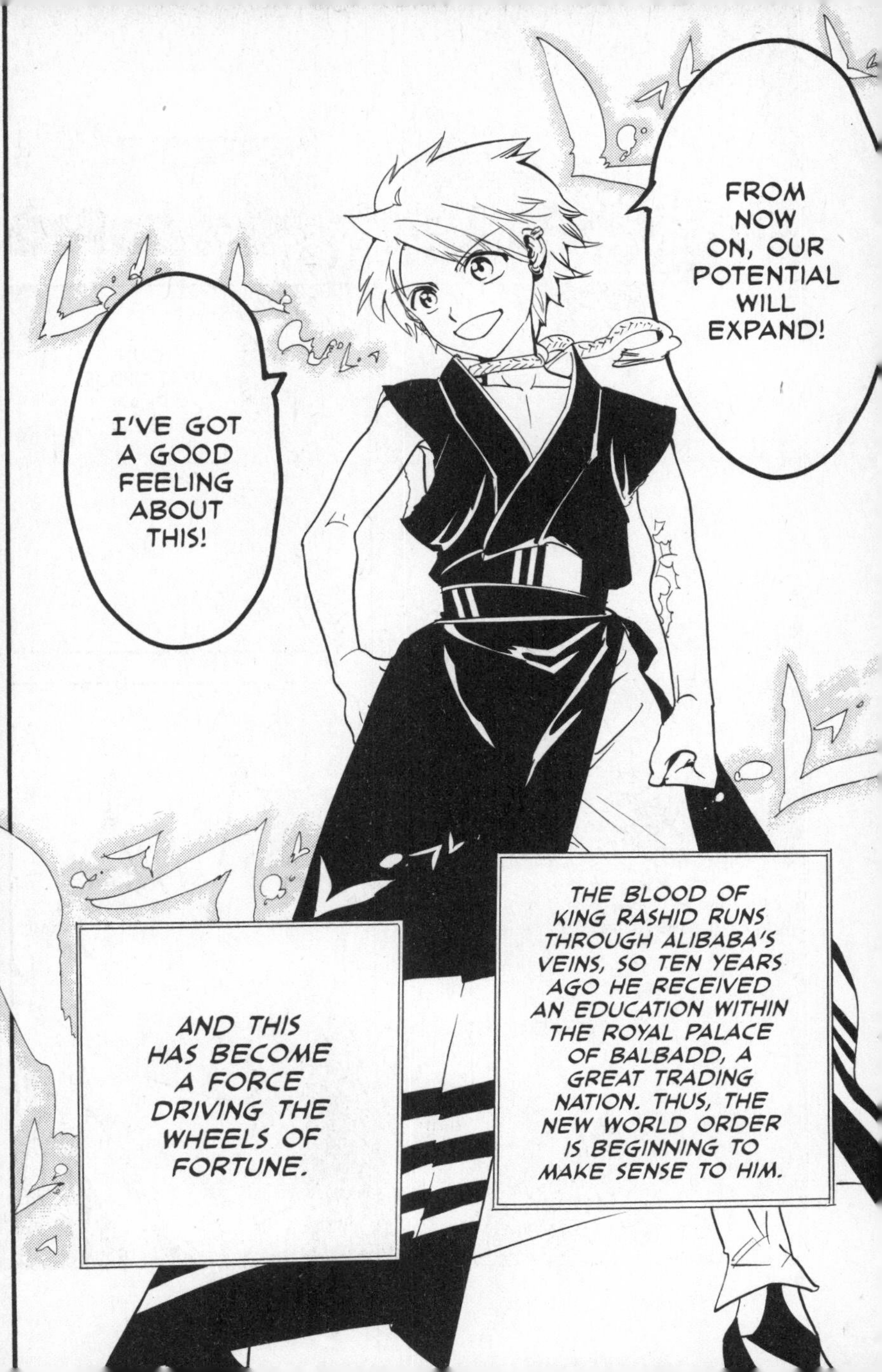
FROM NOW ON, OUR POTENTIAL WILL EXPAND!
I'VE GOT A GOOD FEELING ABOUT THIS!
THE BLOOD OF KING RASHID RUNS THROUGH ALIBABA'S VEINS, SO TEN YEARS AGO HE RECEIVED AN EDUCATION WITHIN THE ROYAL PALACE OF BALBADD, A GREAT TRADING NATION. THUS, THE NEW WORLD ORDER IS BEGINNING TO MAKE SENSE TO HIM.
AND THIS HAS BECOME A FORCE DRIVING THE WHEELS OF FORTUNE.

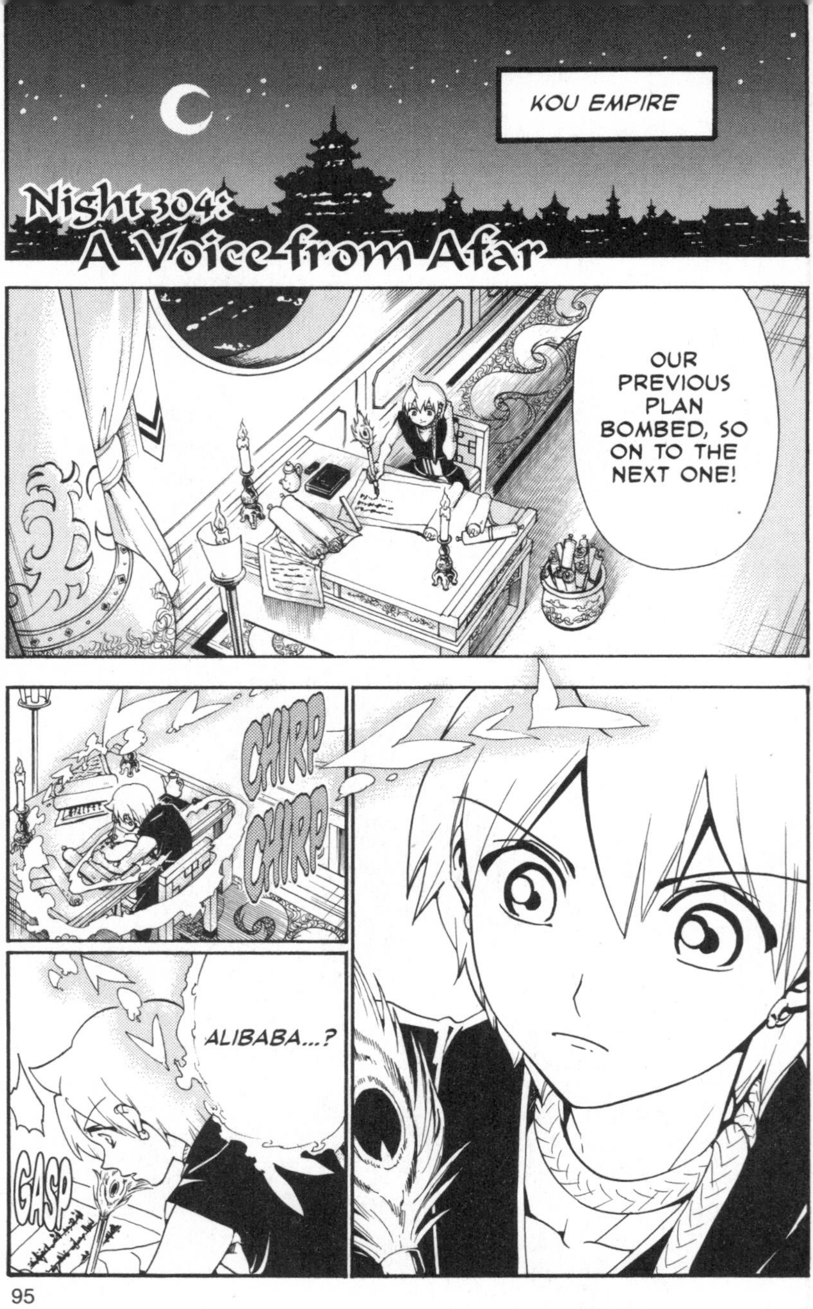
KOU EMPIRE
Night 304: A Voice from Afar
OUR PREVIOUS PLAN BOMBED, SO ON TO THE NEXT ONE!
CHIRP CHIRP
ALIBABA...?
GASP

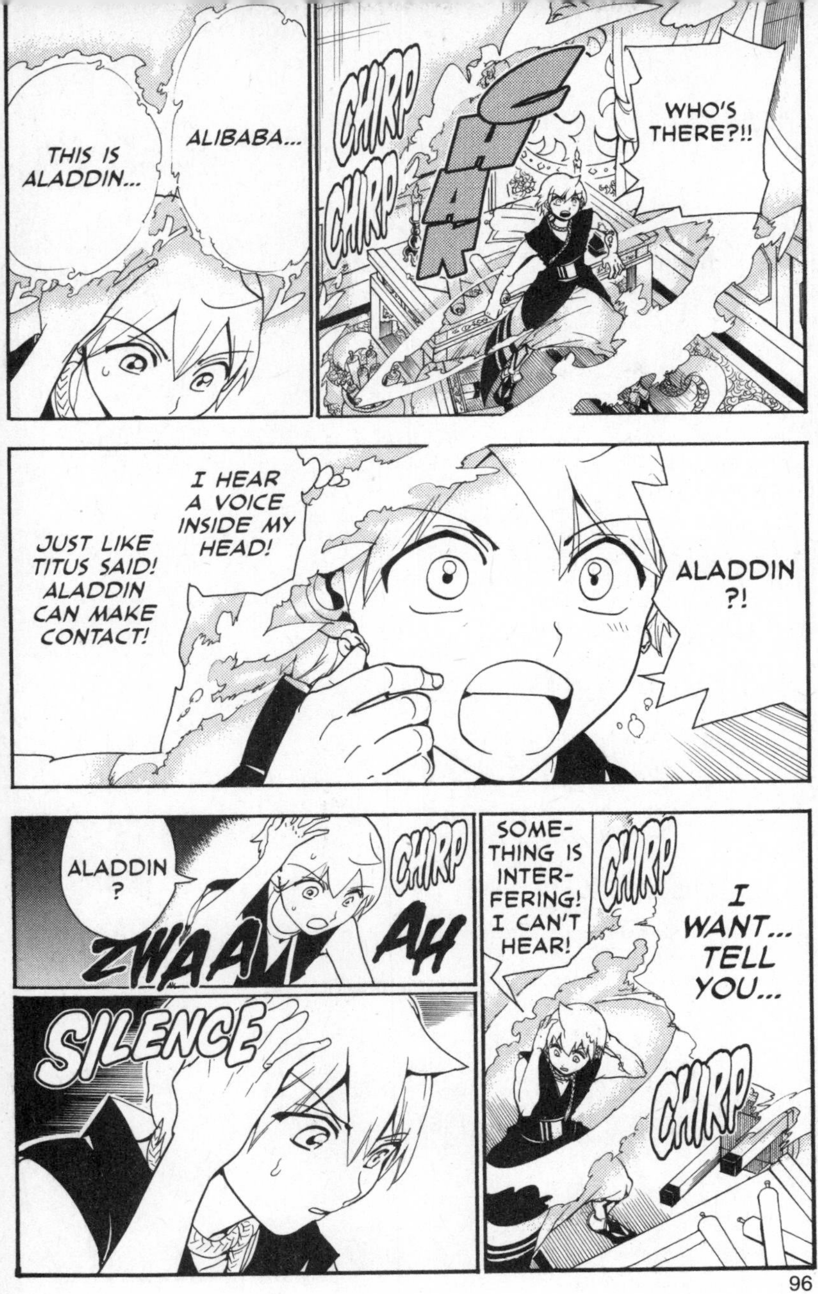
WHO'S THERE?!!
CHIRP CHIRP
CHAK
ALIBABA...
THIS IS ALADDIN...
ALADDIN ?!
I HEAR A VOICE INSIDE MY HEAD!
JUST LIKE TITUS SAID! ALADDIN CAN MAKE CONTACT!
I WANT... TELL YOU...
CHIRP
SOMETHING IS INTERFERING! I CAN'T HEAR!
CHIRP
CHIRP
ALADDIN ?
ZWAAAH
SILENCE

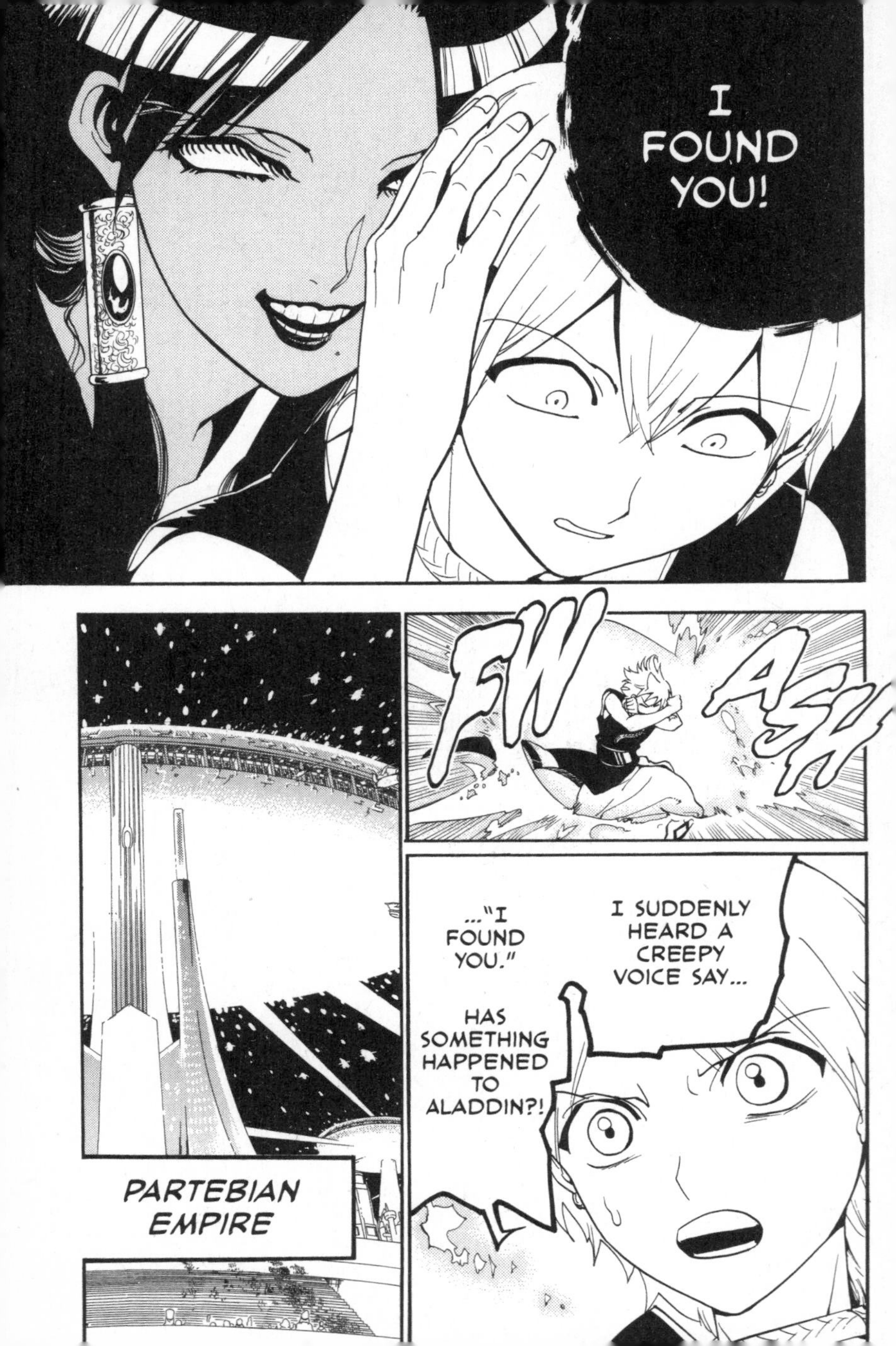
I FOUND YOU!
FWASH
I SUDDENLY HEARD A CREEPY VOICE SAY...
..."I FOUND YOU."
HAS SOMETHING HAPPENED TO ALADDIN?!
PARTEBIAN EMPIRE

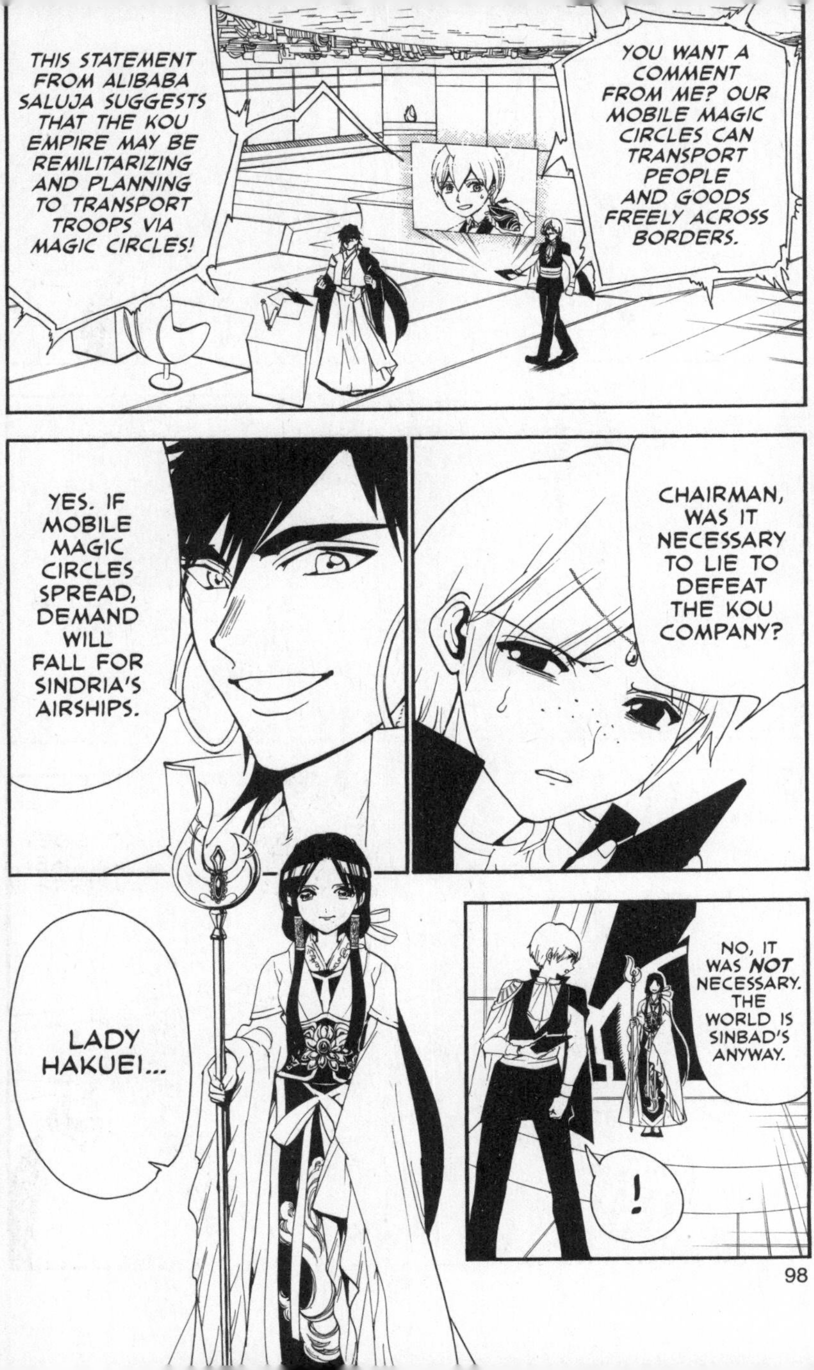
YOU WANT A COMMENT FROM ME? OUR MOBILE MAGIC CIRCLES CAN TRANSPORT PEOPLE AND GOODS FREELY ACROSS BORDERS.
THIS STATEMENT FROM ALIBABA SALUJA SUGGESTS THAT THE KOU EMPIRE MAY BE REMILITARIZING AND PLANNING TO TRANSPORT TROOPS VIA MAGIC CIRCLES!
CHAIRMAN, WAS IT NECESSARY TO LIE TO DEFEAT THE KOU COMPANY?
YES. IF MOBILE MAGIC CIRCLES SPREAD, DEMAND WILL FALL FOR SINDRIA'S AIRSHIPS.
NO, IT WAS ***NOT*** NECESSARY. THE WORLD IS SINBAD'S ANYWAY.
!
LADY HAKUEI...

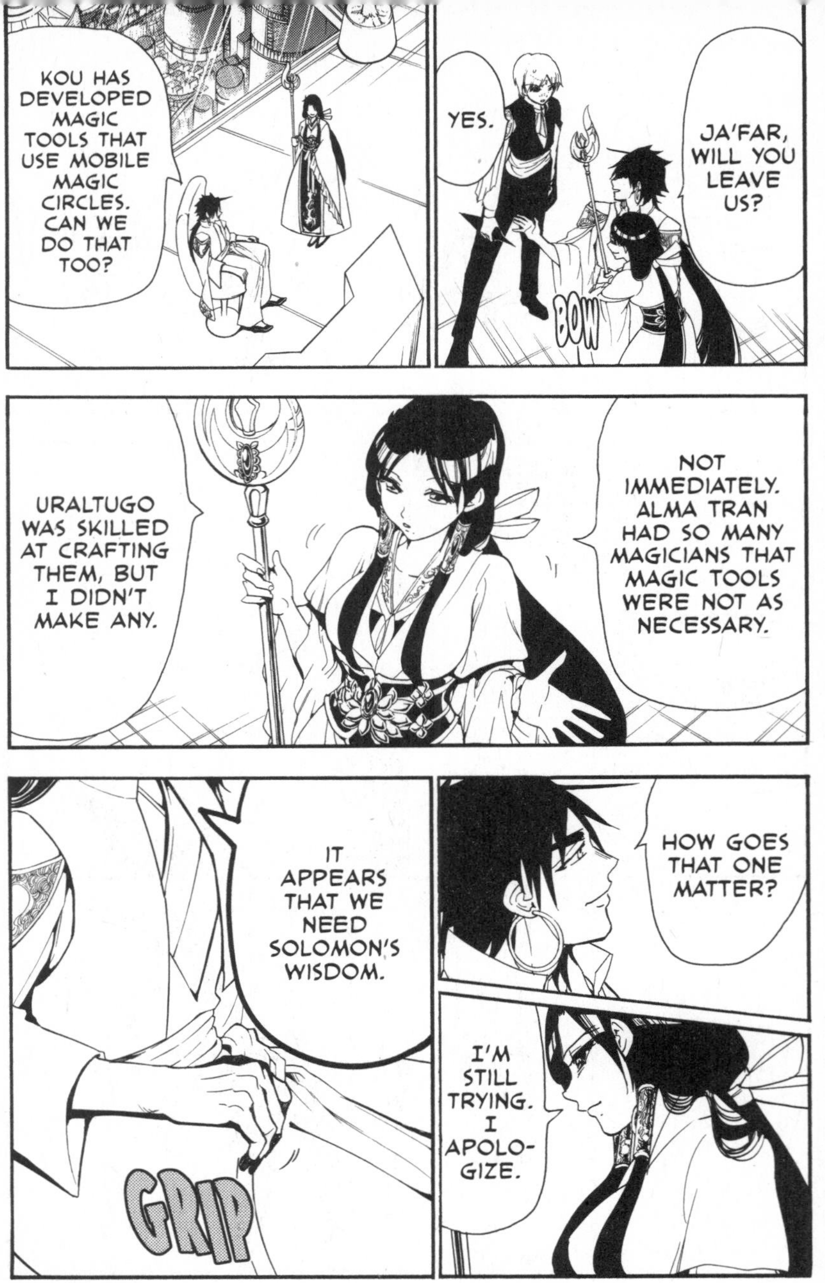
JA'FAR, WILL YOU LEAVE US?
YES.
BOW
KOU HAS DEVELOPED MAGIC TOOLS THAT USE MOBILE MAGIC CIRCLES. CAN WE DO THAT TOO?
NOT IMMEDIATELY. ALMA TRAN HAD SO MANY MAGICIANS THAT MAGIC TOOLS WERE NOT AS NECESSARY.
URALTUGO WAS SKILLED AT CRAFTING THEM, BUT I DIDN'T MAKE ANY.
HOW GOES THAT ONE MATTER?
I'M STILL TRYING. I APOLOGIZE.
IT APPEARS THAT WE NEED SOLOMON'S WISDOM.
GRIP

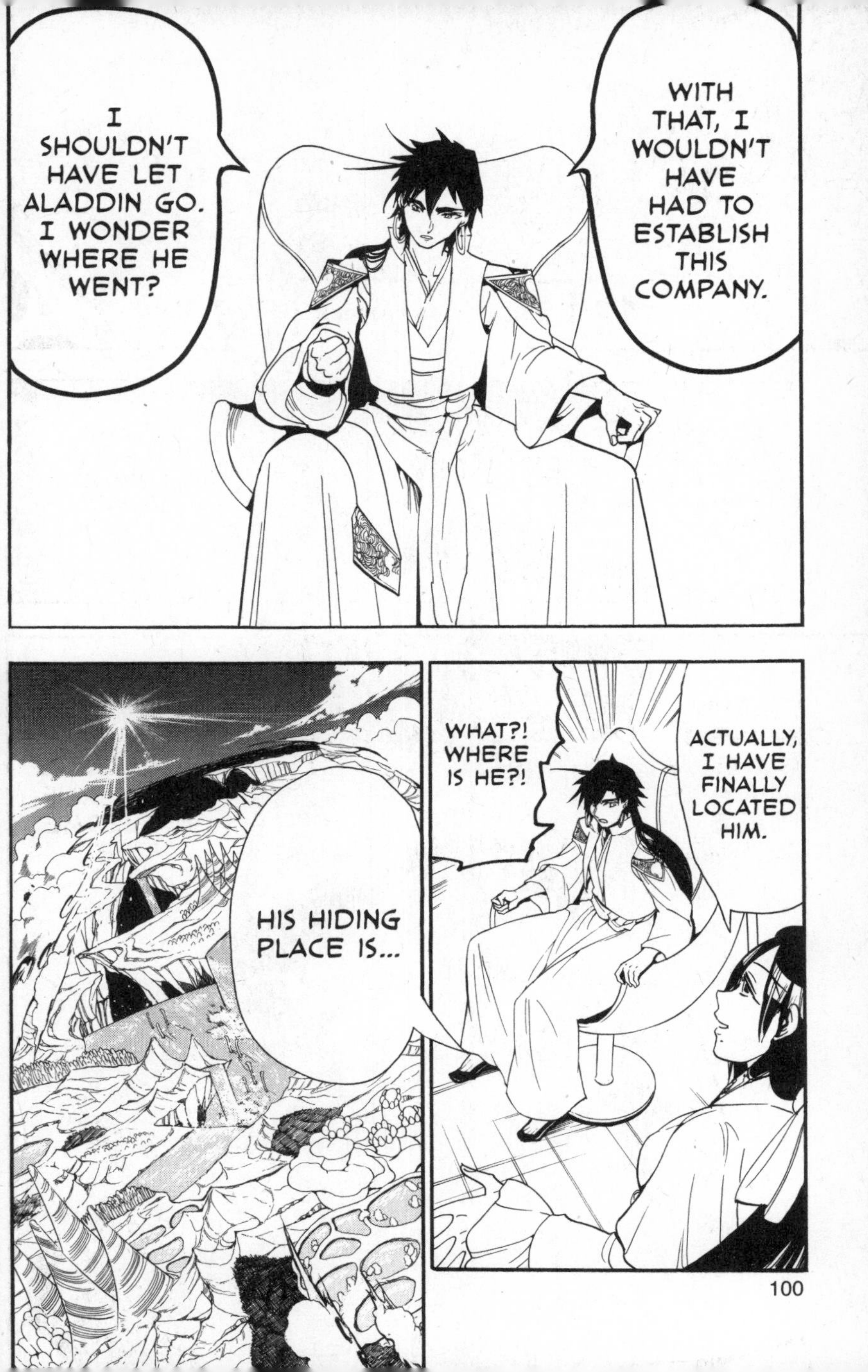
WITH THAT, I WOULDN'T HAVE HAD TO ESTABLISH THIS COMPANY.
I SHOULDN'T HAVE LET ALADDIN GO. I WONDER WHERE HE WENT?
ACTUALLY, I HAVE FINALLY LOCATED HIM.
WHAT?! WHERE IS HE?!
HIS HIDING PLACE IS...

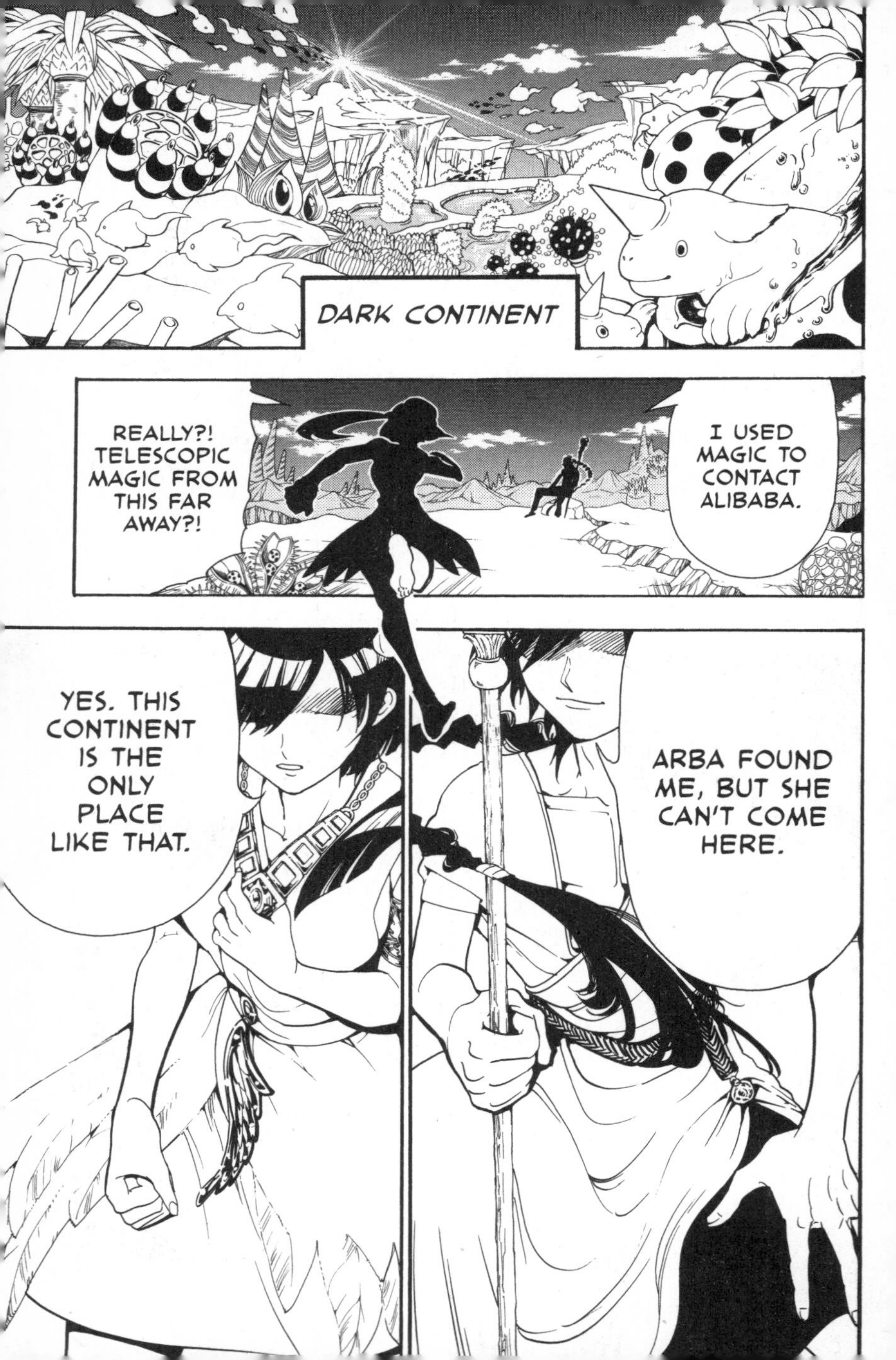
DARK CONTINENT
I USED MAGIC TO CONTACT ALIBABA.
REALLY?! TELESCOPIC MAGIC FROM THIS FAR AWAY?!
ARBA FOUND ME, BUT SHE CAN'T COME HERE.
YES. THIS CONTINENT IS THE ONLY PLACE LIKE THAT.

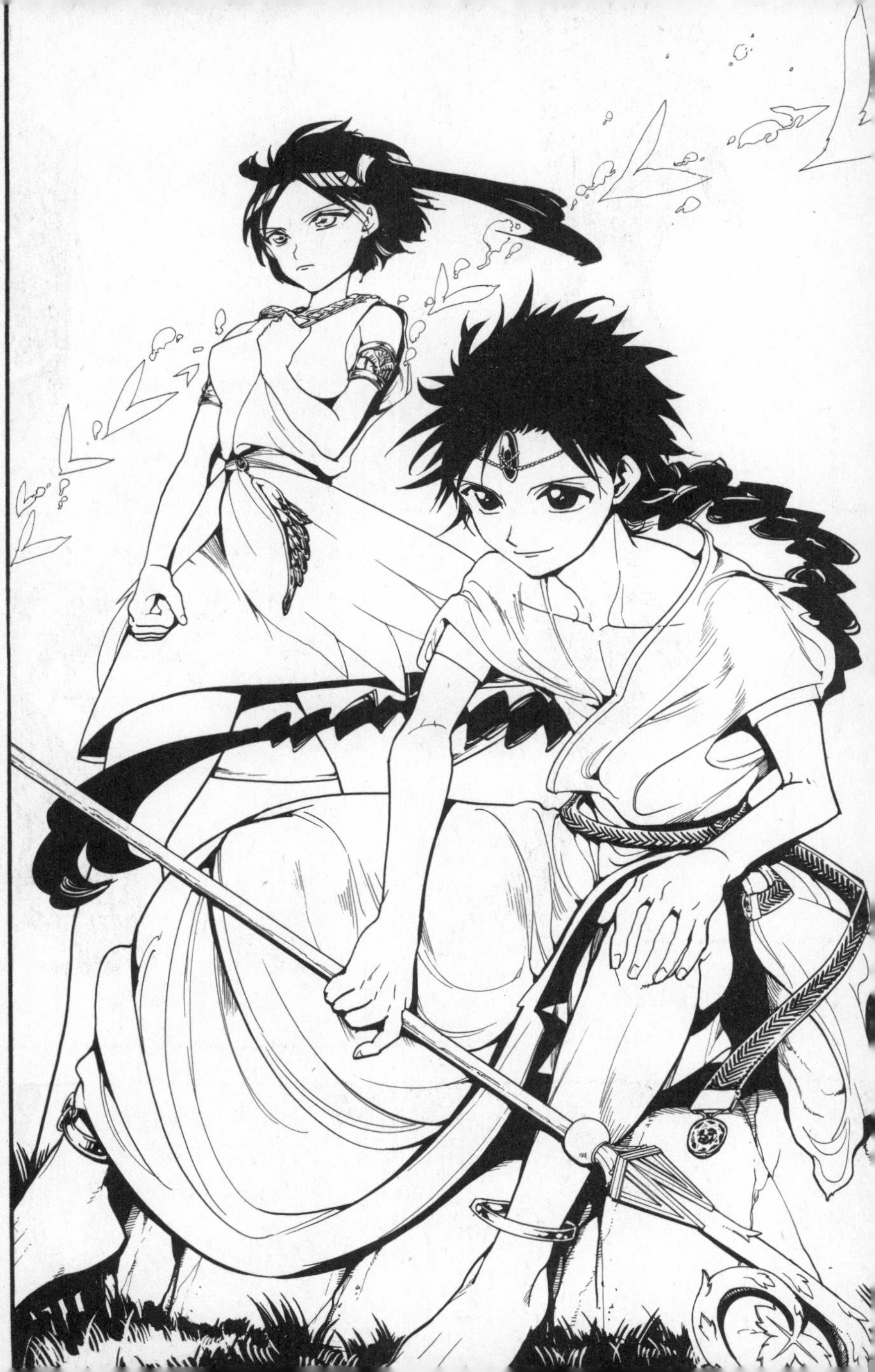

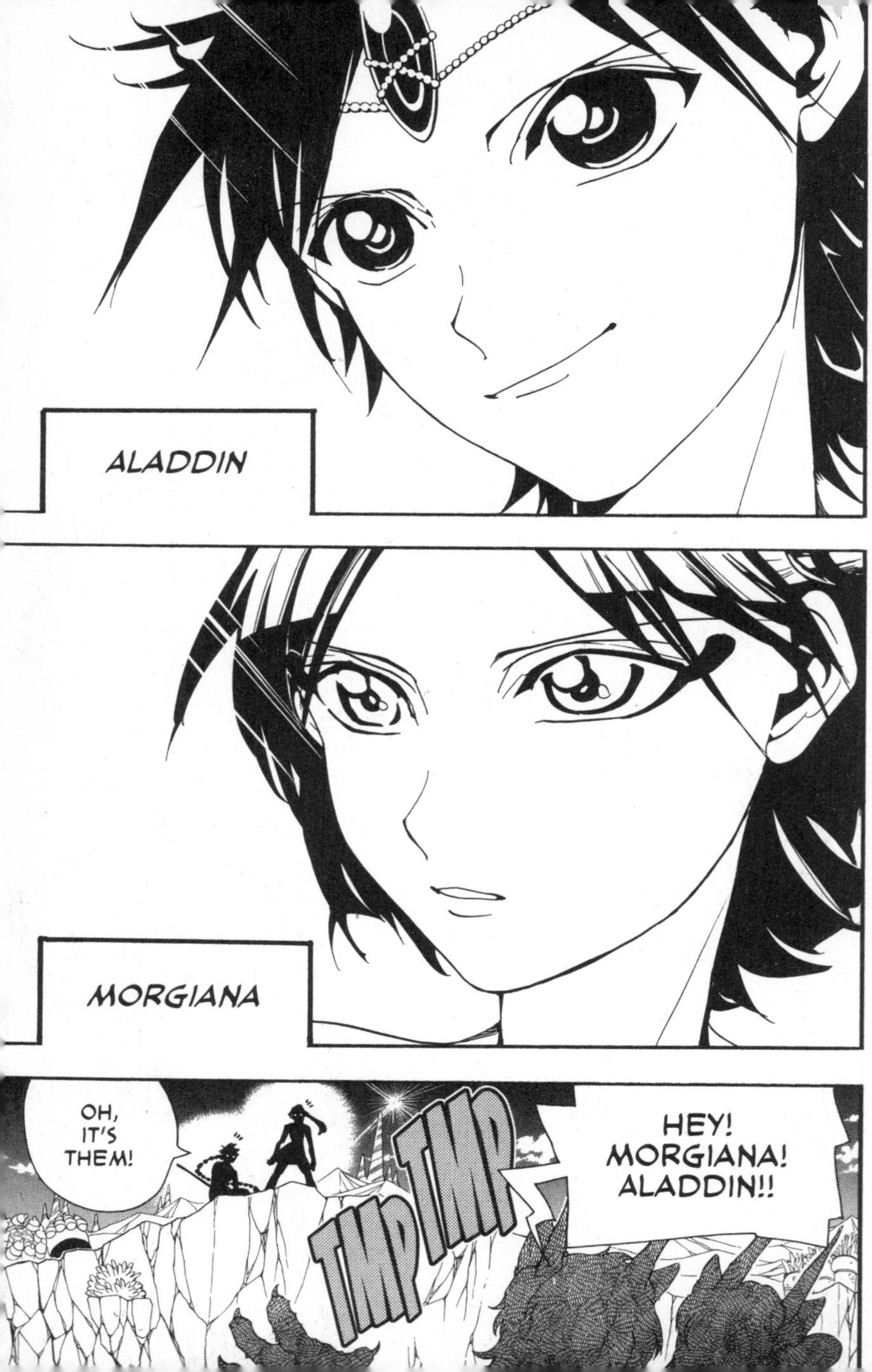
ALADDIN
MORGIANA
HEY! MORGIANA! ALADDIN!!
TMP TMP
OH, IT'S THEM!

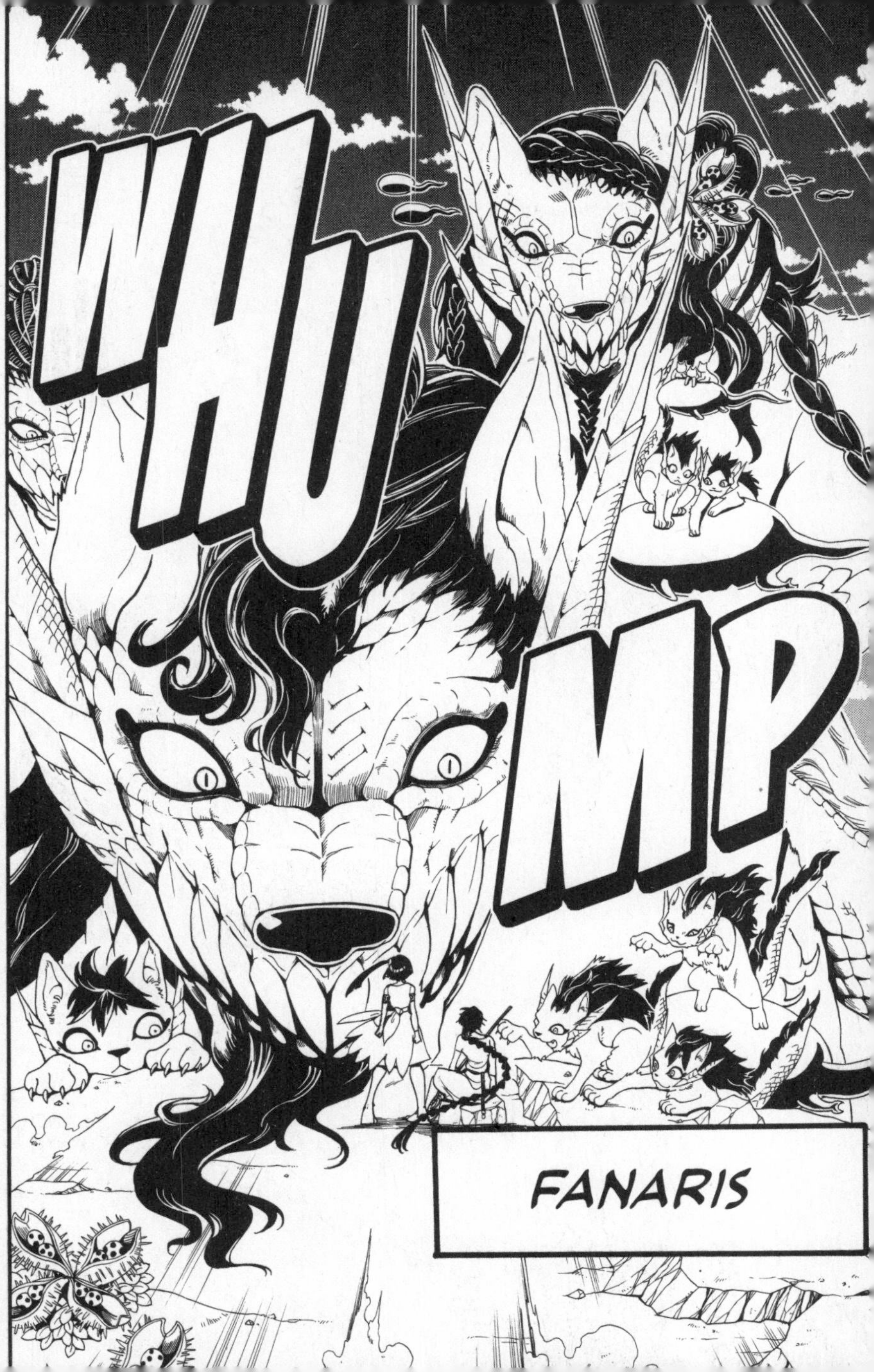
WHUMP
FANARIS

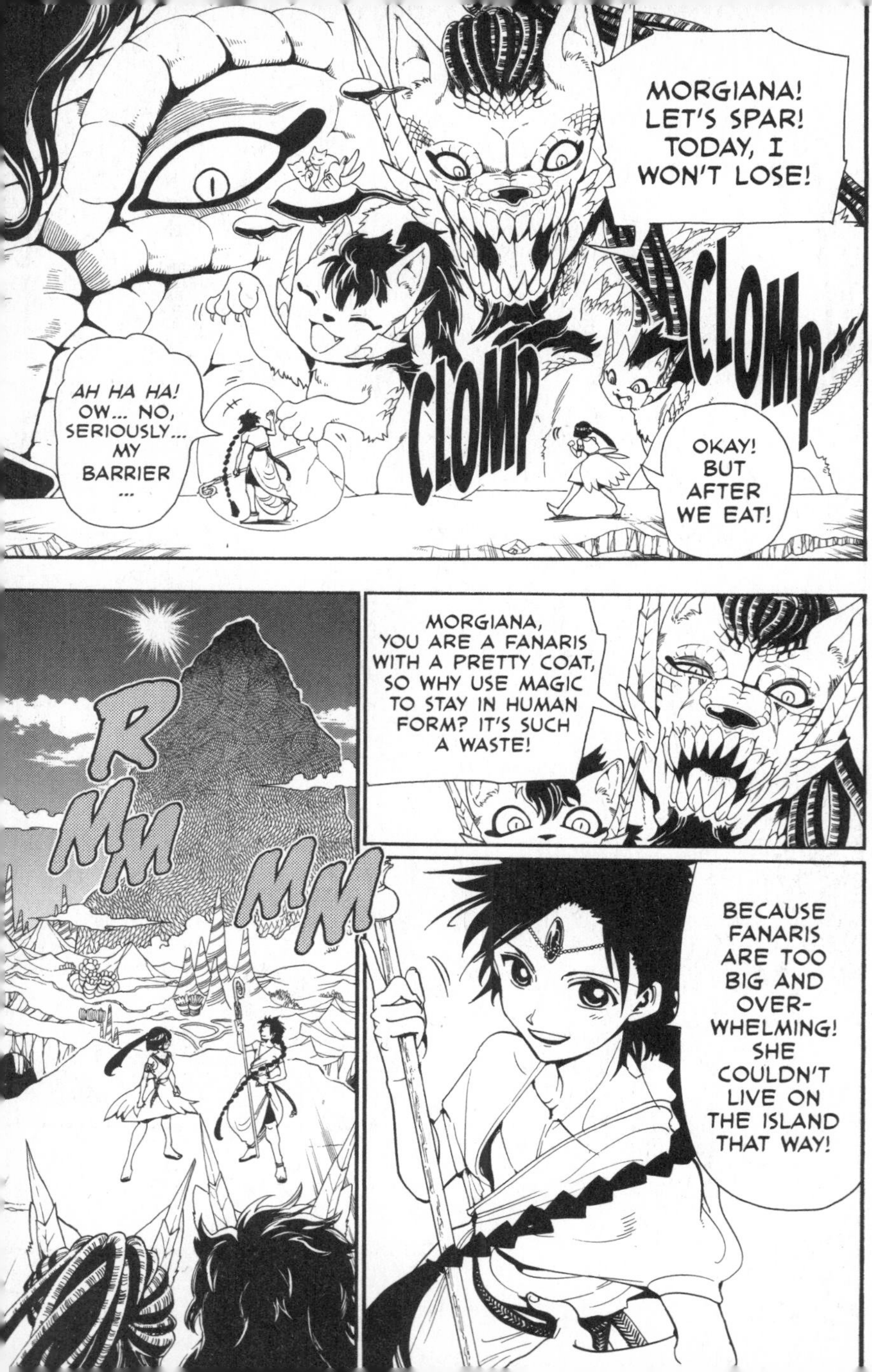
MORGIANA! LET'S SPAR! TODAY, I WON'T LOSE!
CLOMP
OKAY! BUT AFTER WE EAT!
CLOMP
AH HA HA! OW... NO, SERIOUSLY... MY BARRIER ...
MORGIANA, YOU ARE A FANARIS WITH A PRETTY COAT, SO WHY USE MAGIC TO STAY IN HUMAN FORM? IT'S SUCH A WASTE!
BECAUSE FANARIS ARE TOO BIG AND OVER-WHELMING! SHE COULDN'T LIVE ON THE ISLAND THAT WAY!
RMMMMM

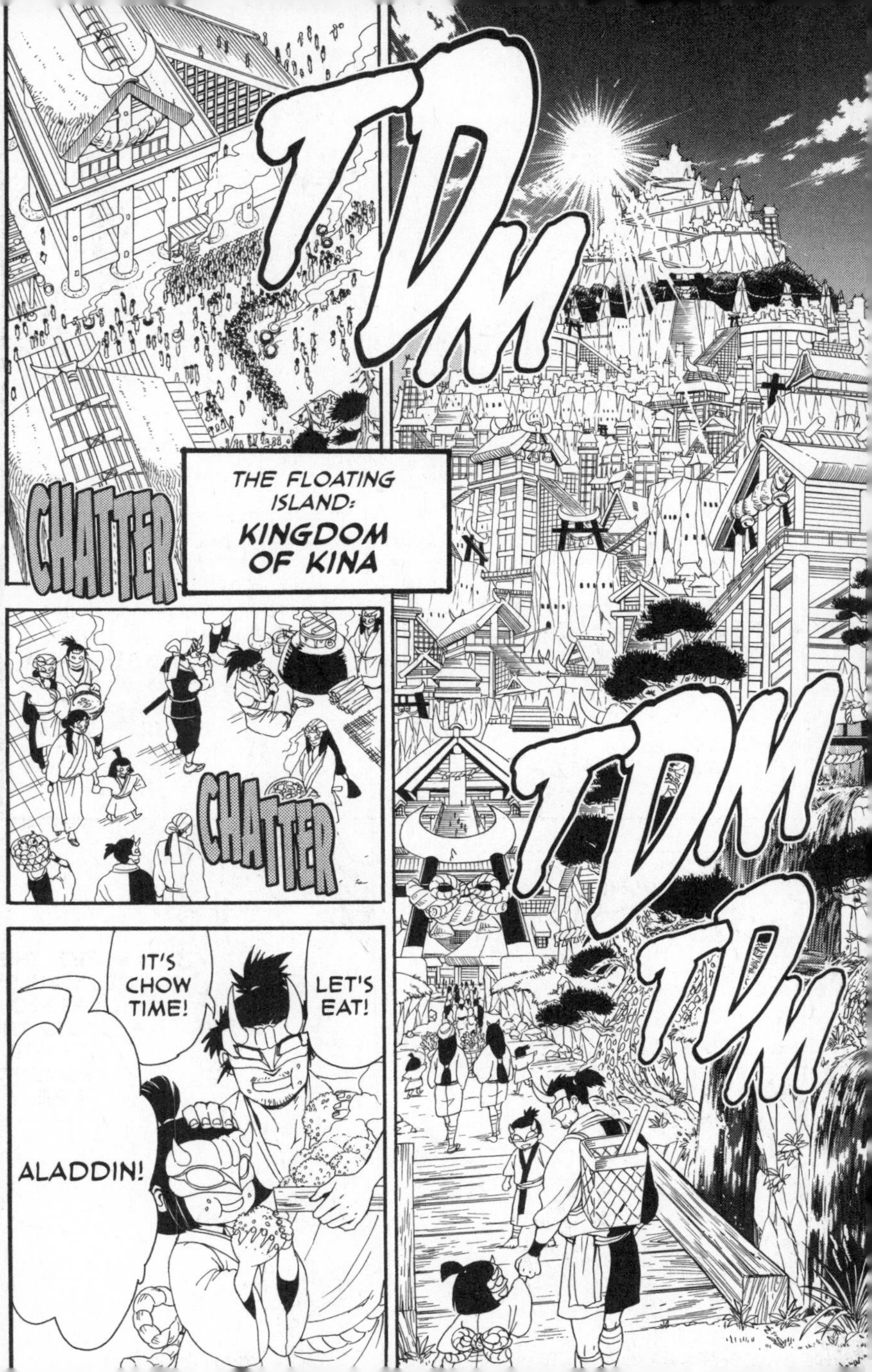
TDM
TDM
TDM
THE FLOATING ISLAND: KINGDOM OF KINA
CHATTER
CHATTER
LET'S EAT!
IT'S CHOW TIME!
ALADDIN!

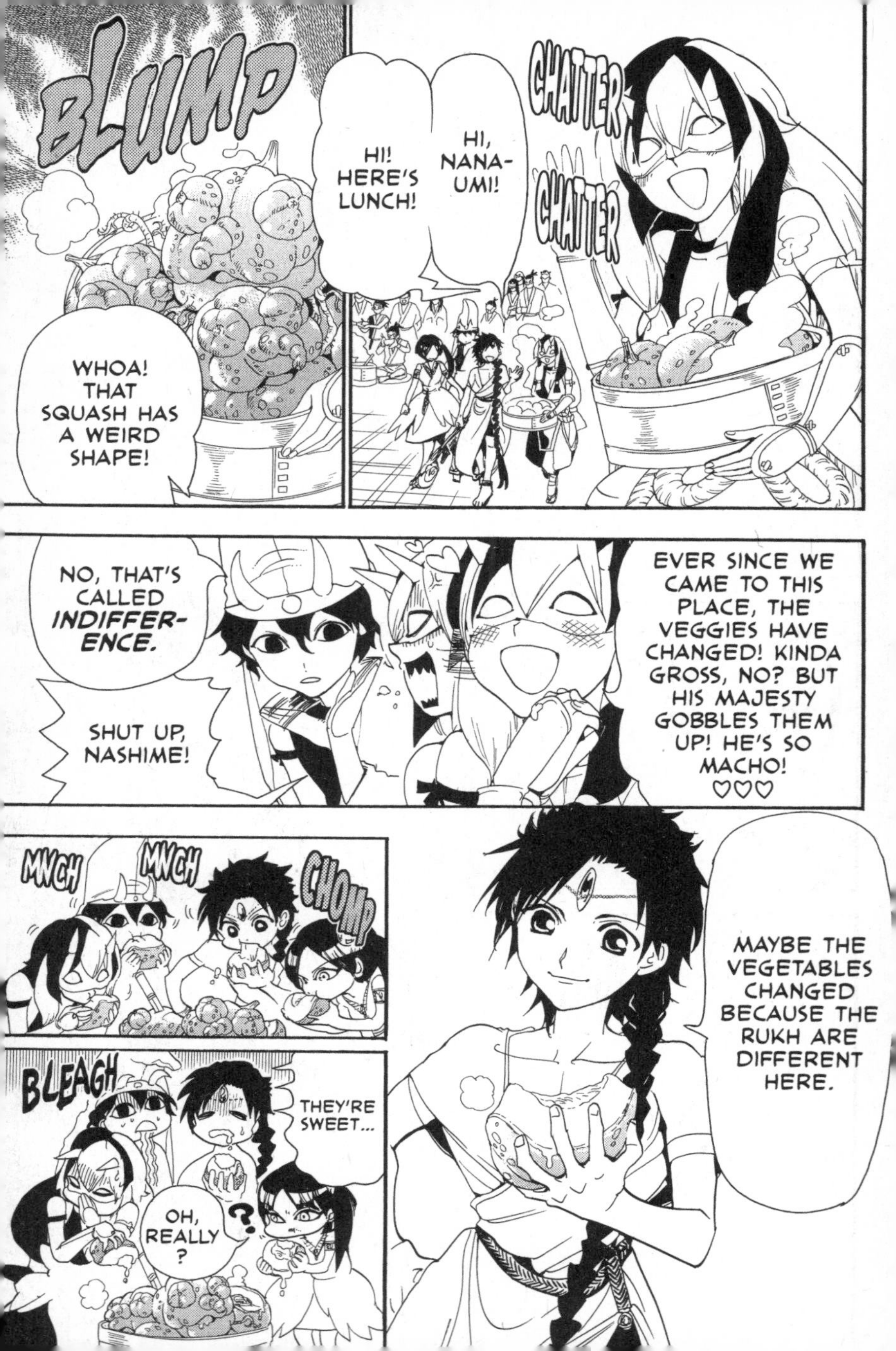
CHATTER
CHATTER
HI, NANA-UMI!
HI! HERE'S LUNCH!
BLUMP
WHOA! THAT SQUASH HAS A WEIRD SHAPE!
EVER SINCE WE CAME TO THIS PLACE, THE VEGGIES HAVE CHANGED! KINDA GROSS, NO? BUT HIS MAJESTY GOBBLES THEM UP! HE'S SO MACHO! ♡♡♡
NO, THAT'S CALLED *INDIFFERENCE.*
SHUT UP, NASHIME!
MAYBE THE VEGETABLES CHANGED BECAUSE THE RUKH ARE DIFFERENT HERE.
CHOMP
MNCH
MNCH
THEY'RE SWEET...
BLEAGH
OH, REALLY?

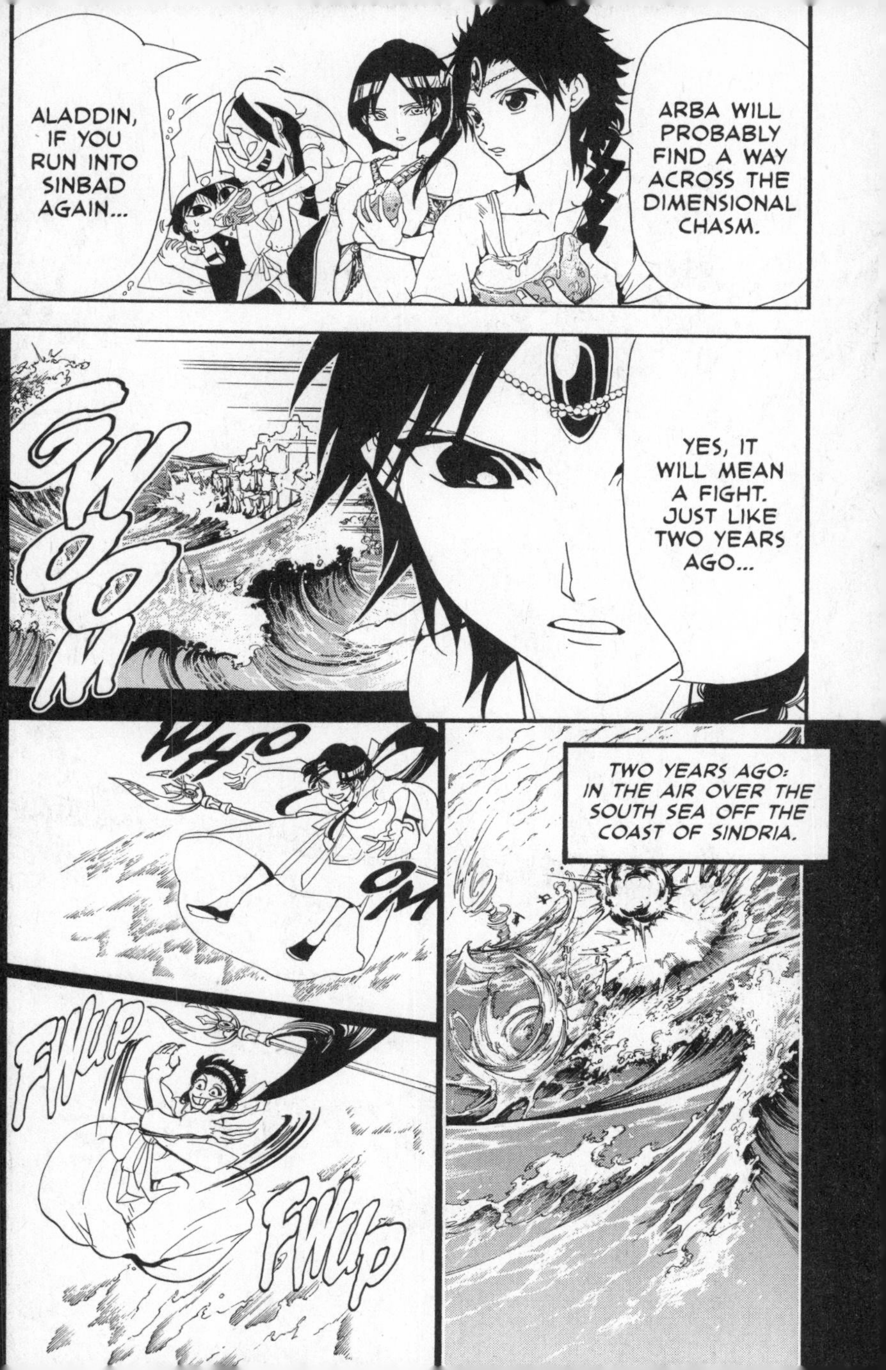
ARBA WILL PROBABLY FIND A WAY ACROSS THE DIMENSIONAL CHASM.
ALADDIN, IF YOU RUN INTO SINBAD AGAIN...
YES, IT WILL MEAN A FIGHT. JUST LIKE TWO YEARS AGO...
GWOOOM
TWO YEARS AGO: IN THE AIR OVER THE SOUTH SEA OFF THE COAST OF SINDRIA.
WHO
OM
FWUP
FWUP

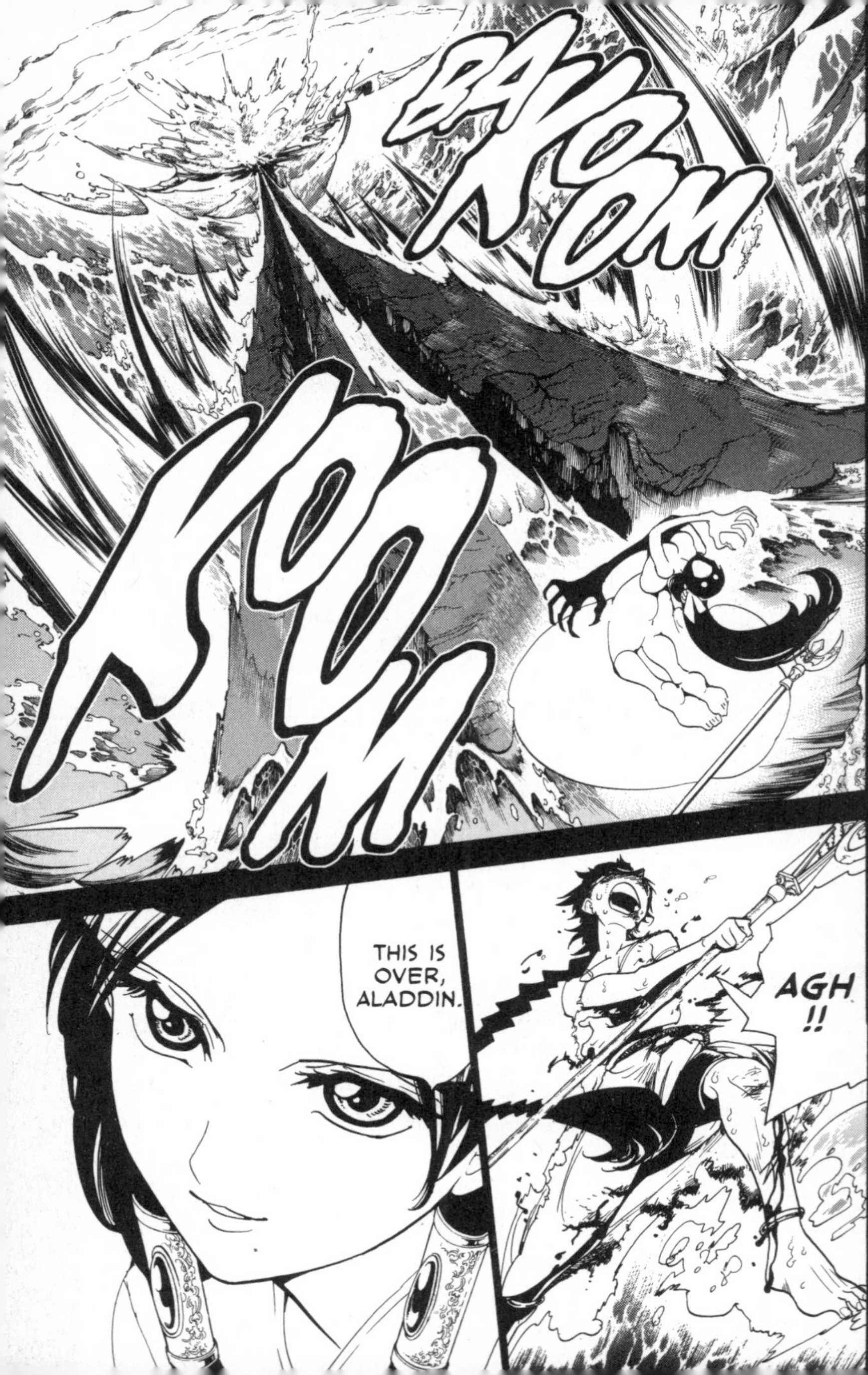
AGH!!
THIS IS OVER, ALADDIN.

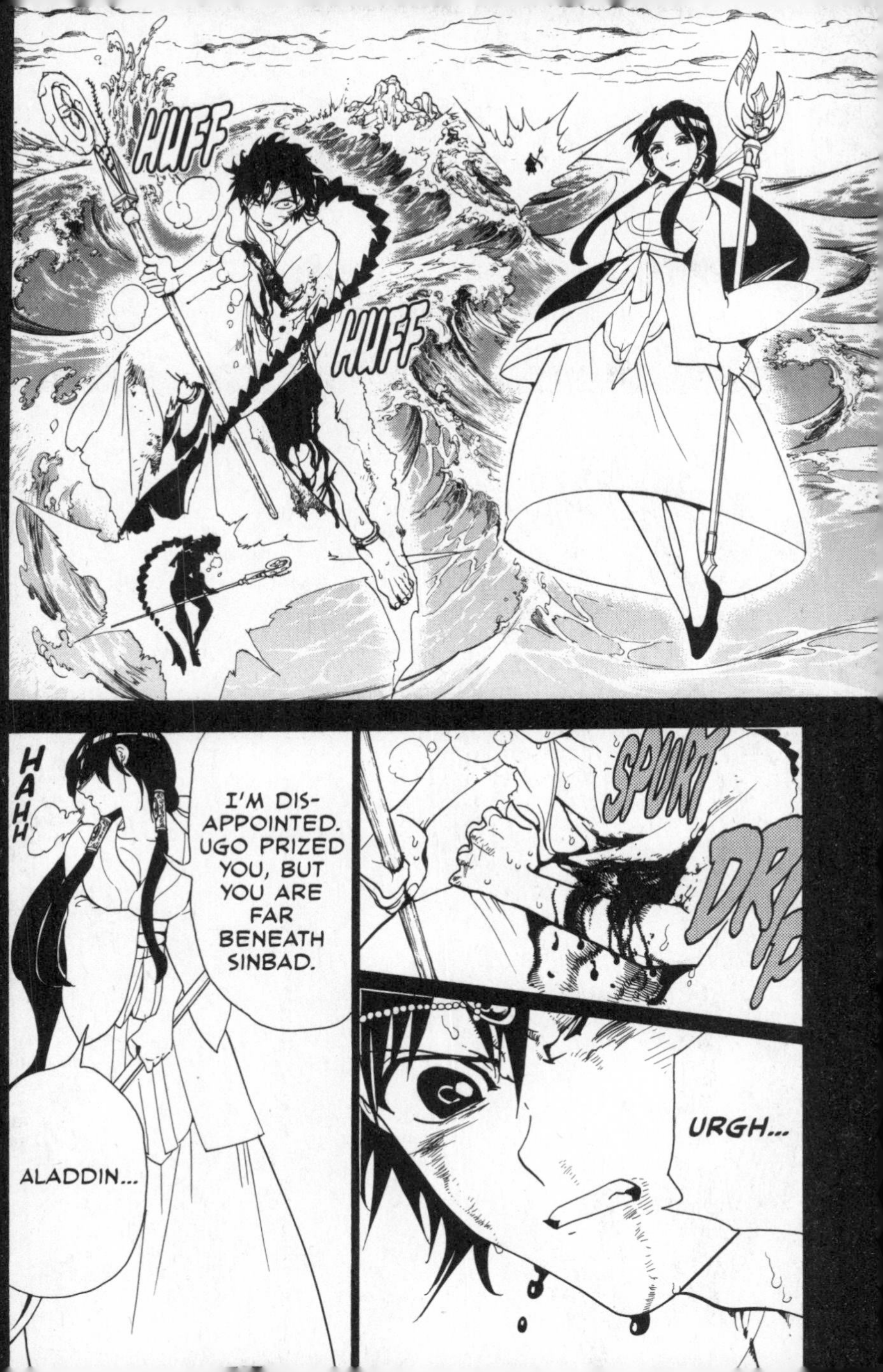
HUFF
HUFF
SPURT
DRIP
URGH...
HAHH
I'M DIS-APPOINTED. UGO PRIZED YOU, BUT YOU ARE FAR BENEATH SINBAD.
ALADDIN...

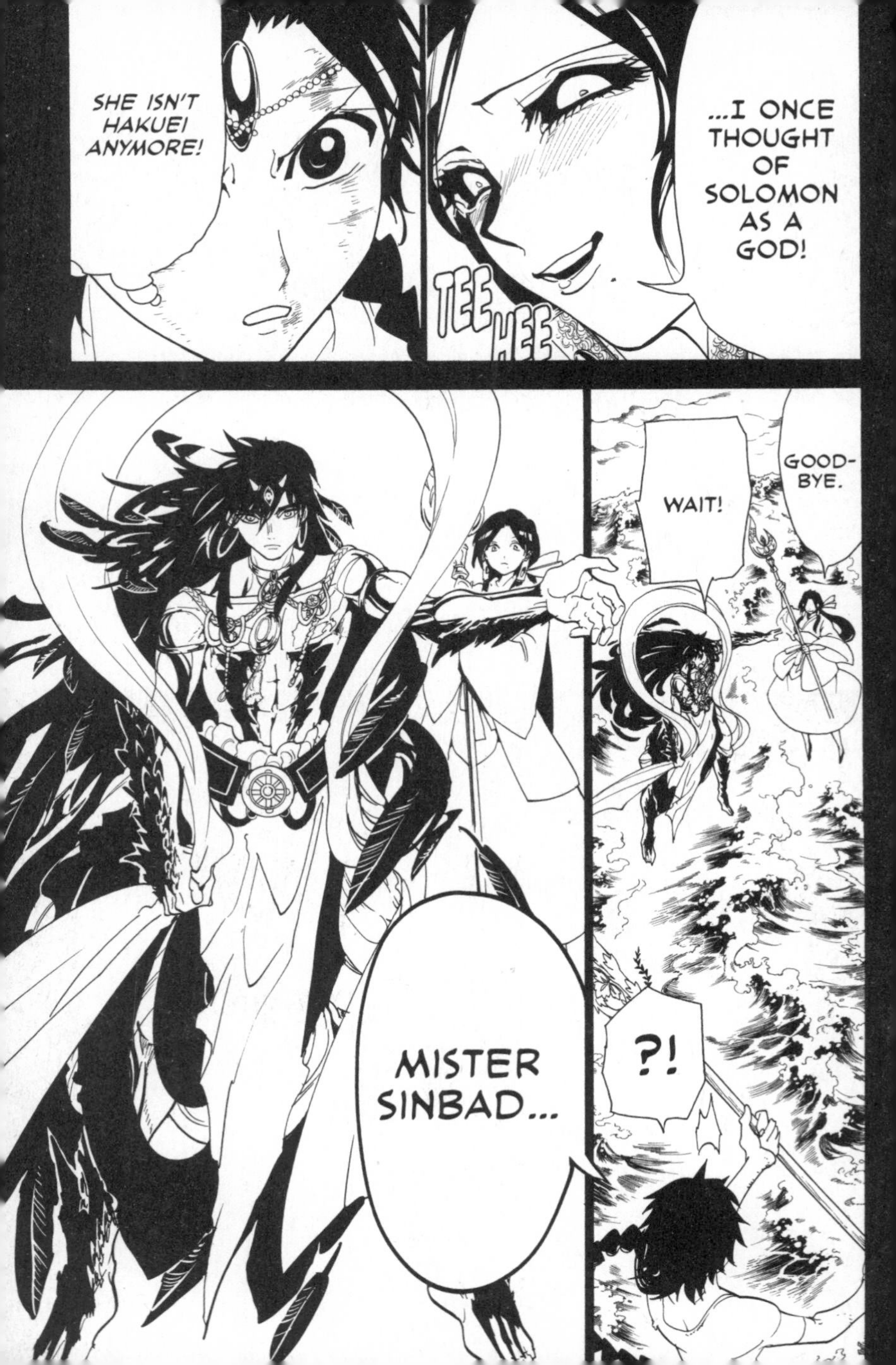
...I ONCE THOUGHT OF SOLOMON AS A GOD!
TEE HEE
SHE ISN'T HAKUEI ANYMORE!
GOOD-BYE.
WAIT!
?!
MISTER SINBAD...

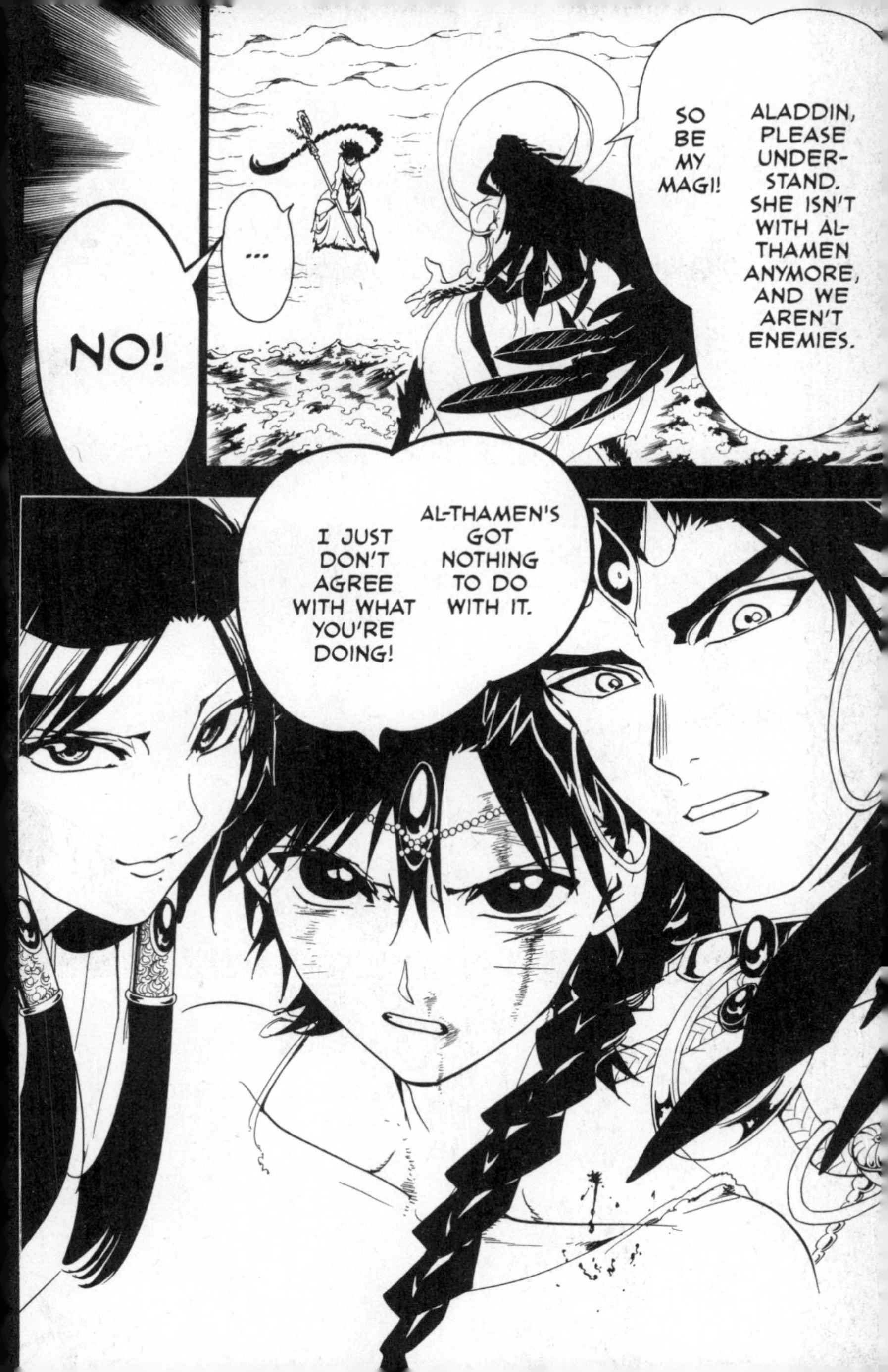
ALADDIN, PLEASE UNDERSTAND. SHE ISN'T WITH AL-THAMEN ANYMORE, AND WE AREN'T ENEMIES.
SO BE MY MAGI!
...
NO!
AL-THAMEN'S GOT NOTHING TO DO WITH IT.
I JUST DON'T AGREE WITH WHAT YOU'RE DOING!

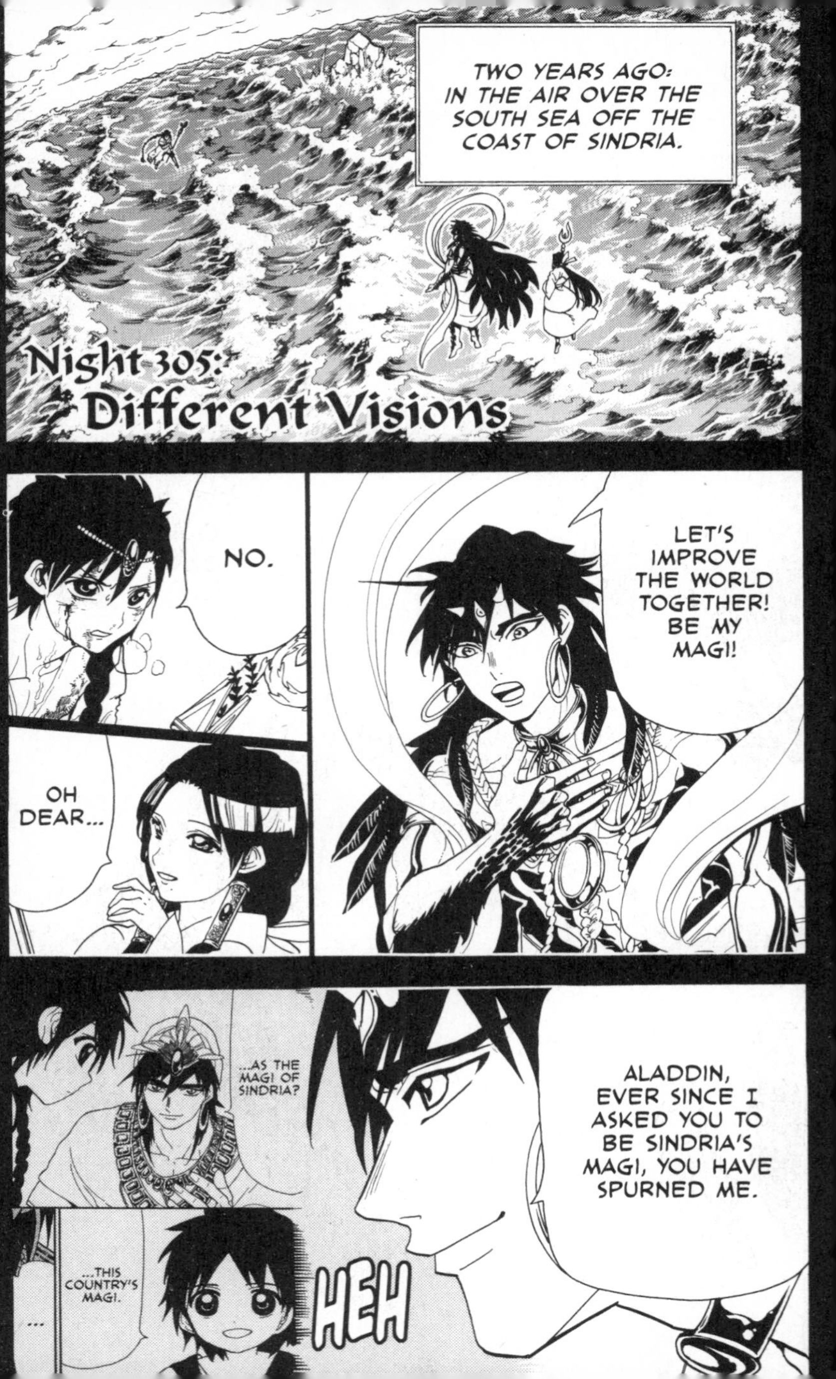
TWO YEARS AGO: IN THE AIR OVER THE SOUTH SEA OFF THE COAST OF SINDRIA.
Night 305: Different Visions
LET'S IMPROVE THE WORLD TOGETHER! BE MY MAGI!
NO.
OH DEAR...
ALADDIN, EVER SINCE I ASKED YOU TO BE SINDRIA'S MAGI, YOU HAVE SPURNED ME.
HEH
...AS THE MAGI OF SINDRIA?
...THIS COUNTRY'S MAGI.
...

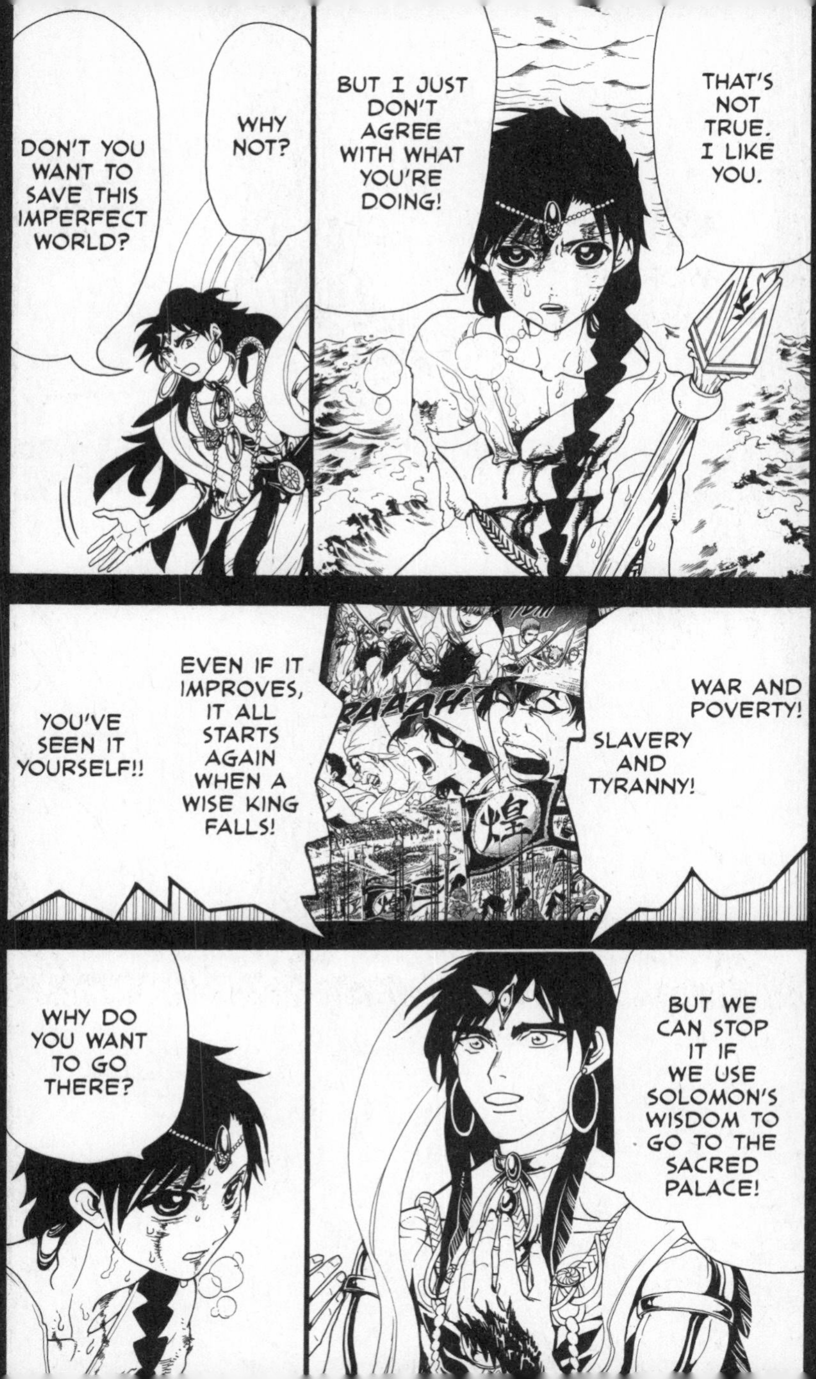
THAT'S NOT TRUE. I LIKE YOU.
BUT I JUST DON'T AGREE WITH WHAT YOU'RE DOING!
WHY NOT?
DON'T YOU WANT TO SAVE THIS IMPERFECT WORLD?
WAR AND POVERTY!
SLAVERY AND TYRANNY!
煌
EVEN IF IT IMPROVES, IT ALL STARTS AGAIN WHEN A WISE KING FALLS!
YOU'VE SEEN IT YOURSELF!!
BUT WE CAN STOP IT IF WE USE SOLOMON'S WISDOM TO GO TO THE SACRED PALACE!
WHY DO YOU WANT TO GO THERE?

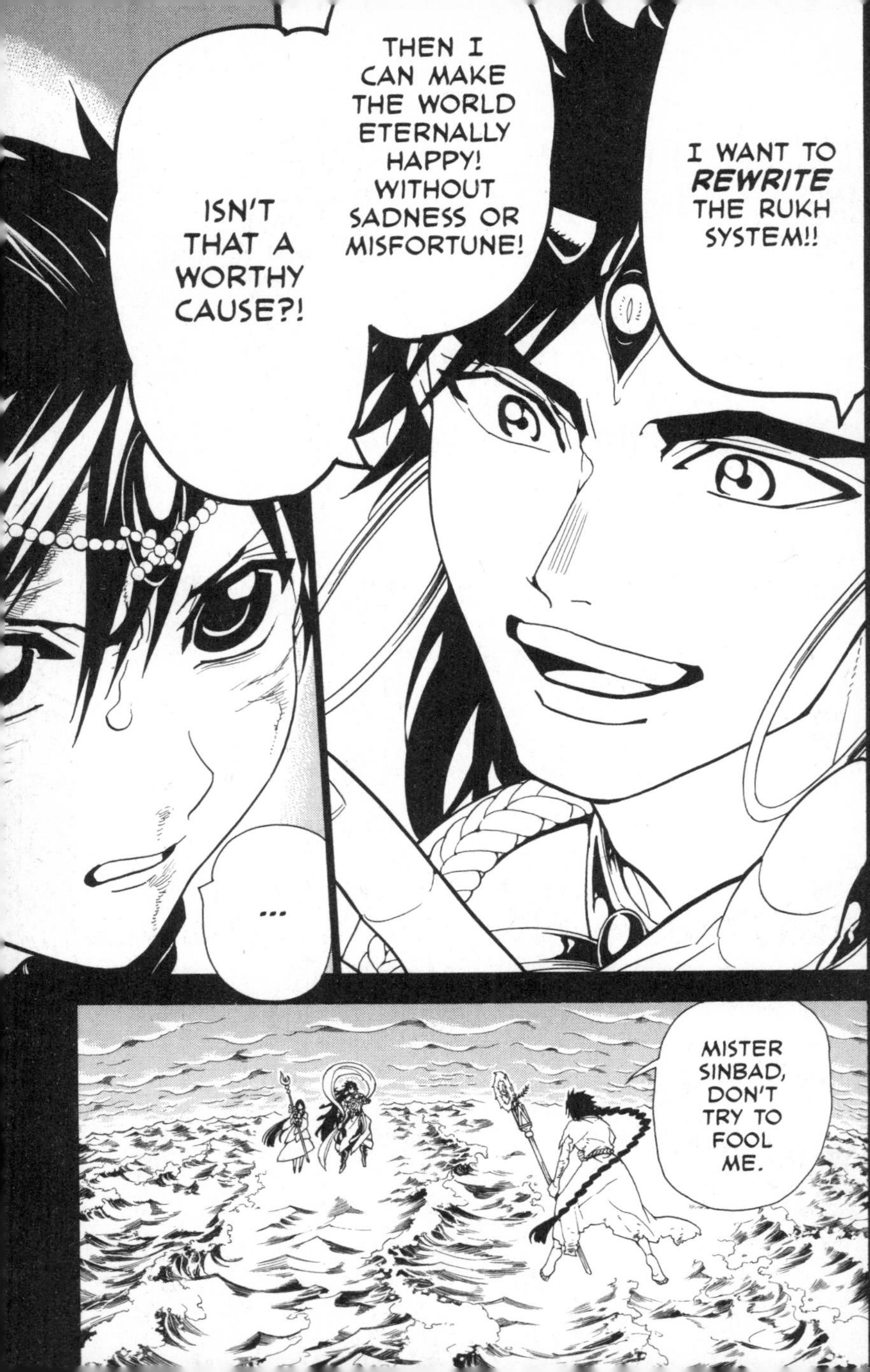
I WANT TO ***REWRITE*** THE RUKH SYSTEM!!
THEN I CAN MAKE THE WORLD ETERNALLY HAPPY! WITHOUT SADNESS OR MISFORTUNE!
ISN'T THAT A WORTHY CAUSE?!
...
MISTER SINBAD, DON'T TRY TO FOOL ME.

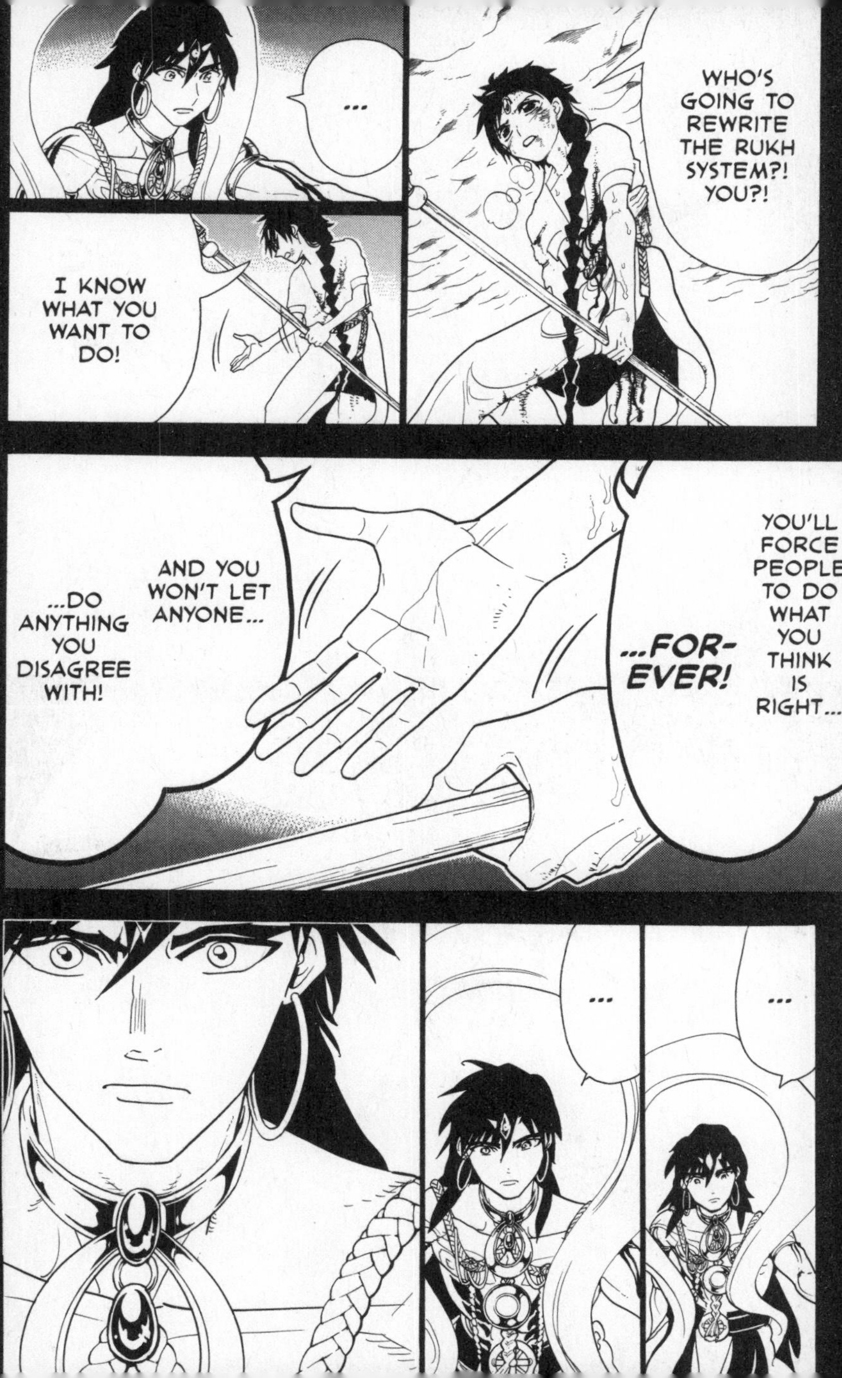
WHO'S GOING TO REWRITE THE RUKH SYSTEM?! YOU?!
...
I KNOW WHAT YOU WANT TO DO!
YOU'LL FORCE PEOPLE TO DO WHAT YOU THINK IS RIGHT...
...FOR-EVER!
AND YOU WON'T LET ANYONE...
...DO ANYTHING YOU DISAGREE WITH!
...
...

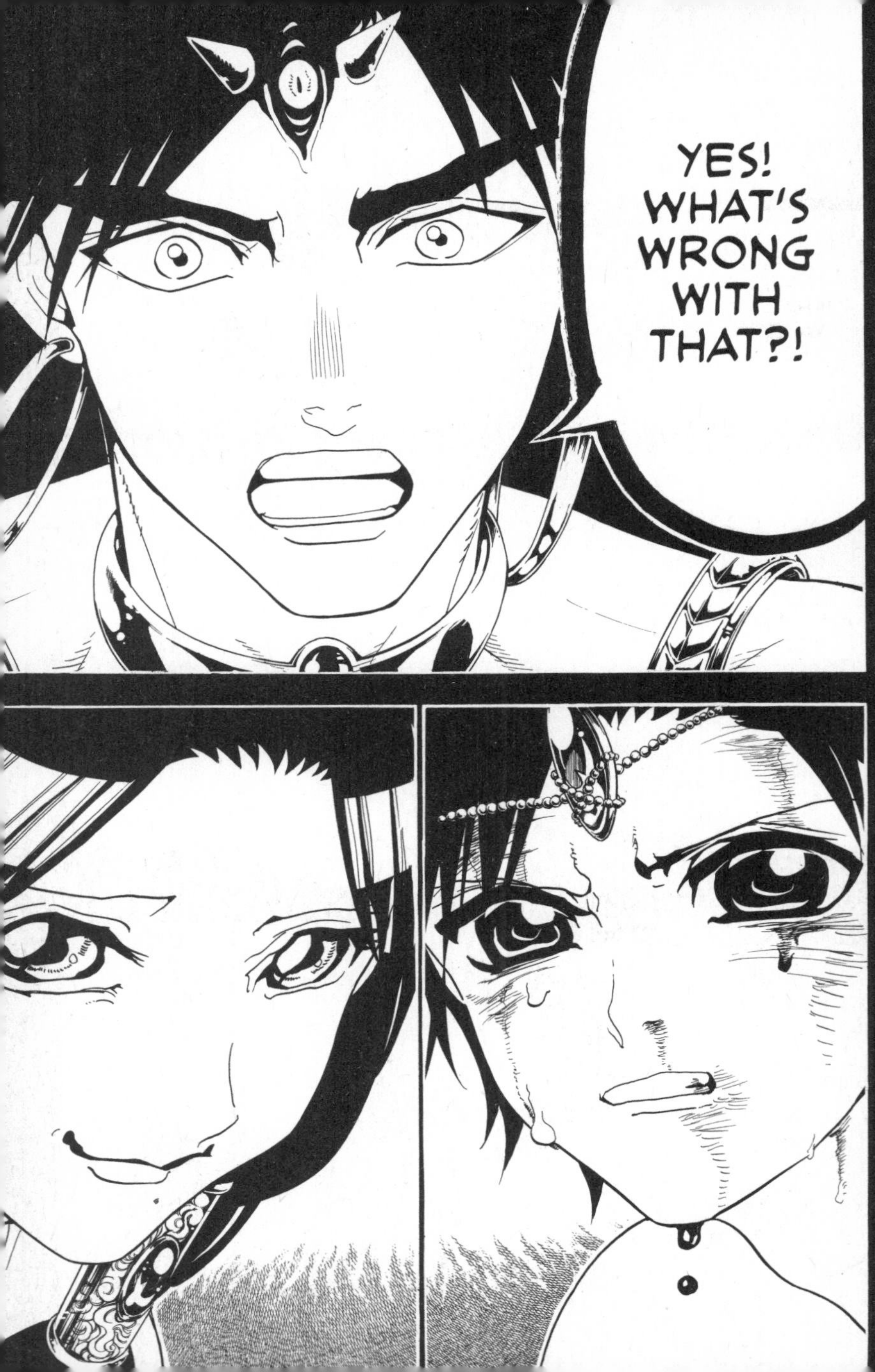
YES! WHAT'S WRONG WITH THAT?!

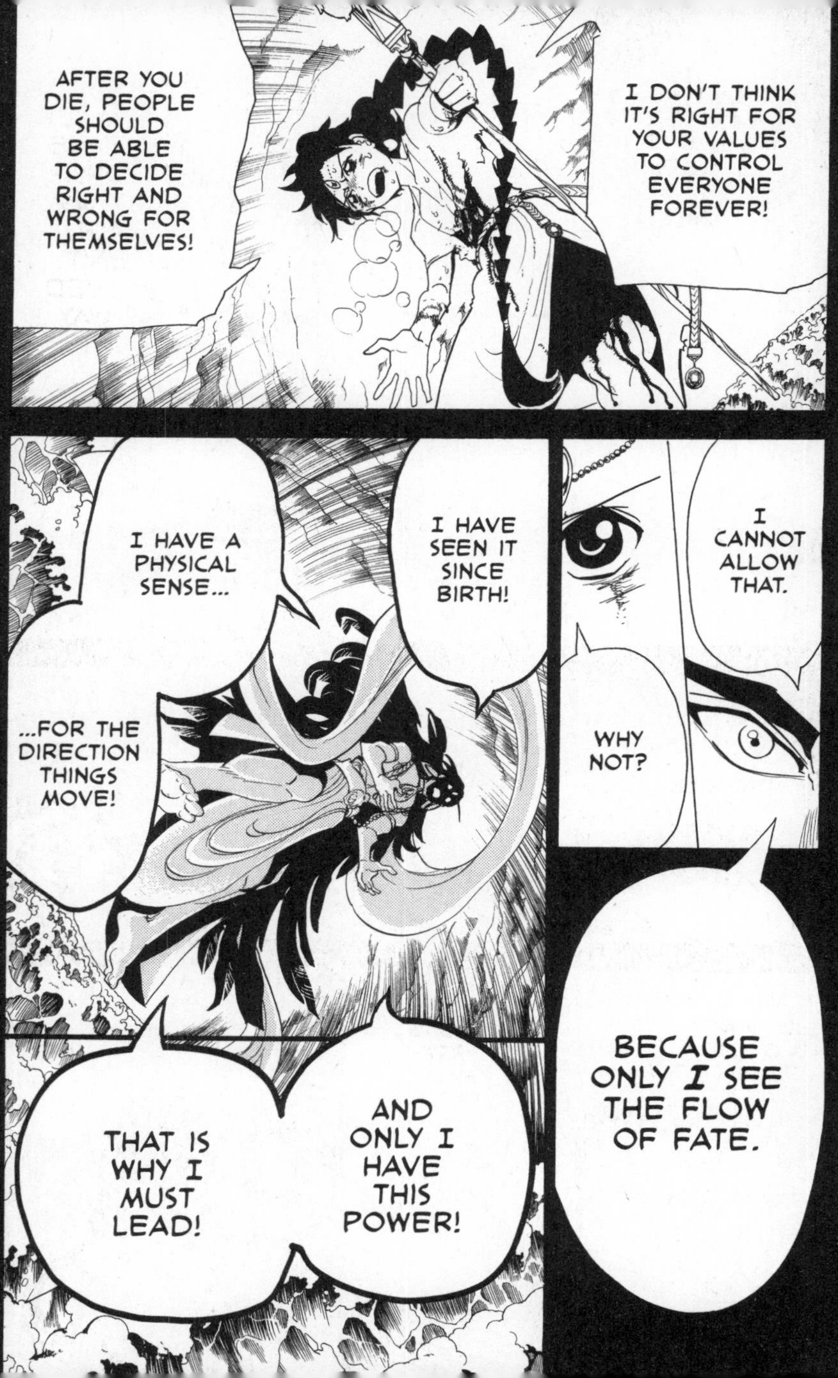
I DON'T THINK IT'S RIGHT FOR YOUR VALUES TO CONTROL EVERYONE FOREVER!
AFTER YOU DIE, PEOPLE SHOULD BE ABLE TO DECIDE RIGHT AND WRONG FOR THEMSELVES!
I CANNOT ALLOW THAT.
WHY NOT?
BECAUSE ONLY *I* SEE THE FLOW OF FATE.
I HAVE SEEN IT SINCE BIRTH!
I HAVE A PHYSICAL SENSE...
...FOR THE DIRECTION THINGS MOVE!
AND ONLY I HAVE THIS POWER!
THAT IS WHY I MUST LEAD!

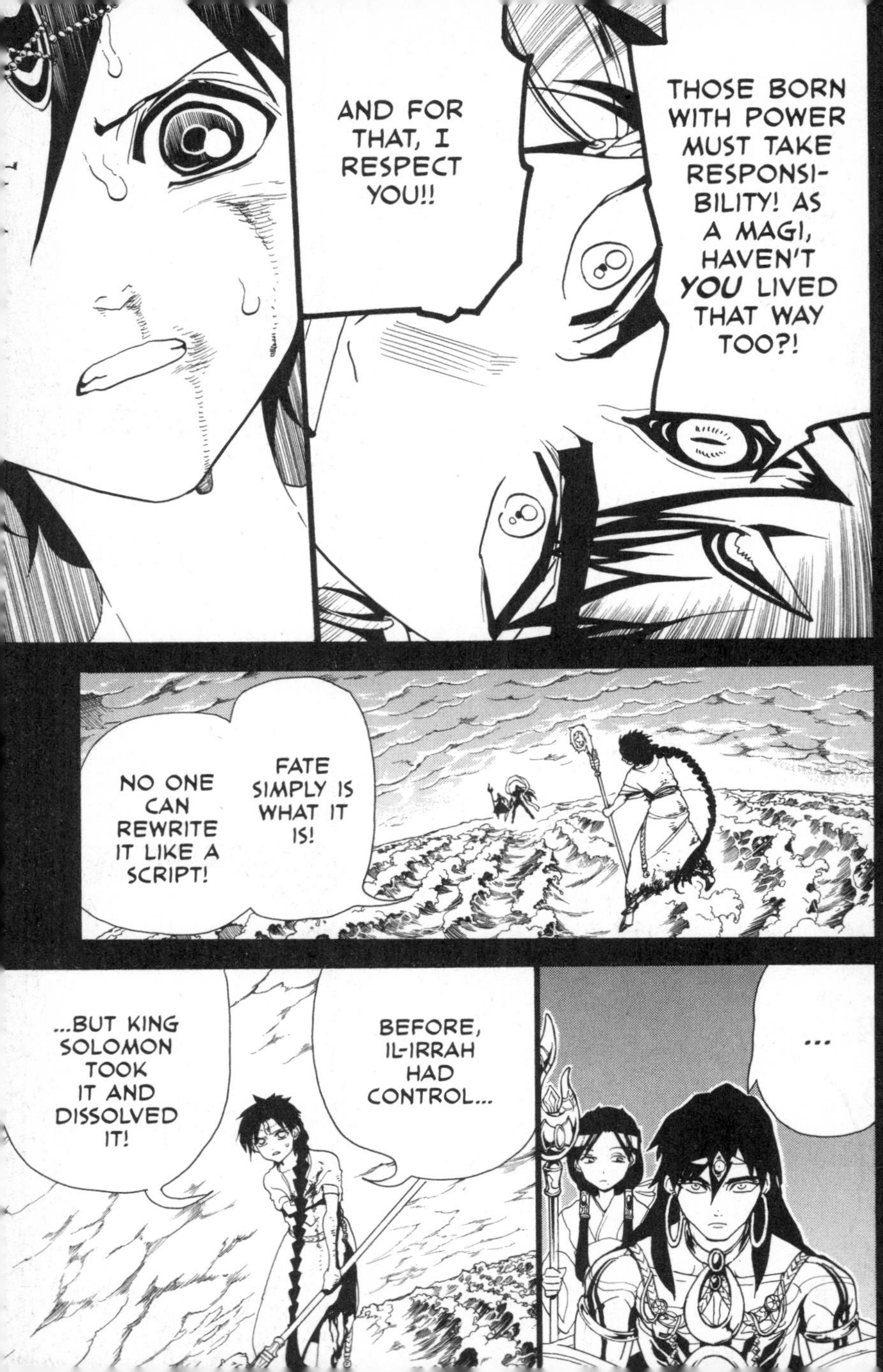

THOSE BORN WITH POWER MUST TAKE RESPONSIBILITY! AS A MAGI, HAVEN'T *YOU* LIVED THAT WAY TOO?!
AND FOR THAT, I RESPECT YOU!!
FATE SIMPLY IS WHAT IT IS!
NO ONE CAN REWRITE IT LIKE A SCRIPT!
...
BEFORE, IL-IRRAH HAD CONTROL...
...BUT KING SOLOMON TOOK IT AND DISSOLVED IT!

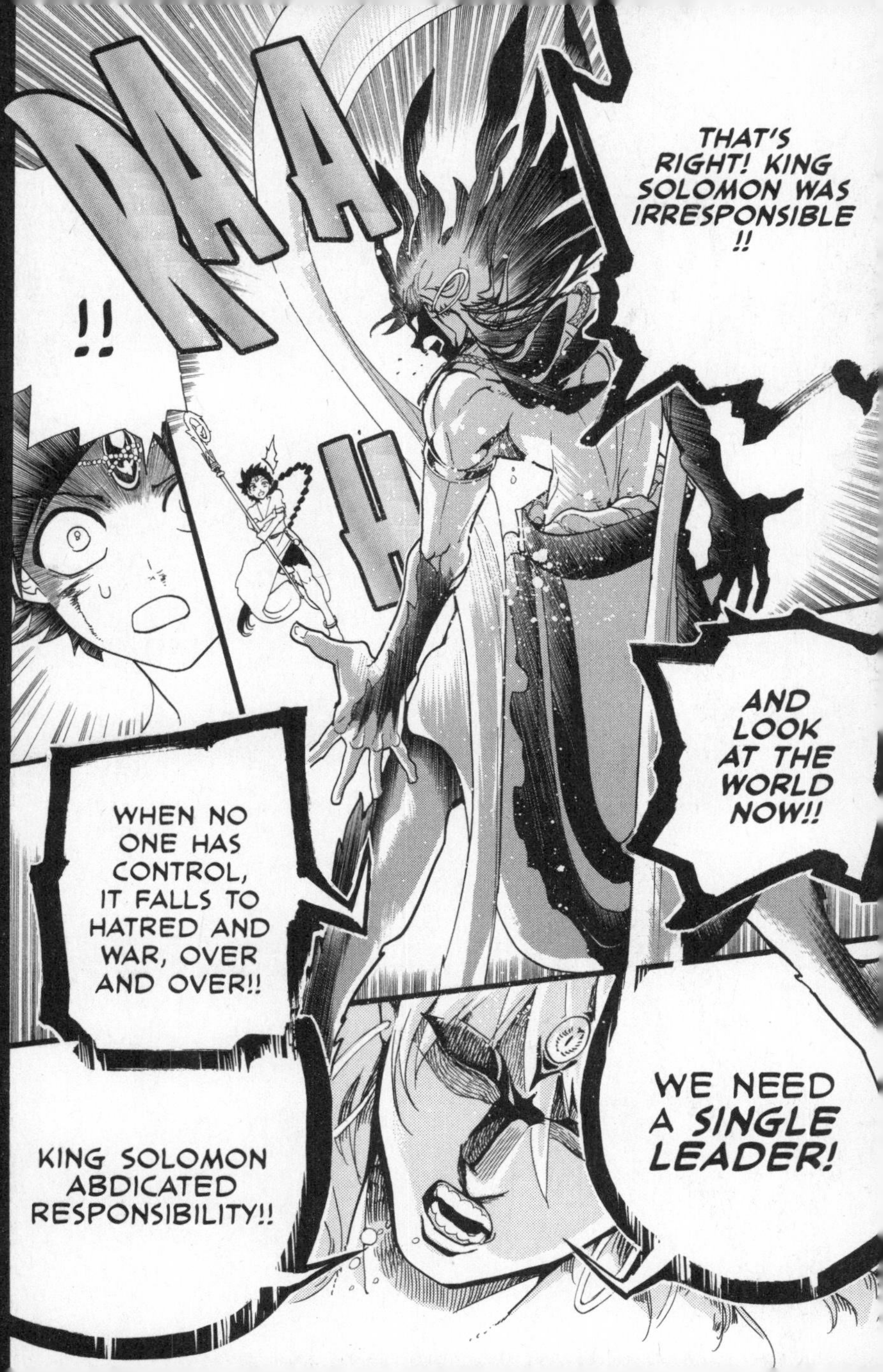
THAT'S RIGHT! KING SOLOMON WAS IRRESPONSIBLE !!
!!
AND LOOK AT THE WORLD NOW!!
WHEN NO ONE HAS CONTROL, IT FALLS TO HATRED AND WAR, OVER AND OVER!!
WE NEED A *SINGLE LEADER*!
KING SOLOMON ABDICATED RESPONSIBILITY!!

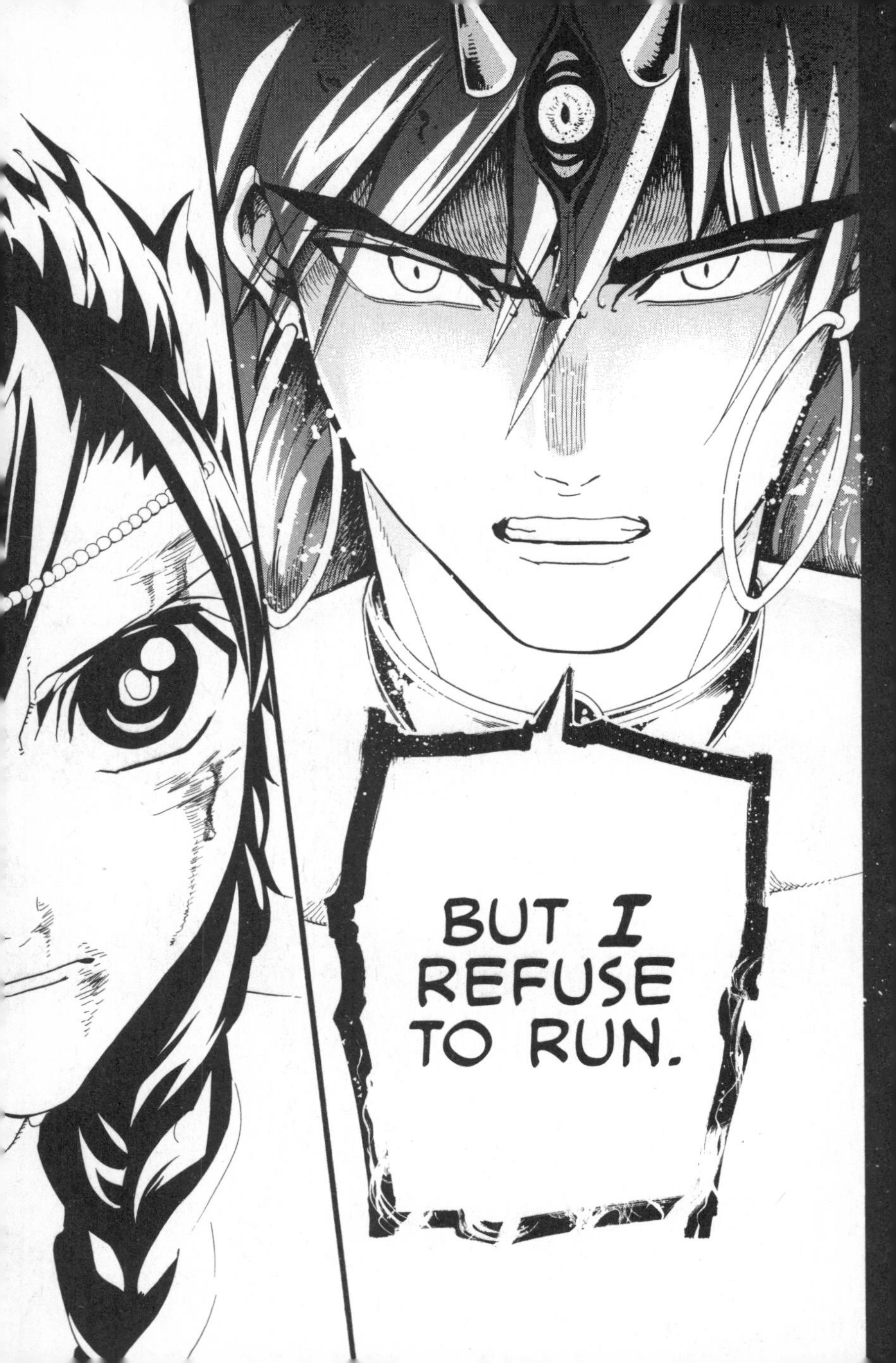
BUT I REFUSE TO RUN.

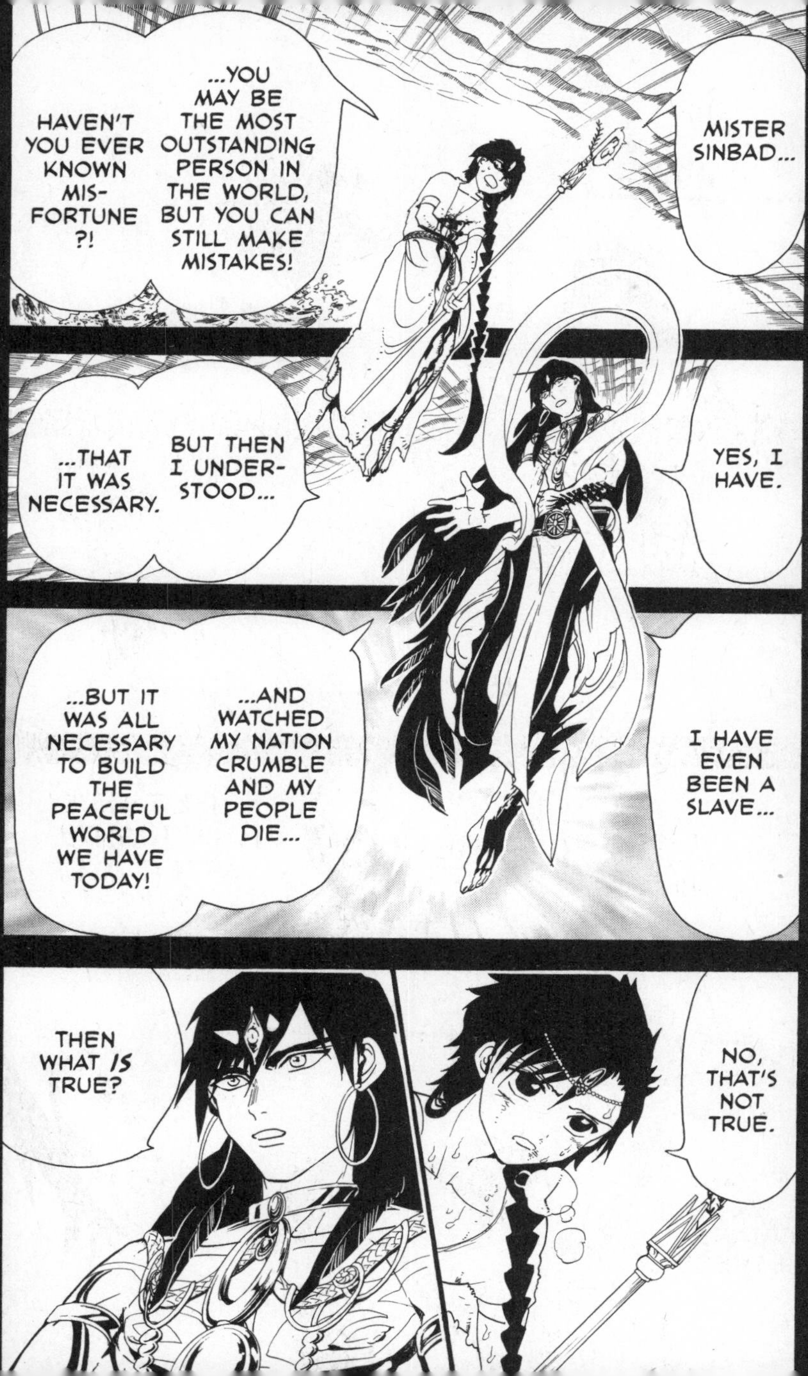
MISTER SINBAD...
...YOU MAY BE THE MOST OUTSTANDING PERSON IN THE WORLD, BUT YOU CAN STILL MAKE MISTAKES!
HAVEN'T YOU EVER KNOWN MIS-FORTUNE?!
YES, I HAVE.
BUT THEN I UNDER-STOOD...
...THAT IT WAS NECESSARY.
I HAVE EVEN BEEN A SLAVE...
...AND WATCHED MY NATION CRUMBLE AND MY PEOPLE DIE...
...BUT IT WAS ALL NECESSARY TO BUILD THE PEACEFUL WORLD WE HAVE TODAY!
NO, THAT'S NOT TRUE.
THEN WHAT *IS* TRUE?

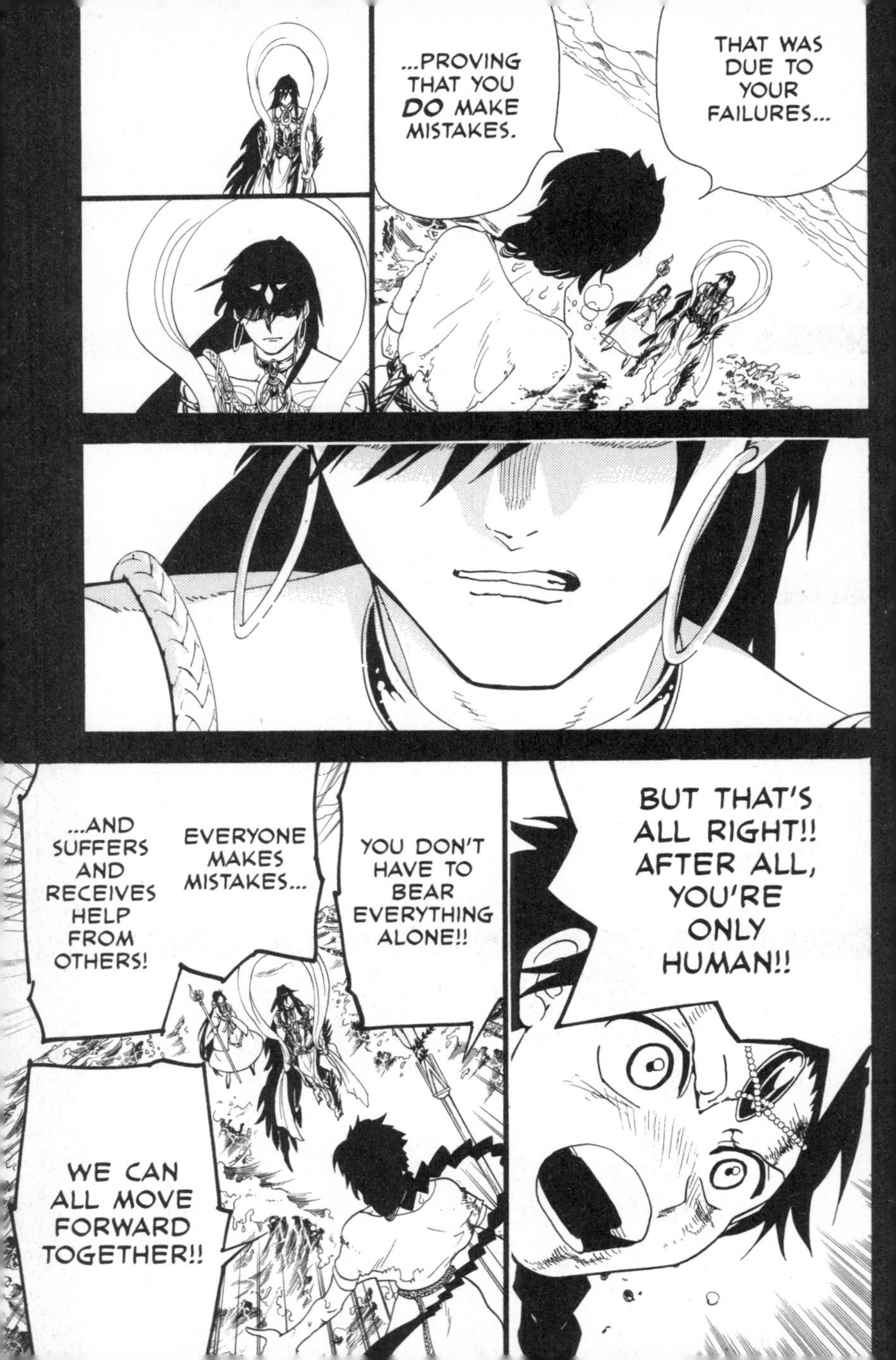
THAT WAS DUE TO YOUR FAILURES...
...PROVING THAT YOU DO MAKE MISTAKES.
BUT THAT'S ALL RIGHT!! AFTER ALL, YOU'RE ONLY HUMAN!!
YOU DON'T HAVE TO BEAR EVERYTHING ALONE!!
EVERYONE MAKES MISTAKES...
...AND SUFFERS AND RECEIVES HELP FROM OTHERS!
WE CAN ALL MOVE FORWARD TOGETHER!!

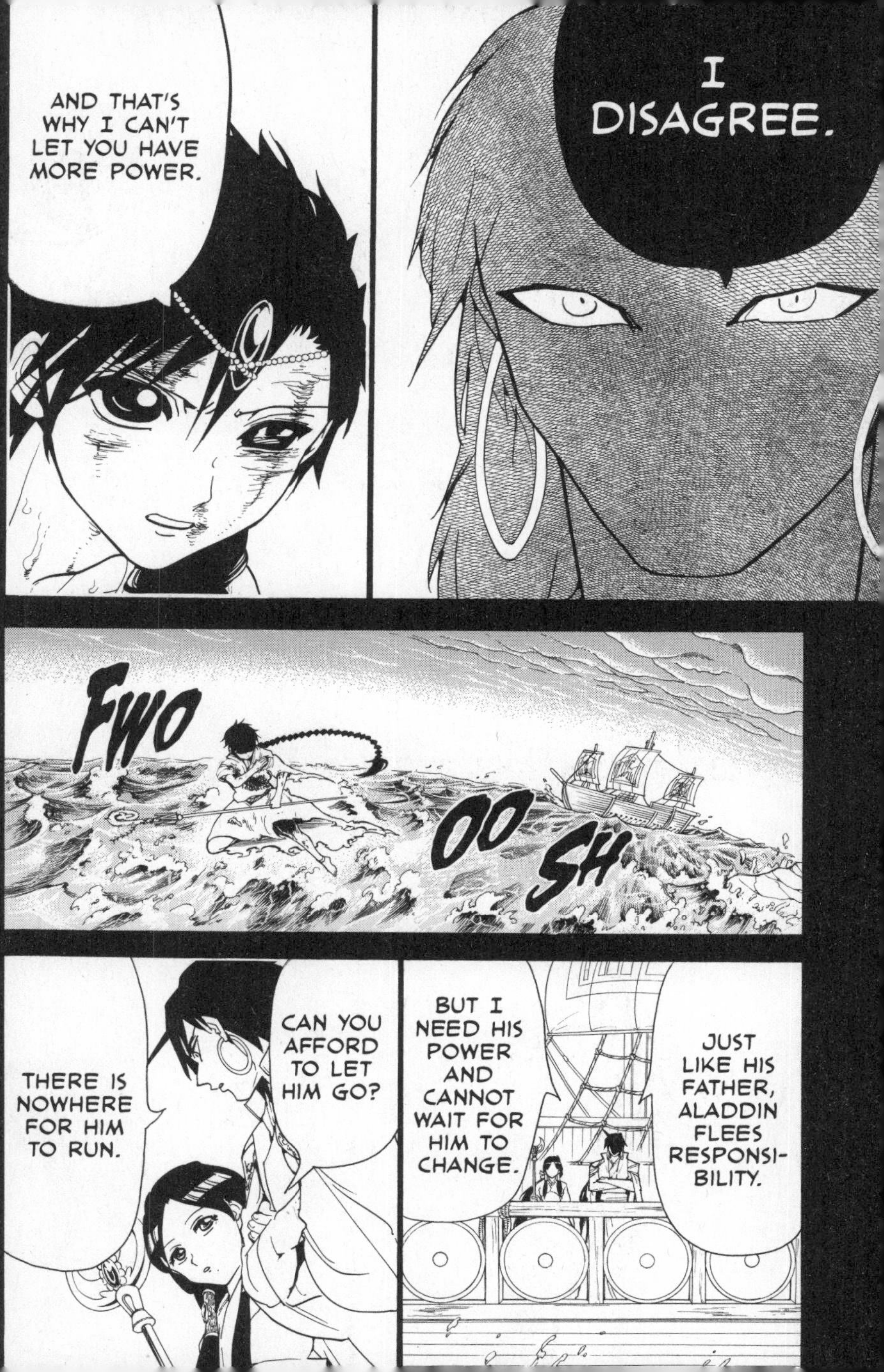
I DISAGREE.
AND THAT'S WHY I CAN'T LET YOU HAVE MORE POWER.
FWOOOSH
JUST LIKE HIS FATHER, ALADDIN FLEES RESPONSI-BILITY.
BUT I NEED HIS POWER AND CANNOT WAIT FOR HIM TO CHANGE.
CAN YOU AFFORD TO LET HIM GO?
THERE IS NOWHERE FOR HIM TO RUN.

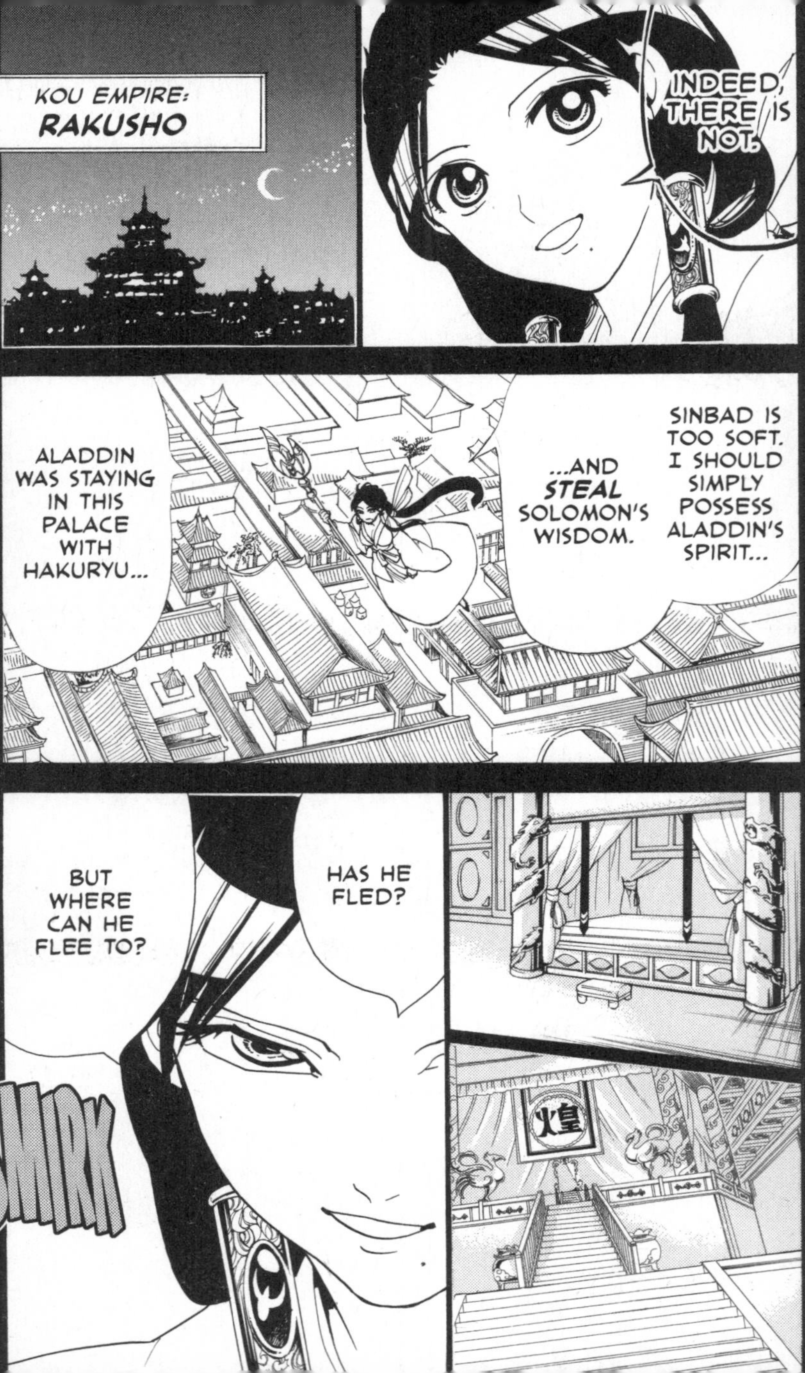
INDEED, THERE IS NOT.
KOU EMPIRE: RAKUSHO
SINBAD IS TOO SOFT. I SHOULD SIMPLY POSSESS ALADDIN'S SPIRIT...
...AND STEAL SOLOMON'S WISDOM.
ALADDIN WAS STAYING IN THIS PALACE WITH HAKURYU...
HAS HE FLED?
BUT WHERE CAN HE FLEE TO?
SMIRK

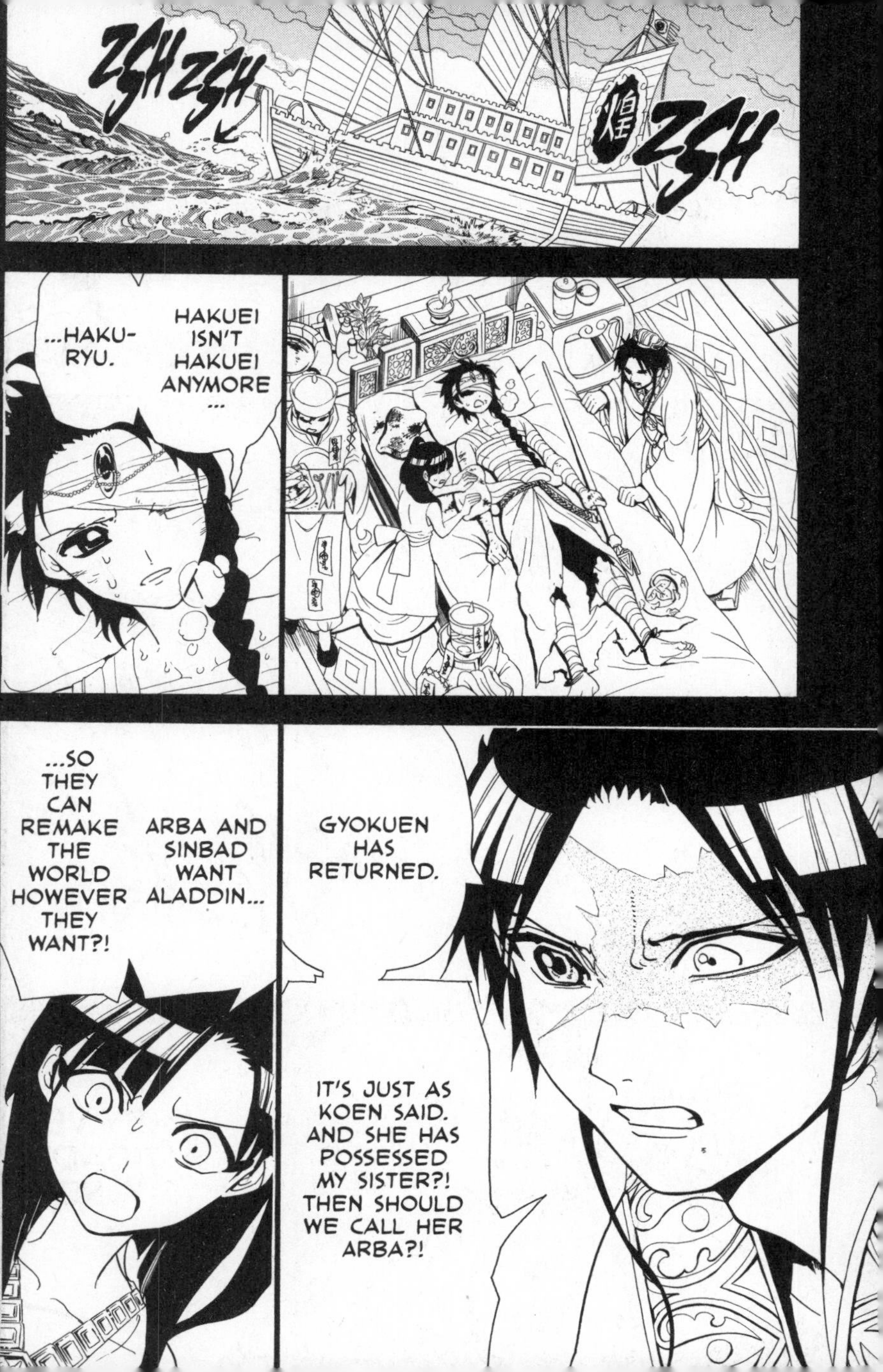
煌
ZSH
ZSH ZSH
HAKUEI ISN'T HAKUEI ANYMORE...
...HAKU-RYU.
GYOKUEN HAS RETURNED.
IT'S JUST AS KOEN SAID. AND SHE HAS POSSESSED MY SISTER?! THEN SHOULD WE CALL HER ARBA?!
ARBA AND SINBAD WANT ALADDIN...
...SO THEY CAN REMAKE THE WORLD HOWEVER THEY WANT?!

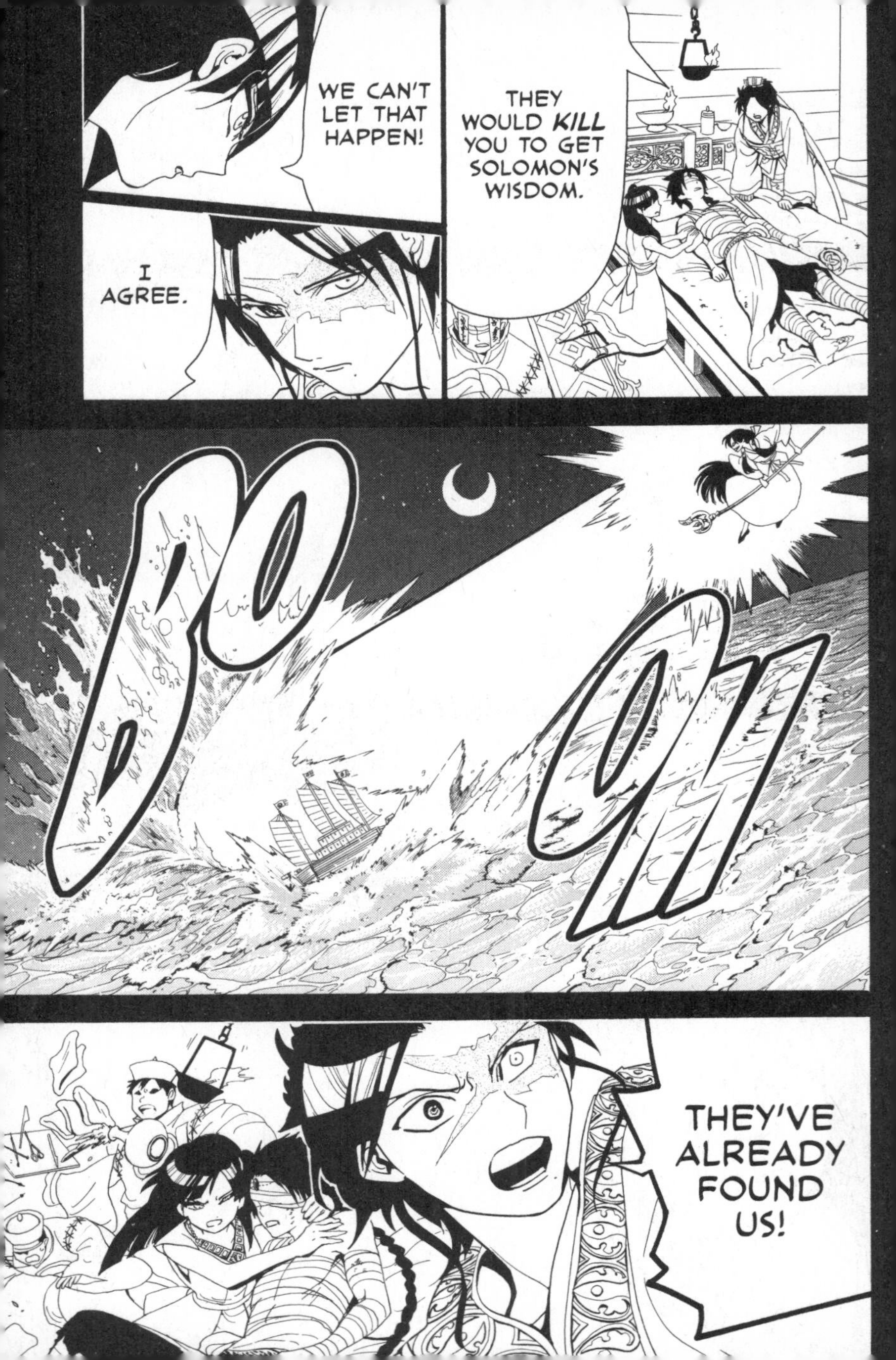

THEY WOULD KILL YOU TO GET SOLOMON'S WISDOM.
WE CAN'T LET THAT HAPPEN!
I AGREE.
THEY'VE ALREADY FOUND US!

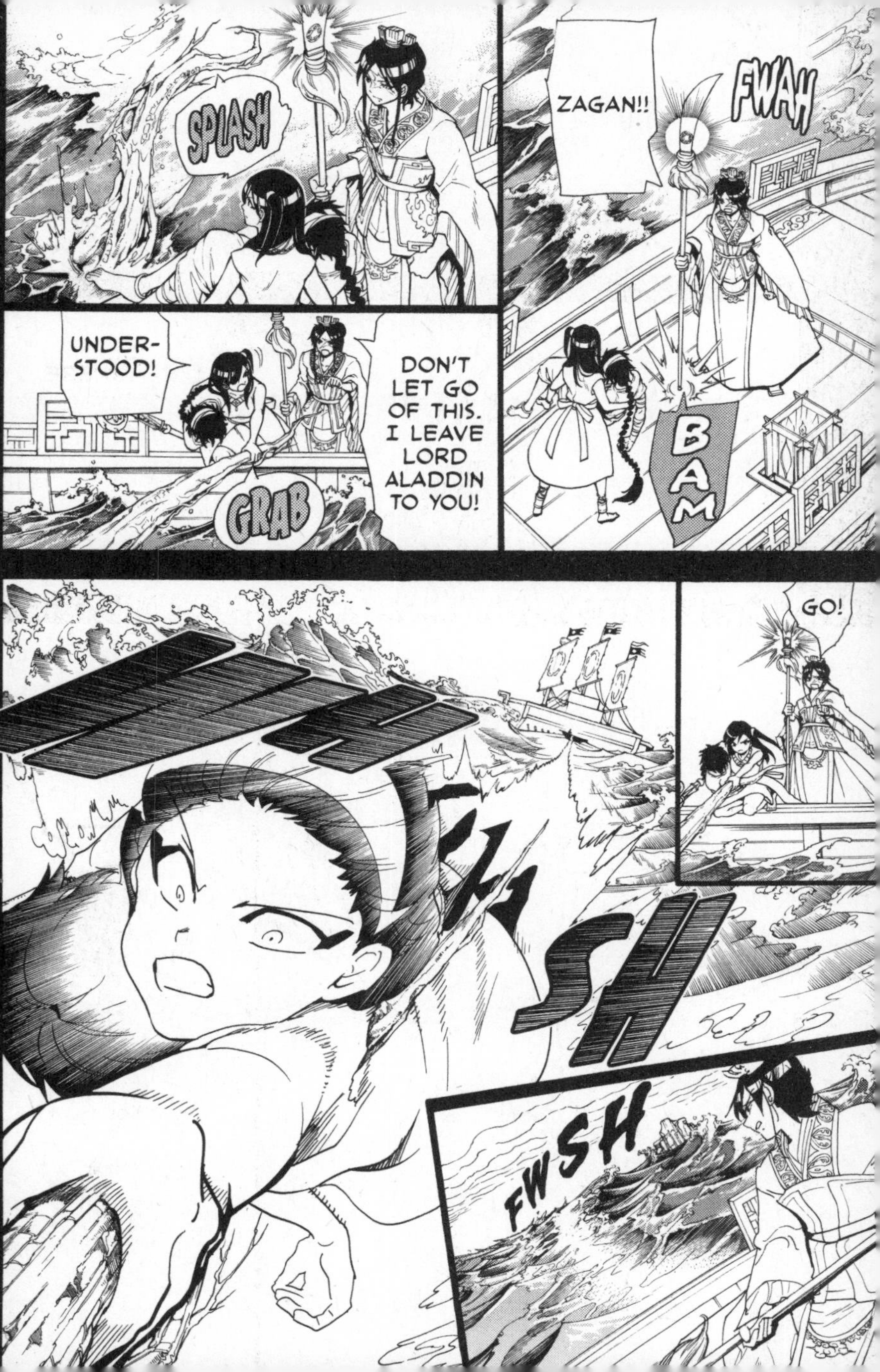
ZAGAN!!
FWAH
BAM
SPLASH
DON'T LET GO OF THIS. I LEAVE LORD ALADDIN TO YOU!
UNDER-STOOD!
GRAB
GO!
FWSH

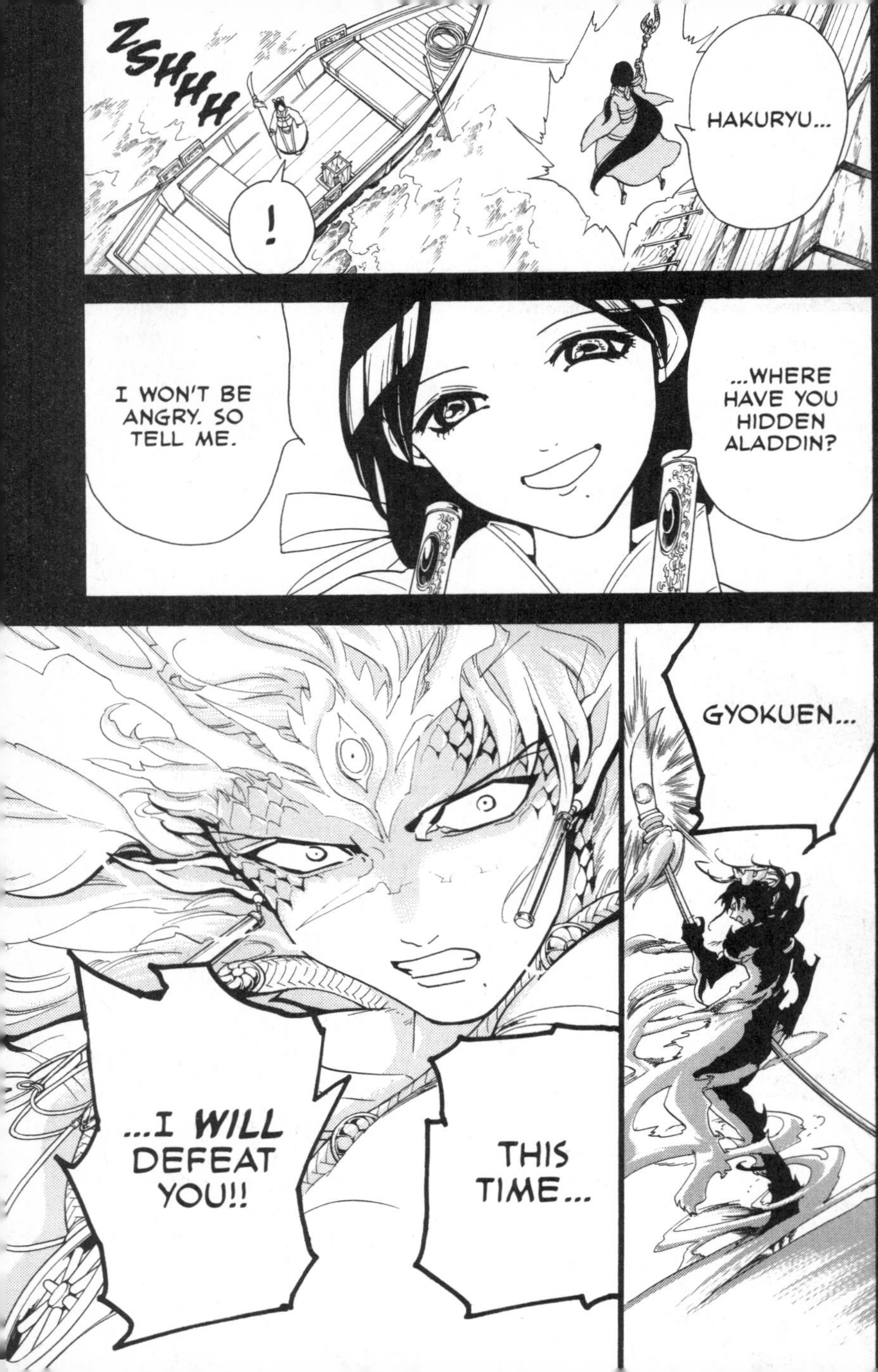
HAKURYU...
ZSHHH
!
...WHERE HAVE YOU HIDDEN ALADDIN?
I WON'T BE ANGRY. SO TELL ME.
GYOKUEN...
THIS TIME...
...I WILL DEFEAT YOU!!

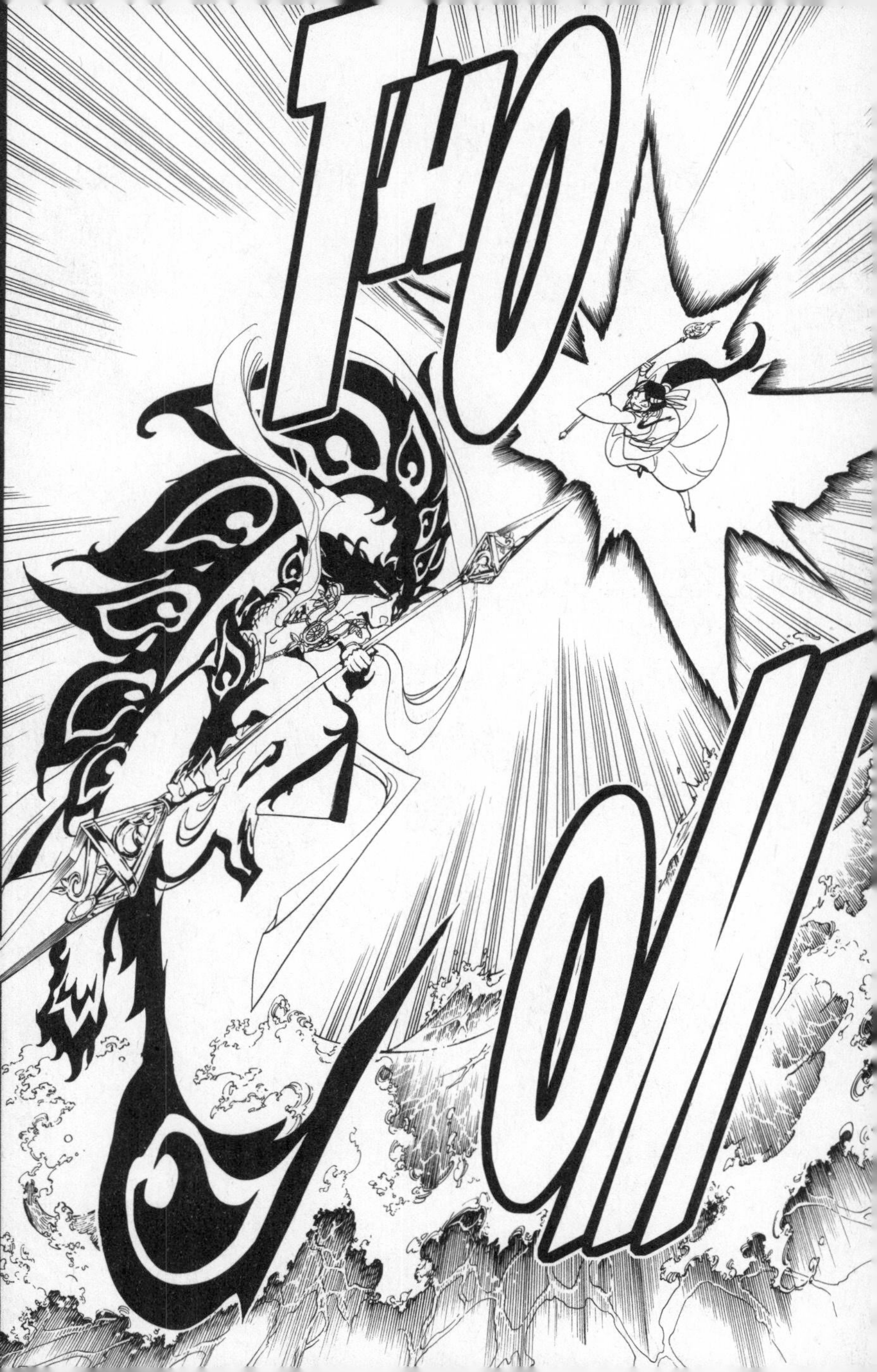
THOOM

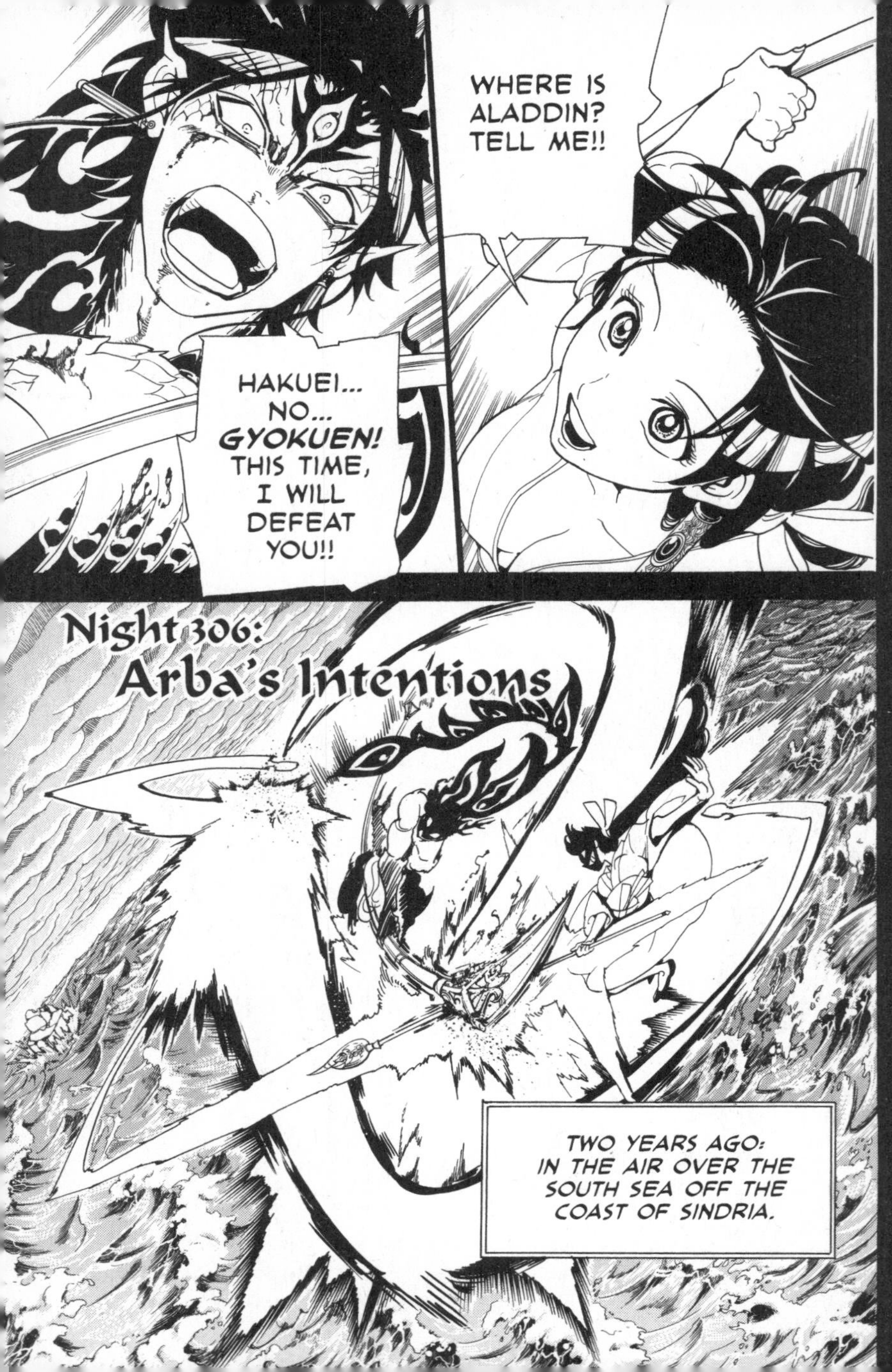
WHERE IS ALADDIN? TELL ME!!
HAKUEI... NO... GYOKUEN! THIS TIME, I WILL DEFEAT YOU!!
Night 306: Arba's Intentions
TWO YEARS AGO: IN THE AIR OVER THE SOUTH SEA OFF THE COAST OF SINDRIA.

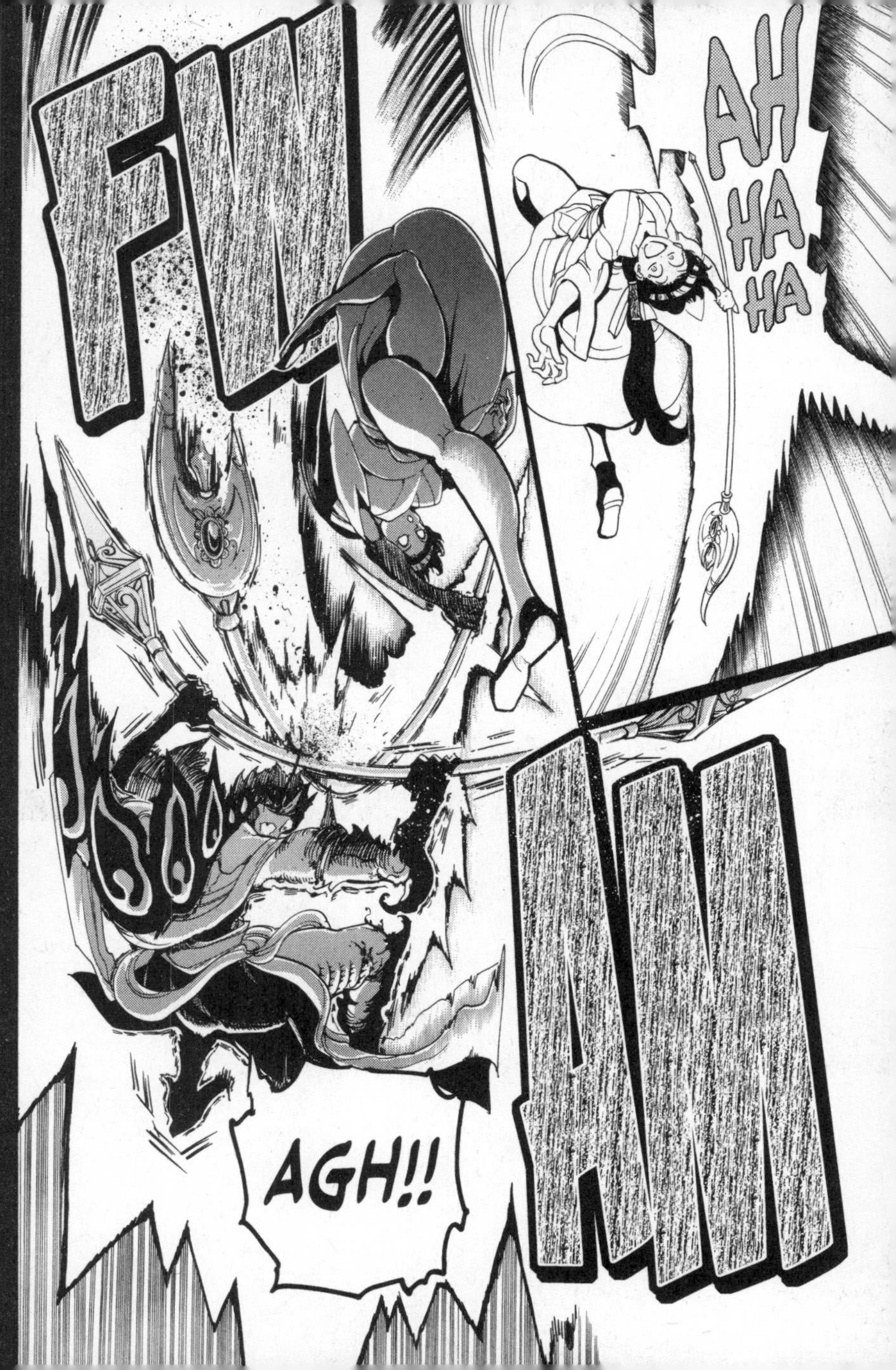
AH HA HA HA
FW
AM
AGH!!

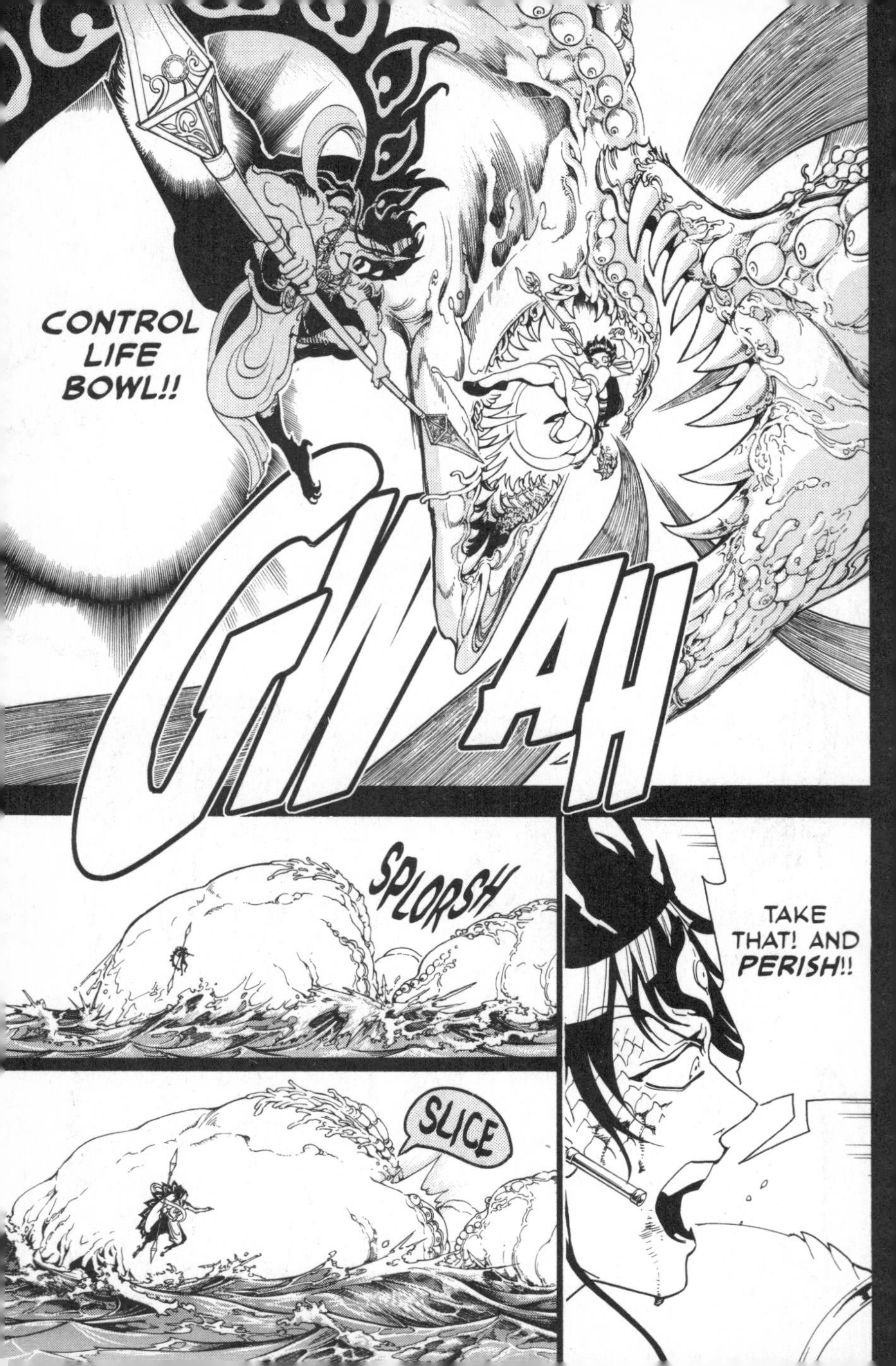
CONTROL LIFE BOWL!!
GNAH
TAKE THAT! AND PERISH!!
SPLORSH
SLICE

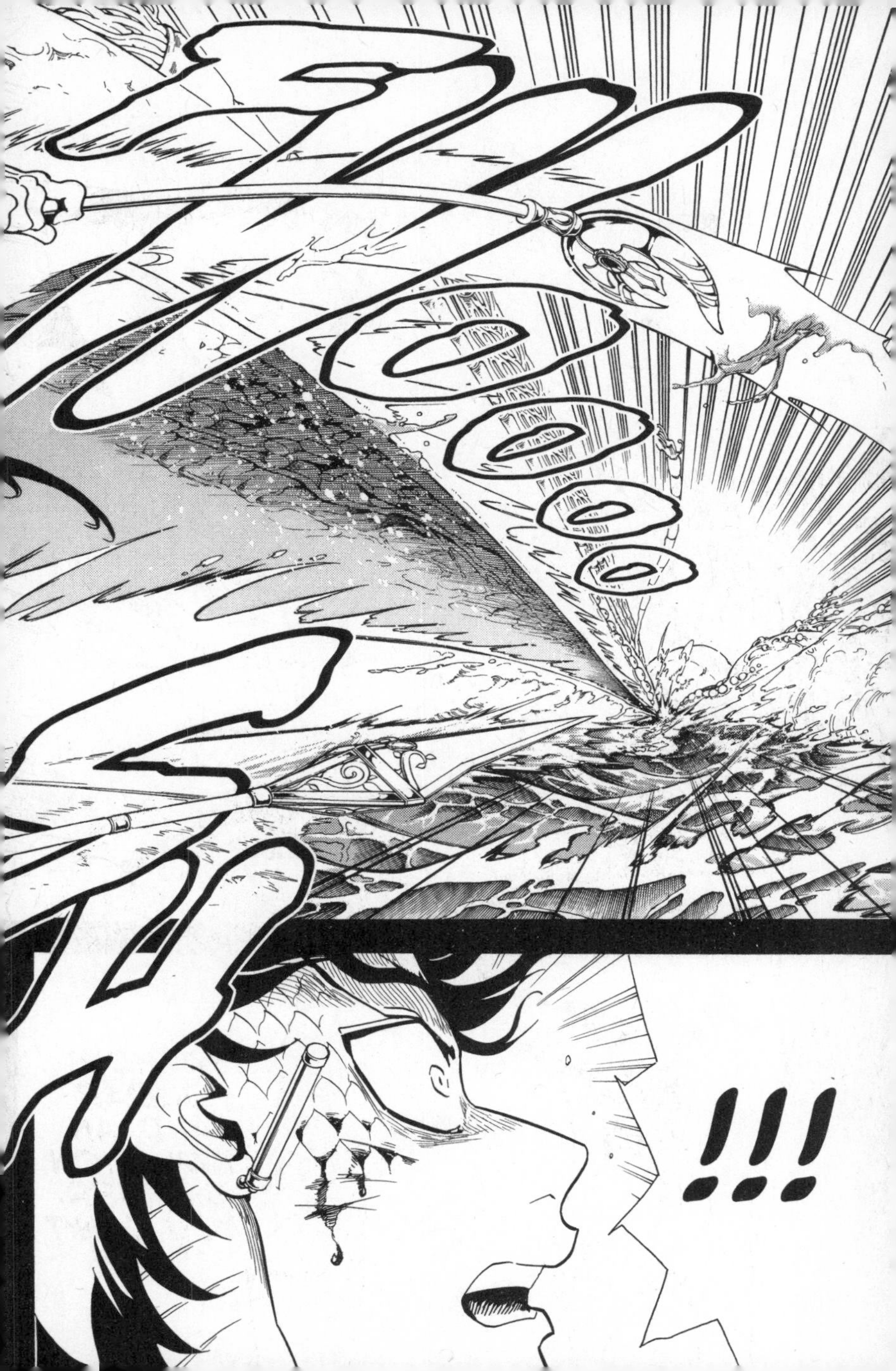
!!!

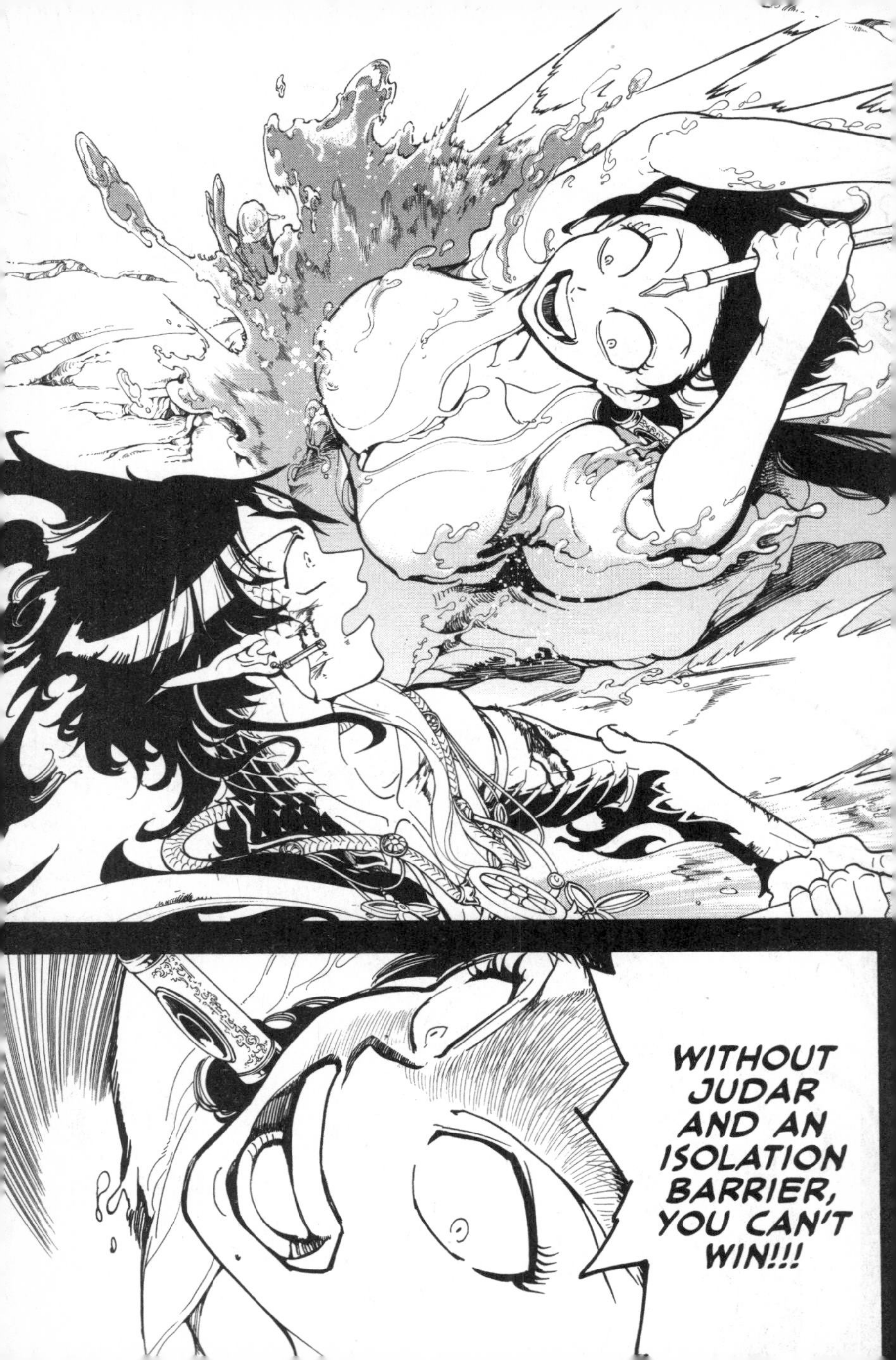
WITHOUT JUDAR AND AN ISOLATION BARRIER, YOU CAN'T WIN!!!

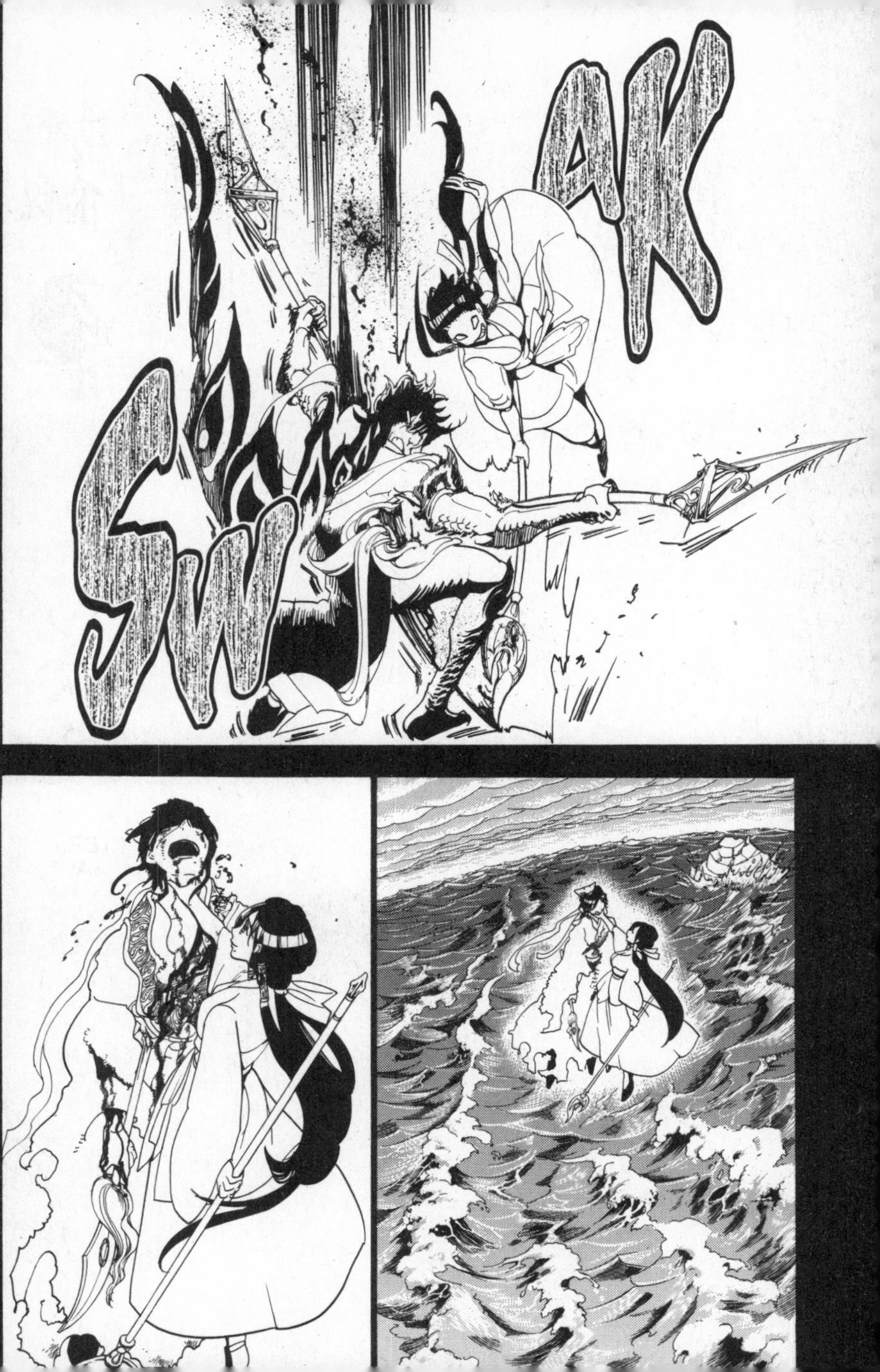
SWAK

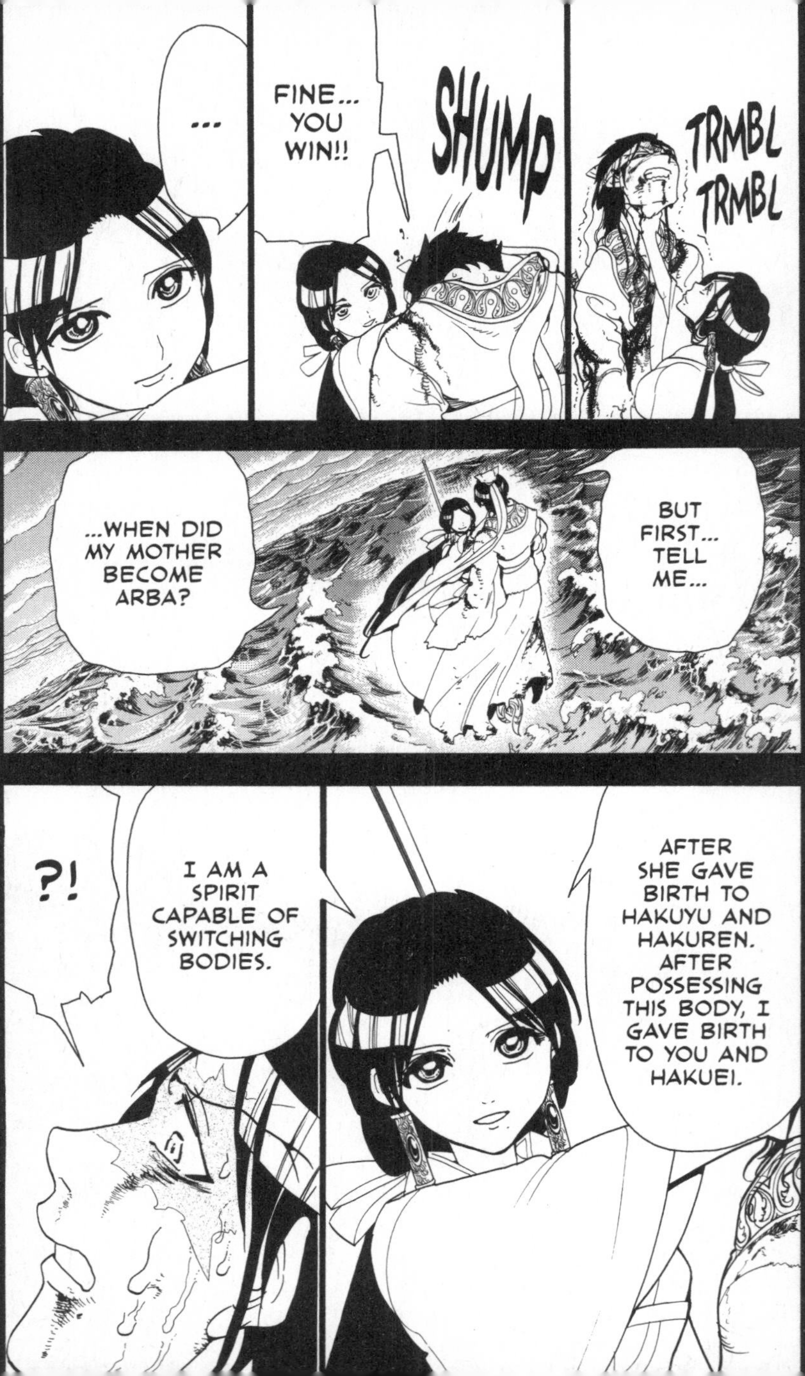
TRMBL TRMBL
SHUMP
FINE... YOU WIN!!
...
BUT FIRST... TELL ME...
...WHEN DID MY MOTHER BECOME ARBA?
AFTER SHE GAVE BIRTH TO HAKUYU AND HAKUREN. AFTER POSSESSING THIS BODY, I GAVE BIRTH TO YOU AND HAKUEI.
I AM A SPIRIT CAPABLE OF SWITCHING BODIES.
?!

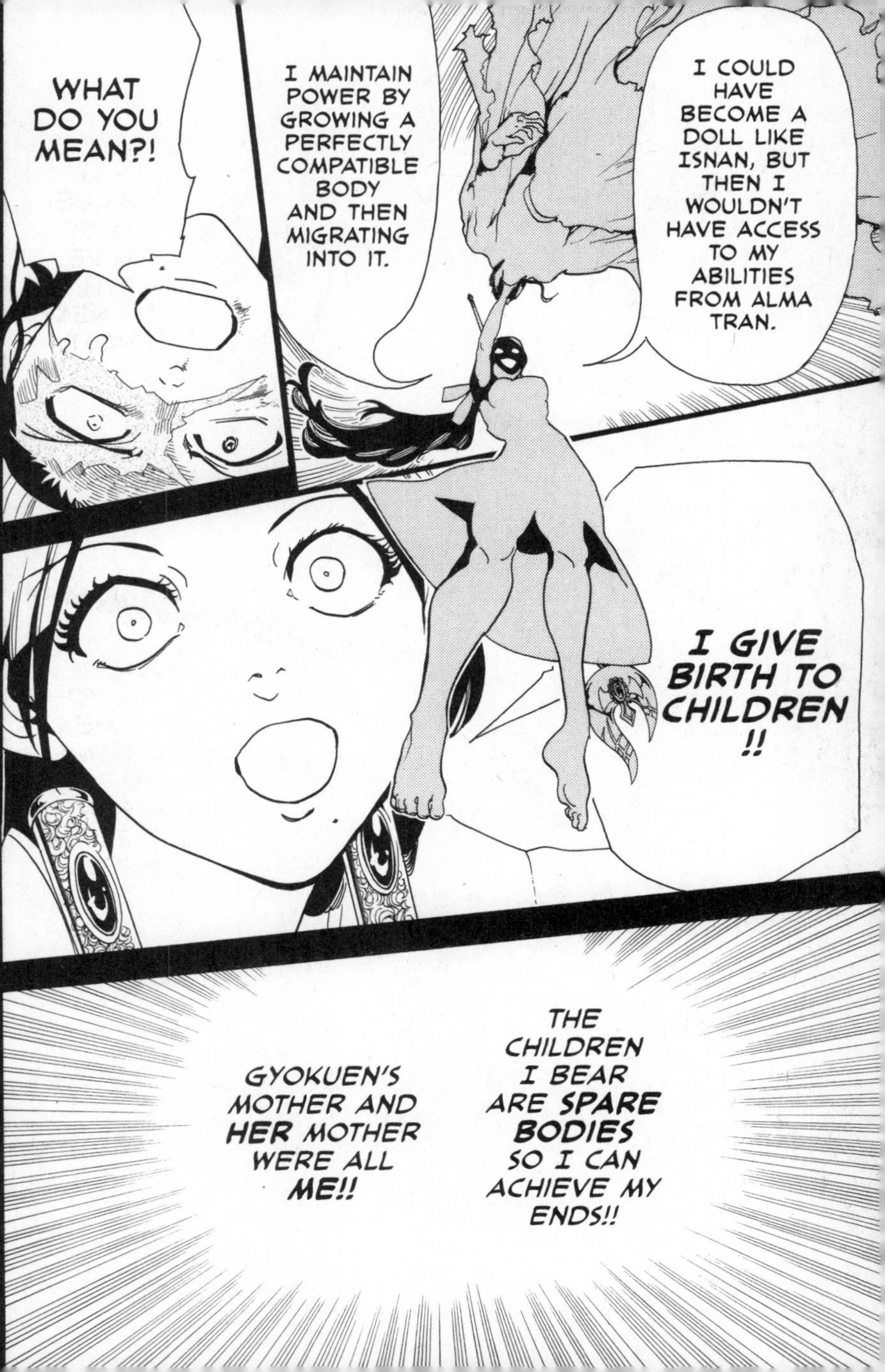
I COULD HAVE BECOME A DOLL LIKE ISNAN, BUT THEN I WOULDN'T HAVE ACCESS TO MY ABILITIES FROM ALMA TRAN.
I MAINTAIN POWER BY GROWING A PERFECTLY COMPATIBLE BODY AND THEN MIGRATING INTO IT.
WHAT DO YOU MEAN?!
I GIVE BIRTH TO CHILDREN!!
THE CHILDREN I BEAR ARE SPARE BODIES SO I CAN ACHIEVE MY ENDS!!
GYOKUEN'S MOTHER AND HER MOTHER WERE ALL ME!!

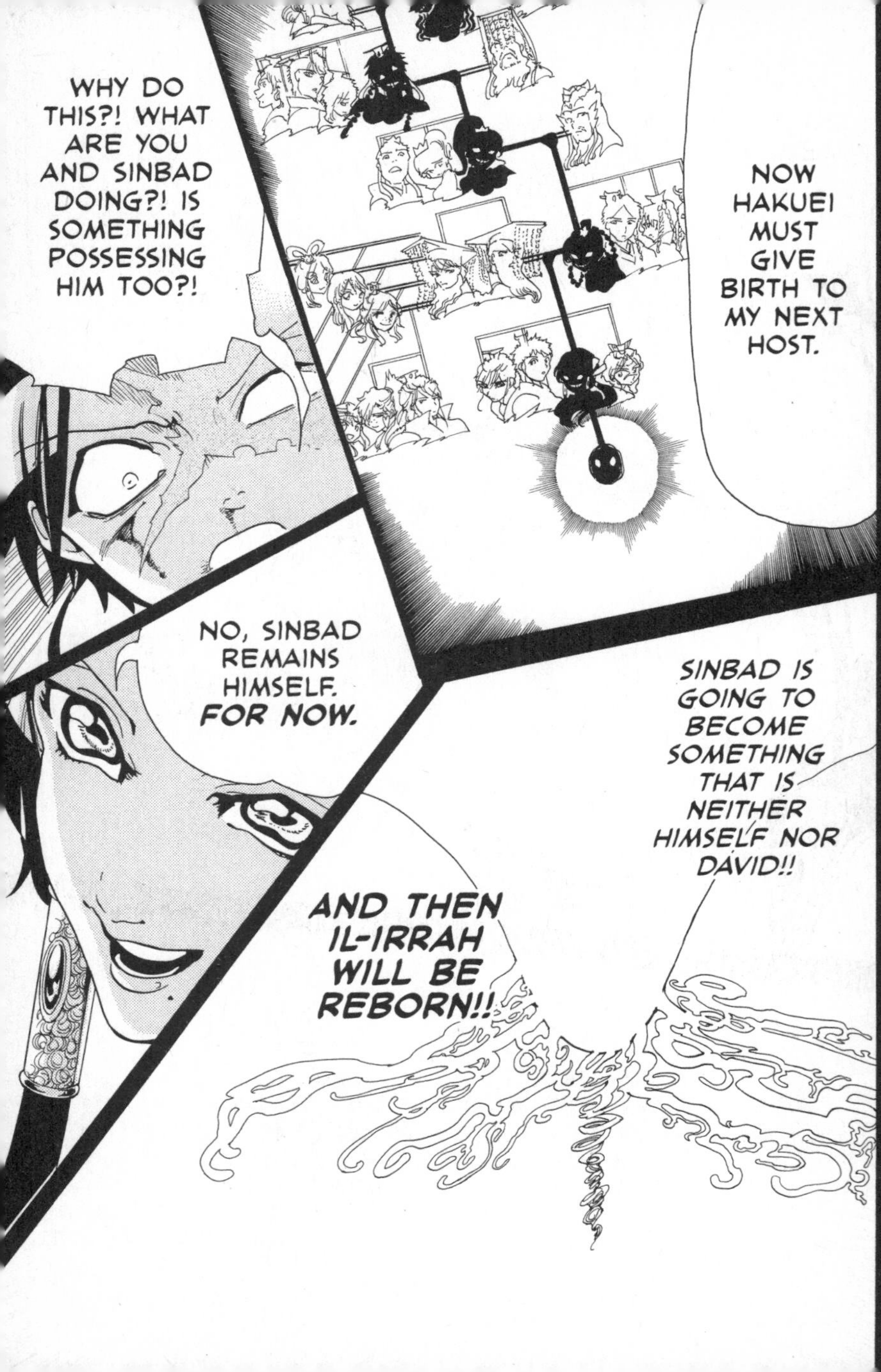
NOW HAKUEI MUST GIVE BIRTH TO MY NEXT HOST.
WHY DO THIS?! WHAT ARE YOU AND SINBAD DOING?! IS SOMETHING POSSESSING HIM TOO?!
NO, SINBAD REMAINS HIMSELF. *FOR NOW.*
SINBAD IS GOING TO BECOME SOMETHING THAT IS NEITHER HIMSELF NOR DAVID!!
AND THEN IL-IRRAH WILL BE REBORN!!

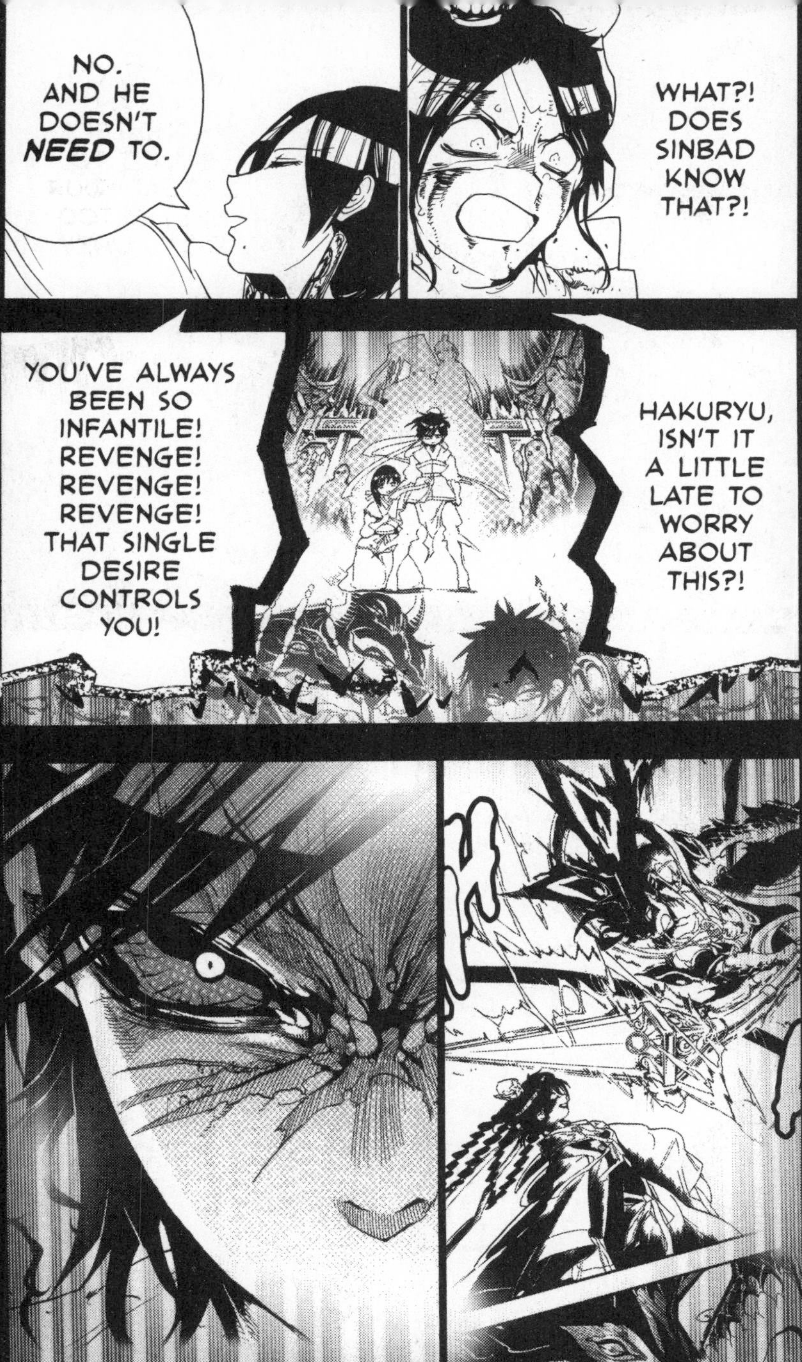
WHAT?! DOES SINBAD KNOW THAT?!
NO. AND HE DOESN'T *NEED* TO.
HAKURYU, ISN'T IT A LITTLE LATE TO WORRY ABOUT THIS?!
YOU'VE ALWAYS BEEN SO INFANTILE! REVENGE! REVENGE! REVENGE! THAT SINGLE DESIRE CONTROLS YOU!

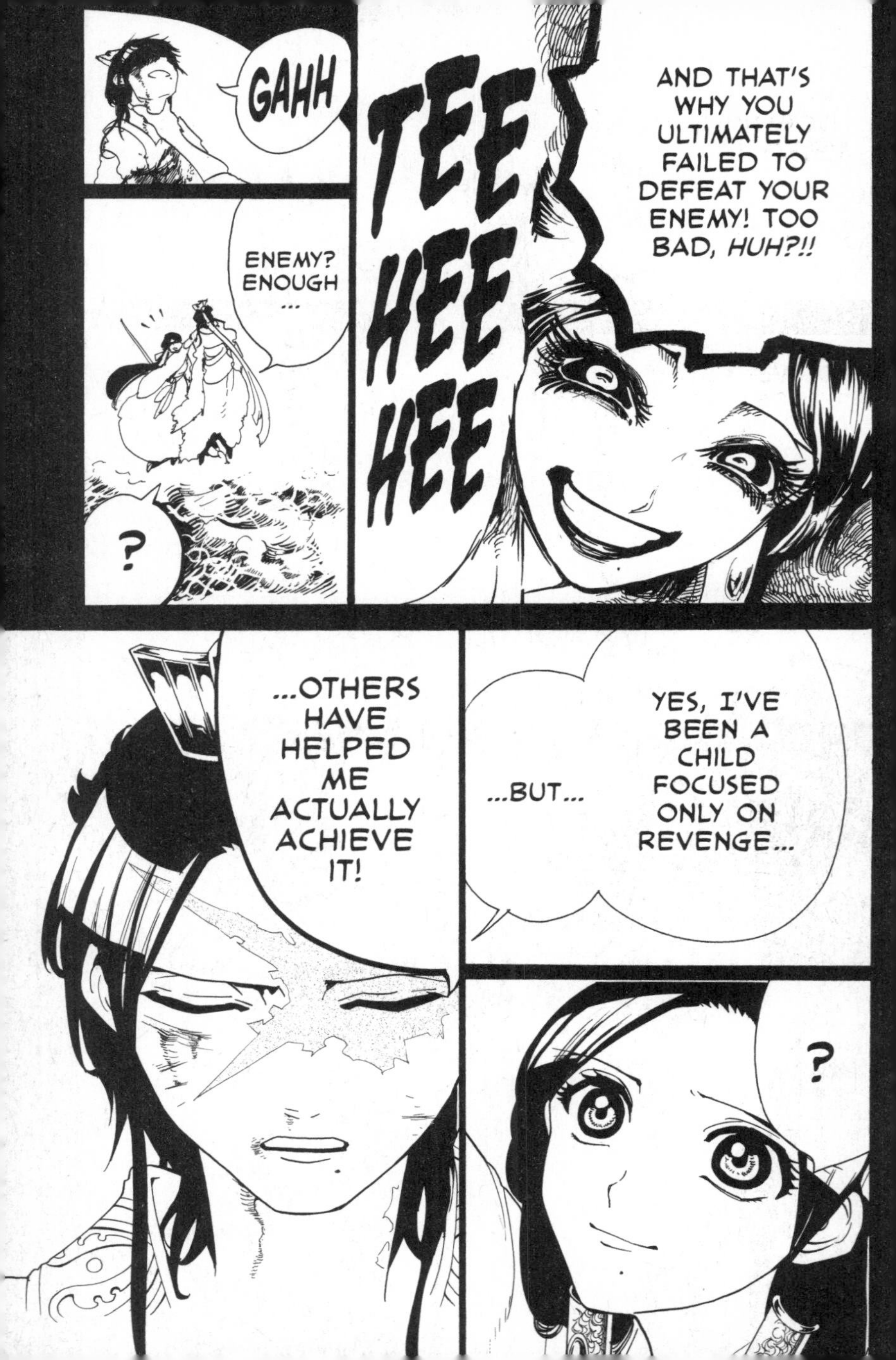
AND THAT'S WHY YOU ULTIMATELY FAILED TO DEFEAT YOUR ENEMY! TOO BAD, *HUH?!!*
TEE HEE HEE HEE
GAHH
ENEMY? ENOUGH ...
?
YES, I'VE BEEN A CHILD FOCUSED ONLY ON REVENGE...
...BUT...
?
...OTHERS HAVE HELPED ME ACTUALLY ACHIEVE IT!

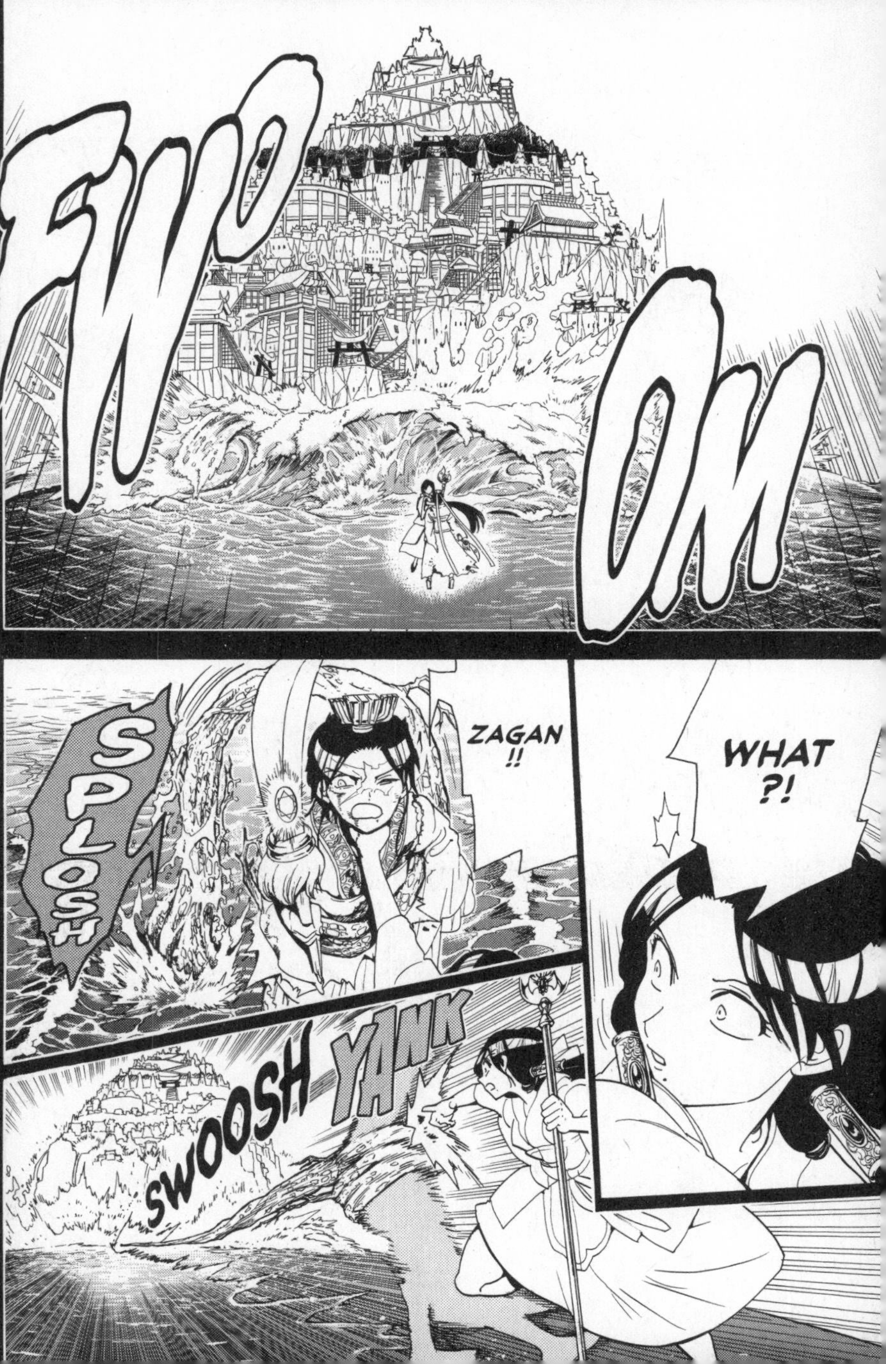
FWOOM
WHAT ?!
ZAGAN !!
SPLOSH
YANK
SWOOSH

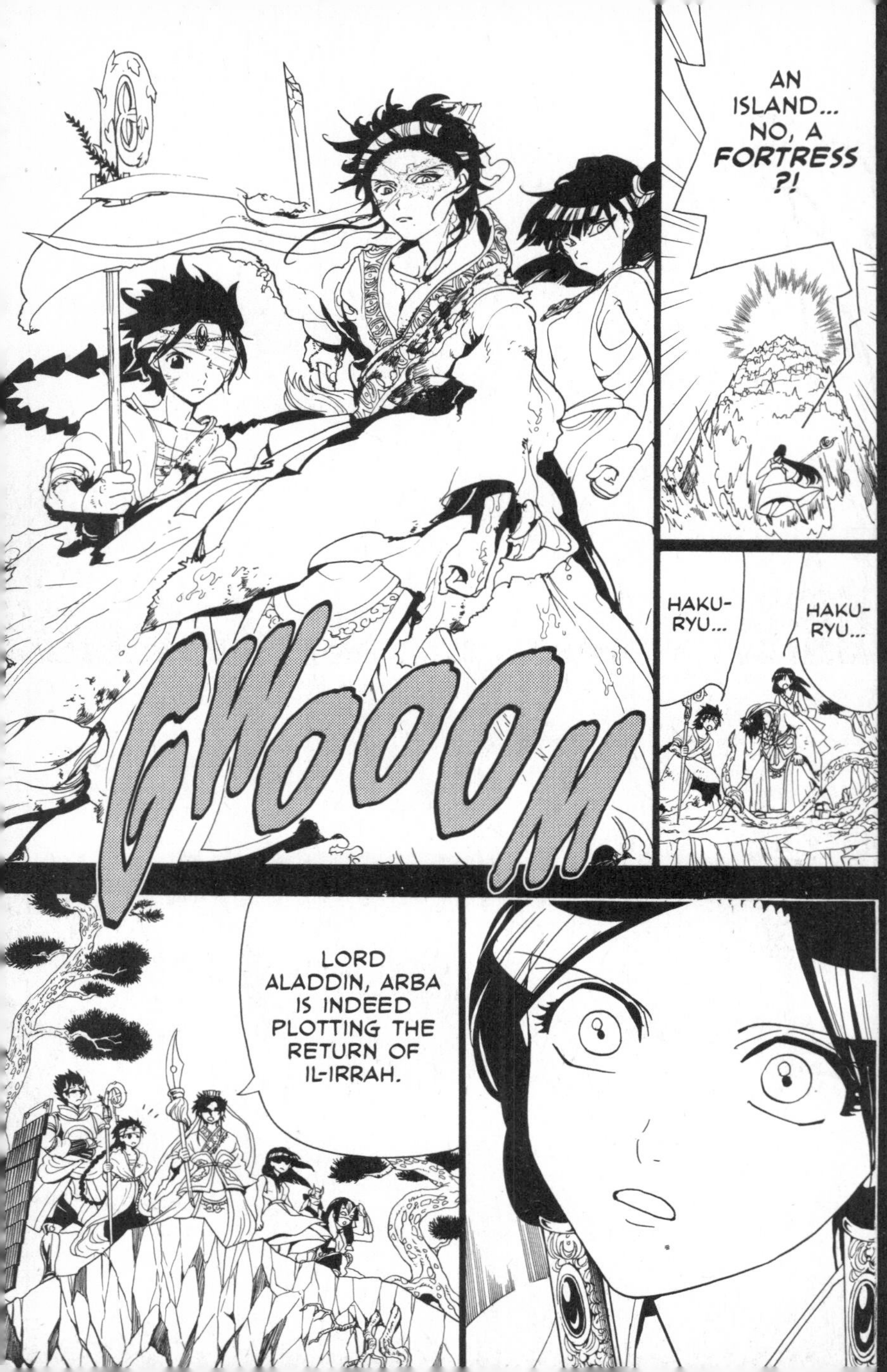
AN ISLAND... NO, A FORTRESS ?!
HAKU-RYU...
HAKU-RYU...
GWOOOM
LORD ALADDIN, ARBA IS INDEED PLOTTING THE RETURN OF IL-IRRAH.

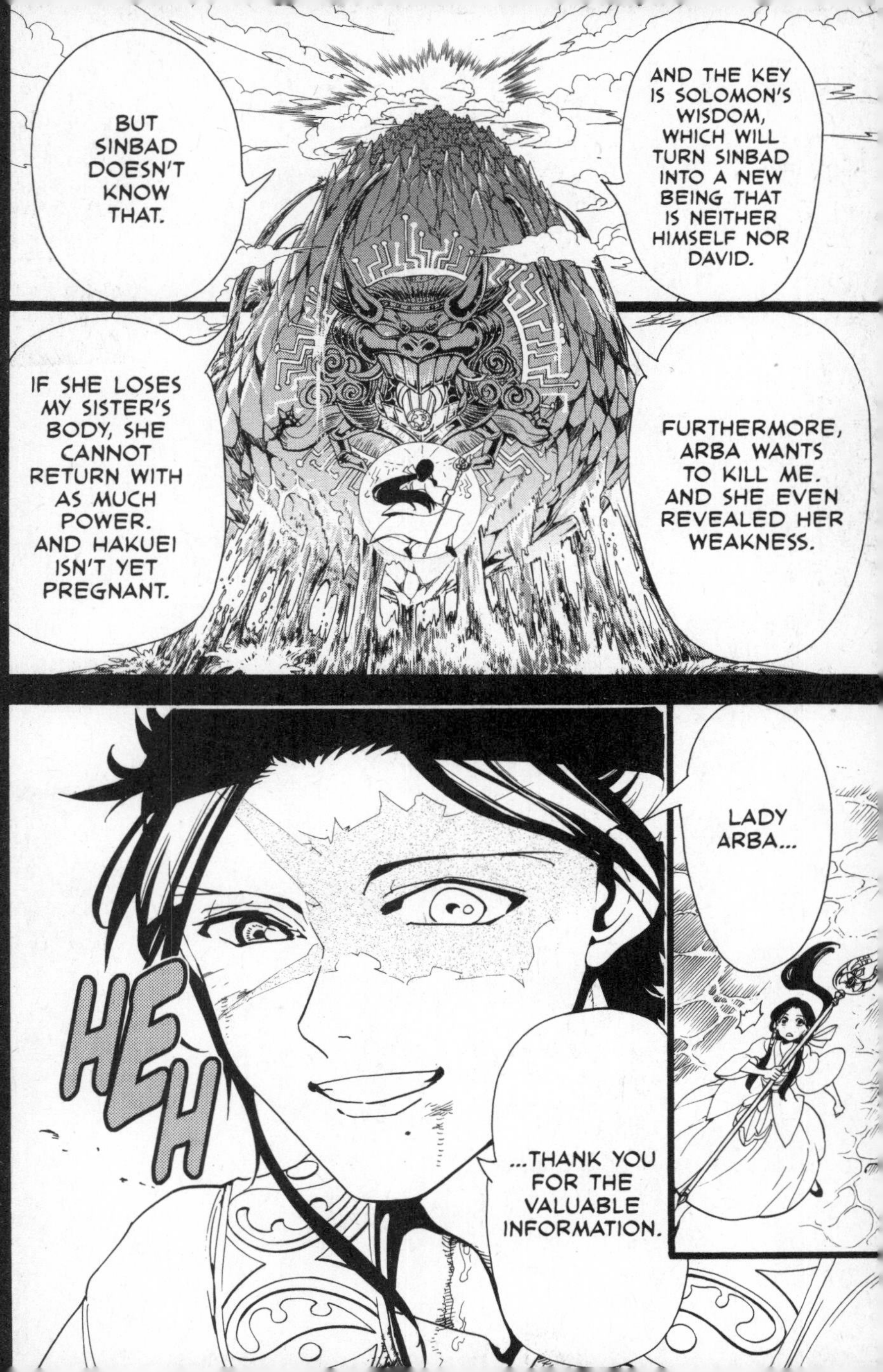
AND THE KEY IS SOLOMON'S WISDOM, WHICH WILL TURN SINBAD INTO A NEW BEING THAT IS NEITHER HIMSELF NOR DAVID.
BUT SINBAD DOESN'T KNOW THAT.
FURTHERMORE, ARBA WANTS TO KILL ME. AND SHE EVEN REVEALED HER WEAKNESS.
IF SHE LOSES MY SISTER'S BODY, SHE CANNOT RETURN WITH AS MUCH POWER. AND HAKUEI ISN'T YET PREGNANT.
LADY ARBA...
...THANK YOU FOR THE VALUABLE INFORMATION.
HEHEH

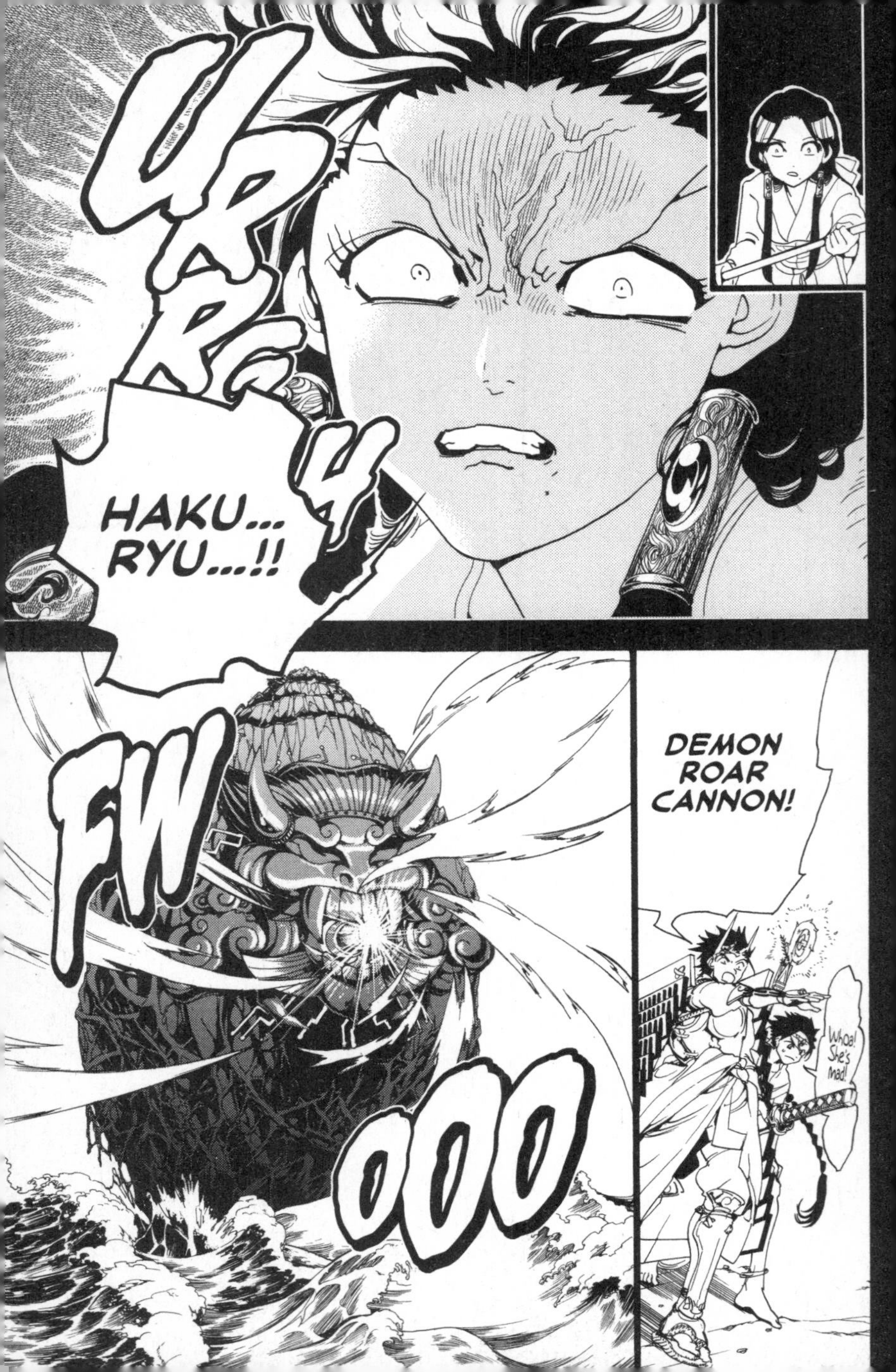
HAKU... RYU...!!
DEMON ROAR CANNON!
Whoa! She's mad!
FWOOOO

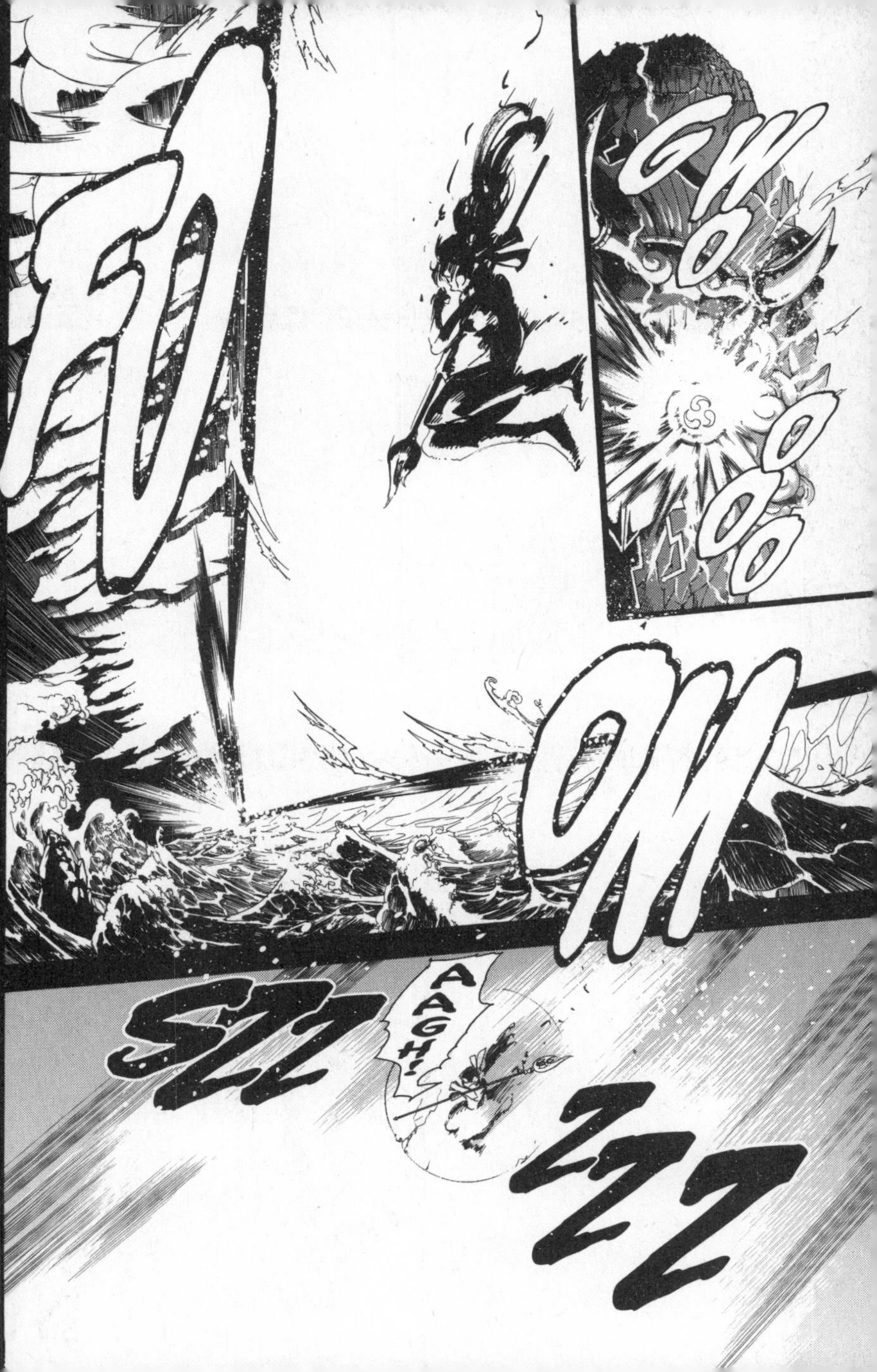
AAGH!

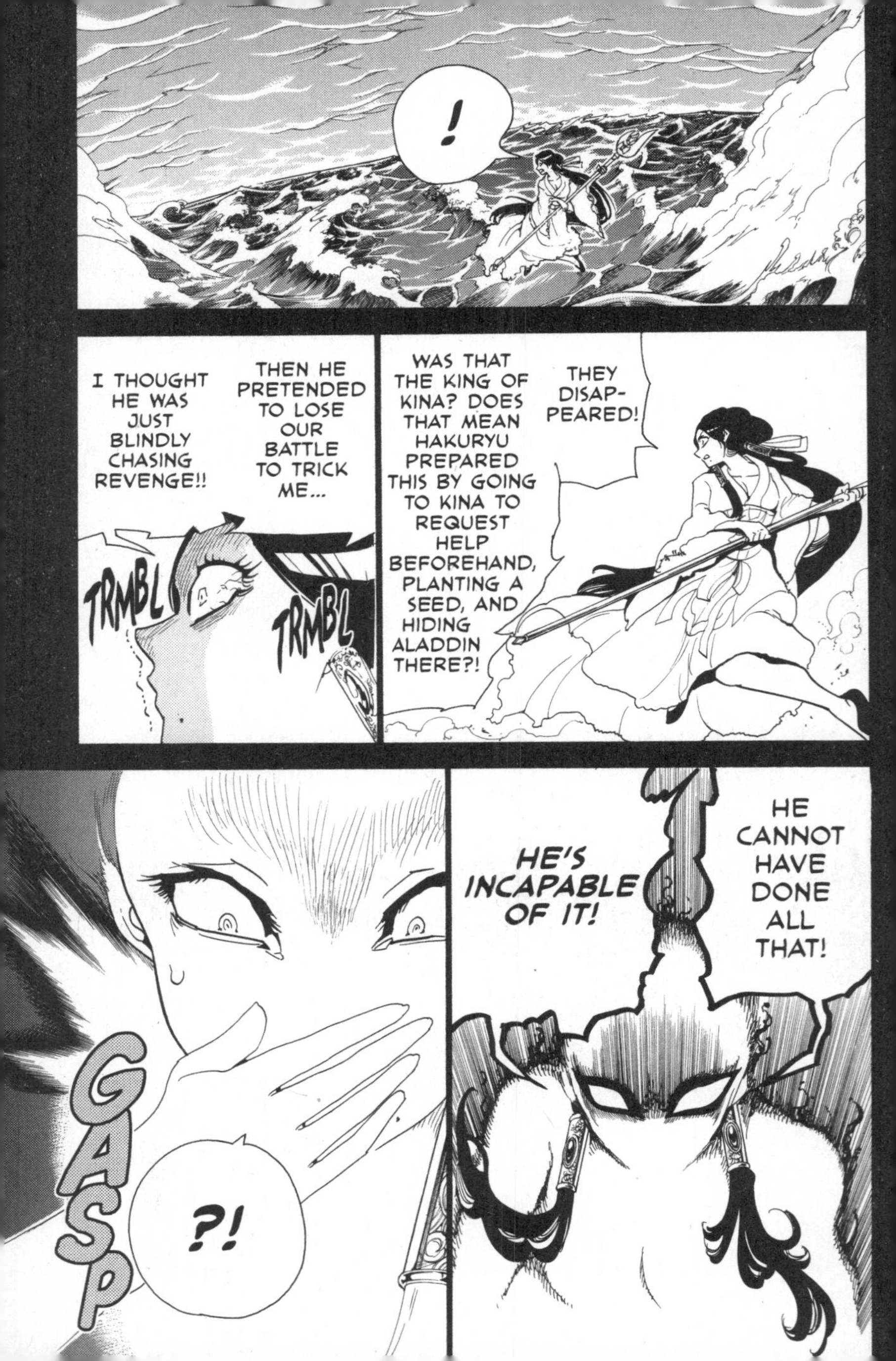
!
THEY DISAPPEARED!
WAS THAT THE KING OF KINA? DOES THAT MEAN HAKURYU PREPARED THIS BY GOING TO KINA TO REQUEST HELP BEFOREHAND, PLANTING A SEED, AND HIDING ALADDIN THERE?!
THEN HE PRETENDED TO LOSE OUR BATTLE TO TRICK ME...
I THOUGHT HE WAS JUST BLINDLY CHASING REVENGE!!
TRMBL
TRMBL
HE CANNOT HAVE DONE ALL THAT!
HE'S INCAPABLE OF IT!
?!
GASP

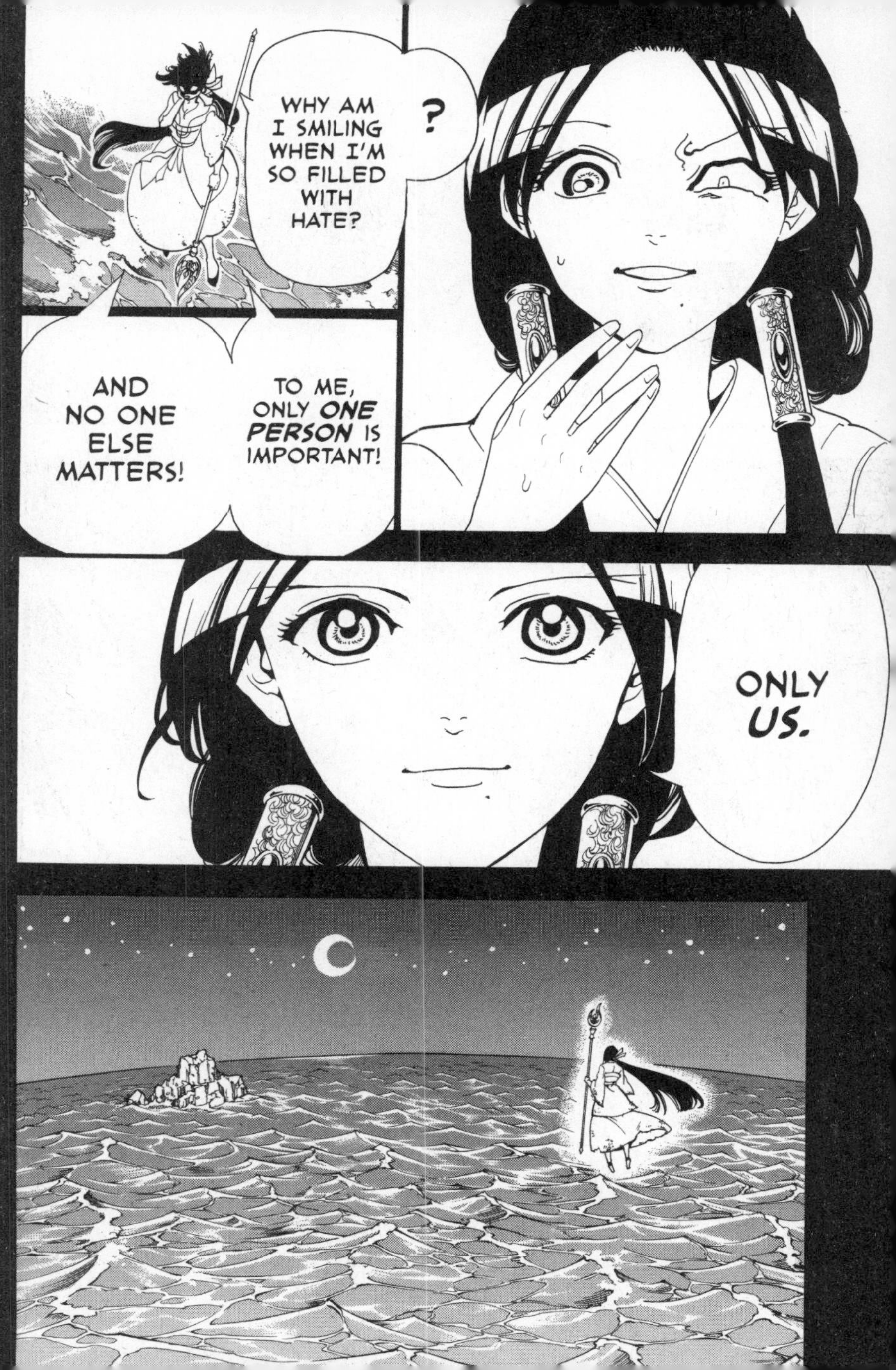
?
WHY AM I SMILING WHEN I'M SO FILLED WITH HATE?
TO ME, ONLY ONE PERSON IS IMPORTANT!
AND NO ONE ELSE MATTERS!
ONLY US.

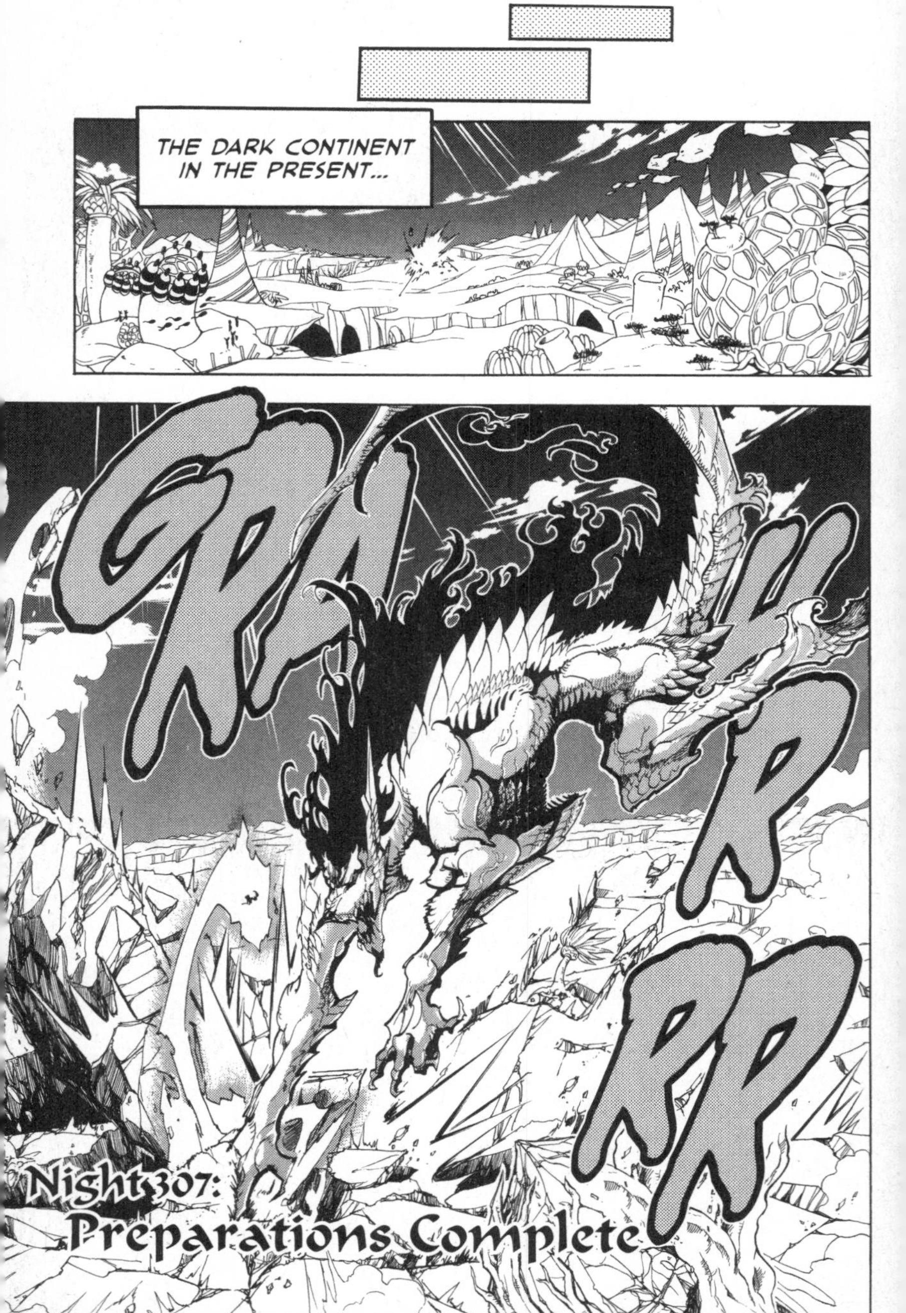
THE DARK CONTINENT IN THE PRESENT...
GRAARRR

Night 307: Preparations Complete

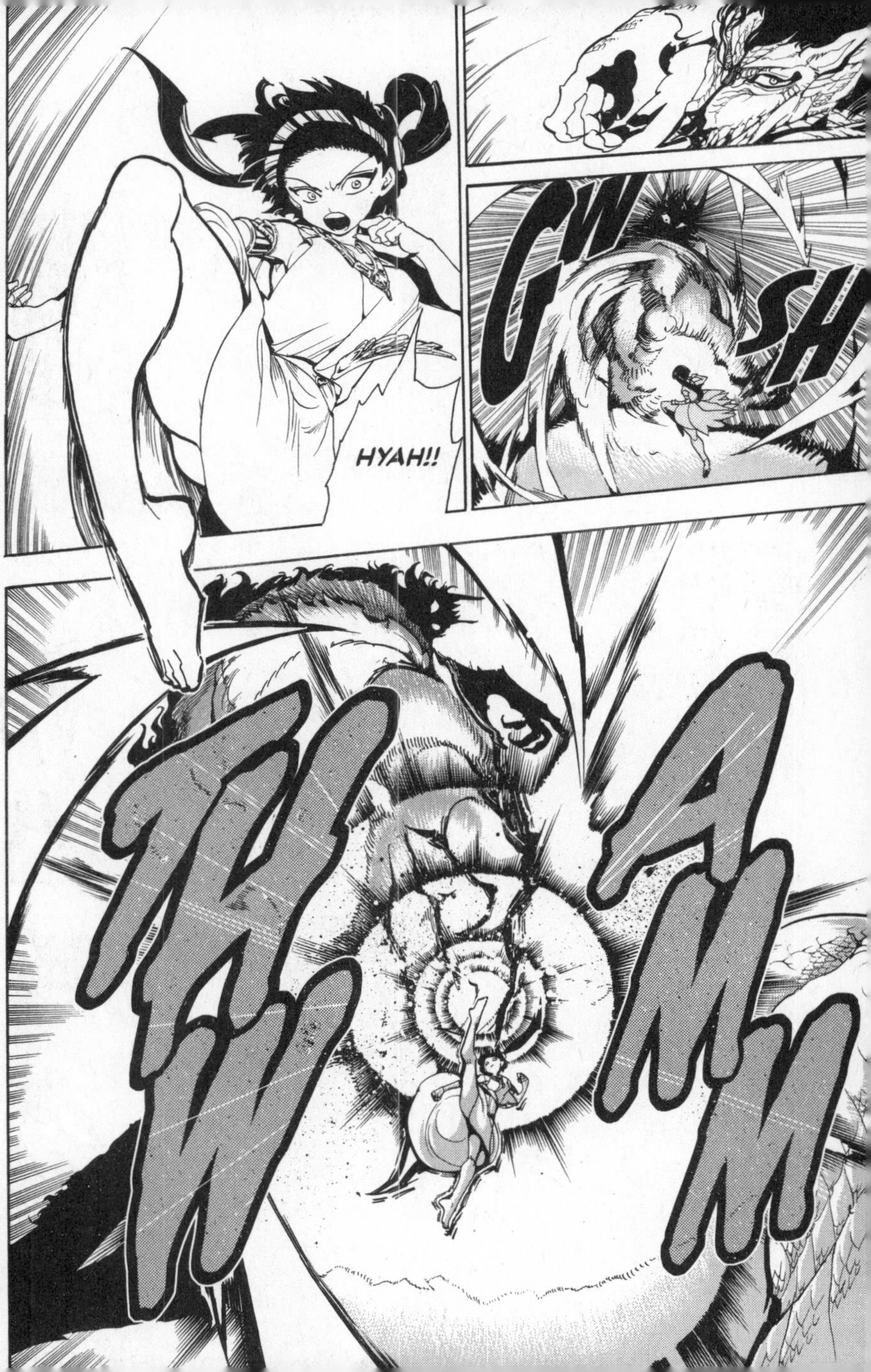
GWSH
HYAH!!
WHAMMM

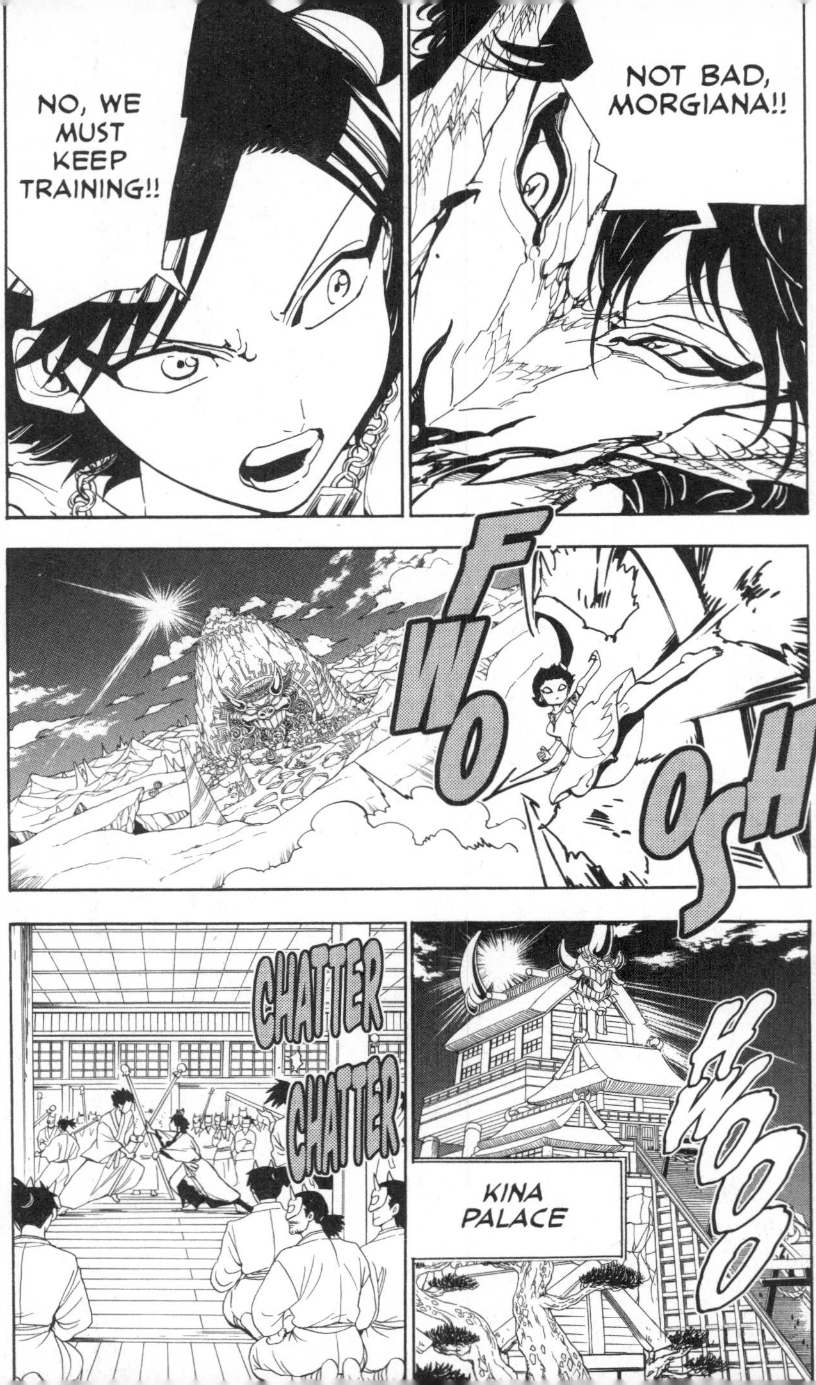
NOT BAD, MORGIANA!!
NO, WE MUST KEEP TRAINING!!
FWOOSH
KINA PALACE
HWOOOO
CHATTER
CHATTER

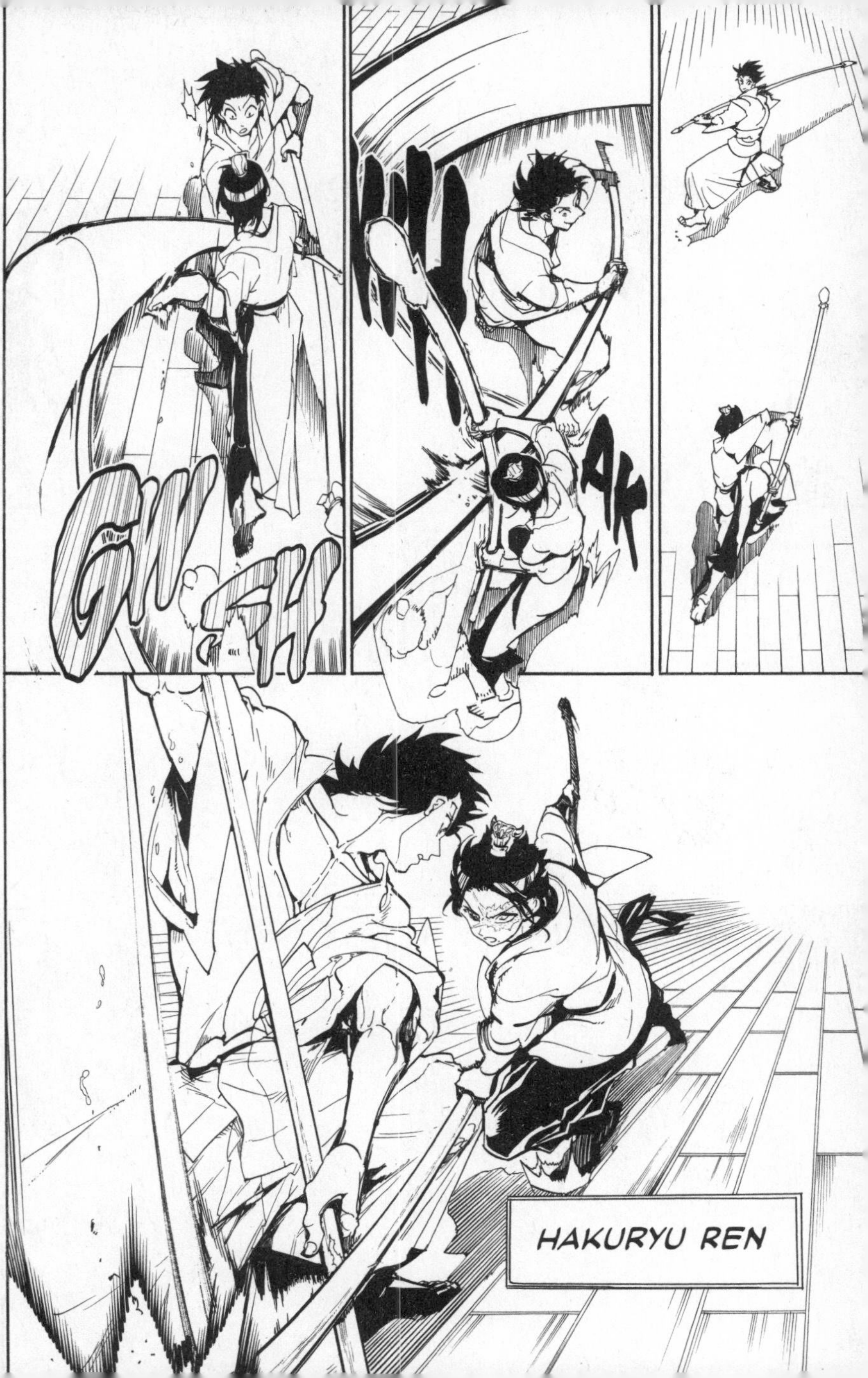
WHAK
GWSH
HAKURYU REN

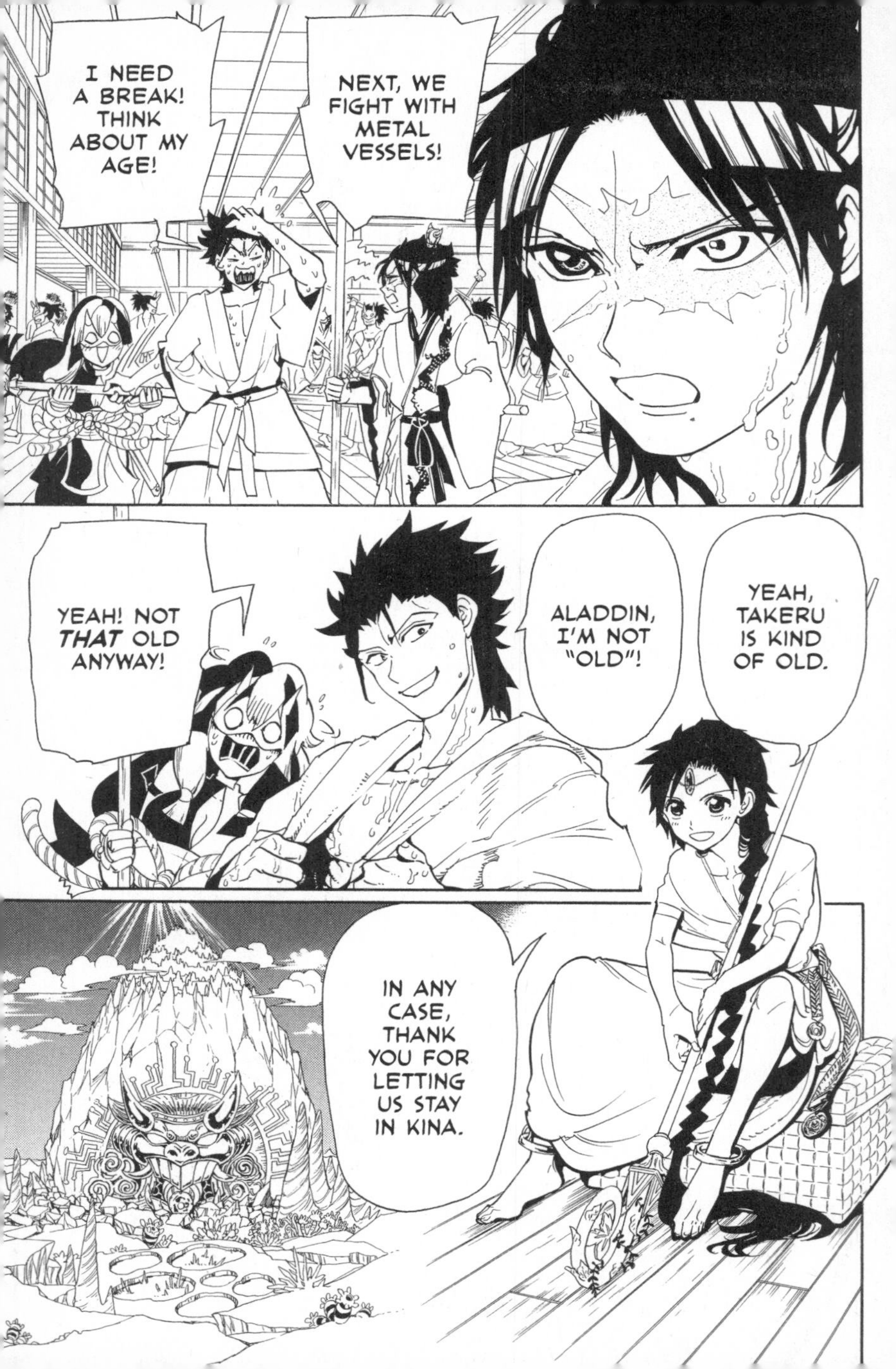
NEXT, WE FIGHT WITH METAL VESSELS!
I NEED A BREAK! THINK ABOUT MY AGE!
YEAH, TAKERU IS KIND OF OLD.
ALADDIN, I'M NOT "OLD"!
YEAH! NOT *THAT* OLD ANYWAY!
IN ANY CASE, THANK YOU FOR LETTING US STAY IN KINA.

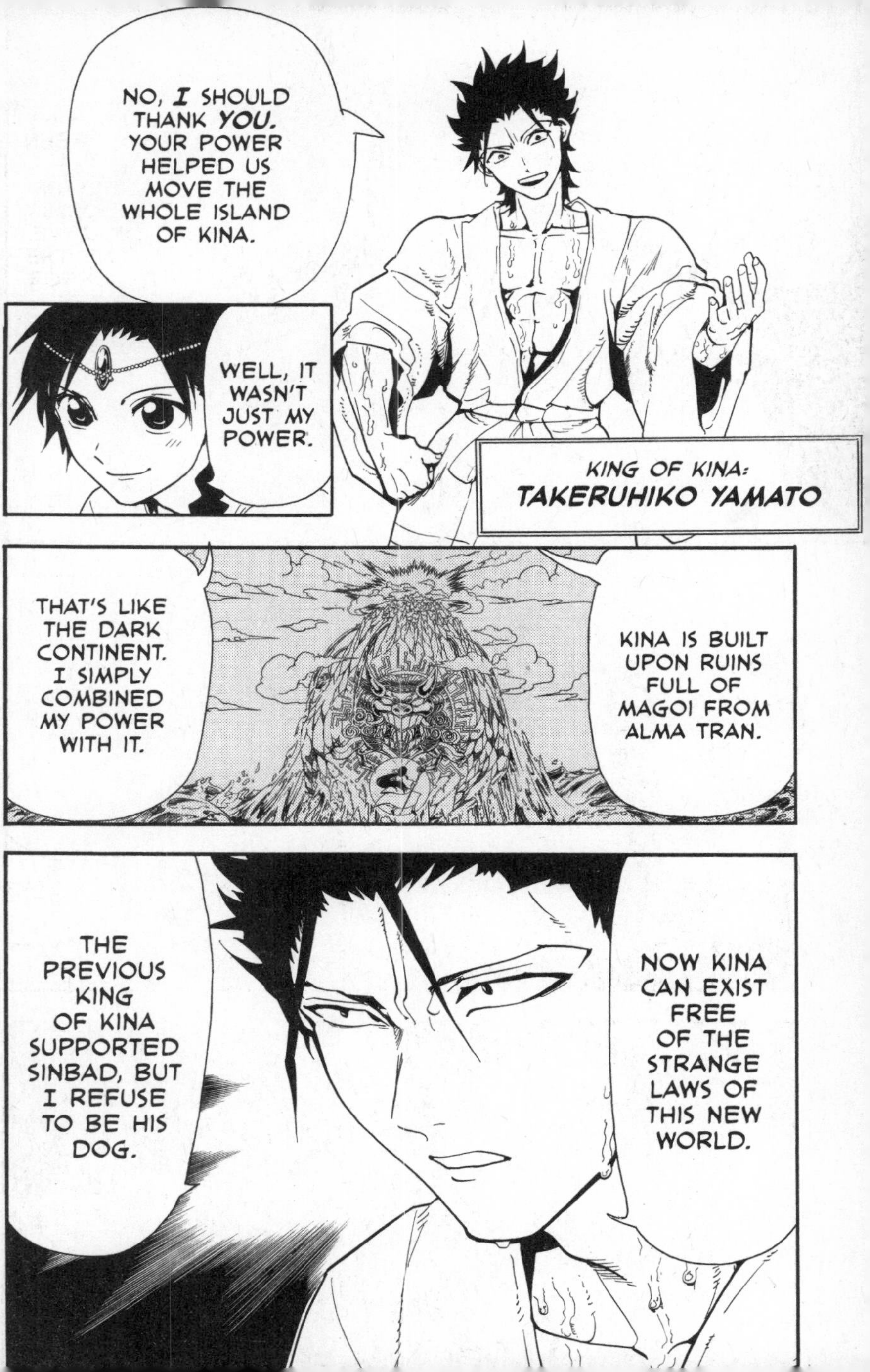
NO, *I* SHOULD THANK *YOU.* YOUR POWER HELPED US MOVE THE WHOLE ISLAND OF KINA.
KING OF KINA: **TAKERUHIKO YAMATO**
WELL, IT WASN'T JUST MY POWER.
KINA IS BUILT UPON RUINS FULL OF MAGOI FROM ALMA TRAN.
THAT'S LIKE THE DARK CONTINENT. I SIMPLY COMBINED MY POWER WITH IT.
NOW KINA CAN EXIST FREE OF THE STRANGE LAWS OF THIS NEW WORLD.
THE PREVIOUS KING OF KINA SUPPORTED SINBAD, BUT I REFUSE TO BE HIS DOG.

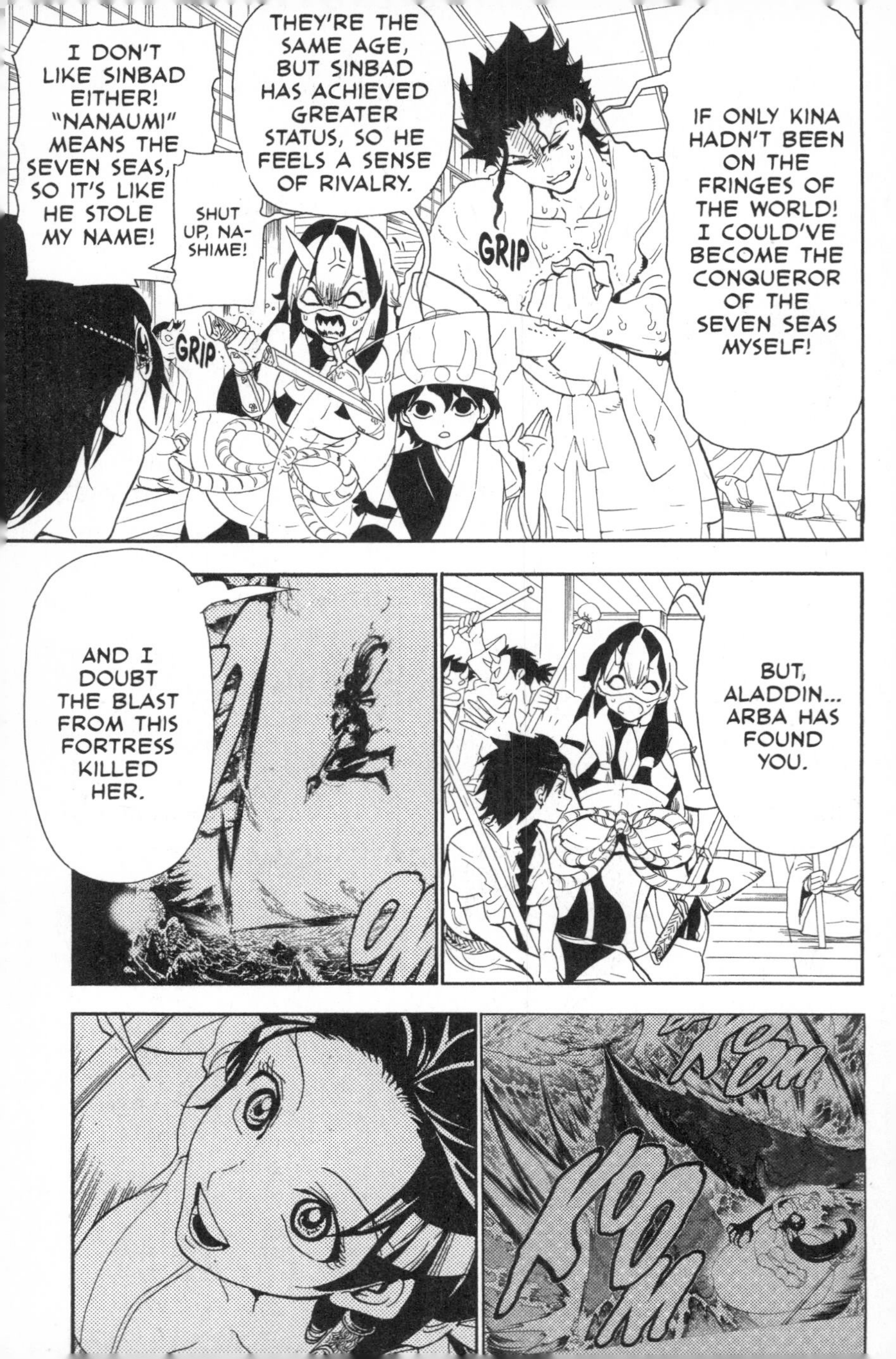
IF ONLY KINA HADN'T BEEN ON THE FRINGES OF THE WORLD! I COULD'VE BECOME THE CONQUEROR OF THE SEVEN SEAS MYSELF!
GRIP
THEY'RE THE SAME AGE, BUT SINBAD HAS ACHIEVED GREATER STATUS, SO HE FEELS A SENSE OF RIVALRY.
I DON'T LIKE SINBAD EITHER! "NANAUMI" MEANS THE SEVEN SEAS, SO IT'S LIKE HE STOLE MY NAME!
SHUT UP, NA-SHIME!
GRIP
BUT, ALADDIN... ARBA HAS FOUND YOU.
AND I DOUBT THE BLAST FROM THIS FORTRESS KILLED HER.

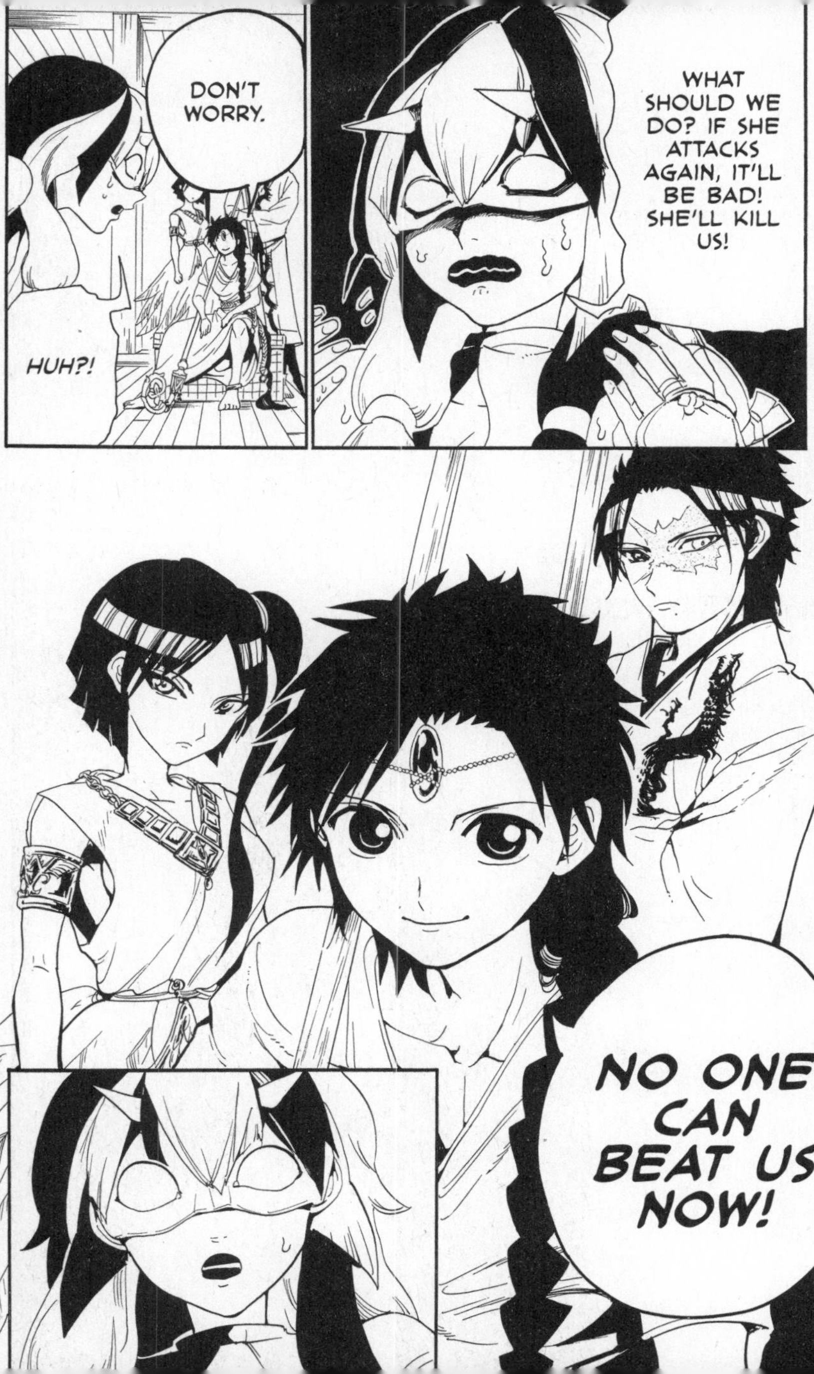
WHAT SHOULD WE DO? IF SHE ATTACKS AGAIN, IT'LL BE BAD! SHE'LL KILL US!
DON'T WORRY.
HUH?!
NO ONE CAN BEAT US NOW!

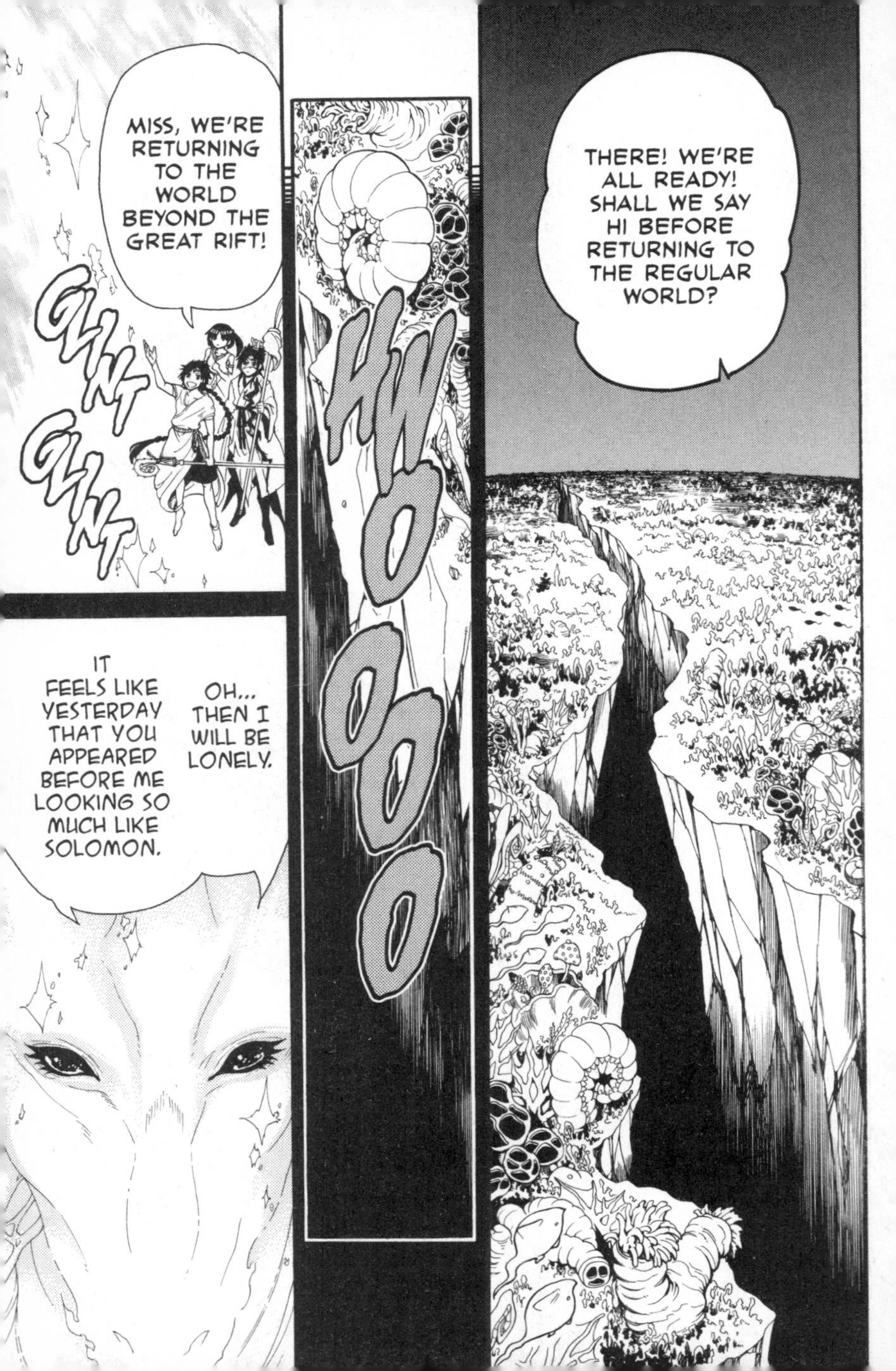
THERE! WE'RE ALL READY! SHALL WE SAY HI BEFORE RETURNING TO THE REGULAR WORLD?
HWOOOOO
MISS, WE'RE RETURNING TO THE WORLD BEYOND THE GREAT RIFT!
GLINT GLINT GLINT
OH... THEN I WILL BE LONELY.
IT FEELS LIKE YESTERDAY THAT YOU APPEARED BEFORE ME LOOKING SO MUCH LIKE SOLOMON.

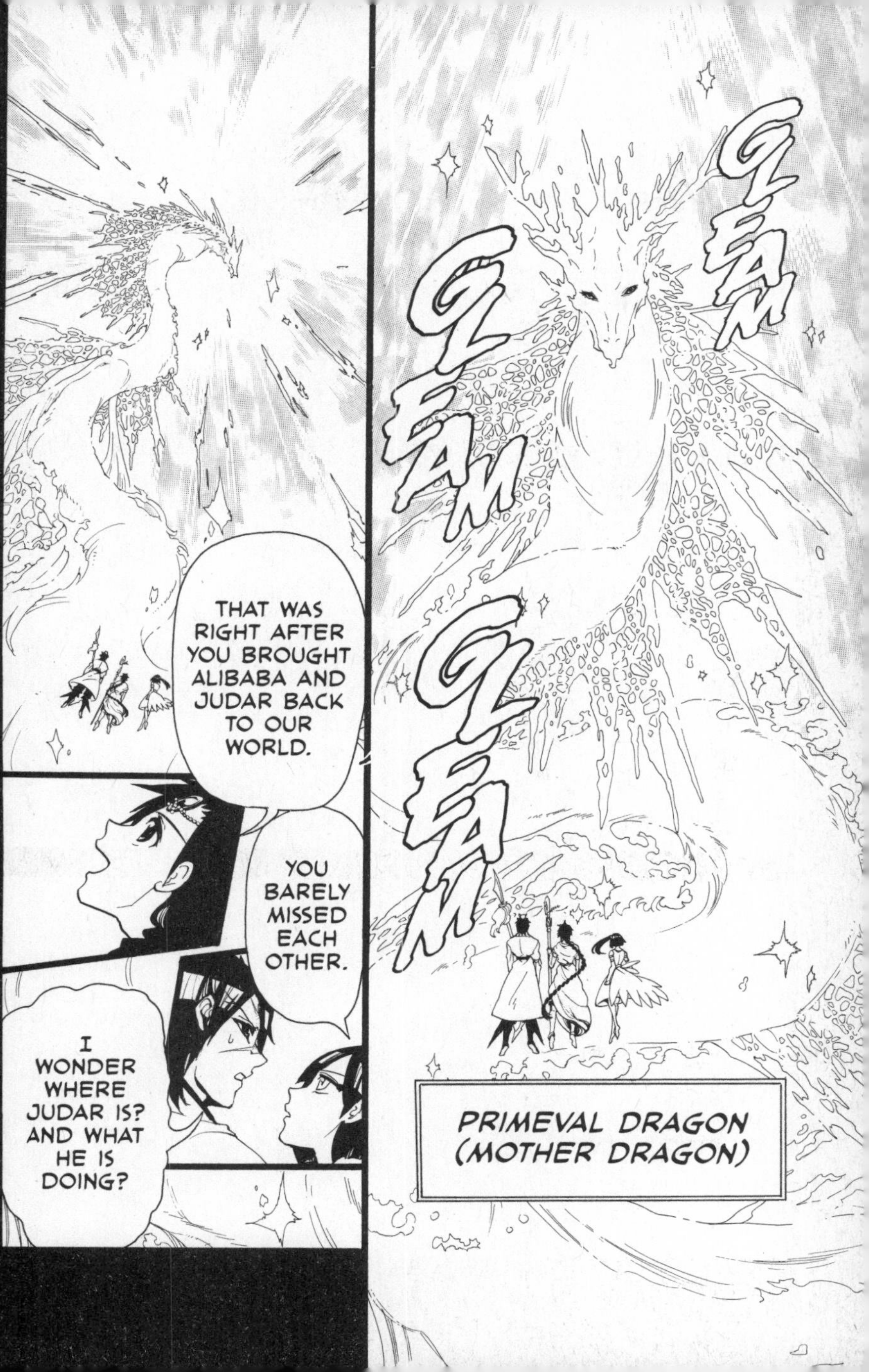
GLEAM
GLEAM
GLEAM
PRIMEVAL DRAGON (MOTHER DRAGON)
THAT WAS RIGHT AFTER YOU BROUGHT ALIBABA AND JUDAR BACK TO OUR WORLD.
YOU BARELY MISSED EACH OTHER.
I WONDER WHERE JUDAR IS? AND WHAT HE IS DOING?

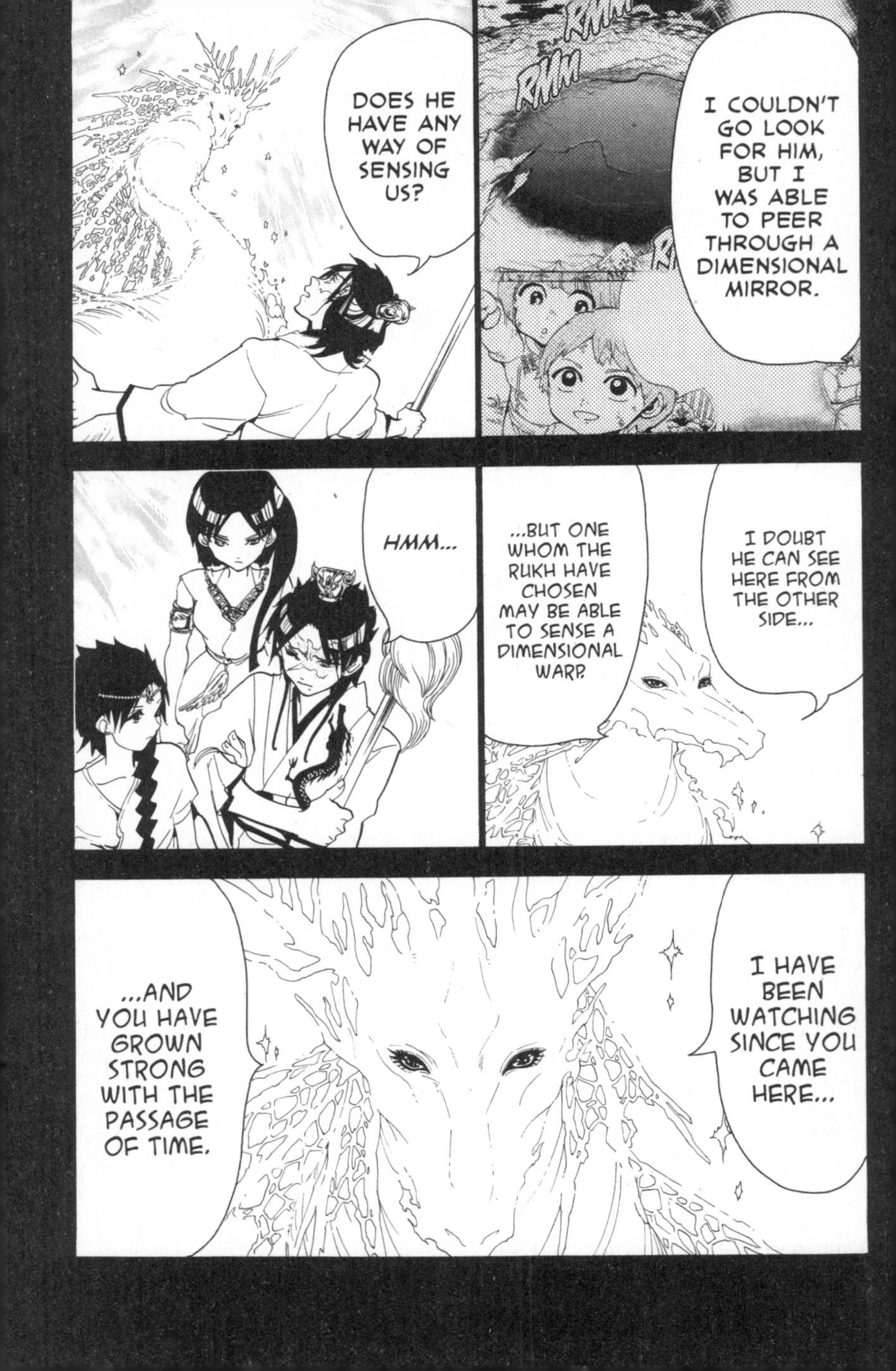
I COULDN'T GO LOOK FOR HIM, BUT I WAS ABLE TO PEER THROUGH A DIMENSIONAL MIRROR.
DOES HE HAVE ANY WAY OF SENSING US?
I DOUBT HE CAN SEE HERE FROM THE OTHER SIDE...
...BUT ONE WHOM THE RUKH HAVE CHOSEN MAY BE ABLE TO SENSE A DIMENSIONAL WARP.
HMM...
I HAVE BEEN WATCHING SINCE YOU CAME HERE...
...AND YOU HAVE GROWN STRONG WITH THE PASSAGE OF TIME.

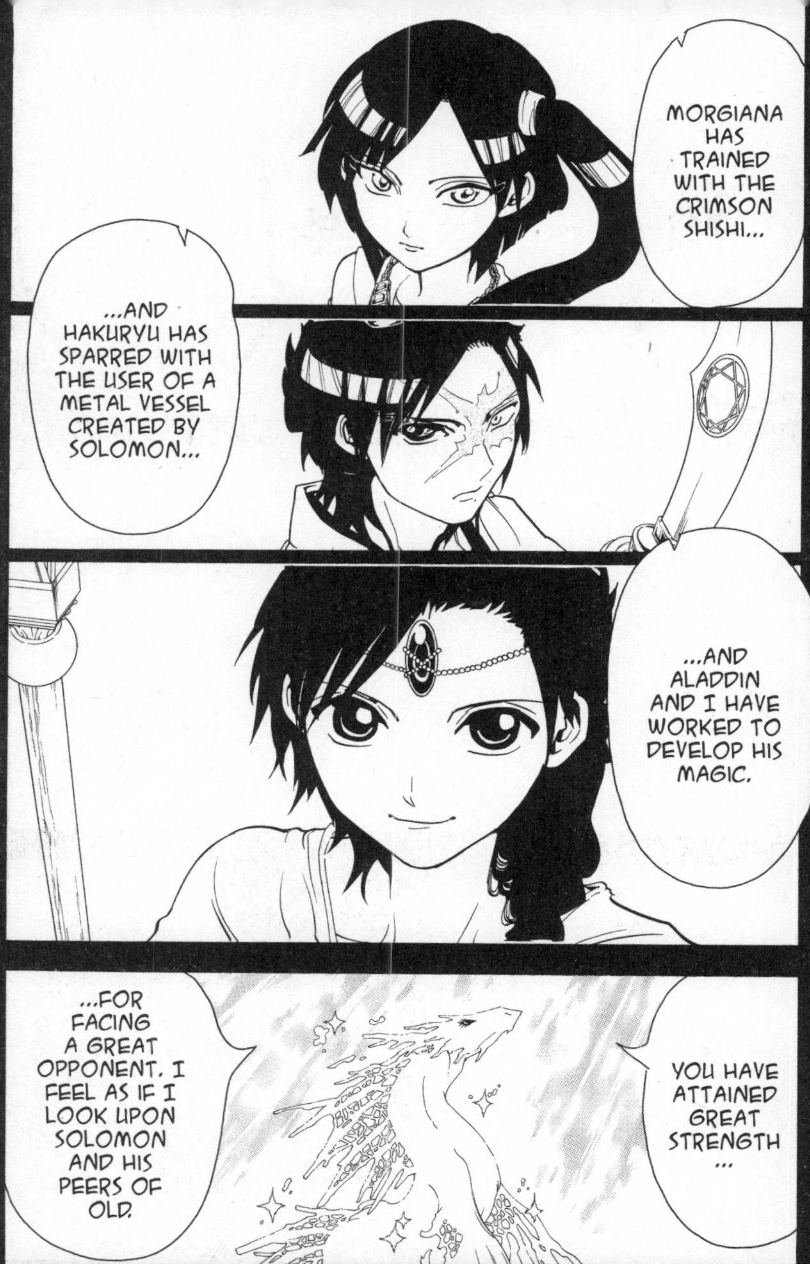
MORGIANA HAS TRAINED WITH THE CRIMSON SHISHI...
...AND HAKURYU HAS SPARRED WITH THE USER OF A METAL VESSEL CREATED BY SOLOMON...
...AND ALADDIN AND I HAVE WORKED TO DEVELOP HIS MAGIC.
YOU HAVE ATTAINED GREAT STRENGTH ...
...FOR FACING A GREAT OPPONENT. I FEEL AS IF I LOOK UPON SOLOMON AND HIS PEERS OF OLD.

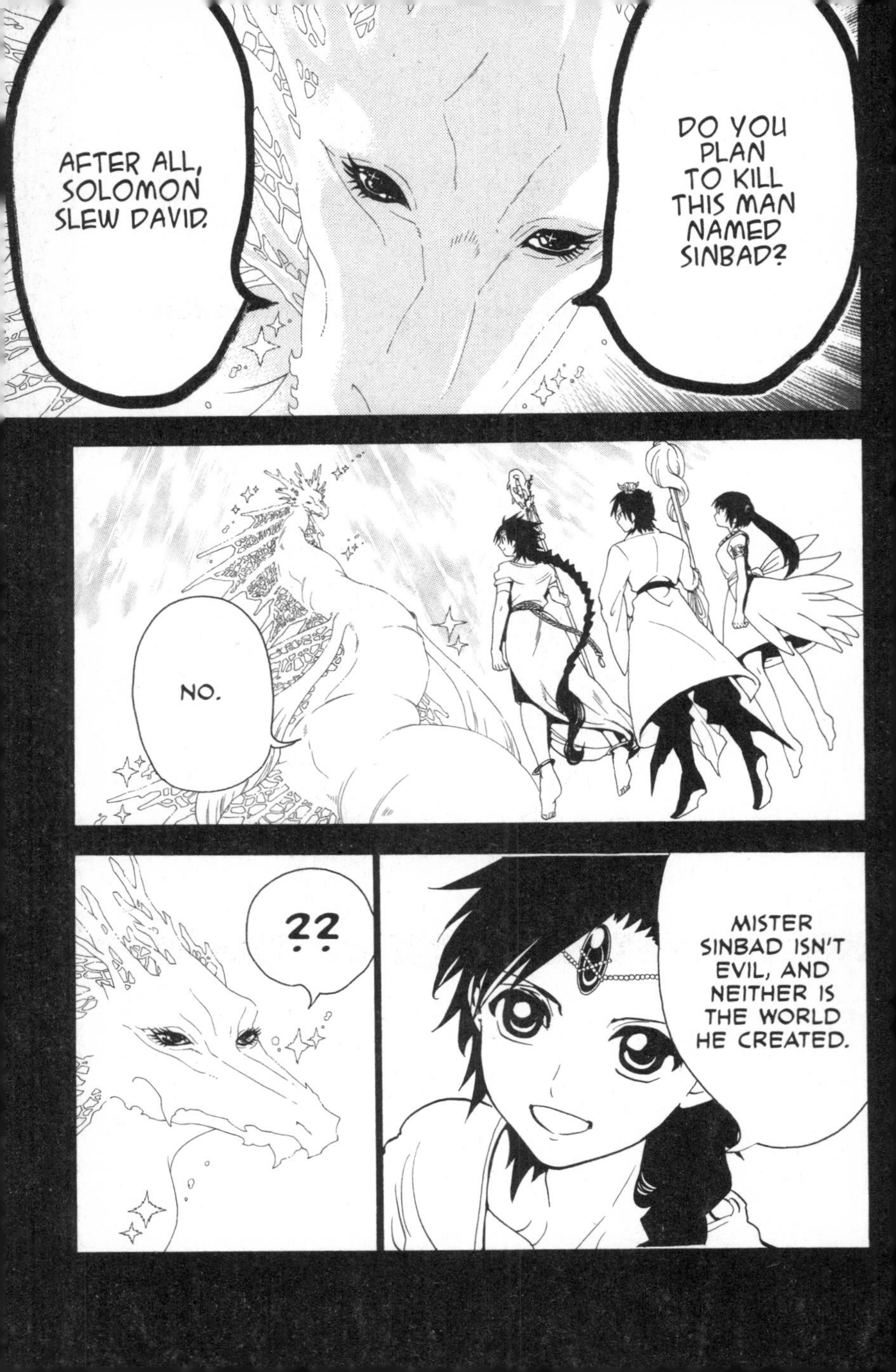
DO YOU PLAN TO KILL THIS MAN NAMED SINBAD?
AFTER ALL, SOLOMON SLEW DAVID.
NO.
MISTER SINBAD ISN'T EVIL, AND NEITHER IS THE WORLD HE CREATED.
??

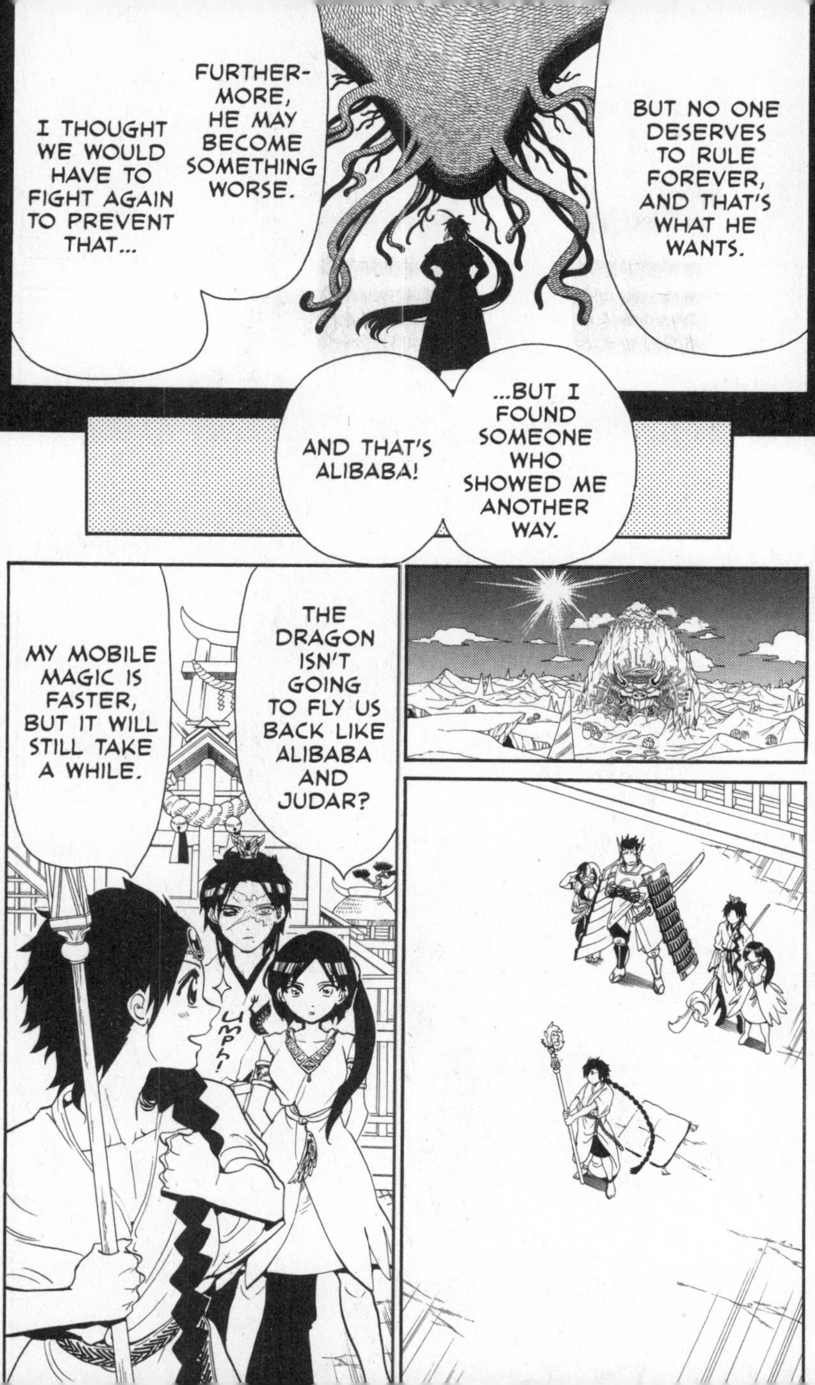
BUT NO ONE DESERVES TO RULE FOREVER, AND THAT'S WHAT HE WANTS.
FURTHER-MORE, HE MAY BECOME SOMETHING WORSE.
I THOUGHT WE WOULD HAVE TO FIGHT AGAIN TO PREVENT THAT...
...BUT I FOUND SOMEONE WHO SHOWED ME ANOTHER WAY.
AND THAT'S ALIBABA!
THE DRAGON ISN'T GOING TO FLY US BACK LIKE ALIBABA AND JUDAR?
MY MOBILE MAGIC IS FASTER, BUT IT WILL STILL TAKE A WHILE.
UMPH!

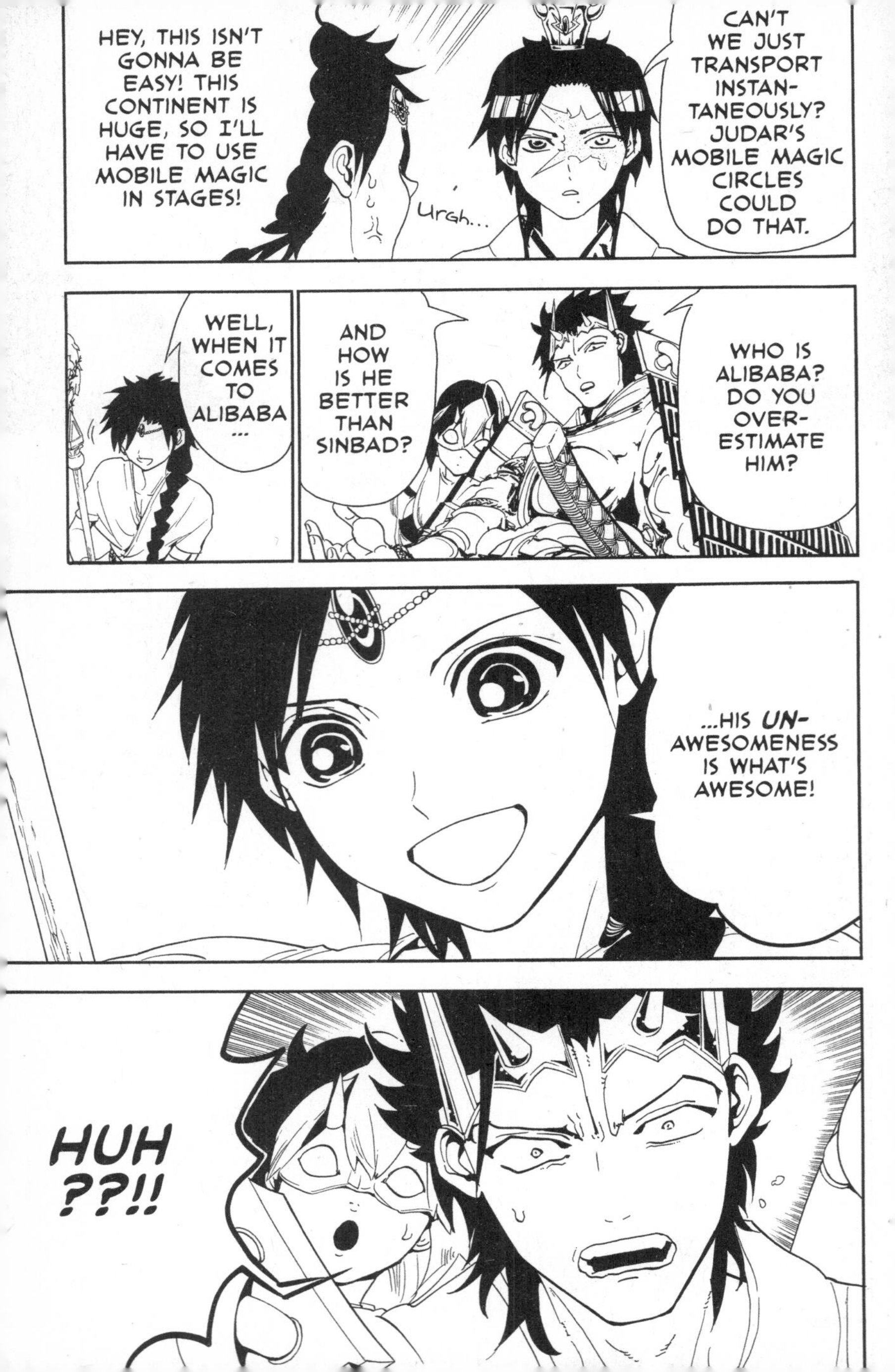
CAN'T WE JUST TRANSPORT INSTAN-TANEOUSLY? JUDAR'S MOBILE MAGIC CIRCLES COULD DO THAT.
HEY, THIS ISN'T GONNA BE EASY! THIS CONTINENT IS HUGE, SO I'LL HAVE TO USE MOBILE MAGIC IN STAGES!
Urgh...
WHO IS ALIBABA? DO YOU OVER-ESTIMATE HIM?
AND HOW IS HE BETTER THAN SINBAD?
WELL, WHEN IT COMES TO ALIBABA ...
...HIS *UN*-AWESOMENESS IS WHAT'S AWESOME!
HUH ??!!

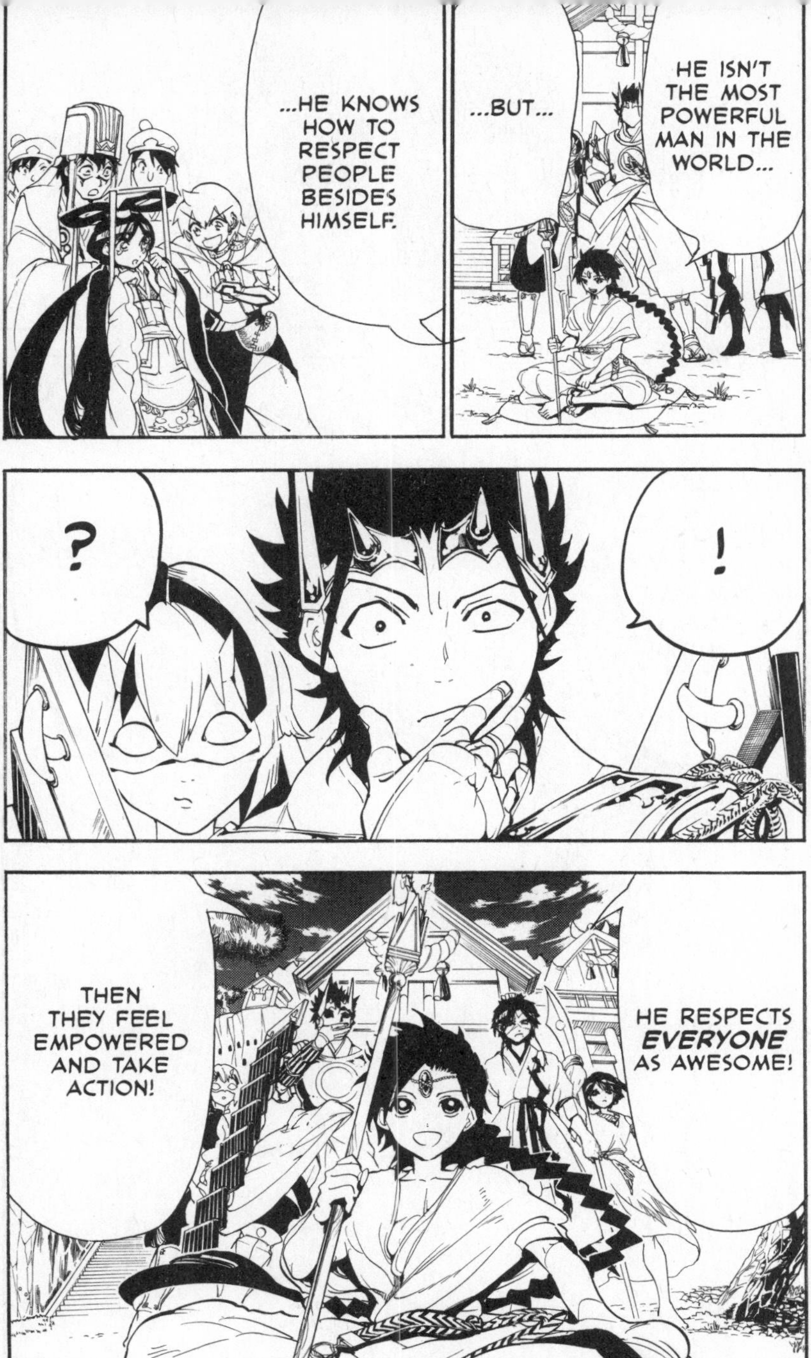
HE ISN'T THE MOST POWERFUL MAN IN THE WORLD...
...BUT...
...HE KNOWS HOW TO RESPECT PEOPLE BESIDES HIMSELF.
!
?
HE RESPECTS *EVERYONE* AS AWESOME!
THEN THEY FEEL EMPOWERED AND TAKE ACTION!

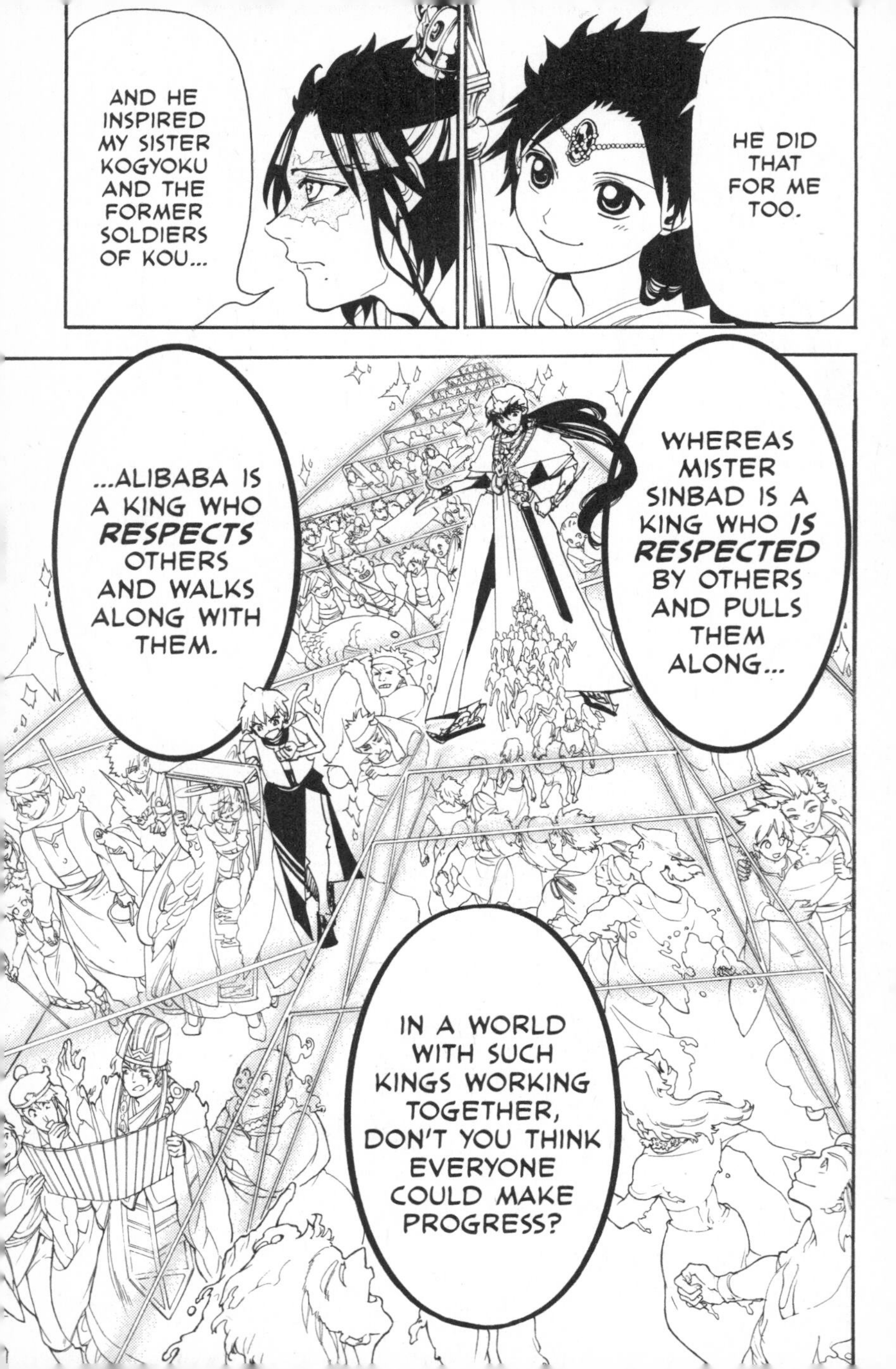

AND HE INSPIRED MY SISTER KOGYOKU AND THE FORMER SOLDIERS OF KOU...
HE DID THAT FOR ME TOO.
...ALIBABA IS A KING WHO *RESPECTS* OTHERS AND WALKS ALONG WITH THEM.
WHEREAS MISTER SINBAD IS A KING WHO *IS RESPECTED* BY OTHERS AND PULLS THEM ALONG...
IN A WORLD WITH SUCH KINGS WORKING TOGETHER, DON'T YOU THINK EVERYONE COULD MAKE PROGRESS?

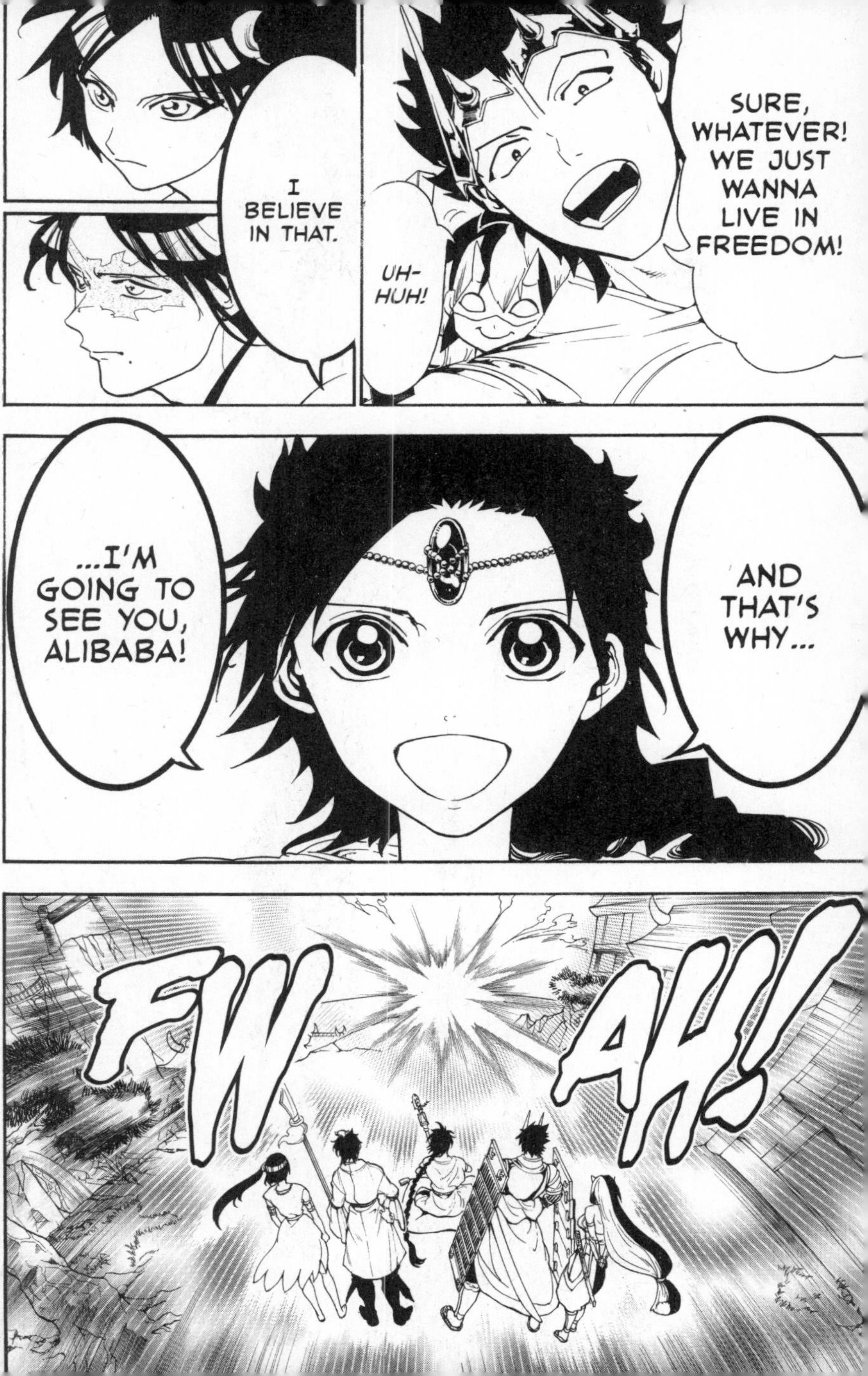
SURE, WHATEVER! WE JUST WANNA LIVE IN FREEDOM!
UH-HUH!
I BELIEVE IN THAT.
AND THAT'S WHY...
...I'M GOING TO SEE YOU, ALIBABA!
FWAH!!

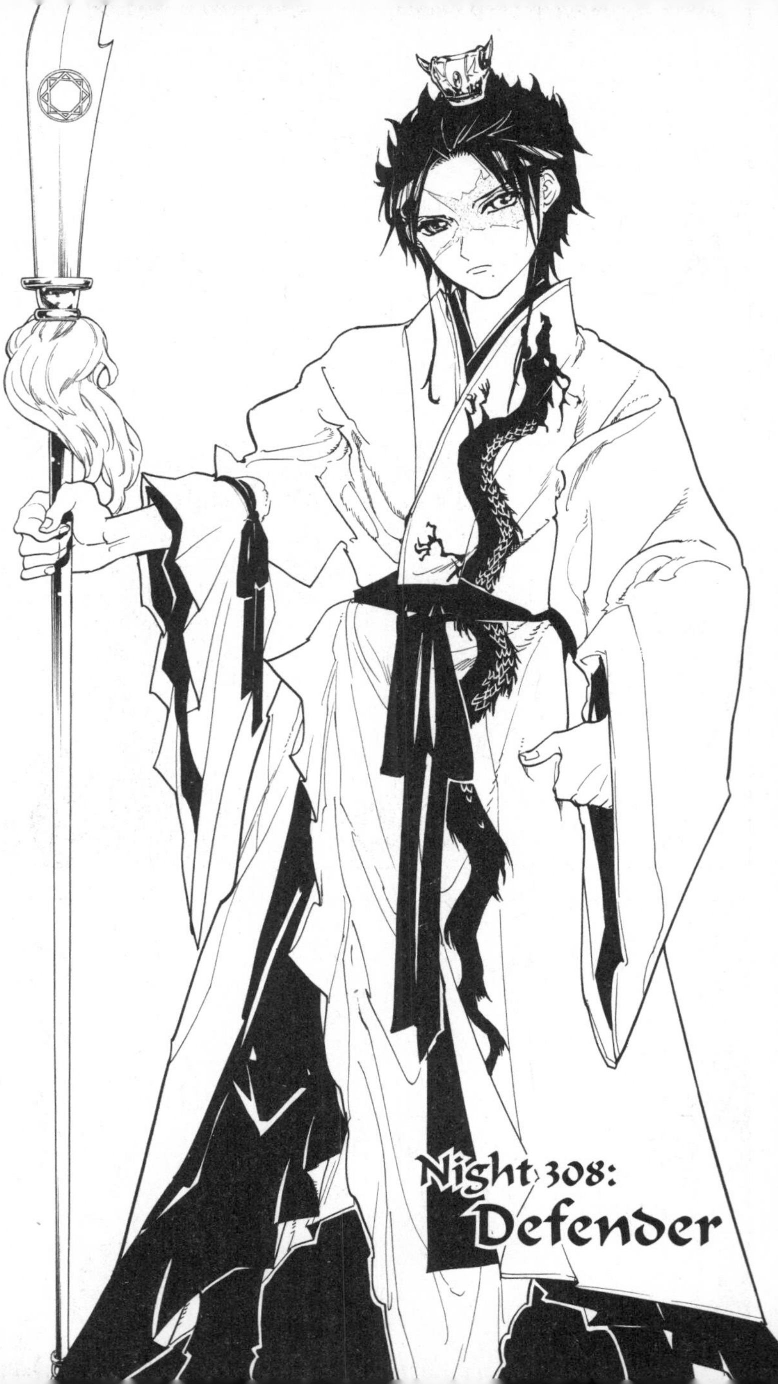

Night 308: Defender

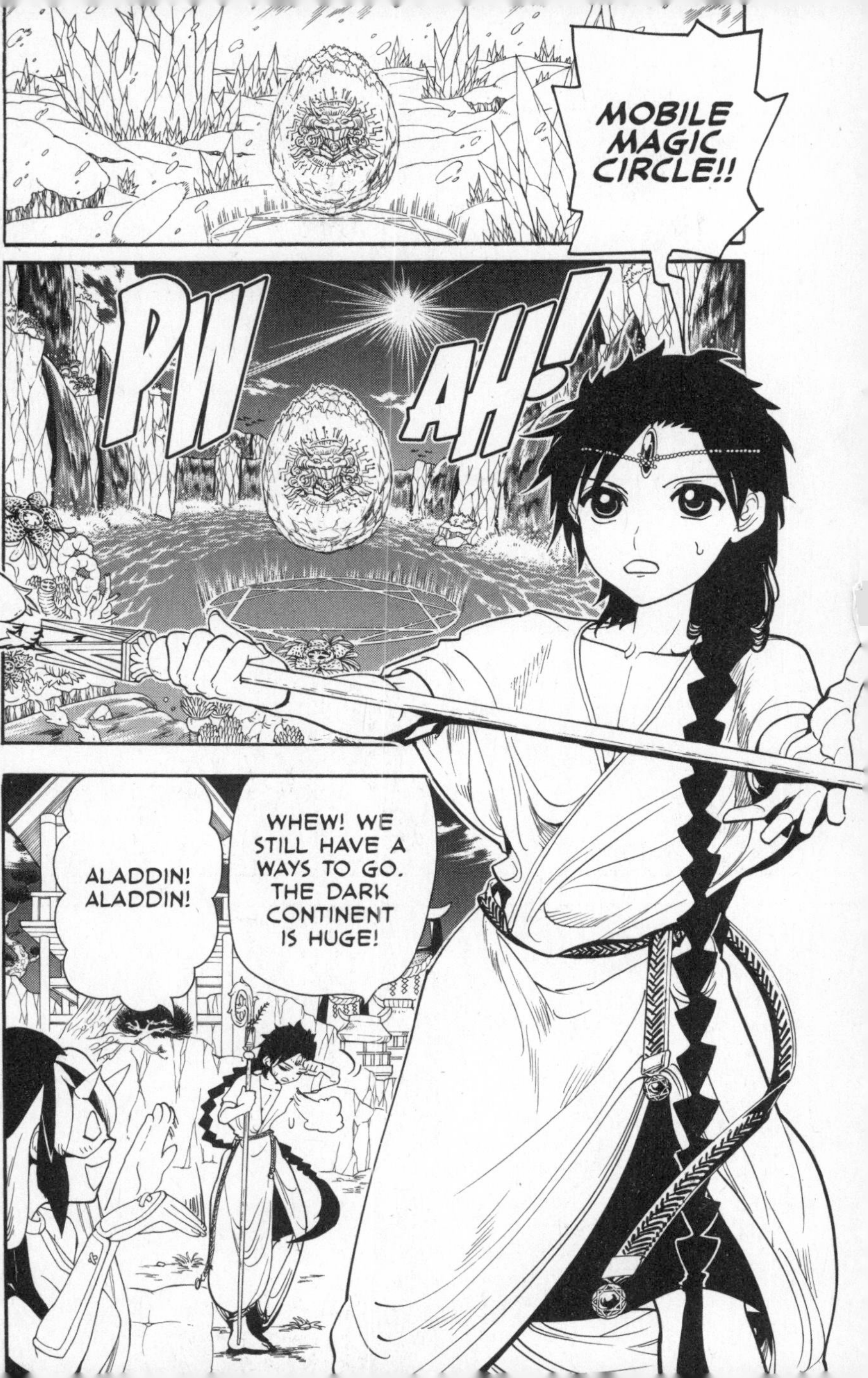
MOBILE MAGIC CIRCLE!!
PWAH!
WHEW! WE STILL HAVE A WAYS TO GO. THE DARK CONTINENT IS HUGE!
ALADDIN! ALADDIN!

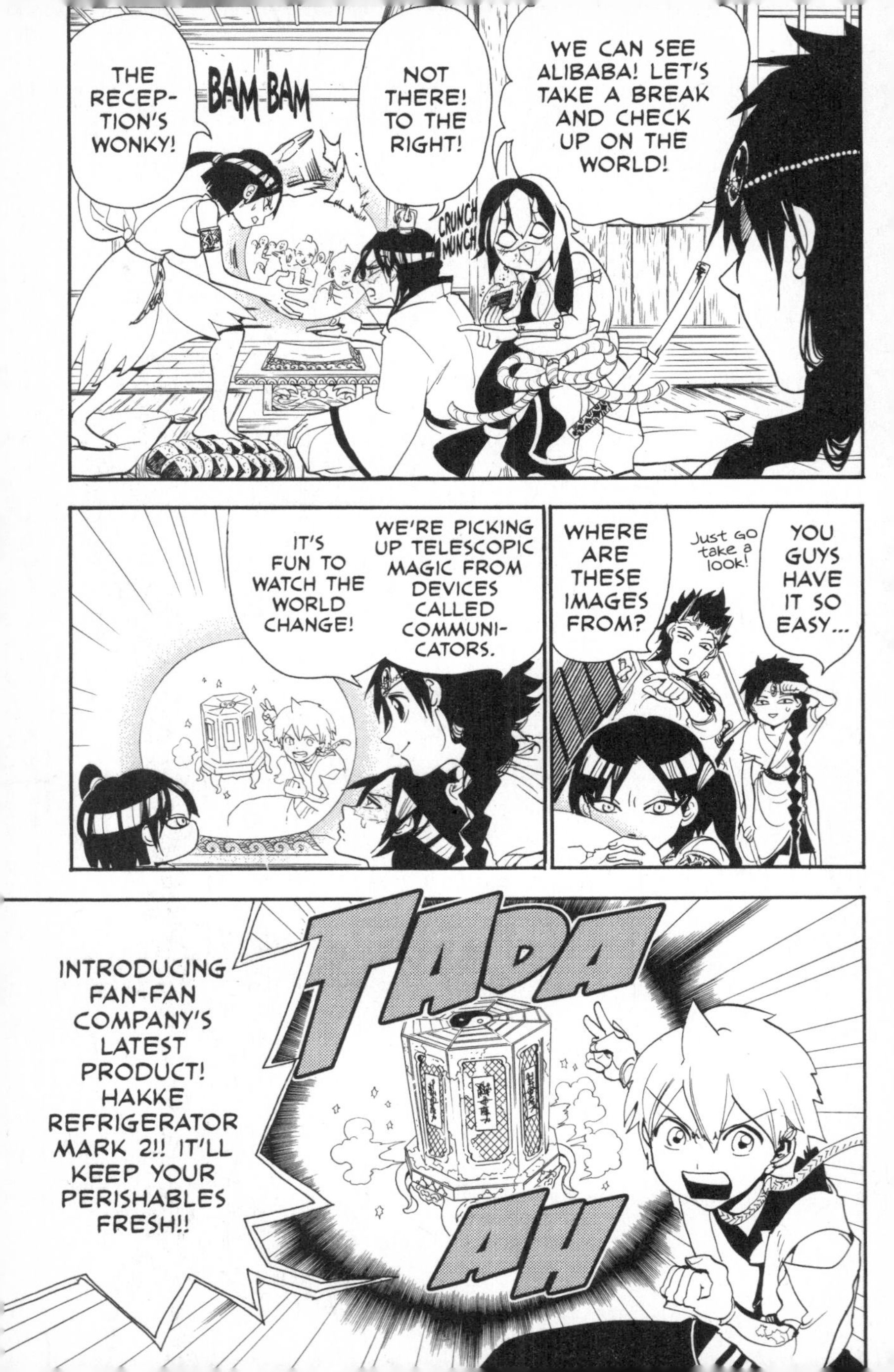
WE CAN SEE ALIBABA! LET'S TAKE A BREAK AND CHECK UP ON THE WORLD!
CRUNCH MUNCH
NOT THERE! TO THE RIGHT!
BAM BAM
THE RECEPTION'S WONKY!
YOU GUYS HAVE IT SO EASY...
Just go take a look!
WHERE ARE THESE IMAGES FROM?
WE'RE PICKING UP TELESCOPIC MAGIC FROM DEVICES CALLED COMMUNICATORS.
IT'S FUN TO WATCH THE WORLD CHANGE!
TADA
INTRODUCING FAN-FAN COMPANY'S LATEST PRODUCT! HAKKE REFRIGERATOR MARK 2!! IT'LL KEEP YOUR PERISHABLES FRESH!!
AH

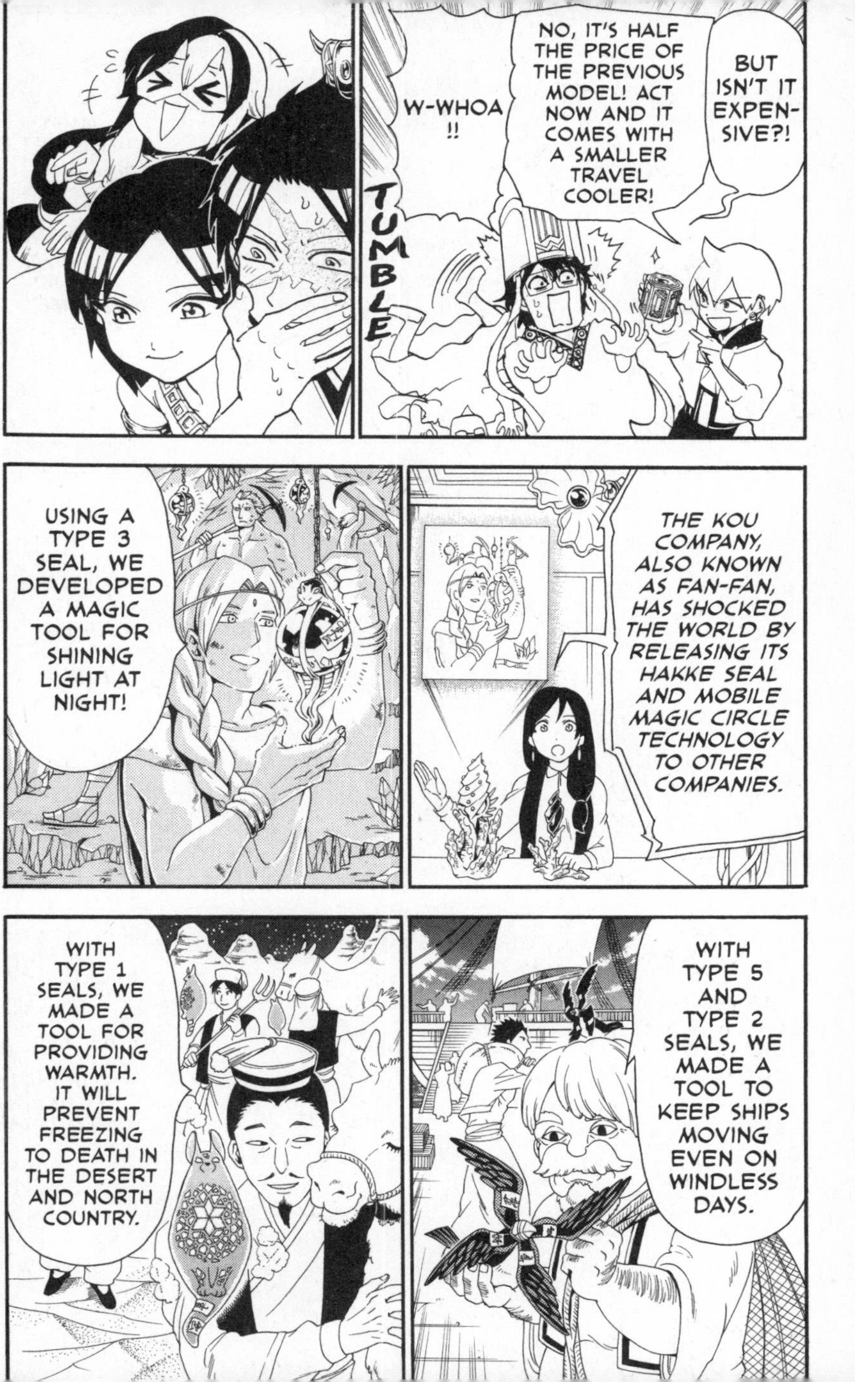
BUT ISN'T IT EXPENSIVE?!
NO, IT'S HALF THE PRICE OF THE PREVIOUS MODEL! ACT NOW AND IT COMES WITH A SMALLER TRAVEL COOLER!
W-WHOA !!
TUMBLE
THE KOU COMPANY, ALSO KNOWN AS FAN-FAN, HAS SHOCKED THE WORLD BY RELEASING ITS HAKKE SEAL AND MOBILE MAGIC CIRCLE TECHNOLOGY TO OTHER COMPANIES.
USING A TYPE 3 SEAL, WE DEVELOPED A MAGIC TOOL FOR SHINING LIGHT AT NIGHT!
WITH TYPE 5 AND TYPE 2 SEALS, WE MADE A TOOL TO KEEP SHIPS MOVING EVEN ON WINDLESS DAYS.
WITH TYPE 1 SEALS, WE MADE A TOOL FOR PROVIDING WARMTH. IT WILL PREVENT FREEZING TO DEATH IN THE DESERT AND NORTH COUNTRY.

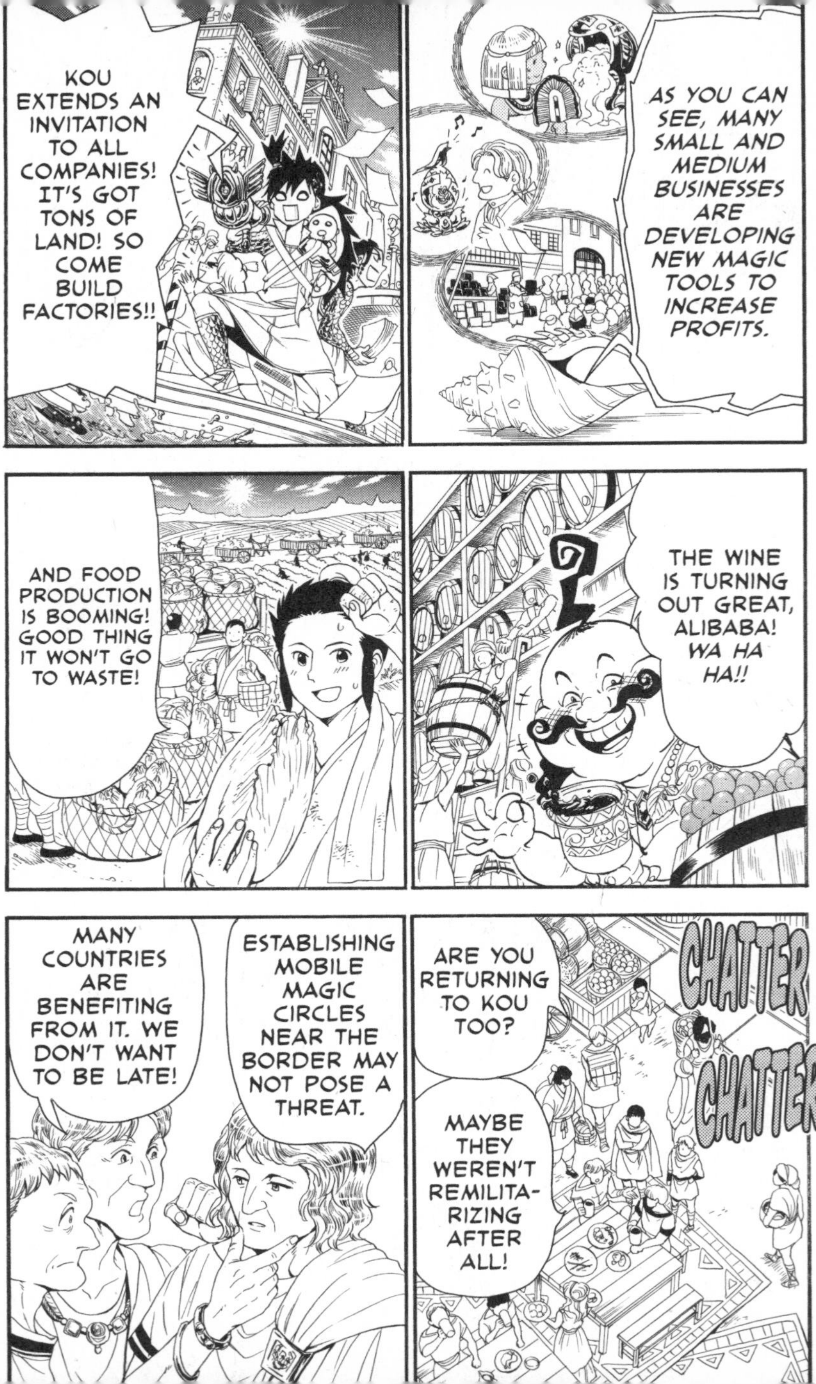
AS YOU CAN SEE, MANY SMALL AND MEDIUM BUSINESSES ARE DEVELOPING NEW MAGIC TOOLS TO INCREASE PROFITS.
KOU EXTENDS AN INVITATION TO ALL COMPANIES! IT'S GOT TONS OF LAND! SO COME BUILD FACTORIES!!
THE WINE IS TURNING OUT GREAT, ALIBABA! WA HA HA!!
AND FOOD PRODUCTION IS BOOMING! GOOD THING IT WON'T GO TO WASTE!
CHATTER
CHATTER
ARE YOU RETURNING TO KOU TOO?
MAYBE THEY WEREN'T REMILITA-RIZING AFTER ALL!
ESTABLISHING MOBILE MAGIC CIRCLES NEAR THE BORDER MAY NOT POSE A THREAT.
MANY COUNTRIES ARE BENEFITING FROM IT. WE DON'T WANT TO BE LATE!

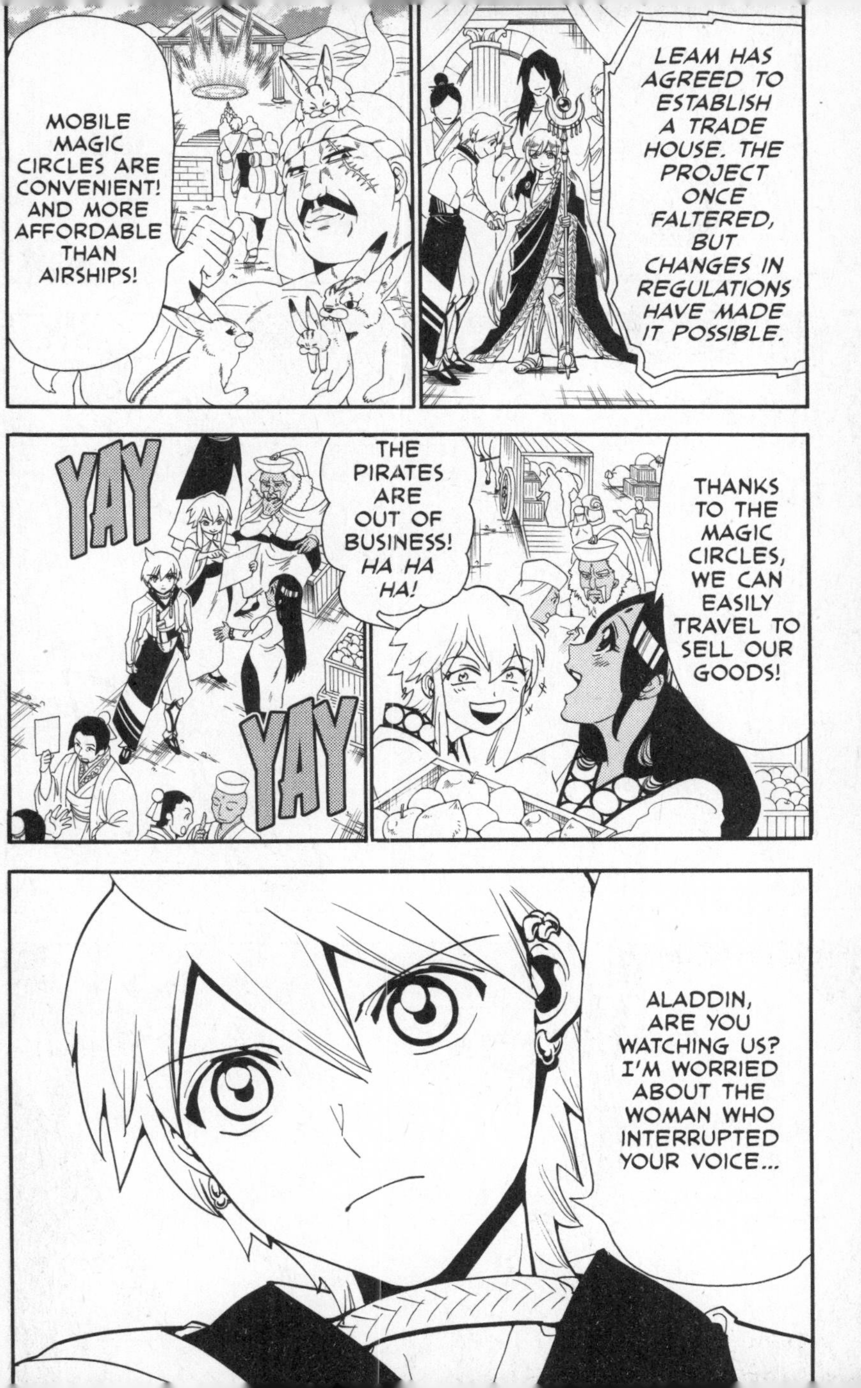
LEAM HAS AGREED TO ESTABLISH A TRADE HOUSE. THE PROJECT ONCE FALTERED, BUT CHANGES IN REGULATIONS HAVE MADE IT POSSIBLE.
MOBILE MAGIC CIRCLES ARE CONVENIENT! AND MORE AFFORDABLE THAN AIRSHIPS!
THANKS TO THE MAGIC CIRCLES, WE CAN EASILY TRAVEL TO SELL OUR GOODS!
THE PIRATES ARE OUT OF BUSINESS! HA HA HA!
YAY
YAY
ALADDIN, ARE YOU WATCHING US? I'M WORRIED ABOUT THE WOMAN WHO INTERRUPTED YOUR VOICE...

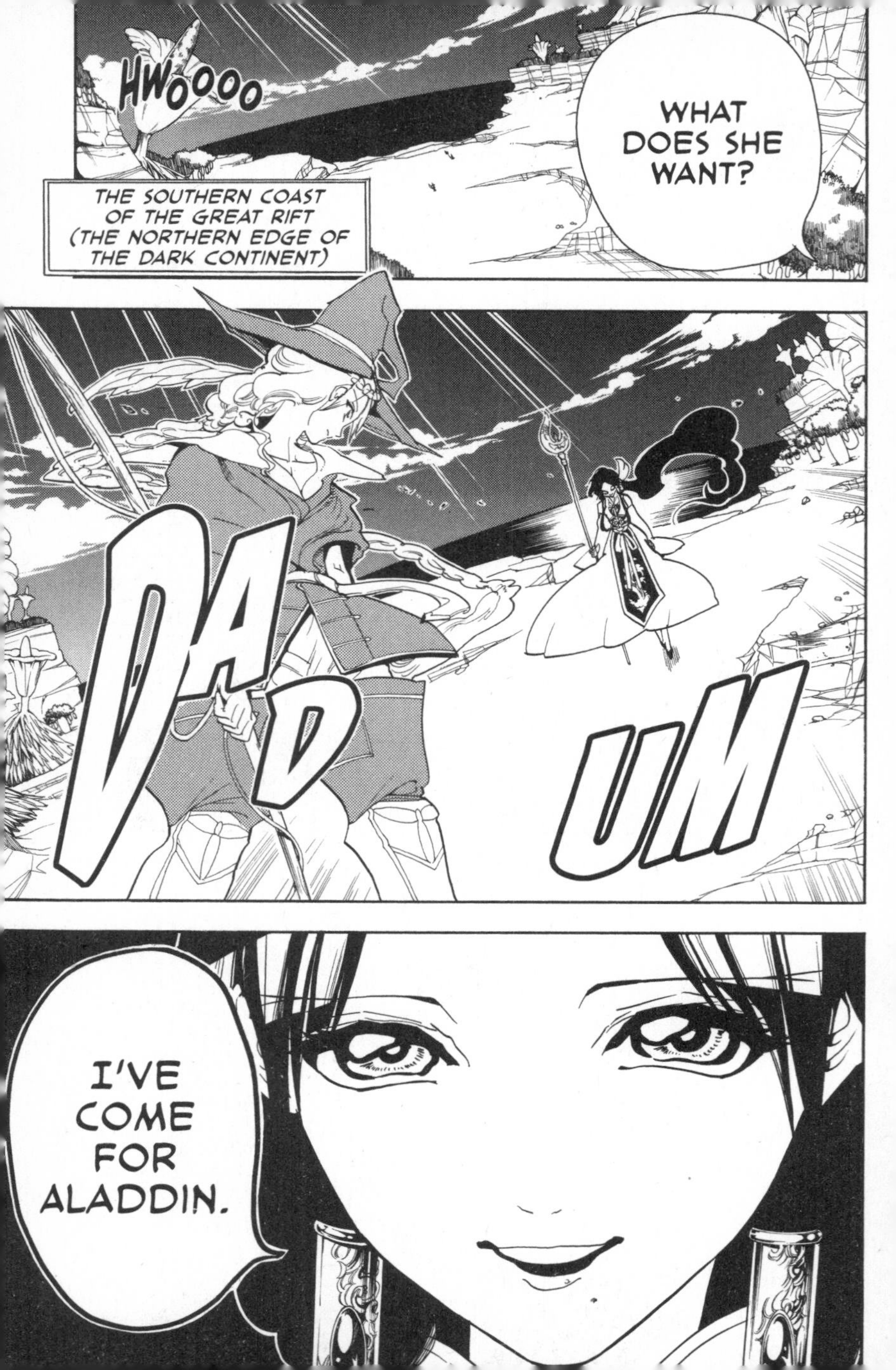
WHAT DOES SHE WANT?
HWOOOO
THE SOUTHERN COAST OF THE GREAT RIFT (THE NORTHERN EDGE OF THE DARK CONTINENT)
DADUM
I'VE COME FOR ALADDIN.

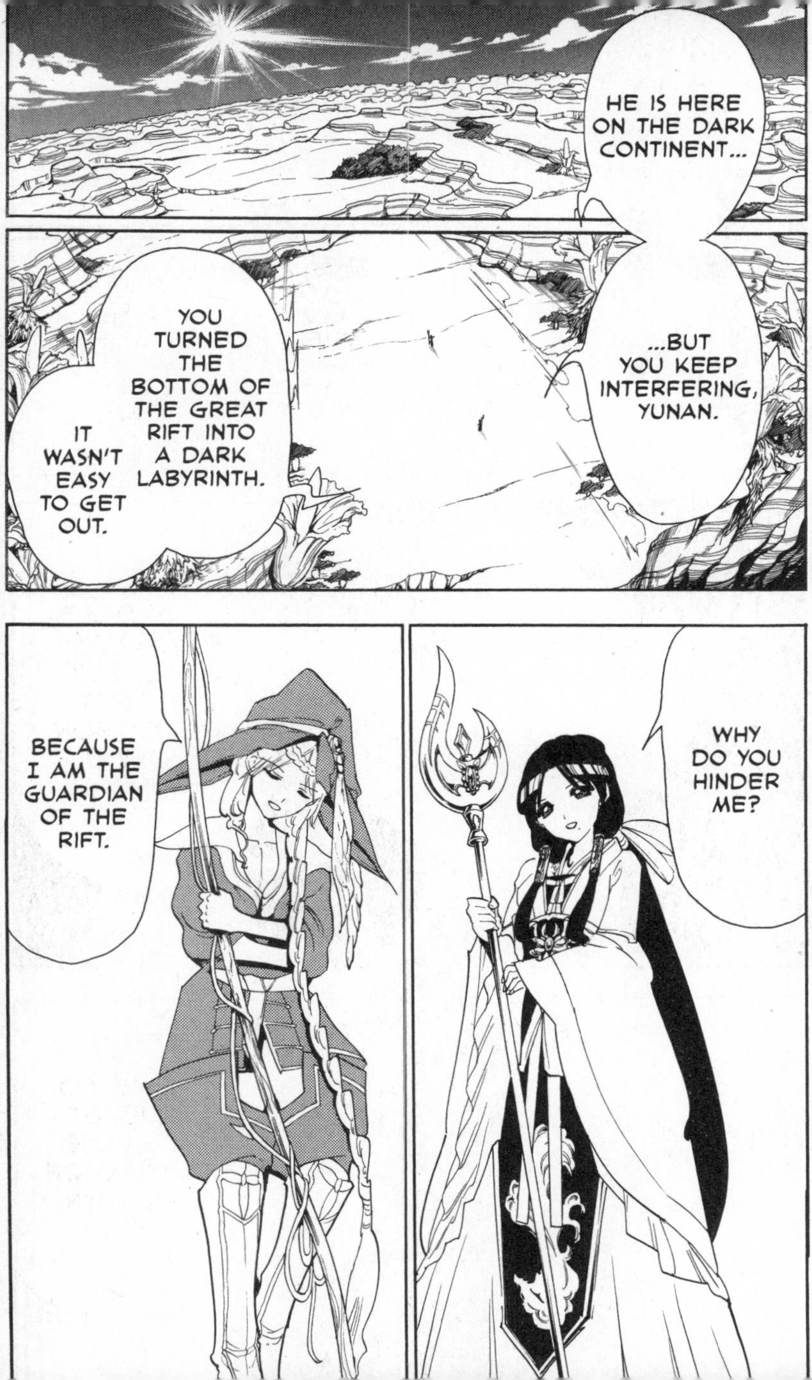
HE IS HERE ON THE DARK CONTINENT...
...BUT YOU KEEP INTERFERING, YUNAN.
YOU TURNED THE BOTTOM OF THE GREAT RIFT INTO A DARK LABYRINTH.
IT WASN'T EASY TO GET OUT.
WHY DO YOU HINDER ME?
BECAUSE I AM THE GUARDIAN OF THE RIFT.

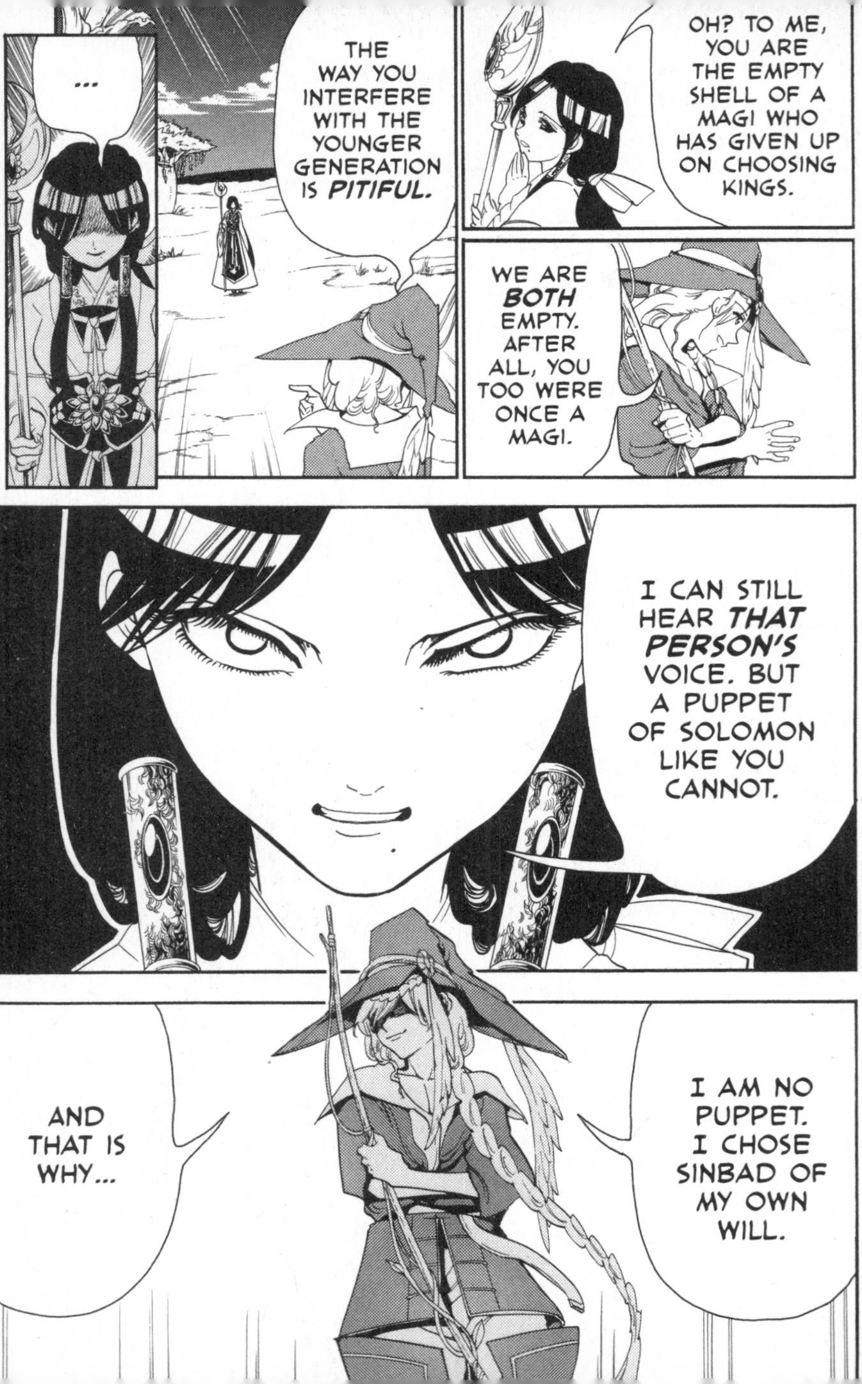
OH? TO ME, YOU ARE THE EMPTY SHELL OF A MAGI WHO HAS GIVEN UP ON CHOOSING KINGS.
WE ARE BOTH EMPTY. AFTER ALL, YOU TOO WERE ONCE A MAGI.
THE WAY YOU INTERFERE WITH THE YOUNGER GENERATION IS PITIFUL.
...
I CAN STILL HEAR THAT PERSON'S VOICE. BUT A PUPPET OF SOLOMON LIKE YOU CANNOT.
I AM NO PUPPET. I CHOSE SINBAD OF MY OWN WILL.
AND THAT IS WHY...

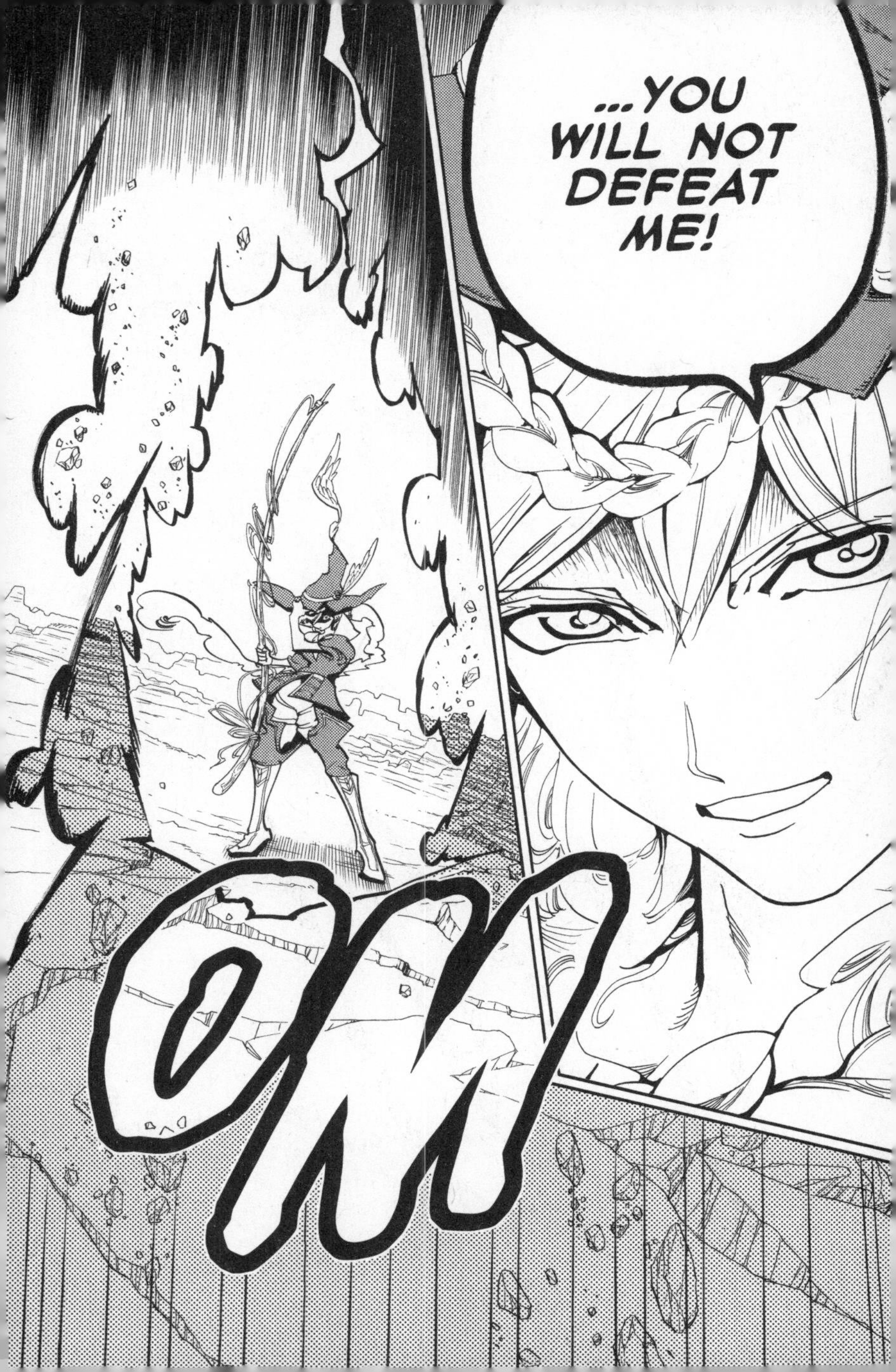
...YOU WILL NOT DEFEAT ME!

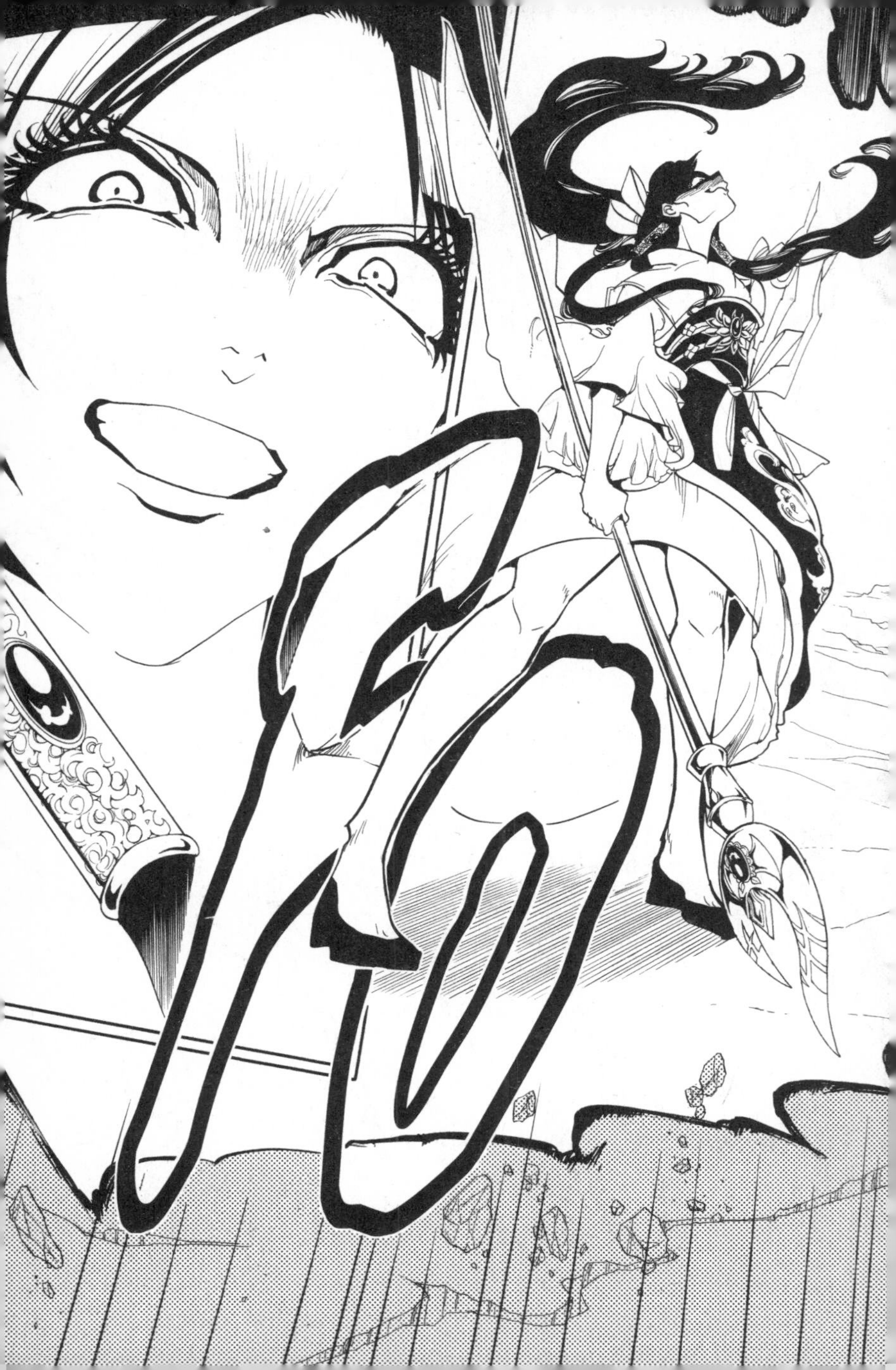

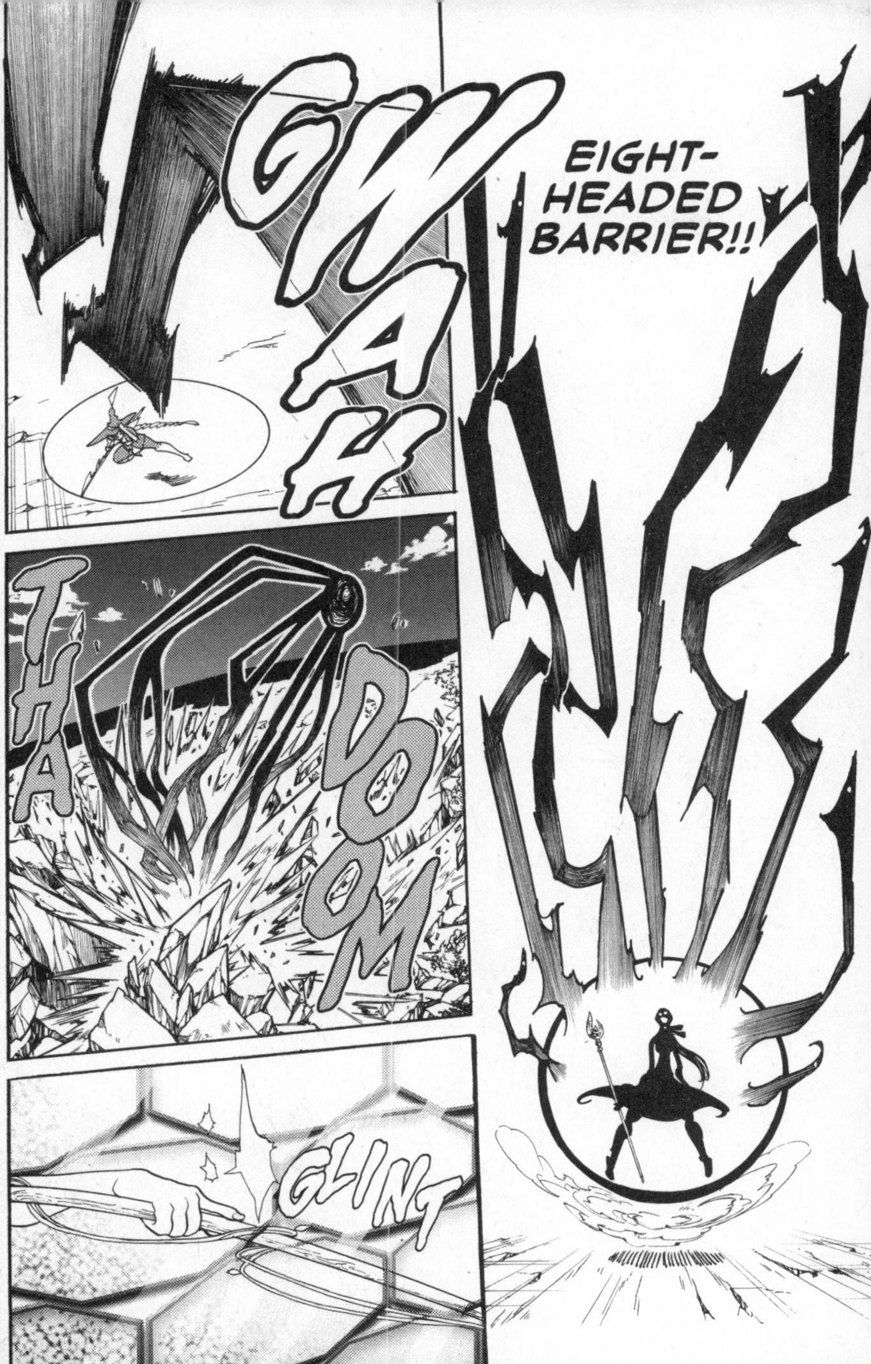
EIGHT-HEADED BARRIER!!
GWAH
THA
DOOM
GLINT

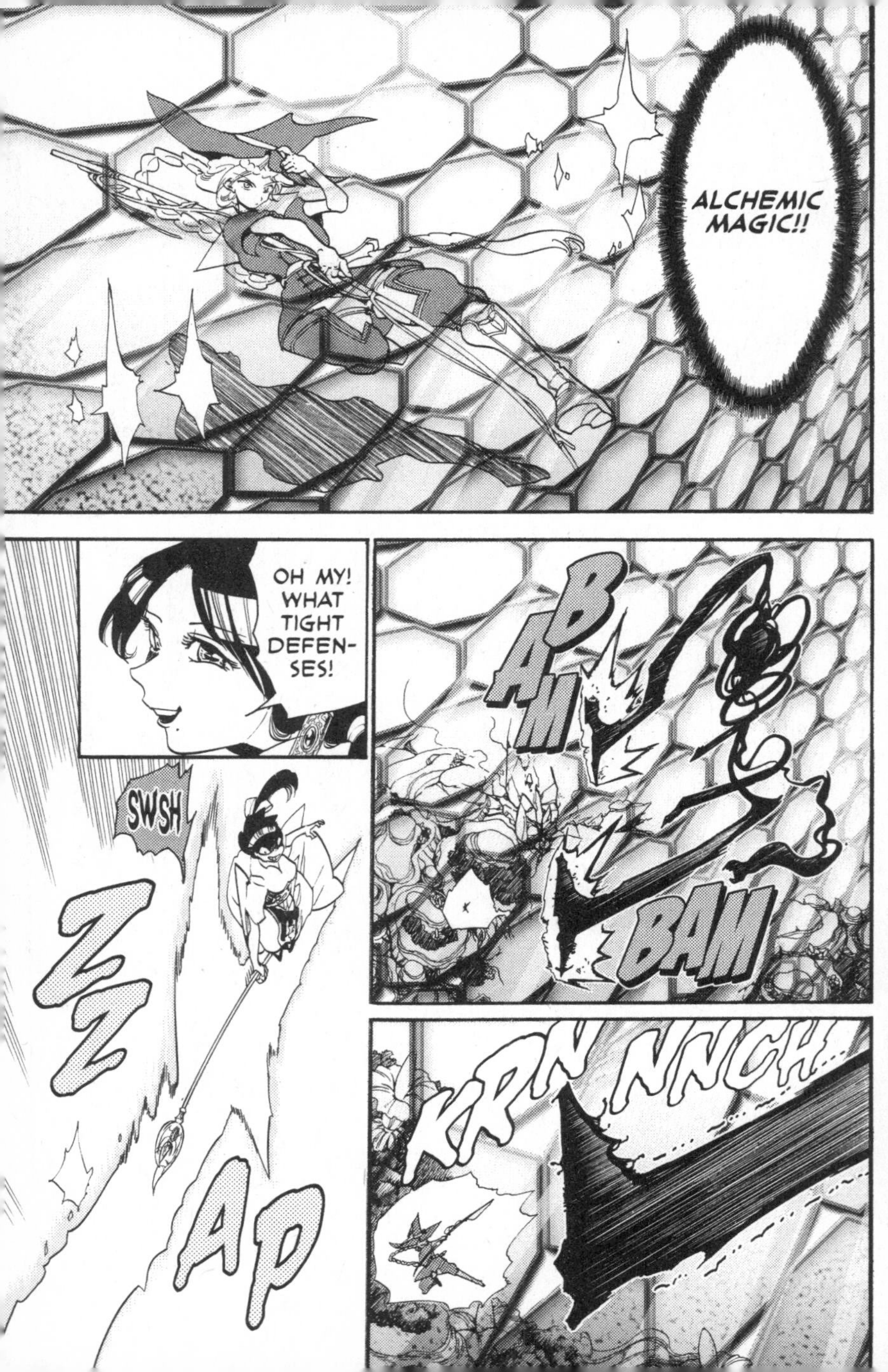
ALCHEMIC MAGIC!!
BAM
BAM
KRNNNCH...
OH MY! WHAT TIGHT DEFEN-SES!
SWSH
ZZAP

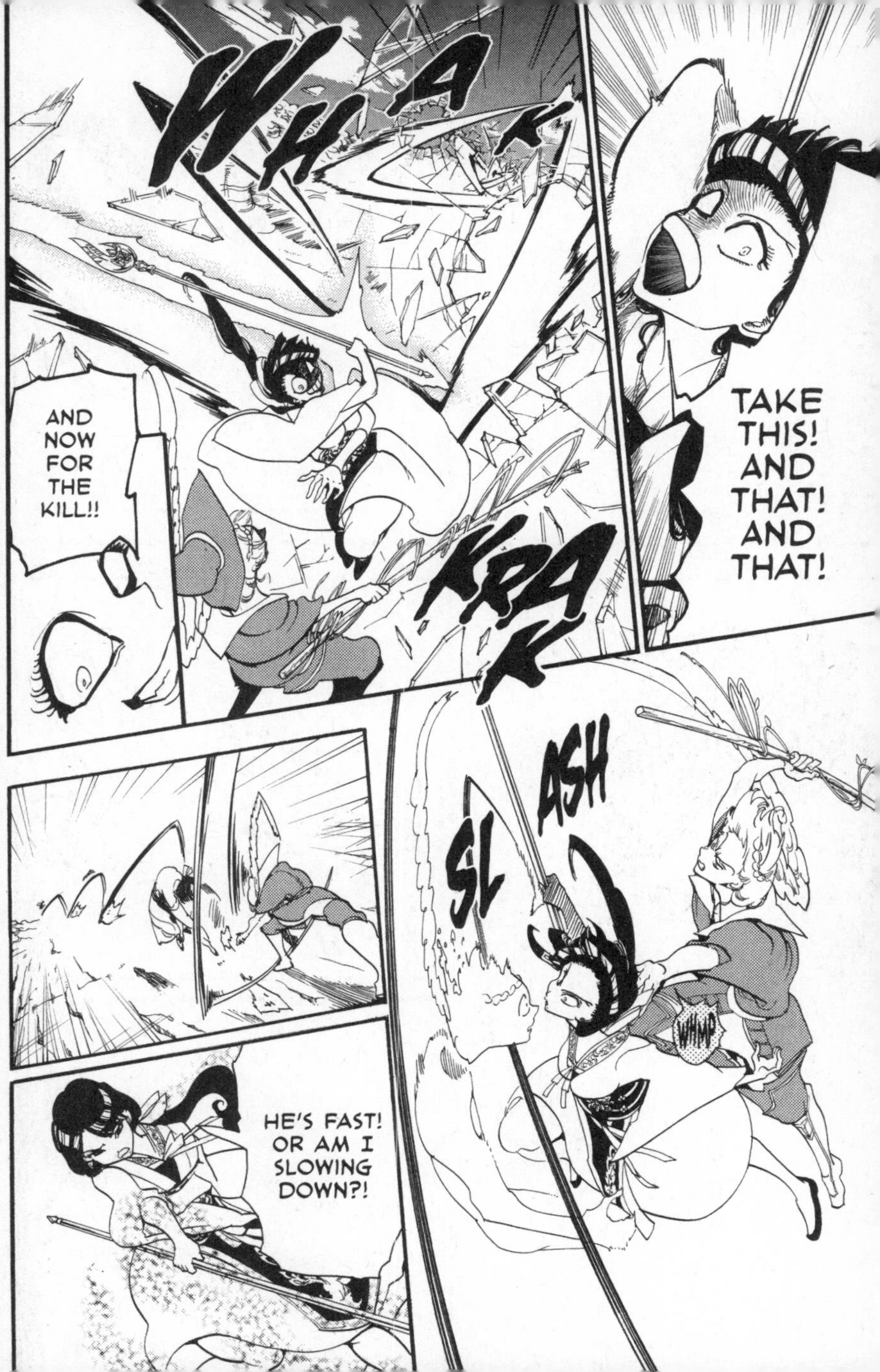
TAKE THIS! AND THAT! AND THAT!
WHAK
KRAK
AND NOW FOR THE KILL!!
SLASH
WHMP
HE'S FAST! OR AM I SLOWING DOWN?!

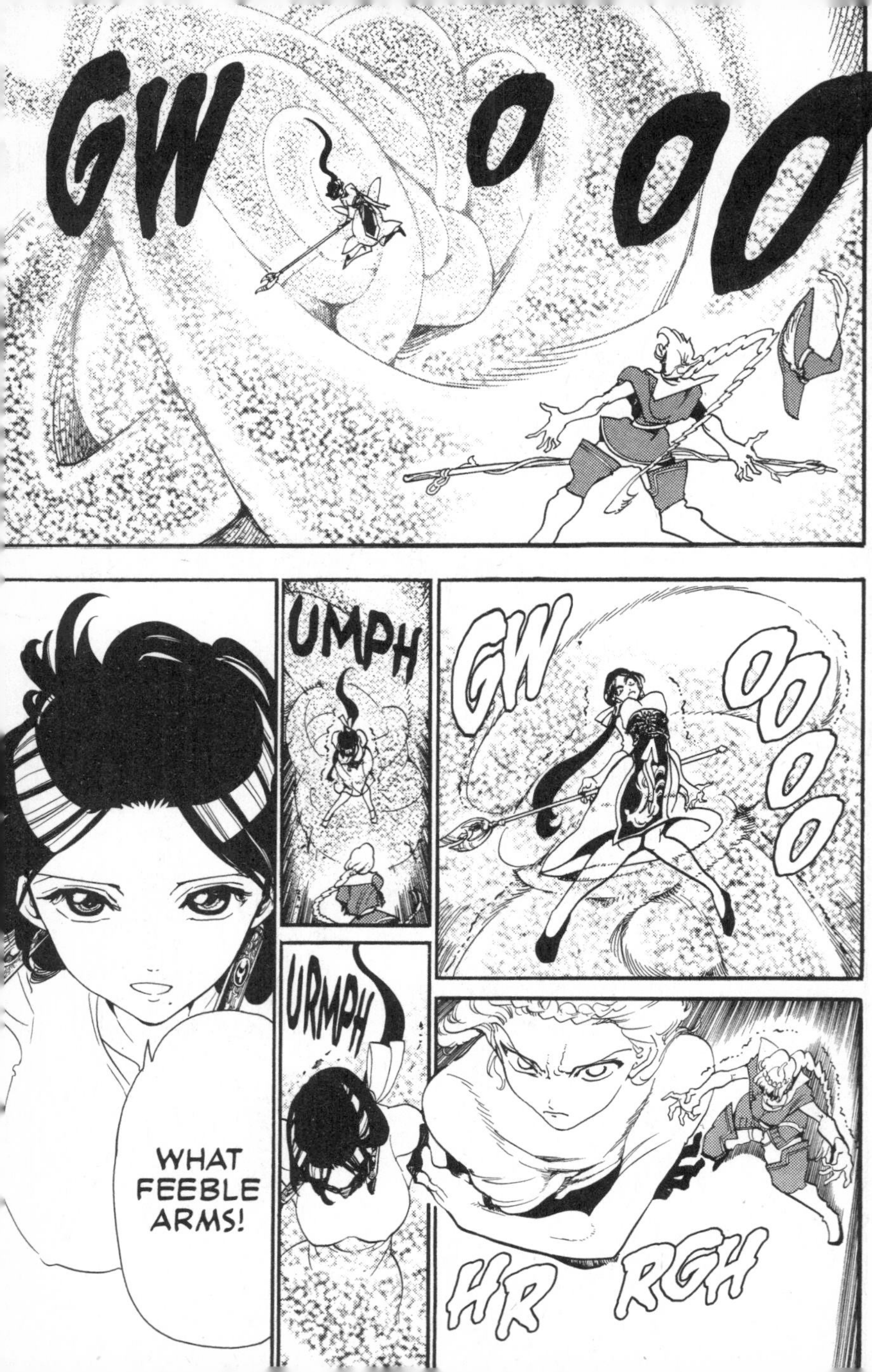

GW OOO
GW OOOOO
UMPH
HR RGH
URMPH
WHAT FEEBLE ARMS!

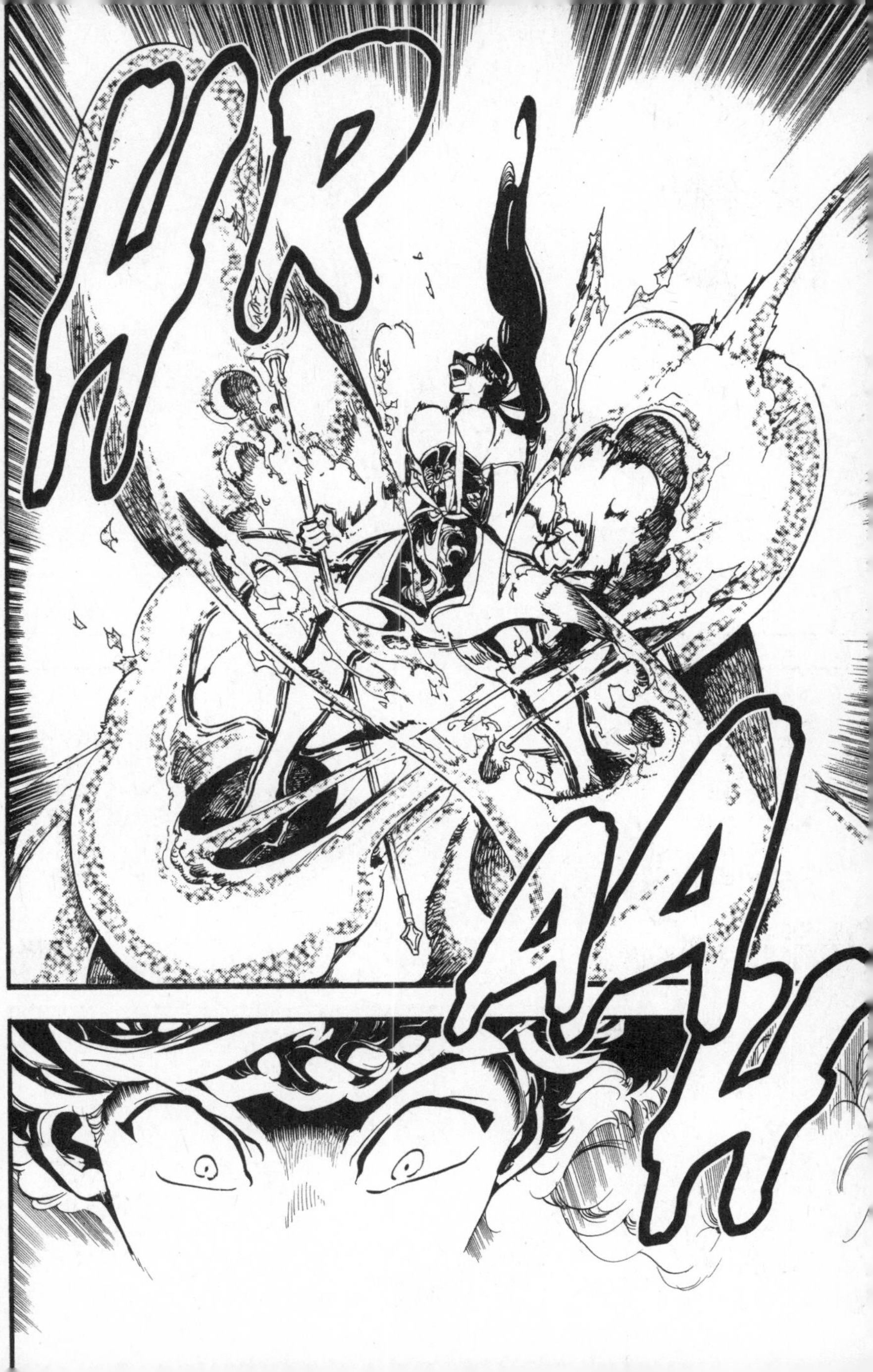
HRAAAH

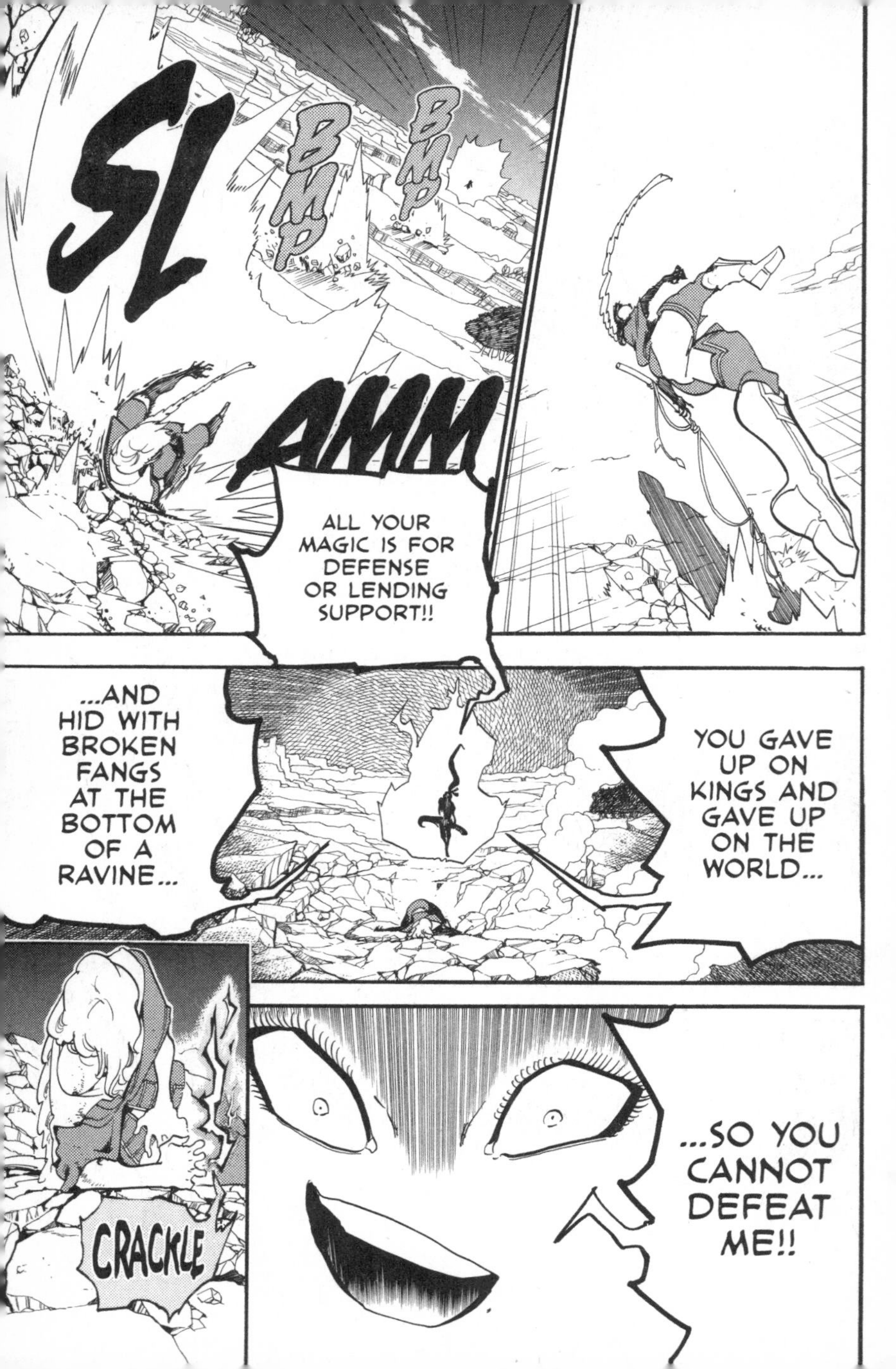
BMP BMP
SLAMM
ALL YOUR MAGIC IS FOR DEFENSE OR LENDING SUPPORT!!
YOU GAVE UP ON KINGS AND GAVE UP ON THE WORLD...
...AND HID WITH BROKEN FANGS AT THE BOTTOM OF A RAVINE...
...SO YOU CANNOT DEFEAT ME!!
CRACKLE

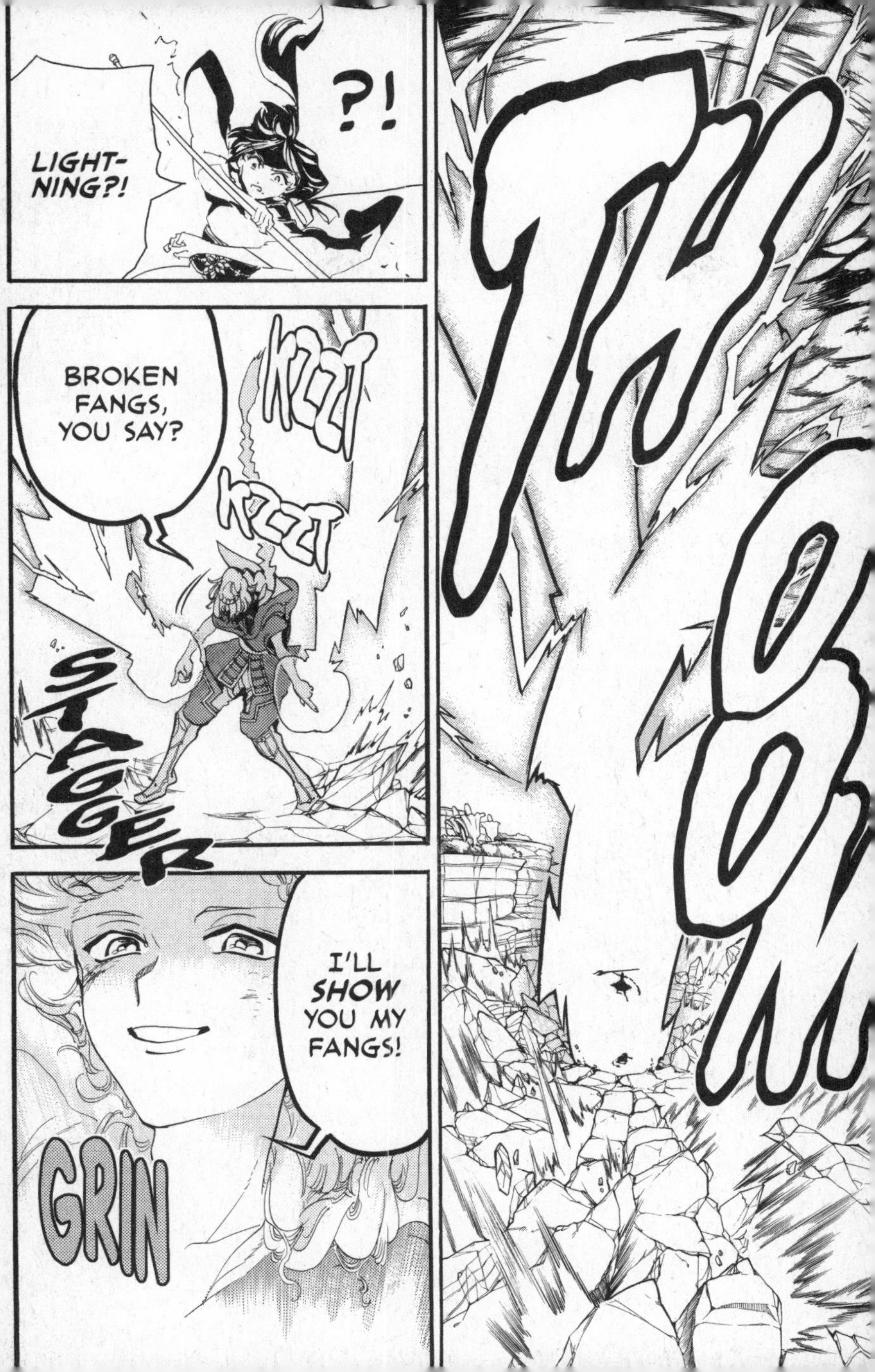
?!
LIGHT-NING?!
BROKEN FANGS, YOU SAY?
KRZZT
KRZZT
STAGGER
I'LL SHOW YOU MY FANGS!
GRIN

MAGI
The labyrinth of magic
31

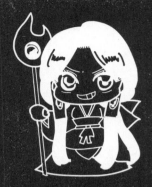

Staff

■ Story & Art

Shinobu Ohtaka

■ Regular Assistants

Hiro Maizima

Yuiko Akiyama

Megi

Aya Umoto

Mami Yoshida

Yuka Otsuji

■ Editors

Kazuaki Ishibashi

Makoto Ishiwata

Katsumasa Ogura

■ Sales & Promotion

Tsunato Imamoto

Yuta Uchiyama

■ Designer

Hajime Tokushige + Bay Bridge Studio

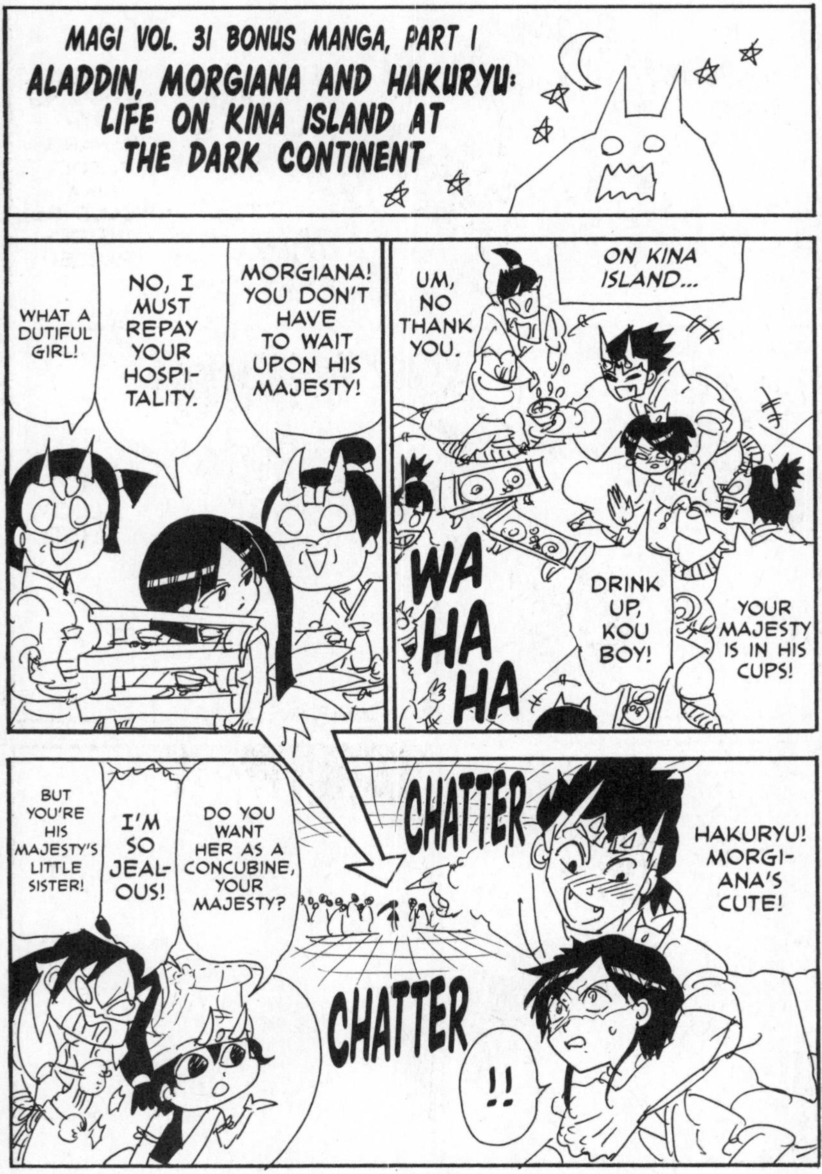
MAGI VOL. 31 BONUS MANGA, PART 1
ALADDIN, MORGIANA AND HAKURYU: LIFE ON KINA ISLAND AT THE DARK CONTINENT
ON KINA ISLAND...
UM, NO THANK YOU.
WA HA HA
DRINK UP, KOU BOY!
YOUR MAJESTY IS IN HIS CUPS!
MORGIANA! YOU DON'T HAVE TO WAIT UPON HIS MAJESTY!
NO, I MUST REPAY YOUR HOSPITALITY.
WHAT A DUTIFUL GIRL!
HAKURYU! MORGIANA'S CUTE!
CHATTER
DO YOU WANT HER AS A CONCUBINE, YOUR MAJESTY?
I'M SO JEALOUS!
BUT YOU'RE HIS MAJESTY'S LITTLE SISTER!
CHATTER
!!

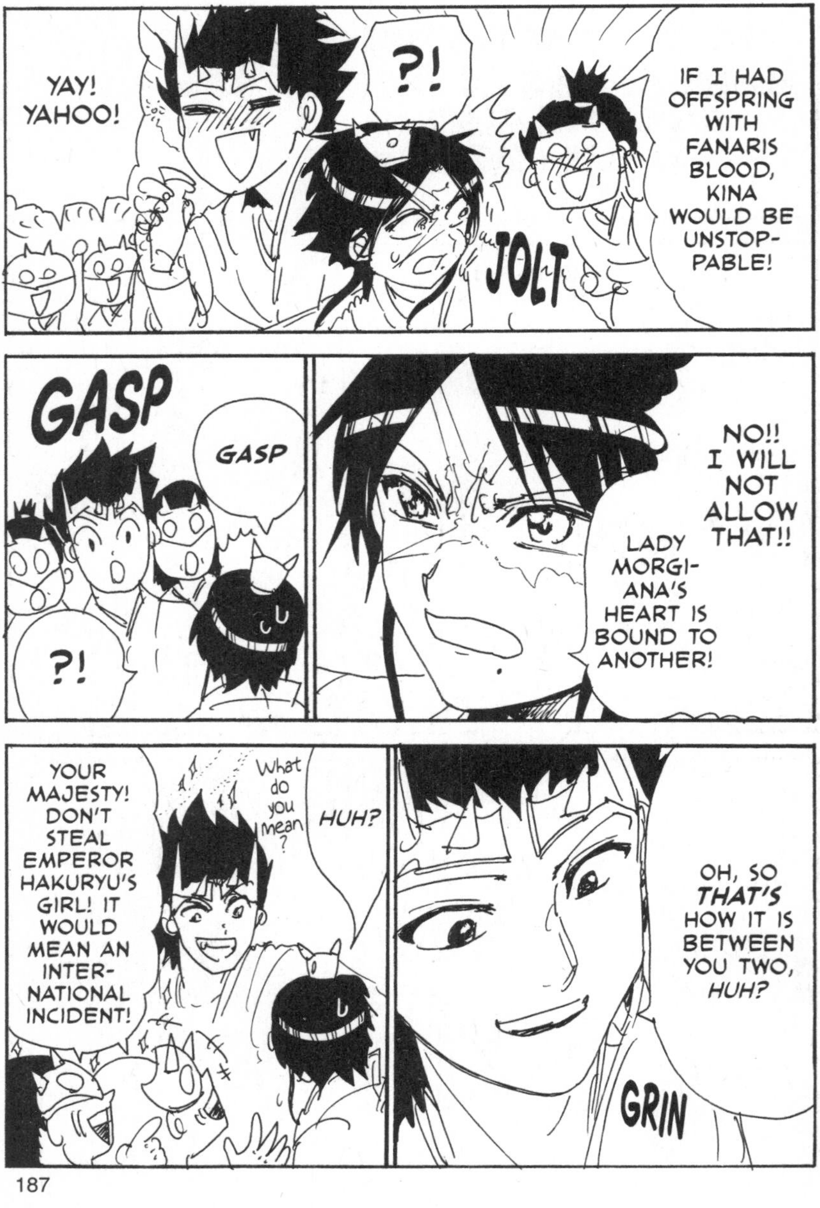
IF I HAD OFFSPRING WITH FANARIS BLOOD, KINA WOULD BE UNSTOPPABLE!
JOLT
?!
YAY! YAHOO!
NO!! I WILL NOT ALLOW THAT!!
LADY MORGIANA'S HEART IS BOUND TO ANOTHER!
GASP
GASP
?!
OH, SO *THAT'S* HOW IT IS BETWEEN YOU TWO, *HUH?*
GRIN
HUH?
What do you mean?
YOUR MAJESTY! DON'T STEAL EMPEROR HAKURYU'S GIRL! IT WOULD MEAN AN INTERNATIONAL INCIDENT!

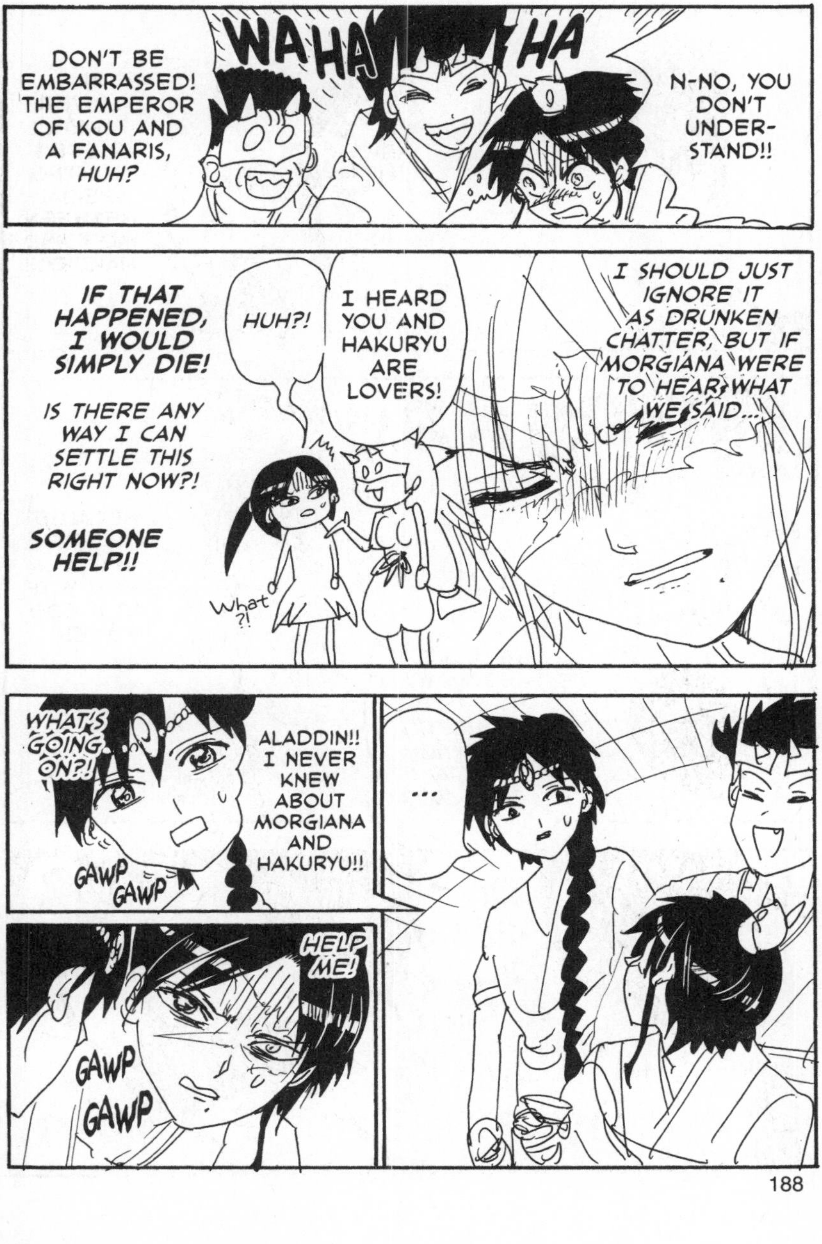
N-NO, YOU DON'T UNDER-STAND!!
WAHA HA HA
DON'T BE EMBARRASSED! THE EMPEROR OF KOU AND A FANARIS, HUH?
I SHOULD JUST IGNORE IT AS DRUNKEN CHATTER, BUT IF MORGIANA WERE TO HEAR WHAT WE SAID...
I HEARD YOU AND HAKURYU ARE LOVERS!
HUH?!
What?!
IF THAT HAPPENED, I WOULD SIMPLY DIE!
IS THERE ANY WAY I CAN SETTLE THIS RIGHT NOW?!
SOMEONE HELP!!
...
ALADDIN!! I NEVER KNEW ABOUT MORGIANA AND HAKURYU!!
WHAT'S GOING ON?!
GAWP GAWP
HELP ME!
GAWP GAWP

NO, MISTER TAKERU! THERE'S NOTHING SPECIAL BETWEEN MOR AND HAKURYU!
HUH? THERE ISN'T?
...
UM...
WHAAAAAT?
...BECAUSE HAKURYU HAS A HAREM WITH ABOUT 600 WOMEN!
HE'S GOT WOMEN BY THE PASSEL! SO THERE'S NOTHING SPECIAL ABOUT MOR!
SHOCK
I'll kill you.
BUT WHAT ELSE COULD I SAY?

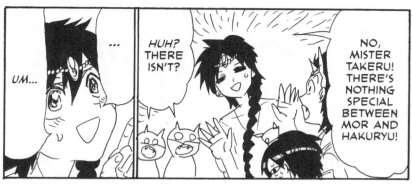

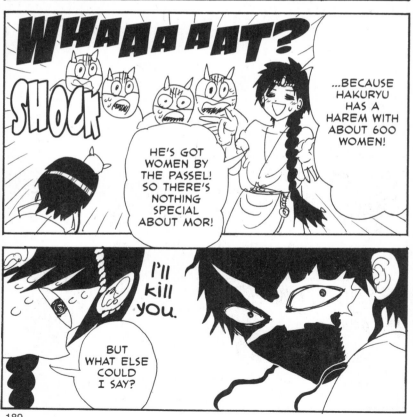

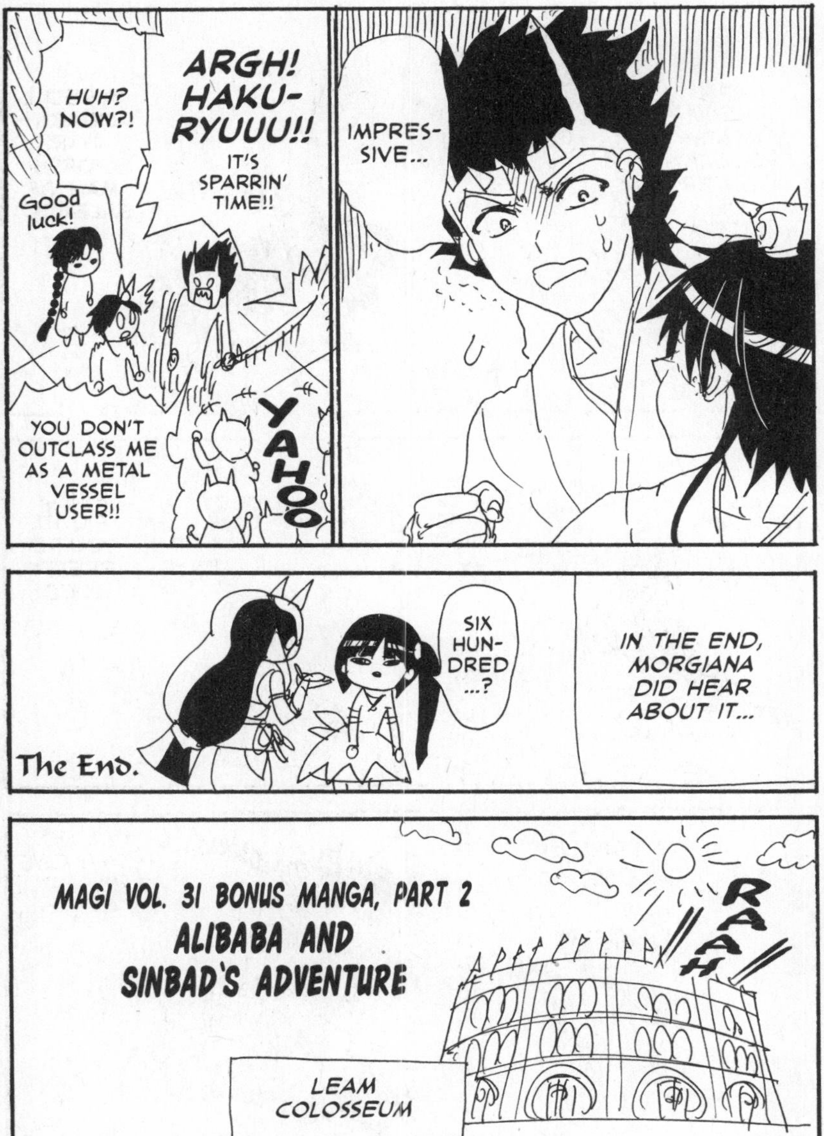
IMPRES-SIVE...
ARGH! HAKU-RYUUU!!
IT'S SPARRIN' TIME!!
HUH? NOW?!
Good luck!
YAHOO
YOU DON'T OUTCLASS ME AS A METAL VESSEL USER!!
IN THE END, MORGIANA DID HEAR ABOUT IT...
SIX HUN-DRED ...?
The End.
RAAAH
MAGI VOL. 31 BONUS MANGA, PART 2
ALIBABA AND SINBAD'S ADVENTURE
LEAM COLOSSEUM

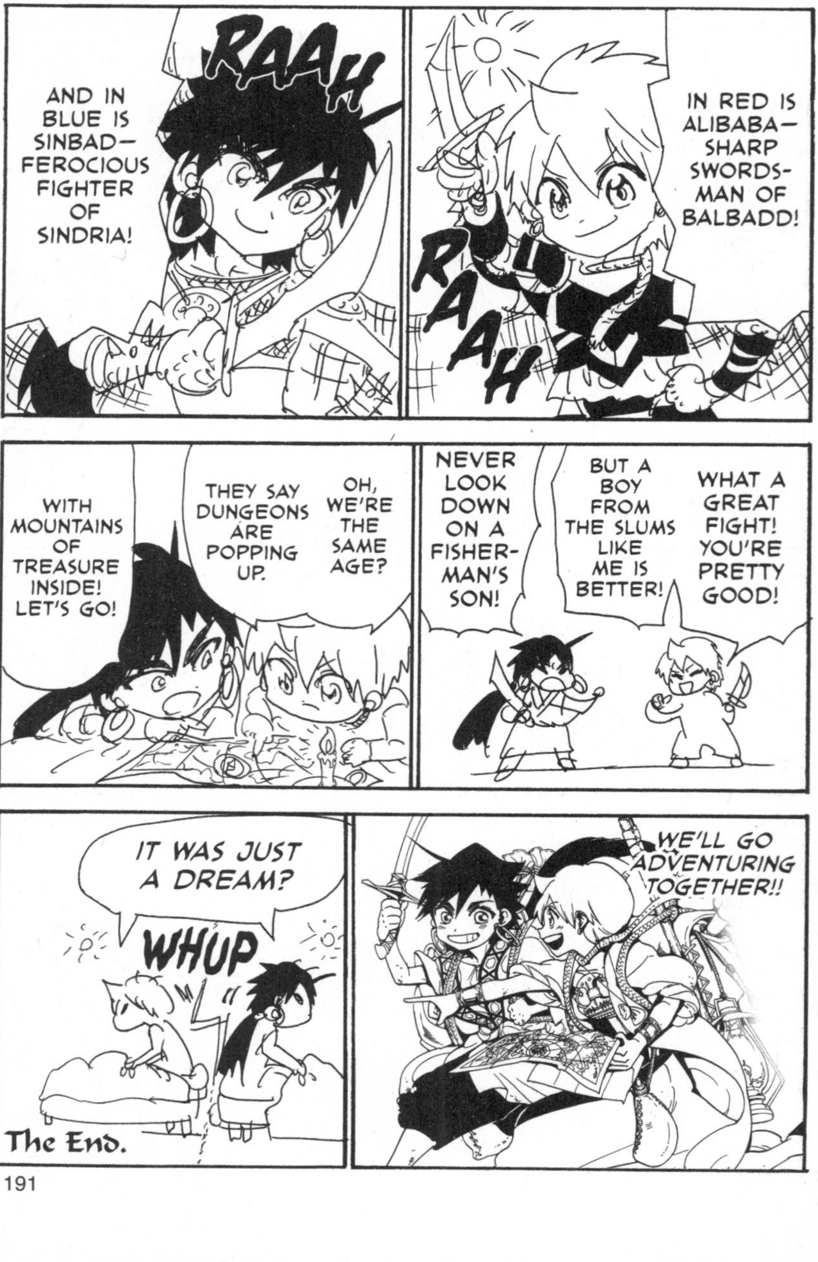
IN RED IS ALIBABA—SHARP SWORDSMAN OF BALBADD!
RAAH
AND IN BLUE IS SINBAD—FEROCIOUS FIGHTER OF SINDRIA!
RAAH
WHAT A GREAT FIGHT! YOU'RE PRETTY GOOD!
BUT A BOY FROM THE SLUMS LIKE ME IS BETTER!
NEVER LOOK DOWN ON A FISHERMAN'S SON!
OH, WE'RE THE SAME AGE?
THEY SAY DUNGEONS ARE POPPING UP.
WITH MOUNTAINS OF TREASURE INSIDE! LET'S GO!
WE'LL GO ADVENTURING TOGETHER!!
IT WAS JUST A DREAM?
WHUP
The End.

You're reading the
WRONG WAY

MAGI reads from right to left, starting in the upper-right corner. Japanese is read from **right** to **left**, meaning that action, sound effects, and word-balloon order are completely reversed from English order.

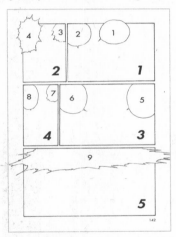